W9-CHB-429

THE ABINGDON
PREACHING
ANNUAL
1995

THE ABINGDON PREACHING ANNUAL 1995

COMPILED AND EDITED BY
Michael Duduit

ABINGDON PRESS
Nashville

THE ABINGDON PREACHING ANNUAL 1995

Copyright © 1994 by Abingdon Press

This book is printed on recycled, acid-free paper.

ISBN 0-687-00571X
ISSN 1047-5486

Scripture quotations, unless otherwise noted, are from the New Revised Standard Version Bible, Copyright © 1989 by the Division of Christian Education of the National Council of the Churches of Christ in the USA. Used by permission.

Those noted GNB are from the *Good News Bible*—Old Testament: Copyright © American Bible Society 1976; New Testament: Copyright © American Bible Society 1966, 1971, 1976.

Those noted KJV are from the King James, or Authorized, Version of the Bible.

Those noted NEB are from *The New English Bible.* © The Delegates of the Oxford University Press and The Syndics of the Cambridge University Press 1961, 1970. Reprinted by permission.

Those noted NIV are from the HOLY BIBLE, NEW INTERNATIONAL VERSION ®. Copyright © 1973, 1978, 1984 International Bible Society. Used by permission of Zondervan Publishing House. All rights reserved.

Those noted NKJV are from The New King James Version. Copyright © 1979, 1980, 1982, Thomas Nelson, Inc., Publishers.

Selected benedictions (pp. 420-21) are reprinted with permission from *Litanies and Other Prayers for the Revised Common Lectionary, Year A:* Copyright © 1989 by Abingdon Press; *Year B:* Copyright © 1990, 1993 by Abingdon Press; *Year C:* Copyright © 1991, 1994 by Abingdon Press.

94 95 96 97 98 99 00 01 02 03 — 10 9 8 7 6 5 4 3 2 1

MANUFACTURED IN THE UNITED STATES OF AMERICA

To my wife, Laura,
whose love and
encouragement
make all the difference

CONTENTS

❧

CONTENTS

FEBRUARY

MARCH

JUNE

CONTENTS

JULY

AUGUST

CONTENTS

SEPTEMBER

OCTOBER

CONTENTS

NOVEMBER

DECEMBER

INTRODUCTION

❧

"The best way to revive a church," said Dwight L. Moody, "is to build a fire in the pulpit."

That advice is still valid, for preaching is at the heart of the church's life and ministry. It is rare to find a vibrant church with a lifeless pulpit, for the preaching of the Word sets a tone and direction for most churches.

Given the centrality of preaching, it is no wonder that most pastors and preaching ministers devote so much thought and attention to the preparation and delivery of sermons. In our own day, when effective communication models are as close as the television news, people expect and the pulpit demands no less in the way of quality communication.

A pastor who recently celebrated thirty years in the same church told me, "After three decades, you'd better find a way to be fresh every Sunday!" The reality is that advice is just as valid in the first year of ministry as in the thirtieth.

In order to build and maintain an effective preaching ministry, the preacher must be a combination of student, detective, reporter, filing clerk, counselor, and prophet. The "detective" role can be particularly important, for as any good speaker will testify, the demand for good resources always seems to outpace the supply. Good preachers are constantly on the lookout for the exegetical insight, the touching story, the challenging phrase that makes the difference between an average sermon and a powerful one.

The purpose of *The Abingdon Preaching Annual* is to provide a quality resource to enable you to strengthen your own preaching ministry. It's not the only resource you'll use or need—that's like asking a surgeon to use only one instrument or a carpenter only one tool—but we hope and expect it will be one of the most helpful.

The format has changed a bit from previous years in an attempt to provide more meaningful assistance to preachers. Rather than providing a single sermon manuscript for each Sunday of the year, we offer three sermon "briefs" for each Sunday—one each for the Old Testament, Epistle, and Gospel readings from the Revised Common Lectionary.

A sermon "brief" (the name is borrowed from legal brief) suggests the outline and direction of a sermon in somewhat abbreviated form. It includes an outline, a suggested approach to the Scripture text (modeled in homiletical form), and an illustration or two. It's not a complete sermon; for example, it doesn't include all the possible development of each point, and it doesn't include all the illustrative material that will be expected, but it shows the preacher one homiletical approach to the passage and gives a good running start. It's an approach developed and used in *Preaching* magazine (which I serve as editor) with positive results for the readers.

The purpose of *The Abingdon Preaching Annual* is not to provide you sermons in a ready-made, easy-to-digest form, ready to carry into the pulpit and pretend they are your own work. There are plenty of "sermon services" out there offering to provide their generic, off-the-shelf sermons for "busy pastors who don't have time to prepare sermons"—although it seems to me that preparing sermons is precisely what God has called us to do! Can you imagine a trial lawyer who didn't have time to prepare a case, or an architect who didn't have time to design buildings?

The sermon brief format offers a suggested treatment and some helpful resources, but the work of fashioning the final sermon is yours, as it should be. The very process of digging through the text and discovering those hidden gems is part of the power and romance of the pulpit, and no substitute for that should ever be sought or accepted.

The writers for this year's *Annual* are a diverse group, representing a variety of denominations, geographical locations, and ministry roles. Those who are pastors come from many different kinds and sizes of churches, ranging from "megachurches" to small congregations. The one constant is that each one shares a commitment to and love for biblical preaching. Their sermon briefs—some abbreviated from longer sermons previously presented, others written specifically for this volume—offer worthy and helpful models for approaching and presenting the truths of Scripture in the pulpit. I appreciate the willingness of each of them to be a part of this project.

Another addition to this year's *Annual* is "Replenishing the Well" by Harriet Crosby. This is a brief guide for pastors in strengthening their spiritual disciplines of prayer and devotional study—yet in a way that is linked to the preaching direction of each month. We hope preachers will find this to be a helpful and encouraging feature.

Special thanks are due to Paul Franklyn, Jill Reddig, Linda Allen, and others at Abingdon Press whose encouragement, patience, prodding, guidance, and suggestions have made this a better resource. Their commitment to help preachers is making a difference in the lives and ministries of many. I also want to thank my wife, Laura, whose understanding and support in the midst of long evenings (often stretching into early mornings) and stacks of paperwork made this project possible.

If you have comments, suggestions, constructive criticism (I dislike the nonconstructive type), or other good words, please let me hear from you. You can write to me in care of *Preaching*, P.O. Box 7728 Louisville, KY 40257-0728.

May *The Abingdon Preaching Annual* be a helpful tool and faithful friend as you preach the Word during the coming year.

Michael Duduit
Editor

THE PREACHER AS POET

❧

Raymond Bailey

Western homiletical thought has been dominated by Aristotelian rhetoric from Augustine to the present. That isn't all bad, but it is unfortunate that preachers have not been as familiar with Aristotle's *Poetics* as they have been, consciously or unconsciously, with his *rhetoric*. The preacher may well have more in common with the poet than with the advocate. The theological implications of the work of such poets as Dante, Blake, Hopkins, and Auden are well known, but the natural affinities between the theologian and the poet—noted by such writers as Tillich, Rahner, Funk, and Heidegger—are not so well known. Karl Rahner has written that "the Perfect Priest and the Perfect Poet are one."[1]

Most preachers are vaguely aware that a third of the Old Testament is in the form of poetry. The Bible itself is largely a collection of sermons, at least testimonies, and demonstrates the connaturality of spiritual content and poetic form. The Bible is primarily a record of human experience that often transcends the limits of ordinary language. J. A. Sanders has reminded us that the Bible is "God's story," but it is the story of God's dealing with humanity. Preachers can draw on the poetry of life experience, which often requires words constructed in a way that moves beyond simple discursive expression.

Among the characteristics that may be shared by poet and preacher are an inner compulsion that drives them to their work, a passionate desire for truth, a recognition that truth transcends that which can be ascertained empirically or rationally, a willingness to be transcended by their work, and an understanding of communication that can evoke an experience rather than convincing with argument.

THE CALL

The concept of "call" to ministry is almost universal among preachers. Of course, there is wide variation in defining what constitutes a call, but nearly all have some notion that the person who preaches should have one. Such terminology would have little meaning to most poets, but each would explain his or her poetry as emerging from some inward drive, however it might be described. Rainer Maria Rilke's response to an aspiring young poet sounds like scores of dialogues between elder pastors and young strugglers:

> You ask whether your verses are good. You ask me. You have asked others before. You send them to magazines. You compare them with other poems, and you are disturbed when certain editors reject your efforts. Now . . . I beg you to give up all that. You are looking outward and that above all you should not do now. Nobody can counsel and help you, nobody. There is only one single way. Go into yourself. Search for the reason that bids you to write; find out whether it is spreading out its roots in the deepest places of your heart, acknowledge to yourself whether you would have to die if it were denied you to write. This above all—ask yourself in the stillest hour of your night: must I write? Delve into yourself for a deep answer. And if this should be affirmative, if you may meet this earnest question with a strong and simple "I must," then build your life according to this necessity; your life even into its most indifferent and slightest hour must be a sign of this urge and a testimony to it.[2]

The poet writes poetry because he or she is a poet; likewise does the preacher preach.

THE TRUTH

One does not choose to be a poet but is one by an accident of individuality. The greatest obstacle to the realization of this vocation is the same as that which obstructs spirituality: the false self. "Many poets are not poets for the same reason that many religious men are not saints: They never succeed in being themselves."[3] One disciplines the self for art in the same way that one prepares the self for the spiritual trek—that is, the impurities and clutter are expurgated to allow the consciousness of the mystery, which will express itself. The artist does not "use" art any more than the spiritual person "uses" the spirit; indeed, artists allow themselves to be used. Each struggles to be free of the pressures, both eternal and external, that interfere with and taint his or her work. The creative spirit strives to escape all forms of domination. The preacher has the same struggle. Poet and preacher must both remain free to be prophetic. They live "in the world" but must not be "of the world." John Kennedy, speaking to honor Robert Frost, noted Frost's words that the poet has "a lover's quarrel with the world." Included in his remarks was a remark by Archibald MacLeish that for poets "there is nothing worse . . . than to be in style."[4]

Preacher and poet are similarly engaged in a passionate quest for truth. Heidegger defined art as "truth setting itself to work."[5] "The nature of poetry," he wrote, "is the founding of truth."[6] Truth is not obtained through rational reflection alone. Perhaps the most important truths are those which lie beyond fact and opinion. God cannot be known as humans are. When Moses asked God for credentials to present to Israel in bondage and Pharaoh in power, he was only given an affirmation of the experience of mystery "just to tell them I AM."

The preacher immerses himself or herself in the spirit to experience the universal unity. Both the poet and the preacher subscribe to a theory that reality lies beneath the surface, the appearance of things. There is a spiritual dimension that invests matter with whatever meaning and value it has. Both the poet and the preacher synthesize the diffused experiences of life into a discernible pattern. The poet appears to create beauty, which may well be, as Hegel concluded, "merely the Spiritual making itself known sensuously."[7] Both art and religion attain "directly to the world of pure being in which all symbols and forms have their transcendent justification."[8] The poet and preacher are concerned with the organic whole of the seen and unseen.

Poet and preacher give form to their experience of truth in order to evoke an experience in the listener. The aim of their work is not to recall experience or the result of an experience but to create experience itself. In spiritual matters the experience itself must be dominant. Here perhaps the poet can learn from the spiritual preacher.

> Religious ascetics have something to learn from the natural asceticism of the artist: it is unselfconscious, organic, integrated in his art. It does not run the risk of becoming an end in itself. But the artist also has something to gain from religious asceticism. It not only raises him above his subject and his material but above his art itself. He can now control everything, even his art, which usually controls him.[9]

21

Art is not truth but a representation of truth (Aristotle called it an "imitation of life") and hopefully a stimulus to an experience of truth.

THE SPIRIT

There is a terrible sameness about sermons that are lectures or arguments. They limit the gospel to human understanding and explanation. This is the failure of rationalism, both secular and biblical. It is the trap in which evangelical Christianity has too often been ensnared. It is the product of a theology devoid of any meaningful doctrine of the Spirit and of transcendency. Archibald MacLeish wrote in his poem "Ars Poetica" that "A poem should be equal to: Not true. . . . A poem should not mean, but be."

Preaching should be at the center of an event. Heidegger said that "poetry is the establishing of being by means of the word."[10] Should preaching be less? The preacher may often communicate a truth that is not factual, one that emerges not through logical persuasion but is evoked from intuitive experience. The measure of a sermon is often not a remembered outline or proposition to live by but a sometimes indescribable experience. The poet provides a vehicle for personal insight and experience. Has a poet failed if a listener discovers in a poem a meaning different from the poet's intended meaning? Does a preacher fail if a sermon evokes meaning or experience different from the preacher's intention?

The poet and the preacher construct myths that portray reality. Does not the preacher call men and women from preoccupation with the mundane, what William James called "a big blooming buzzing confusion?" Artist and preacher each tries to weave together the segments of human experience that flow through consciousness and achieve a mosaic that gives the total experience lucidity, vividness, intensity, and depth.

Poetry and preaching are both communicative acts. W. H. Auden wrote that the first half of art is perception and the second half is telling.[11] Language is the vehicle through which the latter task is accomplished. Here is an area of desperate need for the contemporary preacher, one which can be served by the discovery of poetics. Robert Funk challenges the theologian to escape from "ghetto language, the cloistered tongue of the Christianized age."[12] He urges the liberation of language from "the hegemony of prescriptive thought."[13]

THE IMAGE

Preaching and poetry are similar in the sometimes abstract character of their content but also in the necessity of linguistic form to express it. Both must transcend the limitations of ordinary language because they seek forms to communicate what seems inexpressible. The experience dictates the form of its expression. The poet expresses the inexpressible in extraordinary combinations of words, sounds, and structures.

So it is with the preacher who must rely on metaphorical devices to reveal God, righteousness, and all that transcends the physical. One only has to consider the dreams and visions of the prophets and the parables of Jesus to find biblical examples. Their messages throb with powerful images that arrest the minds of their auditors.

The preacher and the poet are seers both in the technical prophetic sense and in the denotative sense. They not only feel, they see. They have "eyes to see" and "ears to hear" and "mouths to speak." The preacher does well to remember that the sermon, like the poem, is unfinished until it is spoken. Amos Wilder in his important study of the rhetoric of the early church noted the oral tradition of the gospels and the vitality of the speech of Jesus and the evangelists.

This utterance is dynamic, actual, immediate, reckless of posterity; not coded for catechists or repeaters. It is only one aspect of this that it is oral and not written. We find ourselves at first and for a rather long time in the presence of oral and live face-to-face communication.[14]

The language of the sermon should be chosen not only for meaning, denotative and connotative, but also for its aural effect. Bible scholars and teachers have discovered the oral nature of the Bible. Stories that were told before written need to be "told" again to be experienced. Most poets write for the ear and so should preachers. In sermon preparation the scriptures should be read aloud. The Bible and biblical sermons require oral interpretation. The African-American tradition has acknowledged and utilized the power of cadence and rhythm. The Black preacher leads the congregation in sermonic dance and song. Language is used to stir the senses and appeal to both right and left brain functions.

> It must move our emotions, or excite our intellect, for only that which is moving or exciting is memorable, and the stimulus is the audible spoken word and cadence, to which in all its power of suggestion and incantation we must surrender as we do when talking to an intimate friend.[15]

Preaching would be far more effective if preachers would realize that the sermon is to the pulpit what the drama is to the theater. Preaching is an event which requires living language appropriate to the message. The language of the sermon must have the power to inspire as well as inform. Indeed, is not the information of the sermon only a means to the end of inspiration?

NOTES

1. Karl Rahner, "Priest and Poet," *The Word: Readings in Theology* (New York: P. J. Kennedy and Sons, 1964), p. 3.

2. Rainer Maria Rilke, *Letters to a Young Poet* (New York: Norton, 1954), pp. 18-19.

3. Thomas Merton, *New Seeds of Contemplation* (New York: New Directions, 1961), p. 102.

4. John Fitzgerald Kennedy, "Poetry and Power," *Atlantic Monthly* 64 (Feb. 1964): 54.

5. Martin Heidegger, *Poetry, Language, and Thought,* trans. Albert Hofstafter (New York: Harper & Row, 1971), p. 39.

6. Ibid., p. 75.

7. G. W. F. Hegel, quoted in Evelyn Underhill, *Mysticism* (New York: E. P. Dutton and Co., 1961), p. 81.

8. Thomas Merton, "Art and Worship," *Art and Literature,* vol. IV, Collected Essays, p. 22, unpublished.

9. Thomas Merton, *The Sign of Jonas* (Garden City, New York: Image, 1953), p. 56.

10. Robert W. Funk, *Language, Hermeneutic and Word of God* (New York: Harper & Row, 1966), p. 39.

11. W. H. Auden, *The English Auden: Poems, Essays and Dramatic Writings, 1927-1939,* ed. Edward Mendelson (New York: Random House, 1977), p. 359.

12. Funk, *Language,* p. XIV.

13. Ibid., p. XV.

14. Amos N. Wilder, *Early Christian Rhetoric: The Language of the Gospel* (Cambridge, Mass.: Harvard University Press, 1964), p. 13.

15. Heidegger, *Poetry,* p. 327.

PREACHING TRUTH IN AN AGE OF DOUBT

✦

James Earl Massey

Henry Van Dyke, a man of the cloth, was also a man of letters, a noted preacher who had enjoyed a brilliantly successful pulpit ministry nearly a hundred years ago at Brick Presbyterian Church, in New York City. The contents of one of his books was directly related to the Lyman Beecher Lectureship at Yale Divinity School, and the subject was *The Gospel for an Age of Doubt.*

In the sixth edition of Van Dyke's book, and in a new preface, the author explained why he had assessed his times as an "age of doubt." Although Van Dyke was writing a hundred years ago, I call attention to his reasoning because it forms a fitting explanation of our times, an age greatly in need of the benefits of divine truth. Van Dyke wrote:

> In calling the present "an age of doubt," I do not mean that it is the only age in which doubt has been prevalent, nor that doubt is the only characteristic of the age. I mean simply that it is one of those periods of human history in which the sudden expansion of knowledge and the breaking-up of ancient moulds of thought have produced a profound and widespread feeling of uncertainty in regard to the subject of religion.[1]

Henry Van Dyke went on to mention the "questioning temper" that was abroad in the land, and what he termed an "interrogative attitude" toward religion and religious forms, especially the Christian religion. Does not that same assessment fit our times?

The age of doubt in our time is far more widespread, and its effects are so marked. In our time the "questioning temper" and the "interrogative attitude" are more dangerous because the incessant proneness to question and theorize all too seldom lead to any sure end; the emphasis is on exploring in quest for truth, with no agreed norms to guide the search or help to identify the truth being sought. This age of doubt needs to be addressed by persons who have a distinct message about the God of truth and the divine will, a message that rings loud and clear within our own minds and lives; a message that invites scrutiny, prods thought, stirs a reaction; a message that bids one speak out of a settled confidence about its meaning and eternal importance.

TRUTHS TO BE PREACHED

1. There are truths to be preached, even within our churches, among those who doubt or have misgivings about the centrality of Jesus and the cruciality of his cross-experience for an eternal salvation.

Our pulpit work, rightly understood, is to help persons to experience salvation; it is to help them get located in the claiming, saving, life-changing grace of God. The climate of our age does not help us in this quest because, to quote Ellen T. Charry, "the general populace [is] more familiar with secularism or modern expressions of paganism than with Christianity."[2]

The scene we confront in preaching today is like that scene the apostolic company confronted while preaching throughout the Gentile world of the first century. Interestingly, the apostolic message prevailed. The truths those leaders voiced are still with us, and those truths remain worthy of being voiced anew. They prevailed before; they can prevail again!

Now, as when the church began, the mandated agenda for preaching is to proclaim and interpret for each generation the gracious deed of God in Christ Jesus. It is no small matter to help shape persons as "Christians," to travail in prayer for people, as Paul reports he did, until Christ be formed in them. The work of preaching was commissioned to this end, and the purpose of the gospel steadily reminds those of us who preach to keep this motivation central in our concern.

2. There are truths to be preached, to inform and to sustain us as we confront those who question whether there be any absolutes or ultimates to which we can honestly point and reasonably defend.

In this age, variously described as post-Christian, postmodern, and distinctly pluralistic in orientation, the notion is widespread, even among many church members, that we are wise to acknowledge all religious claims as relative. Meanwhile, the truth of the gospel honors human life in ways that evidence God's intention uniquely. The truth of the gospel blesses life; truth reflects its source in the way it rescues from destructive powers, changes one's character, enhances personhood, and grants a true freedom to order one's way in good because of a love for God.

In a day when there seem to be so few places on earth for truth to make its way unimpeded, let those of us who preach make sure that truth finds a broad and ready place of activity within us. Only thus can our pulpit work be what it was intended to be.

3. There are truths to be preached, but the fullest impact from a hearing is when hearing is allied with seeing truth *lived out*. Søren Kierkegaard was pointing to this in his comment that "the truth is a snare: you cannot have it without being caught. You cannot have the truth in such a way that you catch it, but only in such a way that it catches you."[3]

There are those in our time who no longer listen to us with any serious openness and trust. Many people question the veracity and integrity of pastors, asking who is worthy to be trusted. There is a suspicion about us in many minds—suspicions fed by known cases of failure and by an ever-increasing spate of novels about preachers as sneaky schemers, hypocritical money-grabbers, sex-hungry opportunists, and anxious status-seekers. How different our times are from those days when preachers were viewed and known as distinguished, service-minded, truly helpful persons!

Paul's personal stance regarding all of this remains an instructive challenge. Speaking about himself and all others who were mindful of God's mercies and grateful for God's grace, he confessed: "We have renounced the shameful things that one hides; we refuse to practice cunning or to falsify God's word; but by the *open statement of the truth* we commend ourselves to the conscience of everyone in the sight of God" (2 Cor. 4:2, italics added). That apostle not only claimed and preached truth; the truth claimed him, and his open life demonstrated that truth.

BROKER, NOT MANAGER OF TRUTH

In his book *No Place for Truth,* there is a thought-provoking discussion by which author David F. Wells has sought to inform us about the predicament pastors face in the modern world, the factors that he believes produced that predicament, and the effects of that predicament upon the spirit and functioning of the church. As for the predicament, Wells explained that pastors feel homeless, insecure, and impermanent because they have no honored place in a secularized society nor in the church; that because they are purveyors of belief, both the world and the church have shunted pastors to the margins of importance. With both church and world hardly interested in what Scripture reports and commends, many clergy find themselves in search of a niche.

This sense of being dislodged from both the church and society has fed the clergy's need for a sense of security and status. And he further believes that this has led them to a search for importance and validation such as physicians, lawyers, and others know and experience as "professionals." Wells, who is professor of historical and systematic theology at Gordon-Conwell Theological Seminary, has further suggested that this search by some pastors for acceptance and validation might well be one of the reasons for the increasing popularity of the Doctor of Ministry (D.Min.) degree. Instead of being ordered by a sense of standing before God, and the pastoral concern to make God's truth known, Wells argued, many ministers became anxious about their standing in society and have "professionalized" their ministry— aided and abetted by seminary programming that is not centered in the word of God but in career-building. Thus his lament: "The older role of the pastor as broker of truth has been eclipsed by the newer managerial functions."[4]

This is not the place to critique the argument David Wells has offered in that chapter of his strategic statement to the church, but it is surely the time and place to agree with him that careerism in ministry is adversely affecting the spirit of the church and the biblical interests of the gospel. Careerism in ministry is a capitulation to the spirit of the times. It is a giving in to culture.

But so is accepting the false norms that marginalize people, in the very face of the gospel that was given to unify us. There is truth in Scripture about our common humanity, about our common origin, and that truth is in tandem with the truth from our common experience about our common needs. There is a truth to be preached that speaks forthrightly about and against marginalizing—against restrictions based on gender or ethic factors or national origin. There is a truth to be proclaimed in the face of a marginalizing statecraft, all prejudicial politics, and all hegemonic denominationalism. Paul's eagerness to "commend the truth" led him to promote the grace of God in Jesus Christ, on the one hand, and on the other to promote that active goodness that works to overcome evil (see Rom. 12:21).

TRUTH OVER ERROR

Truth is a word that was a constant in the preaching vocabulary of the first-century church. Those believers had experienced Jesus, who founded the church, as someone "full of grace and truth" (John 1:14). Jesus himself talked much about truth and promised that those who received his truth would be set free (John 8:32). Jesus referred to the Holy Spirit as the "Spirit of truth" (John 14:17; 16:13), and he explained that a part of the Spirit's ministry is to "guide [us] into all the truth" (John 16:13). Interestingly, in one of the few recorded references Jesus made concerning his birth, he told Pilate: "For this I was born, and for this I came into the world, to testify to the truth" (John 18:37c).

Paul and other writers in the New Testament echoed that same honored tradition and concern: to testify to the truth. And by the time one reaches the pastoral letters, there is no doubt about what the first Christian preachers understood and sought to convey when they mentioned the word *truth*. In 1 Timothy, that young pastoral leader is reminded that the church within which God has placed him for service must be honored always as "the household of God," and as "the pillar and bulwark of the truth" (1 Tim. 3:15).

The dominical and apostolic emphasis on "the truth" is always set over against the problem of false teaching, error. In Scripture, truth and error are antithetical. In Scripture, error leads to sad, sorry ends, while truth leads to righteousness, peace, and true fulfillment. Truth refutes error, it unmasks deception. Scripture is never unclear nor ambiguous about what is truth and what is error, about what is certain and trustworthy in contrast to what is not. Scripture is concerned to help us know what is genuine and what is not, what is real and what is false, what helps and what hinders, what blesses and what blights. The truth we are commissioned to preach illuminates and distinguishes. As truth it can stand up under any and all scrutiny, and have no fear of being disputed—because it is truth. It needs only to be preached—and lived.

FREEDOM FROM BONDAGE

And why must this truth be preached? Because of the need of everyone in the world to be freed from a threefold bondage, Van Dyke declared: first, from the heavy and erroneous thought that we are creatures whose actions and destiny are shaped by necessity, heredity, and environment; second, from the hounding fear that blind chance and brute force control the world; and third, from the curse of sin, which binds us by selfishness.

> There is a message of religion especially fitted to meet the needs of our times. There is an aspect of Christianity which comes to the world today as glad tidings. There is a newness in the old gospel which shines out like a sunrise upon the darkness and despondency that overshadow so much of modern life. This aspect of Christianity centers in the person of Jesus Christ, as the human life of God.[5]

The truth about Jesus as Savior and God as Sovereign unmasks those errors of determinism, chance, and sin. That truth pierces the darkness of our world with the light that lets us *see* the divine intention and *experience* the delivering, claiming divine will. This is the purpose for preaching.

NOTES

1. Henry Van Dyke, *The Gospel for an Age of Doubt* (New York: Macmillan, 1897), pp. xv-xvi.
2. Ellen T. Charry, "Academic Theology in Pastoral Perspective," *Theology Today* 1, 1 (April 1993): 90.
3. Søren Kierkegaard, *The Last Years,* ed. and trans. Ronald G. Smith (New York: Harper & Row, 1965), p. 133.
4. David F. Wells, *No Place for Truth* (Grand Rapids: Wm. B. Eerdmans, 1993), p. 233.
5. Van Dyke, *The Gospel for an Age of Doubt,* pp. xv-xvi.

1995

अपूर्ण

JANUARY

∾

Replenishing the Well

The People Were Filled with Expectation

All spiritual disciplines or practices, like prayer, fasting, or Bible study, create a bit of sacred time during which we expect to encounter God. In other words, when we practice various spiritual disciplines or exercises, we act on our expectations of meeting God in some way. That sense of expectation is an experience of faith.

Each month, you are invited to practice a spiritual discipline or exercise based on one of the biblical texts in this year's lectionary. The theme of these exercises is *expectation*. Each exercise helps you to expect an encounter with God—an encounter that sustains your ministry of Word and sacrament.

In addition to a Bible, some of the exercises require a blank notebook or journal in which to write. You will also need a quiet, private room where you will not be disturbed as you practice each exercise.

The beginning of each exercise will tell you how much time it will take to complete that exercise as well as identify any extra material or items you will need.

Now you are ready to begin the exercise for January.

Time: 45 to 60 minutes.

Materials: A Bible, your journal, and a pen or pencil.

Exercise:
On January 8, the church celebrates the Baptism of the Lord. Read Luke 3:15-17, 21-22. Now re-read verse 15. Focus on the statement "the people were filled expectation . . . whether he might be the Messiah." In part, the sacrament of baptism is a spiritual practice in which the church expects God to bind himself to the one being baptized. With each baptism we are

33

reminded of our own baptism and our entrance into the community of faith. Some of us are able to remember our own baptism; others, baptized in infancy, are unable to remember it. The purpose of this exercise is to help you reflect on your baptism and the expectations you bring to baptism in the light of the Baptism of the Lord.

In your journal, answer the following questions.

- If you can remember your baptism, describe it in as much detail as possible. What kind of church were you in? What did it look like? Who was present? What were you wearing? How did you feel when you touched the water, heard the words? How did you feel after it was over?
- If you can't remember your baptism, write about it based on what you may have heard from your parents or other relatives present. How old were you? Why did your parents ask to have you baptized?
- How does your own baptism inform or connect with the baptisms you now perform as clergy?
- What expectations do you bring to the sacrament of baptism? What do you expect to experience in performing baptisms?
- When you discuss baptizing a child with parents, what sort of expectations do those parents bring to the baptism?
- Does your congregation express any expectations regarding baptisms? If so, what are they?
- What associations or connections do you make between your own baptism, the baptisms you perform, and the Baptism of the Lord?

Close your journal and offer a prayer of thanks for baptism as an encounter with the Lord. (Harriet Crosby)

JANUARY 1, 1995

❧

New Year's Day

Worship Theme: God's providence gives confidence in all times and in all circumstances.

Readings: Ecclesiastes 3:1-13; Revelation 21:1-6*a*; Matthew 25:31-46

Call to Worship (Psalm 8):

Leader: O LORD, our Sovereign, how majestic is your name in all the earth!

People: You have set your glory above the heavens. Out of the mouths of babes and infants you have founded a bulwark because of your foes, to silence the enemy and the avenger.

Leader: When I look at your heavens, the work of your fingers, the moon and the stars that you have established;

People: what are human beings that you are mindful of them, mortals that you care for them?

Leader: Yet you have made them a little lower than God, and crowned them with glory and honor.

People: You have given them dominion over the works of your hands; you have put all things under their feet,

Leader: all sheep and oxen, and also the beasts of the field, the birds of the air, and the fish of the sea, whatever passes along the paths of the seas.

All: O LORD, our Sovereign, how majestic is your name in all the earth!

Pastoral Prayer:

Lord, we thank you for this splendid, unrenewable gift of one more year of time, packaged in the bright, new ribbons of shiny potential. Time is your best gift to us, but we approach that gift with fear. For such gifts leave us too afraid to clip the ribbons and see the heavy shape of things to come. The future comes so bulky and portentous. What if we find this year our foe? What if this unknown year should prove unkind or dire? Some of those who celebrate with us may not be here this time next year. And some will find it full of grief and stings and pain.

Father, please stay by us, God, as we undo this hopeful, fearful gift. We'll want you there to laugh with us if these unfolding days bring laughter, to cry with us if this year brings us grief. If this be a year of light, stand with us in the sun. If darkness comes, stand close enough that we may feel your presence when the light is scarce. Amen. (Calvin Miller)

SERMON BRIEFS

A TIME FOR EVERYTHING

ECCLESIASTES 3:1-13

There have been occasions in my life when the nature of time has been driven home with a particular poignancy. I have left wedding receptions with all the great celebration that entails to visit the funeral home to console a family in the loss of their husband and father. A visit to the hospital may include calls that run the gamut from rejoicing with a couple that is celebrating the birth of their first child to visiting a church member whose cancer surgery has just been pronounced a success. Those visits may be followed by a visit to the hospice unit where a cancer victim who has lost her battle with that dread disease is struggling not to lose the battle for her faith. I may then try to bring the healing presence of Christ to a couple who want so desperately to share their love with a child but have just suffered their third miscarriage.

I. Everything Has Its Time

Some of these times are joyful and others are not so joyful. In my idealism, I would like to do away with all the not-so-joyful things. Unfortunately, the text for this morning tells us that there will be a time for everything. It's confusing to think about. There's a time for birth and death. There's a time for planting and uprooting. There's a time for love and hate, peace and war. Does this mean that God condones hatred, war, death, and uprooting? Or are these things somehow beyond God's control? On the first Sunday of the new year, it's good for us to think about the meaning of times of our lives.

The preacher of Ecclesiastes smashes some of my idealism. I'd like to think that war, hatred, weeping, and tearing down can be done away with. When I preach, I tell people that God can give them purpose in life. But the preacher of Ecclesiastes says, "Everything is meaningless." I preach and say that some things just make no sense. The writer of Ecclesiastes says that God makes all things beautiful in his time. The message of Ecclesiastes is one of providence. Bad things happen in time, but in time God is able to make all things beautiful.

II. Trust in God's Providence Is Our Only Hope

The writer of Ecclesiastes was puzzled over some of the things that happen in this life here on earth. He knew that life is burdensome. He even implied that God may be the one to blame for these burdensome things. But what is the solution to all of this meaninglessness? A clue comes in verse 11. God has put eternity in the hearts of men and women. God has created us with the sense that this life is not all there is. We know some of the pain and heartache of the bad things that happen to us in time, and that makes us long for the day when time itself will be no more. We long for eternity. We cannot always understand why or how God works. No one knows what the new year will hold for us and our families. It may be a time of planting or of mourning. It may be a time of weeping or of scattering stones, but whatever it is, trust God. We call this providence. If we allow God to be at work in our lives, somehow, some way, God is able to transform the moments of our lives into something beautiful. (Mark A. Johnson)

HE WILL WIPE AWAY EVERY TEAR

REVELATION 21:1-6

That intrepid Viking from the comics, Hagar the Horrible, was trying to lift the spirits of his depressed friend Fast Eddie. "Today the world dumped on you. Today the world humiliated and abused you. But remember, tomorrow is another day!"

Fast Eddie falls down and sobs in despair!

We know the feeling. All around we see pain, hopelessness, and despair. AIDS, drug abuse, poverty, hunger, murder, homelessness, unemployment, child abuse, rape—the list of things we do to each other and to ourselves is endless. Like Fast Eddie, we want to break down and sob in despair.

I. The Bad News Is Sin

Why is there so much hate and violence, so much suffering? Most people don't want to admit the cause. The biblical pronouncement is that the cause of the problems of the world is sin. We are alienated from God and from each other because of our disobedience. We can splice genes; we can put people in space. But we can't seem to end the world's problems. We make matters worse. The farther we move from God, the more painful life becomes.

II. The Good News Is Hope

The good news is that in the midst of our despair comes a vision of hope, the hope of a new heaven and a new earth where every tear will be wiped away, a vision of hope that reminds us of God's offer of reconciliation and redemption.

In the movie *Home Alone,* an eight-year-old boy is accidentally left behind when his family leaves for a vacation in Paris. At first the boy is delighted, but then the house becomes too empty and he misses his brothers and sisters and parents. On Christmas Eve he decides to go to church, and there, he meets an old man.

The boy admits that he didn't always treat his family right, and now he misses them terribly. "Well, this is the place to come when you're feeling bad about yourself," the old man says.

He's right. The church is where we hear the Good News.

These are words of hope from God, who dwells with us and knows firsthand the struggles we face. Christ walked where we walk. He faced death so that we would never face it alone again. Not only did he face it, but he also defeated it. Death no longer has power over us. We are not alone.

A Sunday school teacher read the verse "My yoke is easy" to her class one Sunday and then asked them to describe a yoke. One said it was something you put on the neck of animals so they could pull a wagon or a plow. Then the teacher asked, "What is the meaning of God's yoke?" A little girl answered, "It is God putting his arms around our neck."

That's a great way of thinking of God's yoke. Whatever we face, we face enfolded in God's arms. We are yoked with Christ so that we can know the promise and hope of Revelation.

The good news is that God heard our cry but didn't send technical assistance. Instead, God came in the person of Jesus. He hungered in the wilderness. He was stripped naked on the cross. In hungering with us, God became our bread; and in suffering for us, God became our comfort and strength. This is the mighty and powerful promise of Revelation: *God is with us.* Let God lift the burdens from your heart. Let God wipe away every tear from your eyes. (Billy D. Strayhorn)

FOR THE LEAST OF THESE

MATTHEW 25:31-46

Matthew's recounting of Jesus' public teaching ministry begins in Matthew 5 with the Sermon on the Mount, and ends in Matthew 25 with this sermon on the final judgment. They are like matching bookends: "Blessed are the merciful, for they will be shown mercy" (Matt. 5:7), Jesus said at the beginning of his work. Now as he closes his teaching ministry and prepares for the cross, he reminds his disciples that "whatever you did for one of the least of these . . . you did for me" (v. 40). Both sermons emphasize that the evidence of our faith is loving service.

I. Loving Service Is Practical in Nature

Notice what Jesus refers to: food, shelter, and fellowship. He is affirming those who provide basic human needs for those who are poor and dispossessed.

What more remarkable example is there of modern sainthood than Mother Teresa, walking the filthy streets of Calcutta to find children in need and provide them with food, shelter, and love? Isn't it interesting that if most people were asked to name a "real Christian" they wouldn't think of preachers or theologians or religious leaders, but a simple woman of faith who has given her life in service to "the least of these"?

As the author of James will later remind us, faith is more than belief; it involves putting those beliefs into action. And Jesus calls us here to act out faith through loving service to "the least of these."

II. Loving Service Grows Out of a Merciful Heart

When Christ transforms a human life, a heart transplant takes place. A cold, self-centered heart is one that does not know Christ's presence. By contrast, someone who has experienced the grace of God through Christ is able to see others the way Jesus sees them: through eyes of mercy and compassion.

Notice that those who had served him didn't do so with a religious motive; they didn't even know they were serving Christ through their quiet acts of service. Unlike those who try to earn "religious merit badges" by specific religious activities, Jesus is affirming those whose lives become natural springs of mercy.

III. Loving Service Opens the Doors to God's Presence

The ultimate reward of loving service is eternity in the glorious presence of God. By contrast, those who have lived for their own benefit—who have ignored "the least of these" to focus on their own desires—they already have their reward. Their destiny is punishment, cut off forever from fellowship with their Creator.

In St. Martin's Church in Basel, Switzerland, stands a statue of Martin of Tours, a Roman soldier who had come to faith in

Christ. It is said that a beggar approached Martin on a winter day, but Martin had no money, so he took off his own coat, tore it in half, and gave half to the beggar. In a dream that night, Martin saw Jesus wearing half of a soldier's coat. The Lord was asked by an angel why he was wearing such a thing, to which Jesus replied, "My servant Martin gave it to me."

What better way could there be to begin a new year than to allow God's Spirit to transform our hearts and lives, to give us a new focus and new priorities directed not at our own needs but at the needs of others? What we do for the least of these, we do for him. (Michael Duduit)

JANUARY 8, 1995

❧

Baptism of the Lord

Worship Theme: The Holy Spirit creates among us a community of faith, holiness, and power.

Readings: Isaiah 43:1-7; Acts 8:14-17; Luke 3:15-17, 21-22

Call to Worship (Psalm 29:10-11):
The LORD sits enthroned over the flood;
 the LORD sits enthroned as king forever.
May the LORD give strength to his people!
 May the LORD bless his people with peace!

Pastoral Prayer:
 Lord, today all is declared! The world knows who you are! This is the day to stop the Temple traffic and shout: This is he! This is our Christ! But Lord, what if they should say, "Please don't talk about him here, this is a place too public, a place of commerce. This is that special area where we talk about our own pursuits"?

 Lord, if this should happen, make us like Anna and like Simeon. Let us cry in that bright joy they knew, "We have found him." Make our courage bright as magi's gold. Make it flow like myhrr itself. Let it lie as sweet as frankincense that balmed the desert air.

 Lord, we want the world to know you so it may come to you. As wise men made long journeys, long ago, let us at least cross some small lane and cry, "Today all is declared, we have found him." Amen. (Calvin Miller)

SERMON BRIEFS

WHAT A HOMECOMING

ISAIAH 43:1-7

 It was the Christmas season of 1991, and the eyes of the world were focused on the Rhine-Main Air Force Base in Germany.

There a very touching drama was playing out on our television screens as Terry Anderson, the AP Bureau Chief in Beirut who had been held hostage for nearly seven years, ran into the arms of his sister Peggy Say, who had labored so diligently for his freedom. For that family, Christmas was a celebration that they will never forget. Their loved one had been held in a foreign land against his will for more Christmases than they cared to think about. But now he was free and was on his way home.

It's always special to go home. There's no agony quite like homesickness. The people to whom the prophet Isaiah was speaking must have known what it was to feel homesick. Their nation had been defeated by Babylon, and many of them had been carried off into exile. They were forced to live in a land that was not their own. They endured the taunts of people who asked them to sing some of the songs of Zion. Didn't these oppressors know that they couldn't sing the songs of Zion in a foreign land? You see, they believed that to be cut off from their homeland, from the Temple in Jerusalem, was to be cut off from God's very own presence.

Isaiah wanted to reassure the people that God was indeed with them and would continue to be with them. There was no price that God would be unwilling to pay for their deliverance.

Isaiah reminded the exiles of God's presence with them. The chapters prior to this one have a tone of judgment. In order to help the people see beyond judgment, however, God began to encourage them about his promise to bring them home. While obstacles stood in the way of their homecoming, nonetheless, God would be with them on their journey homeward.

After stern words of rebuke, Isaiah said to them, "[God] created you, O Jacob,/he who formed you, O Israel" (v. 1). In spite of all their difficulties, God was calling them by name, and he had not forgotten them. Even though they were hundreds of miles from their homeland and their Temple, God was still with them. God says, "I will always be with you, and I will bring you home. You can pass through waters and you can pass through fire but even these dread obstacles will not keep my presence from being with you."

Not only does God promise to be with the people, but he also promises to pay any price for their ransom. God tells them, "You are precious in my sight, and honored, and I love you" (v. 4). God

43

was willing to pay a price as great as all the riches of Africa to bring his chosen people back to their homeland.

The value of any object is determined by what price someone is willing to pay for it. God looked at sinful humanity and determined that the cost to bring us "home" would be the blood of his own dear Son—the most precious thing he had. (Mark A. Johnson)

PASSING ON THE FLAME

ACTS 8:14-17

A Sunday school teacher taught her class to recite the Apostles' Creed by giving each child one phrase to learn. At the Sunday school presentations, the class was asked to give their recitation. They began beautifully: "I believe in God the Father Almighty, maker of heaven and earth," said the first child.

"I believe in Jesus Christ his only Son our Lord," said the next. They went on perfectly until they came to the child who said, "He ascended into heaven, and sitteth at the right hand of God the Father Almighty; from thence he shall come to judge the quick and the dead." At that point an embarrassed silence fell until a little girl spoke up and said, "Uh, the little boy who believes in the Holy Spirit is absent today."

Just as the Creed came to a halt without the Holy Spirit, so too did the ministry of the believers in Samaria. So they waited. The apostles in Jerusalem had experienced the promise of Jesus at Pentecost. The breathtaking promise of Jesus blew and rushed its way into the disciples and breathed new life into their breathlessness. The Holy Spirit blew into their hearts and danced the sacred dance of God's presence and deliverance. The pillar of fire that had guided the children of Israel through forty years in the wilderness subdivided and settled in the hearts and souls of the disciples to empower their ministry. They in turn passed on the fire to the believers in Samaria.

I. We Require Power from Above

A crow saw a turtle sitting on top of a fence post. Curious, the crow flew down and asked the turtle, "How did you get there?" And the turtle said, "Well, obviously not by myself."

The Samaritans didn't get to this point by themselves, either. Through the laying on of hands, John and Peter empowered them with the power of the same Holy Spirit who descended upon Jesus at his baptism and filled the disciples on Pentecost.

Whenever anyone is baptized, whenever someone joins the church we are reminded that we are a people set aside, God's own children. What we do is very holy. We pass on the flame.

II. With Power Comes Accountability

Alone, we're unable to be the children God wants us to be. So the Spirit dances into our lives, touches our hearts, and causes us to sing the Lord's song. The Spirit empowers us to carry out the privilege of living our faith in front of each other. We keep each other accountable.

In ancient Israel, six "cities of refuge" were founded. The Law of Moses declared that if one person killed another, without malice or premeditation, he or she could flee to one of those cities and live there without coming to any harm until the death of the high priest. Then the person would be free to go home. The rabbis had an interesting tradition about those cities. Once a year the roads leading to those cities were repaired and cleaned of any obstacles so the person fleeing for his or her life would have nothing to hinder the way to the refuge.

The same is true of the church. Our "city of refuge" is Christ. Our mission is to clear the roads so that others won't stumble. Every church should be a road that points the way and helps people on to the refuge that can only be found in Christ. Live your faith before others and empower them. Pass on the flame of the Spirit. (Billy D. Strayhorn)

THE AGRICULTURE OF PRAYER

LUKE 3:15-17, 21-22

John and Jesus—two men on a mission for God. One is famous, the other is unknown. They meet at the river's edge and walk into the water. When they emerge, roles have been reversed, but the mission remains: harvest the field. But what of the means? A fiery clearing of wheat and chaff? A parable of wheat falling and dying and rising enacted by the Sower himself? John's mission is to prepare Israel for God through repentance. The people must be winnowed and straightened so that God may have direct access to their hearts, minds, and souls. John will baptize with water. Jesus will baptize with "the Holy Spirit and fire." John calls for a conflagration of apocalyptic conversion. The people will burn with shame and be saved or be consumed by the Spirit's fire. The task of the Lukan community is to discover the difference that grace makes in this fiery rhetoric. Turning up the heat and giving light are different methods of the same mission. John and Jesus—one led into the water; the other, named "Beloved," will lead into life.

I. Prayer Before Harvest

John began his mission with a fiery call to repentance and a scorching rebuke to the religious elite. He mocked those who pray publicly for private ends.

Jesus joined sinners in an act of public repentance, and as he prayed, his identity and mission were revealed. Prayer precedes the reception of the Holy Spirit. The Spirit led Jesus into the wilderness. In the Gospel of Luke, every mission of Jesus begins with prayer.

Prayer is not a private experience. Prayer, even when most private, is corporate. Prayer is preparation for action and the way that action is informed by the will of God. The Spirit, received through prayer, will lead Jesus into the wilderness and then into the field white with harvest. To "bring good news" and to "proclaim release to the captives" is thus a full realization of the power of the Spirit received in prayer.

Prayer should be labeled: "Use for results beyond caution." When we pray for the Spirit we pray carefully, because the Spirit will make us careful in our actions. We will be called, led, winnowed, and ripened in the service of God and neighbor.

II. Prayer as a Harvest

The Spirit is not achieved; it is given. Jesus was conceived through the Holy Spirit, but received the Spirit in his baptism.

His baptism was like his prayer. It opened his life to the Spirit, who formed, nurtured, and then led him into God's harvest.

The point of contact between Jesus and the Spirit is the blessing given and a need created. Jesus is the gift, the beloved child of God. He is God-given, and with him comes the blessing of creation. God is well pleased. This echoes the original blessing of creation, which God had blessed as "good, and very good."

To what, then, does the Spirit respond? Prayer. To join in the harvest of the Spirit requires an openness to receive the blessing of God. In the Gospel, all this "agriculture of prayer" is discovered and expressed in the mission of Jesus. Just as Jesus receives his blessing and mission in the midst of his baptism, so also we begin our "harvest" in the water. Prayer begins, forms, and is reformed through the Spirit. This blessing of water and fire and Spirit also creates a need: to love God with heart, mind, soul, and strength. The harvest is waiting. Pray that the laborers come. (Heather Murray Elkins)

JANUARY 15, 1995

❧

Second Sunday After Epiphany

Worship Theme: God has given us diverse gifts that we might all have a place of service in his Kingdom.

Readings: Isaiah 62:1-5; 1 Corinthians 12:1-11; John 2:1-11

Call to Worship (Psalm 36:7-9):
How precious is your steadfast love, O God!
   All people may take refuge in
     the shadow of your wings.
They feast on the abundance of your house,
   and you give them drink from
     the river of your delights.
For with you is the fountain of life;
   in your light we see light.

Pastoral Prayer:
   O Lord, our Teacher and Comforter, as we stand in your presence, may we be encouraged and uplifted so that we may bring forth fruit for your glory. We deplore our lack of zeal for you and your Kingdom. We have believed more in self-assertion than self-sacrifice. We have wronged good causes by our indifference, by our suspicions, and by our cold, critical words. We have grown weary in well doing. Grant us the gift of the Holy Spirit that he may teach us to acknowledge our sins, sincerely to repent of them, and to receive your forgiveness so that we may serve you and our fellows in newness of life. Inspire us with the true desire to glorify you in all the works of our hands. May we fight the good fight and be faithful unto death, so that we may receive at last the crown of eternal life. Amen. (John Bishop)

SERMON BRIEFS

GOD'S CINDERELLA

ISAIAH 62:1-5

When I was a sophomore at Wake Forest University, there was a great air of excitement on our campus. Our lowly football team had won only one game the previous season and had lost ten. That season, however, we started out with victories against two smaller schools. Some folks said, "Well, we really are a sorry team if we can't beat these guys. We'll see how we do against some real competition."

As the season progressed, we beat Maryland, Duke, our arch-rival the despised North Carolina Tarheels, and before you knew it, we had cracked the AP Top Twenty. On Homecoming Day, we fell behind Auburn by eighteen points at halftime. The mood in the stands was "It was fun while it lasted. I guess the glass slipper's for someone else." In the second half, the Demon Deacons scored three touchdowns and a two-point conversion to win the game 42-38. We were touted in *Sports Illustrated* as the Cinderella team of the nation and went on to play in the Tangerine Bowl—the first time that had happened in thirty years. Wake Forest, the poor stepsister of ACC football, had gotten to dance at the ball after all.

Who doesn't resonate with the story of Cinderella? Who hasn't felt like the poor stepsister at times? Maybe that's why little girls love to hear the story of an ordinary girl who gets to dance with the handsome prince.

It seems that God has a thing for unwanted stepsisters. He told Israel that they weren't chosen because they were the most wonderful people on the face of the earth. Quite the contrary. God picked them because they were lowly. They probably never felt any lowlier than during the waning years of the Babylonian exile. Disobedient and rebellious, they found themselves in a God-forsaken country where their enemies made fun of them.

How do you turn a perennial loser into a winner? Through persistence, hard work, and determination. As Coach John Mackovic and his positive outlook, coupled with his football genius,

49

turned the Deacons into Cinderellas, Isaiah's faithfulness to God's call helped to transform the exiled band from Judah. He prayed for his people. He continued to prophesy to them, even in difficult circumstances. He told them, "I'm going to keep on preaching and praying until your righteousness shines like the dawn, until your salvation is as obvious as a blazing torch."

Isaiah reminded God's people that God wasn't through with them. "One day," Isaiah may have written, "every nation and person on earth will know that you are righteous." God promised to give a new name to the people. Their name had been desolate. They had felt the numbing agony of God's judgment. Their name was Desolation. But like a parent who visits the child that had been sent to his room to assure the child of the parent's love, God visited his people with words of reassurance for them. "Your new name will be Beulah. I will delight in you. You will be married to me. You're my prize."

God promised his people that there would be a wedding feast. Weddings are such sentimental times. A young man and a young woman dream about the person they will marry, and the time finally comes when, after a period of courtship, they commit to each other with all of the hopes for a "happily ever after."

God is preparing another wedding feast for a lot of other Cinderellas—people just like you and me. It's called the marriage feast of the Lamb for those who come to him through Jesus Christ. (Mark A. Johnson)

SEASONING THE CHURCH

1 CORINTHIANS 12:1-11

The Corinthian Christians wrote to Paul, asking about every aspect of living the faith. But their primary question concerned the work of the Holy Spirit in the life of the Christian and in the life of the church. Paul helped them to understand the work of the Holy Spirit within the individual Christian and in the church.

I. The Spirit Provides a Variety of Gifts

To paraphrase Paul, the church is like a variety store of the gifts of the Spirit. We aren't created with the same talents. Some folks sing in the choir, some sing in the congregation, and some don't sing at all.

Dick Van Dyke told the story, in *Faith Hope and Hilarity,* of a woman taking her nephew to church. She whispered to him as they approached the pew: "Can you genuflect?" "No," he said, "but I can somersault!"

Young and old alike, we're all given a different set of gifts. Some can sing, some can play an instrument, some can pray or preach or visit, some can genuflect, and some can somersault. We are created with a variety of talents, not for uniformity but for unity.

II. We Have a Variety of Gifts, but We Share One Spirit

We are all one-of-a-kind designer originals. Our gifts and abilities come from and are inspired by "the same Spirit, the same Lord, the same God." There might be a diversity of gifts, but there is only one God. And through the diversity of our gifts, there can be unity of faith and purpose.

III. The Spirit Gifts Us to Serve and Glorify God

Each of our gifts adds spice to life and enhances the flavor of the church. Have you ever tasted a dish and known that there was something missing? It's not bad; it just doesn't taste right. Without the seasoning of our gifts within the stew of the church, something is missing. Our gifts are needed.

When we each do our part and add our talents to the work of the Kingdom, it enhances the flavor of the whole church and of life itself. Paul wrote: "To each is given the manifestation of the Spirit for the common good" (v. 7).

Dennis the Menace and his pal Joey were standing beside Mr. Wilson's chair. Dennis and Joey both had on identical striped shirts and were wearing Mickey Mouse ears. Mr. Wilson had an "Oh, no!" look of shock on his face. And Dennis said, "I'm training him to be just like me!"

We're called to serve and glorify God, maybe not with the intensity of Dennis the Menace but certainly with the enthusiasm. We're called to be the salt of the earth, adding spice to the life of the church and to the life of the world.

We're called to enhance the flavor of life by showing others that faith is real, that guilt is meant to be redeemed and sin to be forgiven.

A farmer had two mules. One was named Willing, and the other was named Able. Willing wasn't able, and Able wasn't willing. Consequently, the farmer didn't get much done.

Paul challenges us with a picture of a church filled with people who have breathed deeply of the Spirit and are united in Christ. The church needs people who are both willing and able to add their seasoning to the pot so that all can be fed. The challenge is simple: The church needs you. Yours may be the one missing ingredient. Add the seasoning of your gift to the stew pot of the church. (Billy D. Strayhorn)

STANDING IN LINE FOR WINE

JOHN 2:1-11

The miracle at Cana is one of the most frequently mentioned, yet most neglected, stories of Jesus. Every couple who made it down the aisle, hoping that it won't take long but will last forever, has heard about Cana. Every caterer of a reception has a latent memory of this water/wine solution. But what of the theological context of this overly heard text? Why does this Gospel begin with a small crisis of hospitality and claim that this narrative of Jesus as a reluctant miracle worker "reveals his glory"?

I. Jesus Pronounces Creation Good Again

This miracle recreates the original blessing of creation, male and female. Jesus' presence at a wedding is life-affirming, restoring the connection between the human community and the created order.

The first sign of the Word made flesh is not that of a magician, or even a Messiah. Wine, the ancient means of blessing, is restored to the human community by the One through whom "all things came into being." God, in Christ, is the life of this party.

II. New Wine Won't Wait

The new wine of the Spirit can't be labeled for long. Every year planes in Paris are placed on alert as spring wine is rushed from vines to market. Lines of people in cities around the world gather to purchase a bottle of this fresh ferment of spring. Just like spring wine, the work of the Spirit cannot be kept waiting.

The immediacy of the gospel is evident in this miracle at Cana. The water is poured in; the wine is poured out; the hearts of the guests are made glad.

III. Do What He Tells You

The Christ of John's Gospel is the divine revelation, the eternal Word, the Holy One of God. This passage provides one of the few intimate insights into a mother-and-son relationship. She asks him to help. He hesitates, seemingly refusing. She persists. The miracle is performed. It is difficult to avoid the temptation to psychologize this text out of context. The meaning of Mary to John's community is difficult to translate into a contemporary Protestant setting. What is evident is that Jesus was moved to · enact his first miracle with its sacramental images within a human celebration.

There are many traditions of spiritual formation and corporate discipleship. Each generation of believers explores ancient methods of prayer and invents new structures of mission. The simplest guide of all can be found in Mary's instruction: "Do what he tells you."

There are many ways to wait in line. There is usually only one reason—you want whatever is at the place where the line begins. Charles Wesley wrote hundreds of hymns for the Methodists to sing while they were waiting in line, the communion line. The early Methodist movement produced a community that transformed their world, "doing what he told them." They visited prisons, formed schools, fed the hungry, opposed slavery, prayed unceasingly, and stood in long lines in order to receive the new wine of the Spirit served at the Lord's Table. It is, remember, the finest spring wine on earth and in heaven. (Heather Murray Elkins)

JANUARY 22, 1995

~

Third Sunday After Epiphany

Worship Theme: God's Word brings unity and understanding to God's people.

Readings: Nehemiah 8:1-3, 5-6, 8-10; 1 Corinthians 12:12-31*a*; Luke 4:14-21

Call to Worship (Psalm 19:7-9):

Leader: The law of the LORD is perfect, reviving the soul;

People: the decrees of the LORD are sure, making wise the simple;

Leader: the precepts of the LORD are right, rejoicing the heart;

People: the commandment of the LORD is clear, enlightening the eyes;

Leader: the fear of the LORD is pure, enduring forever;

All: the ordinances of the LORD are true and righteous altogether.

Pastoral Prayer:
O Lord, you have spoken to us in so many ways: in the beauty of creation, in the truth of your Word, and most wonderfully in your Son and our Savior. What a wonder that the Creator of all seeks to communicate with us! Yet how tragic, Father, that we so often ignore your truth in order to bow down at the altars of culture and possession and self. Forgive us our foolishness and our selfishness, and draw us unto yourself that we might know afresh your love and grace. Amen. (Michael Duduit)

54

SERMON BRIEFS

THE POWER OF THE WORD

NEHEMIAH 8:1-3, 5-6, 8-10

Why do you come to church? What does church really mean to you? If you were to pose that question to a variety of people, you would get a variety of answers. An eighty-year-old grandmother might respond with great surprise that you would ask such a question. A teenager in the youth group would say, "I like the kids that come here. We have fun together." A young mother with small children whose husband has just left her may say, "This is the only place where I find people who really seem to care about what happens to us."

But suppose that your church building was taken from you—perhaps destroyed by a fire or a tornado. Suppose that for some reason you and your fellow church members had been dispersed by some government resettlement program and after a period of years you all returned to your town and attempted to get on with the business of being the church. What would be the most important element of your celebration? I would hope that it would be to reestablish your fellowship around God's Word.

I. We Gather to Hear the Word of God

The scenario I have just described to you is not unlike the scene in our text. After the people of Israel had been in exile in Babylon, they returned to Palestine. Many of these "returnees," however, had been born in Babylon and had never seen their "homeland." What they found upon their return looked nothing like the wistful stories that had been told to them by their elders. Jerusalem was in ruins.

The books of Ezra and Nehemiah tell the story of the community reestablishing itself in the Promised Land. Nehemiah tells how he wept when he surveyed the scene. After an appropriate period of mourning, he realized that his tears would not rebuild the wall—there was work to be done. So he rallied the forces, and they got to work.

In the seventh month, the people gathered together and did a most interesting thing. They asked the chief priest to read the book of the Law to them. And that's what Ezra did. Now, when I counsel a new believer to read the Bible, I encourage that person to start with the New Testament—one of the Gospels, either Mark or John. I also counsel the person to avoid starting at Genesis and attempting to read straight through, because some of the stuff in Leviticus and Numbers gets pretty slow.

Yet these people had been unable to worship for so long, they had suffered the consequences of their rebellion against God for so long that they had an insatiable hunger to hear God's instruction for them. They all stood from early morning until noon, listening to their "preacher" read the Bible to them. All the people listened attentively to the law. This wasn't just the stories of the Creation or of Noah or of Abraham. No, it also included laws about mildew, descriptions of the priestly garments, the regulations for the building of the tabernacle, and the dietary laws. Why would the people stand for six hours to listen to this?

II. The Word Produces in Us Power and Celebration

Throughout their reading of the scripture, emphasis was placed on explaining to the people what was being read so that they could understand it. They celebrated because they understood the words of God.

Have you ever struggled with a problem, maybe some principle in mathematics when you were in school? It seemed so difficult as you pondered it until, all at once, the lights went on and the bells rang as understanding broke through. That's a wonderful feeling.

God's people suddenly understood in a new and exciting way that God loved and cared for them, even in the most mundane and ordinary corners of their lives. And just as the reading of the Word helped them to understand their place in God's world, so also the study of the Word in our lives helps us gain new insight that will make a difference in our lives each day. Such an understanding in your life will be a cause for great celebration! (Mark A. Johnson)

STRIVE FOR THE GREATEST GIFTS
1 CORINTHIANS 12:12-31*a*

In a "Peanuts" cartoon Lucy is berating Charlie Brown: "And I don't care if I ever see you again! Do you hear me?" Linus turns to Charlie Brown and says: "She really hurt your feelings, didn't she, Charlie Brown? I hope she didn't take all the life out of you."

Charlie Brown answers: "No, not completely. . . . But you can number me among the walking wounded!"

Some of us know about the walking wounded. The church is full of them. And the sad part is that many of the wounded have been hurt in the church. That's what Paul is addressing in this letter.

I. There Is Strength in Our Diversity

One of the great biblical affirmations is that we are created in God's image. And we are each unique. Each part of the body is unique. While the left hand and the right hand are both hands, each is different from the other. We've all known people who we have said have two left feet, but imagine really having two left feet or even two right hands. Each part of the body has been tested and approved and was created for a specific purpose. We can function without certain parts or with artificial parts, but we work best when all the parts are in their place and functioning.

The same is true in the church. Every Christian has been given gifts and talents. Within the Body of Christ, the church, there should be no distinction as to the importance of any single gift over another. All are important. All have been tested and approved. All have been designed and given for a specific purpose.

When a portion of our body is broken or sick, the whole body suffers. An ingrown toenail or an earache affects the whole body. The same is true in the church. "If one member suffers, all suffer."

II. We Seek Unity in the Midst of Diversity

Paul says we should "strive for the greater gifts." That greater gift is the unity of the body. As members of the Body of Christ, we are called to strive for unity despite and in the midst of our diversity.

One of the greatest instances of Christian unity I've ever witnessed was in Israel in 1992. On a tour of the Holy Land, our group—made up of United Methodists, Presbyterians, Disciples of Christ, and Roman Catholics—stopped at the Church of the Nativity in Bethlehem on Russian and Greek Orthodox Christmas Eve, our Epiphany. Attached to the church is an ancient monastery. There in the cell occupied by Jerome, the Roman Catholic priest who translated the Old and New Testaments from the Greek and Hebrew into the Latin Vulgate, making the Bible accessible to ordinary people, we paused to sing Christmas carols. While we were singing, a group of Korean and German Christians joined us, and in mixed tongues and mixed denominational affiliations, we celebrated the birth of the Savior of us all. In the midst of our vast diversity, there was unity.

This is the kind of unity Paul described. We can have different belief systems. We can worship and serve God in different ways. Christianity is not one person or one idea over another. It is life inspired and empowered by the Holy Spirit to serve the Lord and Savior of us all. "Strive for the greater gift" of unity in Christ. (Billy D. Strayhorn)

WHEN THE PERSONAL IS POLITICAL: THE POLITICS OF COMPASSION

LUKE 4:14-21

How can the gospel be politically relevant without being defined by party politics? In politics, our labels often turn into libels. He is politically liberal. She is fiscally conservative. New Age. Stone age. Left, right, left of right, right in the middle, somewhere between here and there—we cannot live without labels. They place us in relation to each other. But a social or political map may subdivide and even balkanize our social relations. Often a label obscures the real people and the real needs that make politics necessary. The art of politics, the "science of economics," are the means through which communities seek the common good. But the common good is more than the common human denominator. The God of Israel also has a vested interest in politics and economics. The politics of God are the politics of compassion. The spiritual economy of God's sovereignty establishes new possibilities for individual and social relations.

I. The Personal Is the Political

In this passage Jesus is presented with a personal crisis in his ministry. He faces the difficulty of proclaiming the spiritual economy of God's sovereignty in his own community. The difficulty he must confront is that the people may confuse the messenger with the message. It has been reported that he is "filled with the power of the Spirit." People expect miracles. What he does or says will be evaluated in terms of their previous expectations.

The personal is the political. The community will not recognize the radical possibilities of personal and social transformation created by the spiritual economy of God's sovereignty. Compassion requires intimacy, knowing the stranger as neighbor, recognizing God in the least and the lost. The personal is the political, but Nazareth does not recognize how true this slogan really is.

II. Economics Is Transformation

A simple definition of *economics* is "a study of how money changes hands." Economics was once called the dismal science because in studying patterns of exchange it also detailed patterns of human misery. Money changed hands and changed the hands that it crossed. Some prospered, but many more did not. In choosing to read from the prophet Isaiah with his echoes of the year of the Jubilee, Jesus redefined economics on the economy of God.

In the Jubilee year, it was required that those who had lost their land or freedom be restored what they had lost. This was the human community modeling the economy of creation and God's liberation from slavery for the promised land.

Economics consists of patterns of exchange. Yet politics can revolutionize any economy. The politics of compassion (e.g., the parables of the sower, the unjust steward, the prodigal son) constitutes God's spiritual economy. This is the economy that determines a pattern of transformation as well as a pattern of exchange: as we have freely received, we freely give.

The fundamental need that makes politics political is conflicting perspectives on achieving the common good. This is the reason why we can be so deeply disappointed by politics and politicians. When private interests and party loyalty replace a commitment to the common good then it may appear impossible to trust our lives to others. All is reduced to calculations of self-interest. There is no valued self left to take an interest in. Politics becomes the politics of private passion, not a search for the compassion.

With God, however, the political is the personal. In his reading of Isaiah, Jesus proclaimed the compassion of God. The people were expectant because Jesus personally assumed the responsibility of proclaiming the compassion of God for all "the poor," "the captives," "the blind," and "the oppressed." The ordinary expectations of a leader have been met. Jesus, the local boy, had performed a miracle of healing. The real miracle, however, is that Jesus initiated the economy of God's grace. Jesus will fulfill all that is implied in this proclamation. The politics of compassion will lead Jesus from a crisis in Nazareth to the cross in Jerusalem. His personal is political. His passion of compassion will ultimately lead to the transformation known as the resurrection.

(Heather Murray Elkins)

JANUARY 29, 1995

❧

Fourth Sunday After Epiphany

Worship Theme: Because God has loved us, we are empowered to love others.

Readings: Jeremiah 1:4-10; 1 Corinthians 13:1-13; Luke 4:21-30

Call to Worship (Psalm 71:15-16):

My mouth will tell of your righteous acts,
   of your deeds of salvation all day long,
     though their number is past my knowledge.
I will come praising the mighty
     deeds of the Lord GOD,
   I will praise your righteousness, yours alone.

Pastoral Prayer:

Lord God, because we are richly blessed by having Christ in our lives, we pray for others in these moments. Help us to share Christ in the world, through both our words and our actions. Help us to touch others with love and compassion as we daily work and shop and talk and live, always mindful of our call to be "doers of the Word." Help us to give according to our means to the work of Christ, freely and without compulsion. Help us to pray daily for peace in our troubled world; for peace in family and personal relationships; for peace in our own troubled and chaotic lives. May the peace that passes understanding be ours. Help us to speak kindly of those who hurt us; to walk softly when our desire is to make a big noise; to listen when we want to state our opinions; to worship you when we feel we ought to be "worshiped." You have given us freedom. Help us to use it wisely. Amen.
(Steven R. Fleming)

SERMON BRIEFS

ACCEPTING GOD'S CALL

JEREMIAH 1:4-10

"God loves you and has a wonderful plan for your life." These are words that we all believe, I'm sure. God has a plan for each of us, but many times we wrongly tend to limit God's call to preachers and missionaries. Although Jeremiah thought himself unqualified, God chose him to be God's messenger.

I. God Had a Purpose for Jeremiah

Jeremiah was to be God's mouthpiece in a time of great turmoil. It should not surprise us that God would be at work in a situation of turmoil, but it may shock some to know that God did not choose to make his voice heard through the world superpowers. Instead, he spoke through a young man who lived in the unknown town of Anathoth. There was a priestly community there, and Jeremiah was probably the descendant of a priestly family.

It's interesting that Jeremiah starts by saying, "The word of the LORD came to me" (v. 4). This is the basis for any effective service. Nothing we have to say or do is of any value if it is not deeply rooted in God's call. Jeremiah was not called to voice his own opinions but to speak for God.

It's significant to note that God's purpose went back long before Jeremiah was even born. God says to Jeremiah and to us:

> "Before I formed you in the womb, I knew you,
> and before you were born, I consecrated you."

The fact that God wanted to use Jeremiah was too much for the young prophet to take in. Hence, the desperation in his voice as he says, "Ah, Lord GOD! Truly I do not know how to speak, for I am only a boy." But God is no respecter of persons. He says,

> "Do not say, 'I am only a boy';
> for you shall go to all to whom I send you,
> and you shall speak whatever I command you." (v. 7)

The assurance is "Do not be afraid . . . I am with you" (v. 8).

Isn't that the last thing Jesus told his disciples before he ascended into heaven? The last part of the Great Commission says, "I am with you always" (Matt. 28:20). What else do we need? There's a lot of despair and purposelessness in the lives of people in the 1990s. But God has a purpose. We don't have to be afraid. Age and social standing don't matter. What matters is finding ourselves in obedience to God.

II. God Had a Commission for Jeremiah

Much like the assurance that God would be with him, God assured Jeremiah that God would put the words in the prophet's mouth. God says that Jeremiah would be appointed to do some unpleasant things.

I don't know about you, but I'd rather be a positive person. When I accepted God's call to ministry, I had visions of building great churches, seeing multitudes saved, and generally making a difference in the community. If this had been the call that I received, I don't know how I would have responded. It's painful to have to be prophetic at times and speak harsh words of judgment to people who you know won't accept what you say.

Jeremiah's call was much like that of Moses, Joshua, Isaiah, and others we read about in scripture. In times of human inadequacy, God not only promises his presence, but he also promises to give us the words to say. God's call is something that comes to us every day. He gives us the opportunity to accept it or reject it, and he assures us of his grace, which will enable us to bring it to completion. (Mark A. Johnson)

IF IT DOESN'T RAIN NEXT WEDNESDAY

1 CORINTHIANS 13:1-13

A young man wrote his sweetheart a love letter: "Dear Jennifer, I love you so much I'd climb the highest mountain just to see your smile. I'd swim the deepest river, infested with piranhas, just for one of your kisses. I'd cross the widest sea for one of your hugs. I'd cross the burning desert just to look upon your face.

With neverending love, Frank. P.S.: I'll be over to see you next Wednesday, if it doesn't rain."

Are you a fair-weather lover? Our whole purpose is to be agents of love; not James Bond type agents of love, but agents whose lives and behavior are ruled by Christlike love.

I. We Love Because Christ First Loved Us

Alone we can't begin to understand what love *really* is, even with a definition like Paul's. This love can be understood only in the context of a faith relationship with Christ. Only in this relationship can we be empowered to love.

Love is the central message of Christianity. We can do everything that a church is supposed to do, but if we don't have love and express that love to each other, then we have nothing. God's love, the sacrificial love we experience in Christ, moves and transforms us into Christlike people.

II. We Love Through Our Actions

As Christians, all we have is this power of love. This is what makes us different and sets us apart from all the other religions; not our worship and preaching, not our singing and Sunday schools. What sets us apart is this quality of love that begins with God and empowers everything we do.

Christian love is more than a warm, fuzzy feeling. It is being patient whether you feel like it or not. It is being kind even when you want to be mean—*especially* when you want to be mean. It is refusing to be boastful. It is forgiving when you want to get even. It's not a feeling; it is a way of acting and living.

December 21, 1990, in Mount Vernon, Missouri, was a bitterly cold day. Outside the local hospital, protesters maintained an around-the-clock vigil. They were protesting the court-granted right of Nancy Cruzan's parents to shut down life support systems and let the thirty-three-year-old woman die after being in a coma for seven years.

Nancy Cruzan's father came outside and met briefly with the protesters. He could have resented their presence and their protests, but he didn't just think of himself. He brought out a coffee pot, cups, and an extension cord. His thoughtfulness and love extended even to the people who were protesting against him.

Mr. Cruzan was expressing his faith in a powerful way. Only the love of Christ in our lives can transform our thoughts and actions like that. There is no other way for Christians.

The highest, most exalted act of life is to love. When we allow Christ into our lives, we become more Christlike in our attitude and behavior, not like the young lover, pledging undying love if doesn't rain next Wednesday.

Let Christ's love grow and multiply in your heart. Reach out in love, not because others deserve it, but because you were loved when you didn't deserve it. Let love, Christian love as described here in Paul's letter, guide your every action and thought. (Billy D. Strayhorn)

NOT GOOD ENOUGH FOR GOOD NEWS

LUKE 4:21-30

There ought to be a law: Nobody preaches this passage unless he or she was born and raised in the place where he or she is preaching. No outsider can be faithful to this text. You have to know, in your bones, what it's like to stand in front of those who raised you, who fed and forgave you, who changed you, or chased you out of their kitchen or classroom or store. There's no getting around the knowing. These are the ones who heard you learn to talk, and now you're going to tell them something they don't know.

I. Good News Isn't Home-Grown

Where strangers heard the sound of a "fulfilling" gospel, Jesus' friends and neighbors heard the extravagant claims of a son who'd gone "strange." Adherence to local custom is a powerful test of sanity. Was this home boy crazy or spirit-led? Prophet or prankster? No-good Nazareth, filled with self-deceit and self-despair, refused to believe that the good news had come bearing its accent, wearing its clothes.

Charity should begin at home. Part of the anger in that congregation came from disappointment. Jesus had healed elsewhere. Why not at home? Jesus had fed strangers. Why not his own?

Prayer cannot live in an atmosphere of spiritual provinciality. When we demand a localized example of grace, we smother the very breath of the Spirit. Charity, our charity of heart, is necessary for any miracle of faith and hope and love.

II. No News Is Good News

One of the disturbing developments of the media industry is the dissolving of the distance between reporting and public relations. The hiring of a former Pentagon official as a headline maker for a major news network is seen as good business, not bad practice. Keeping a news source happy is the current method of truth retrieval. Suppression of disturbing information is the guarantee of a long and happy relationship. No wonder they wanted to push Jesus off the highest cliff they could find. He had the bad taste to remind them of all the good news that had happened somewhere else. Why didn't their local paper carry stories about the long drought of God's Word? Why wasn't there any gossip about a neighborhood healing? Because no news is never good news when it comes to God.

III. What We Need Is a Lot, Not a Little, Good News

The classic song "What We Need Is a Little Good News Today" by Anne Murray is a wistful expression of our desire for some word of life, some evidence of good. We have grown numb to the news of war. The global voice can be heard hour by hour, reciting narratives of horror or honor, but the net effect is a flatline reading on our heart. What we need is a lot, not a little, good news.

The congregation in Nazareth wanted a little spice to their life, a local manifestation of the transcendence of God. What the local rabbi wanted was some confirmation of the good work he'd done with the youth. What we all want, even now, is a private revelation of our ultimate importance. What Jesus offers is the news of all time being fulfilled for all people. The justice that will reorder the universe has begun in our sight. The peace that will surpass all local forms of appeasement has been offered. The love that called creation into life has begun a new world right in the midst of our aisle. May God help us to recognize the news that is better than good—the gospel of Jesus, our Christ. (Heather Murray Elkins)

FEBRUARY

ᕀ

Replenishing the Well

Expect to See God

Epiphany is a season of revelation, a time when God is revealed to the world. During Epiphany, we expect to see God revealed in Scripture, in the community of faith, in our daily lives. Expect to see God this day in Epiphany. The following exercise helps you to expect a personal Epiphany.

Time: 45 minutes.

Materials: A Bible, your journal, and a pen or pencil.

Exercise:
Read Luke 6:17-26 carefully. Close your Bible. Read through the rest of this exercise before you begin.

Get into a comfortable position in your chair, both feet flat on the floor, your hands quietly in your lap. Close your eyes. Imagine you are one of Jesus' disciples gathered on the plain. Feel the crowd surrounding you, jostling you out of the way to touch Jesus. Like the rest of the crowd, you have come to see Jesus for healing. The crowd catches you up and surges forward toward Jesus. You turn around, and suddenly you are face to face with Jesus. You realize he is speaking directly to you, "Blessed are you. . . ." Jesus goes on to tell you how you are blessed. Listen carefully to Jesus.

Then, after a pause, he begins speaking to you again, saying, "Woe to you . . ."—words of admonition, even warning. Listen carefully as Jesus lists reasons you have for woe.

Jesus is finished speaking to you, and you are left behind in the crowd.

Now slowly open your eyes and open your journal. Remember, in the scene you have just imagined you came to Jesus for healing. You will now record Jesus' healing words to you.

On a fresh page, write "Blessed are you," then fill in your name after that and complete the sentence. For example, "Blessed are you, Jane, for you have known pain and soon you will know healing." You may write several such "Blessed are you" sentences. When you've finished, write "Woe to you"; fill in your name after that and complete the sentence. For example, "Woe to you, Andrew, for your sharp tongue will bring you trouble." You may write several such "Woe to you" sentences. After you've finished, close your journal.

Conclude this exercise by offering a prayer of thanksgiving for Jesus' healing words and ask for strength and guidance. (Harriet Crosby)

FEBRUARY 5, 1995

❧

Fifth Sunday After Epiphany

Worship Theme: The resurrection of Jesus Christ provides us victory over life and death.

Readings: Isaiah 6:1-8 (9-13); 1 Corinthians 15:1-11; Luke 5:1-11

Call to Worship (Psalm 138:7-8):
Though I walk in the midst of trouble,
> you preserve me against the wrath of my enemies;
you stretch out your hand,
> and your right hand delivers me.
The LORD will fulfill his purpose for me;
> your steadfast love, O LORD, endures forever.

Pastoral Prayer:
Father, in Jesus you defeated death. And through faith in him, you enable us also to live in victory over death. Forgive us for the times when we do not live in the knowledge of the eternal life you have already given us. Renew our understanding of Jesus' resurrection so we may rejoice in our resurrections with full vigor, to the glory of Jesus in whose name we pray. Amen. (Robert R. Kopp)

SERMON BRIEFS

EMPOWERED BEYOND OURSELVES!
ISAIAH 6:1-8 (9-13)

Wally Chappell once said, "There is a difference between running from something and running to something." The vision shared in this powerful revelation comes to a man who finds himself in personal need. The power of this passage is discovered as God seeks to meet Isaiah where he is. It is through this vision that Isaiah is moved—beyond his grief, beyond his despair, beyond his guilt, beyond his suffering—to a point of going and doing for the Lord.

People are in pain! Their lives are broken. They're struggling to make some sense of it all. I have discovered that often, through such events and experiences, persons are open and listening for the voice of God in a way as never before. Moses was tormented that his people were enslaved. God called him beyond that pain to lead his people. Martin Luther King, Jr., hurt for the condition of black people. In King's concern and struggle, God called him forth to lead the civil rights movement that swept across America. Sometimes, God meets us in our pain and moves us beyond it, to make a difference.

Isaiah came, in pain, seeking after God. Apparently Isaiah had this vision from God in the Temple. The revelation that came as a part of this vision involves a powerful and majestic display on God's part. In the presence of God, Isaiah saw himself as he really was. His words are "Woe is me! I am lost, for I am a man of unclean lips, and I live among a people of unclean lips" (v. 5). God's revelation brings a sense of Isaiah's unworthiness and the unworthiness of his people.

Bruce Larson, author and preacher, talks about how David was a man after God's own heart. The reason for God's favor toward David is, in the words of Larson, "David knew what to do with his unworthiness." Isaiah, in the convicting presence of God, was overwhelmed with a sense of unworthiness. Isaiah's honest admission and confession in the presence of God invoked God's forgiveness. Isaiah also knew what to do with his unworthiness. Are we doing anything with our unworthiness? Are we in touch with the spirit and movement of God's own self-disclosure enough in our lives that we have let down our defenses to the point that we can honestly admit who we are and what we have or haven't done, as God's person? Such a movement is crucial for us to ever get to a place in our lives where we trust God with all of who we are. God help us to know what to do with our own unworthiness!

The drama now moves to God and his response to Isaiah. God forgave him and shared God's concern by asking of Isaiah,

"Whom shall I send, and who will go for us?" (v. 8). These questions imply God's concern for Isaiah's community of faith. The progression of this drama has now moved from the personal need of Isaiah—his grief—to his coming to the Temple seeking after God, to God's revelation to him as God discloses himself, to the honest confession by Isaiah of his own unworthiness, to forgiveness, and now to God involving Isaiah as God discloses his own concern as to who can go to the people with his Word. It is a sweeping story that describes, in detail, the call of this prophet of God. Some who have received this same call will see their own story here. The power of this call is discovered as Isaiah is moved beyond his own need, through forgiveness, to being invited by God through the petition to participate with God in bringing his Word to the community. God leads Isaiah throughout the story beyond himself and his situation.

As Isaiah ran to God and not from his struggle, God empowered him to move beyond the struggle. Sometimes in the journey of life, our own healing comes, as we seek to follow God's lead, to the power of helping others. Isaiah was a person of faith in desperate need. While in the Temple, he was overwhelmed by a vision from God. Through that vision, Isaiah moved beyond his need to a place where he could answer the penetrating question of God with, "Here am I; send me!" With God's help, we are enabled to move beyond our own hurts, pains, struggles, doubts, and fears to become persons sent forth in the name of the One who calls. Through our own encounters with this God who loves us, may we come to realize that we, too, are a sent people! May we stop running from life and start running to this God who "empowers us beyond ourselves!" (Travis Franklin)

FACING OUR BIGGEST FEARS
1 CORINTHIANS 15:1-11

The resurrection of Jesus Christ equips us to face the two biggest fears in the world: the fear of *dying* and the fear of *living*. However deep your grief may be coming from those necessary and unnecessary losses in your own life, the very bottom line of the Christian faith is that Jesus Christ is Victor over both life and death.

One of the most important facts of the Christian faith is the bodily resurrection of Jesus Christ. The very existence of the Christian church bears witness to the fact that something happened to transform a broken, beaten group of losers into men and women who gave their very lives for Christ, whom they witnessed in his resurrection power.

More than all the factual data we could muster in our endeavor to prove the literal resurrection of Christ is the very fact that he, right now, is in the business of changing lives. He is equipping people to die. He is equipping people to live. Our Christianity is not just an ethical system that helps us survive in this world. The fact is that Christ is risen, and that makes a tremendous difference.

I. The Resurrection of Jesus Christ Equips You to Die

You and I are equipped to live only when we are prepared to die. We are all in the process of dying. Granted, it will catch up with some of us sooner than others. We bet that our turn will come up later. In reality, we are all part of a frantic string of refugees clutching to our few possessions and trying to find a safe place to live.

The resurrection of Jesus Christ releases us from having to deny the reality of death. In fact, it equips us to die in at least three ways.

First, God promises that there is life beyond this life. Paul refers to Jesus as being "the first fruits of those who have died" (v. 20). His resurrection stands as evidence that life does not end with death. Christ is Victor.

Second, God promises hope. Jesus promised that we will be with him, united with our loved ones in heaven. We are promised new bodies, spiritual bodies. It will be a different existence, free from the pain and sorrow we know here. Our hope is of a reunion with our Savior. We will see him face to face and experience a quality of life that goes beyond anything we can try to imagine.

Third, God promises that you and I need not face the specter of hell. Jesus died to set us free from that ominous alienation from God Almighty. Christ's resurrection assured us a place in heaven with our Savior. The sting of death is removed. The notion of punishment, the notion of condemnation, which is universal to the human existence, is canceled in what God has done for us in Jesus Christ.

II. The Resurrection of Jesus Christ Equips You to Live

The Christian is the one who is prepared both to die and to live. First, God promises meaning in life. A friend of mine describes his life before he came to Christ as one in which, "I was going around in circles. Circles of emptiness, with me at the center." I am convinced that Jesus Christ is the missing piece in the puzzle called life.

Second, God promises authentic forgiveness. The resurrection of Jesus Christ takes the sting out of death and exposes us to that freeing catharsis of confession. Guilt is removed. You have acknowledged that you are a sinner who needs this forgiveness. There is nothing you have done that cannot be forgiven.

Third, God promises you strength. Jesus said that we will receive power when the Holy Spirit comes upon us. Divine energy is ours. We have the strength to live, for we are not alone. We are special to God. Our confidence is in a risen Lord who wills to walk with us as an intimate friend. (John A. Huffman, Jr.)

AN EXTRAORDINARY CALL
FOR ORDINARY PEOPLE

LUKE 5:1-11

More than anything else, the story about the miraculous catch of fish is a story of a call to discipleship. Jesus had, so far, been doing his ministry alone. It is here, in Luke 5, that he begins to enlist his followers, disciples. The striking message of this passage is that God calls ordinary people to do the extraordinary and empowers them to do it.

Jesus climbed into a boat and called these fishermen to fish for people. But it was only *after* they realized Who was in the boat with them that their call came. And the call is just like ours—to serve.

I. The call of God forces us to confront our inadequacies. When Simon Peter realized Who was in the boat he fell down in front of Jesus and said, "Go away from me, Lord, for I am a sinful man!" (v. 8). He knew he was in the presence of God (he called Jesus "Master" in v. 5 but "Lord" in v. 8) and had no right to be there. He's not up to the task.

Like Isaiah, Peter was immediately conscious of his unworthiness in the face of God. None of us, by our own merit, can stand before the God of the universe with our heads held high. Any person who has accepted God's call as an adult has had this over-whelming sense of unworthiness. The past floods one's con-sciousness, and the person will echo Peter, "Depart from me! I am sinful, O Lord." We are all inadequate and unworthy.

II. But the call of God comes anyway, with the assurance of God's presence and power. Once Peter realized this was no ordi-nary man in the boat with him, he feared for his life. But Jesus offered him the soothing words that God has said several times already in Luke. To a trembling Zechariah, God's words of seren-ity: "Do not be afraid." To Mary, the panic-soothing word of God: "Do not be afraid." To an ordinary Peter, the freeing, empower-ing words: "Do not be afraid."

God says to us when we realize our undeservedness, "Do not be afraid. My grace is sufficient for you, for my power is made perfect in weakness." Jesus said to Simon Peter, "It's okay. I know you don't have what it takes. That's why I've called you." Before Peter's empowering, he was no more capable of catching people than he was capable of catching fish the night before. But God's enduring presence ("I am with you always") enables us (the ordinary disciples) to do the extraordinary and answer the call to discipleship.

III. Finally, the call of God comes with the ultimate challenge: Leave everything. "From now on" (v. 10) is not a time reference but refers to a fundamental change in the state of affairs. Peter has met the Lord and can never be the same again. He can't go back to just fishing. It's as if Jesus was saying, "*Now*, you're ready to catch people."

There is a Roman coin that has inscribed on it a picture of an ox facing both an altar and a plow with the words "Ready for either" inscribed around it. Discipleship requires the ultimate sacrifices of life. While we probably will not be required to die for our faith, the yoke of servitude awaits us. The challenge is the same: It will cost everything we have. Nothing comes before our Lord. For the three disciples and for us, it's all different now. Ordinary people must now do the extraordinary—leave it all to follow him. (Blake Harwell)

FEBRUARY 12, 1995

✌

Sixth Sunday After Epiphany

Worship Theme: Christ calls us to a radical transformation of life and values.

Readings: Jeremiah 17:5-10; 1 Corinthians 15:12-20; Luke 6:17-26

Call to Worship (Psalm 1:1-2):
Happy are those
   who do not follow the advice of the wicked,
or take the path that sinners tread,
   or sit in the seat of scoffers;
but their delight is in the law of the LORD,
   and on his law they meditate day and night.

Pastoral Prayer:
   Lord, as we reflect on the past seven days, each of us has something for which we can give thanks: the touch of a friend; a new insight; the chance to share what we have with others; a beautiful sunset that filled our hearts. Whatever it was that gave us joy, we give thanks. We thank you for the great joy that is ours in Jesus Christ, your Son, who was sent to bring us good news about life and your love. He has shown us the way of salvation and life abundant. Yet how little we thought about him this week! Draw us closer to Jesus through the power of the Holy Spirit. Shape us in Christ's image—an image of love and compassion, forgiveness and mercy, truth and justice, faithfulness and holiness. We give thanks for his model for our lives and ask courage to seek after him. Amen. (Steven R. Fleming)

SERMON BRIEFS

IN WHOM DO WE TRUST?

JEREMIAH 17:5-10

   Frank Freed tells the story of two boys who grew up in the family of an alcoholic. One of the boys became successful with his life. The other boy became an alcoholic. Each of the boys was asked why his life had turned out the way it had. Each of the boys responded with, "Well, with my background, what would you expect!" Choices are made *by* us or *for* us. One way or the other, they are *our* choices!

Jeremiah's prophecy reminds us of the fact that we must decide about our lives, and at the heart and soul of our decision is the basic idea of whom and of what we will trust. God's judgment, spoken by Jeremiah in the verses that precede our passage today, comes as a result of Judah's choice as to whom the people have sought to trust. Our scripture reading for today is a reminder to the people that they have a choice to make in life regarding whom they will trust. That choice is to trust in the ways of humans or in the way of God. Each choice carries with it a natural effect in terms of the life events that follow. Both God's favor and God's curse are ultimately expressed in terms of the choices people dare to make.

Our passage today reminds us of the contrast between the folly of placing our trust in human wisdom and placing our trust in God. To trust humanity is to live a life of illusion and error. To trust God is to live a life of blessedness and favor. This is a basic "rule of thumb" for life. It gets at the heart of who we are, who God is, and how life works. Goodness and evil, judgment and blessing, are built into the very fabric of the life we are given the opportunity to live. Our choices in terms of whom and what we trust have a natural, caustic result. The New Testament expresses it as "You reap what you sow." Richard Halverson, the chaplain to the United States Senate, expressed a similar understanding when he said, "Mastered by God, I am the master of myself and my circumstances. Mastered by anything less than God, I become the victim of myself and my circumstances." The daring question for us then becomes "Whom are we allowing to master us?" For one boy in an alcoholic family, the choice *was not* alcohol. For the other boy, the choice *was* alcohol. It was their choice. It was Judah's choice as to whom they trusted. And it is our choice as well!

The powerful images that Jeremiah used to illustrate his point show that trusting in humanity is like a bush in the wastelands; it will not see prosperity when it comes. Trusting humanity is like dwelling in parched places of the desert, in salt land where no one lives. Trusting God, on the other hand, is like a tree planted by the water that sends its roots by the stream. It does not fear when heat comes; its leaves are always green. This trusting of human wisdom found expression in the world of Judah in pursuing the worship of false gods created by human hands. Such trusting made a mockery of the people's relationship to the God of covenant. As we consider these images, they beg the question of us and our lives as to whom we worship and to whom we trust our lives. Asking such a question can lead us to confession, renewal, and hope. Or such a question can lead us to anger, denial, and curse. We live in a world consumed with the latter. Such brokenness takes on extreme and distorted expression—murder, suicide, apathy, alcoholism, drug abuse, divorce, bitterness, unhealthy relationships, sex in place of love, and all other sorts of sick expressions of life.

Life is a choice. That choice confronts us in the daily routines of our lives, as it did the people of Judah. Ultimately, in those routines we must answer the persistent question, "In whom do we trust?" (Travis Franklin)

WHAT IF THERE WERE NO EASTER?

1 CORINTHIANS 15:12-20

After years of study and dedication to her goal, Mary stumbles over a word she knew in the district spelling bee and has to sit down. At his initial "at bat" in the Major Leagues, Johnny hears the umpire bellow "Strike three!" after the first pitch! "What?" Johnny exclaims. "Sit down, rookie, you came to bat with two strikes against you!"

What if life were like a spelling bee—one mistake and you're gone? What if you began with two strikes against you with no second chance? In response to their questions about the resurrection, Paul asked the church at Corinth to imagine what it would be like to live in a world where there is no Easter.

I. If There Is No Easter, Life Has No Purpose (vv. 13-14)

If Christ was not raised, our faith is in vain, religion is a joke, the church is a sham, the Bible is full of idle wishes, and Jesus was just a man. If Christ was not raised, there is no God, so there is no goodness and tomorrow is confined to yesterday's tragedy. What if the rich young ruler was right, "Grab all you can. The one with the most toys wins"? But if there is no resurrection, winning is futile.

II. If There Is No Easter, We Are Still in Our Sins (v. 17)

If Jesus is still dead, we are slaves forever to our sins and suffer hopelessly under a burden of debt we can never repay. We are like a person who vainly tries to run from his or her own shadow. If there is no Easter, our faith is in vain; we are still in our sins, and life is "a tale told by an idiot, full of sound and fury, signifying nothing."

III. If There Is No Easter, Life Has No Permanence (vv. 15, 18)

Write over our situation "no hope." We wish it were different. We climb on skinned knees, with bated breath, and grasp with white knuckles to peer over the edge of eternity, only to see the sign "No Exit!" Judas was right! We might as well give up because there is no second chance. There is no hope.

IV. If There Is No Easter, We Are of All People Most Miserable (v. 19)

Why? It is bad enough to have never had something good. It is worse still to lose something that we once thought we had. The regret of the bowed head in the soup kitchen is not so much the tastelessness of the soup but the memory of better meals once enjoyed but now thrown away.

Do you sense what Paul is doing? Do you feel the hopelessness, gloom, despair, and darkness of a world without the resurrected Christ?

V. But Christ Is Raised, the First Fruits of the Resurrection (v. 20)

Because he lives, we can know joy, love, forgiveness, and an eternity with God. Our destiny is linked with Jesus' resurrection. As God's children, one day everything Jesus has will be ours because we are "heirs of God and joint heirs with Jesus." God has created in us something designed to live forever. And it shall be because God has loved us through the birth, life, death, and resurrection of God's Son.

Paul Tillich tells a story that came to light during the Nuremburg War Trials. In the village of Wilna, Poland, people began to hide from the Nazis. One such hiding place was a nearby cemetery. In one of those graves a woman gave birth to a son, assisted only by an eighty-year-old grave digger. The old man exclaimed, "Oh Lord, has thou finally sent the Messiah? For only the Messiah could be born in a grave!"

As Jesus was reborn from the open grave on Easter morn, so were our hopes and dreams of life and life eternal. (Gary L. Carver)

THE DAY THE WORLD TURNED UPSIDE DOWN

LUKE 6:17-26

Most of us get pretty comfortable with the way things are, don't we? We may not like everything about the way the world works, but over the years we come to accept things and acclimate ourselves.

That's nothing new—it's human nature. The people who gathered that day to hear Jesus teach—even his disciples—had a pretty good understanding of how the world worked. They understood the difference between the "haves" and the "have nots"—and they knew it was a lot better to be a have!

That's why these words of Jesus were so revolutionary. Anybody who had settled in on a lawn chair to hear another *nice* sermon must have nearly fallen out of it when Jesus started talking about the way things were in his Father's Kingdom. It was as if the world had turned upside down, as Jesus pointed out that in God's Kingdom the values of the world have been reversed.

I. Kingdom Living Has a New Set of Values

Poverty was no more esteemed in first-century Israel than in our own day. Indeed, the closest thing to a "safety net" for the

79

poor was the willingness of passers-by to offer alms to the poor beggars on the street.

Yet Jesus says, "Blessed [or happy, fortunate] are you who are poor, for yours is the kingdom of God" (v. 20). This is not a reference to the "poor in spirit" as in Matthew, but to the literal poor; because Jesus is talking to disciples and would-be disciples, he is identifying those whose poverty is lived out in a setting of discipleship. Many would actually suffer economically and physically for their faithfulness, but that was to be affirmed, not grieved, for God would bless those who suffered for the sake of the Kingdom.

While the world sets the highest value on wealth and possessions, God honors highest those who have willingly sacrificed because of their discipleship. Have you and I done without anything on behalf of the Kingdom?

II. Kingdom Living Has a New Set of Priorities

The book *The Day America Told the Truth,* by James Patterson and Peter Kim, offers data on a major survey of American attitudes and values in the 1990s. One of the most interesting revelations is that when asked if they could change one thing about their lives, fully 64 percent responded that they want to be rich. Wealth was far and away the top answer; the desire to be a "better person" didn't even record enough responses to make the top fifteen list!

It's likely that a similar book in Jesus' time—Maybe *The Day Israel Told the Truth?*—would have recorded a similar result. The desire for wealth is not an exclusively modern priority.

Yet Jesus says that in the Kingdom of God, priorities are reversed. The desire for wealth and material gain has no place. Persons who have lived their lives with a priority of accumulating possessions have already received their reward in this life.

Jesus is speaking to a mind-set—a set of values and priorities—that is captive to a desire for more and more. It is modeled in a comment attributed to John D. Rockefeller. When asked how much money was enough, he replied, "A little more." Those for whom riches are the driving priority can never be satisfied; they never find satisfaction, either in this life or in the next.

By contrast, the person whose priorities are on serving God

and his Kingdom are free to enjoy the abundance of life in the spirit of Christ. Although this life may well carry a measure of sacrifice and pain, we know that "joy comes in the morning." Whatever we hoard for ourselves we will ultimately lose; whatever we give for Christ is multiplied beyond our wildest dreams. (Michael Duduit)

FEBRUARY 19, 1995

❧

Seventh Sunday After Epiphany

Worship Theme: True joy and satisfaction come to us through the surrendering of our lives to the will of God.

Readings: Genesis 45:3-11, 15; 1 Corinthians 15:35-38, 42-50; Luke 6:27-38

Call to Worship (Psalm 37:3-5):

Leader: Trust in the LORD, and do good; so you will live in the land, and enjoy security.

People: Take delight in the LORD, and he will give you the desires of your heart.

All: Commit your way to the LORD; trust in him, and he will act.

Pastoral Prayer:

Father of our Lord Jesus Christ, we admit that our lives are full of poor beginnings and bad endings. We mean well; we are full of good intentions, but we give up too easily, too quickly. We are burdened by the guilt of our lost commitment, of our waning enthusiasm, of our halfhearted efforts. Forgive us, Lord, and stir the dying embers of our passion to new flame. Breathe your Spirit into us, that we may seek you and love you with our whole hearts. Grant us the blessing of your Presence, of your mercy, and of your grace through our Lord Jesus Christ. Amen.

SERMON BRIEFS

LIVE THE MYSTERY!

GENESIS 45:3-11, 15

I saw a poster that read "God's Will, Nothing More, Nothing Else, Nothing Less." The will of God is at work in the story for

82

our consideration today. The will and providence of God are the thread that holds this surprising and refreshing story together; ultimately, the will and providence of God bring a fresh, new opportunity of beginning to a potentially disastrous series of events.

The will of God throughout human history has received a lot of bad press. All sorts of human pain and misery have been blamed on the will of a judgmental and angry God. Even today, in a more civilized and sophisticated world, we still hear at the death of a loved one that trite and judgmental proclamation uttered by someone to those grieving, "You just have to accept that it was the will of God." How many persons have turned their backs on such a God that wills the death of someone they love? I can't say that I much blame them.

Joseph did not explain the providence and will of God so much as he sought just to trust his life to it. The story gives us some insight into Joseph's own feeling and understanding of the providence and will of God as it sought expression in his life. Such disclosure on the part of Joseph can help us to recognize and to respond to God's will as it finds expression in our own lives as well. Several ideas concerning the will and providence of God seem apparent in this passage.

The story asserts that God's purpose is finally sovereign. While it may be delayed in expression, it ultimately works with and through every human action. The climax of the story is discovered in Joseph's own sense of that fact, as he recalled and witnessed to the power of God's providence, when he continued to assert three separate times in this story "for God sent me." Joseph's own understanding of his life and his place in this moment in history is the direct result of God's providential will expressing itself in the stuff of his life. His "aha!" experience is his own understanding and affirmation of the powerful way in which God has been present with Joseph throughout his life. The power of our lives can be discovered in our own sense of God's will in our lives. Regardless of whether we agree or fully understand what is happening, ultimately life comes down to whether we trust that God knows what God is doing in our life. Joseph proclaimed with great confidence, "God sent me!"

As God's providential will finds expression in our lives it

brings to us a sense of newness and freshness. The excitement in Joseph's tone has something to do with his own sense that God's providential will has now opened a new window of opportunity for renewal, the preservation of life for the family, survival, and reunion. The author of Revelation attempted to describe this action of the providential will of God as he proclaimed, "See, I am making all things new" (Rev. 21:5). We serve a God who, through his will, constantly seeks to make us a new creation.

A large part of what Joseph experienced is done as mystery. Even when it was happening, Joseph did not understand what was happening from the perspective of God's will. That revelation came later. His understanding was not a condition of God working his will in Joseph's life. The point is that God is working. Mystery is part of that, not because God doesn't want us to know, but primarily because we are so caught up with other things about life. The "aha!" experiences come in our life when we, like Joseph, begin to see the mystery of God's way even though we do not understand it. As Frederick Buechner says in his book *Wishful Thinking*, "Live the mystery!"

The thread that holds our fragile lives together is this mysterious providential will of God. Joseph didn't seek so much as to explain this mystery as he did to live it. Yes, in this story today, some of it now even makes no sense to him as he in retrospect sees the hand of God so clearly. And yet, that is not the point. The point is that throughout, Joseph never gave up trusting God. He allowed that providential will of God to lead him. The bold affirmation of this story today is in the words of Buechner, "Live the mystery!" (Travis Franklin)

A BODY FOR ALL SEASONS

1 CORINTHIANS 15:35-38, 42-50

I was talking with a friend whose father-in-law had died a few months before. "How is your wife feeling about her father's death?" I asked.

"It's funny you should ask," he said. "Last night in the middle of dinner she began to cry. We had had a beautiful day. In fact, we had spent most of the day planting flowers. Then, suddenly, without any warning, she just began to cry. I asked, 'What's the matter, honey?' She said, 'I was thinking about Daddy. I'm afraid he's cold out there in the ground.' "

Letting go of the earthly body is not easy, is it? We have deep attachments to it. We cannot imagine what it will be like to transcend the body, to leave it behind.

Neither could Christians in the earliest days of the church. "How are the dead raised?" they asked when Paul preached about the resurrection to them. "With what kind of body to they come?" (v. 35).

These were Greeks, people who had been raised in the best traditions of Hellenistic thought. Their philosophy taught a strict dualism between the mind and the body. Their minds were like the ethereal bird imprisoned in the body. When the body died, the bird was free to fly away. Yet, to them this was not a joyous occasion. They could not imagine that existence for the mind would be very pleasurable without the body. The idea of the resurrection must have struck them with great promise, but they could not begin to comprehend it.

And Paul told them (v. 37) that what we shall be when we die is somehow contained in who we are while we live, but it is more than that. As the apple tree is far more than the seed from which it grew, so we shall be far more than anyone could tell by looking at us now.

Receiving a heavenly body is not automatic. It is not something everybody has a right to. God gives it (15:38). Eternal life is centered on God and God's power. We have no automatic right to live forever. But God wills that those who have been saved through his Son Jesus have an eternal form beyond this life.

And what a form it will be! (See vv. 42-44.) The body, which dies, is *perishable, contemptible,* and *weak.* The older we become, the more perishable, contemptible, and weak we think of ourselves as being. But this body is only the seed; the body that is raised up—the spiritual body—is another story! It is *imperishable, glorious,* and *powerful.*

It is imperishable. It will never die. No accident or illness can touch it. It will go on forever. It is glorious. It is like the "Hallelujah Chorus" in the flesh, embodied in a person. And it is powerful. Traditionally, the grave has been thought of as the place where one has no power, where all strength has gone. But Paul said that the body that is raised up is powerful.

Our faith is centered in a God who has the power to raise up our weak and perishable bodies after death and convert them into strong and everlasting bodies of a new kind, of a heavenly kind, so that we may worship and glorify God forever. We shall become what it is in us now to become but what we cannot become until we have died and the seed has been raised up by God into an incredible flowering! (John Killinger)

THE MOST DIFFICULT COMMANDMENT

Luke 6:27-38

This passage contains what may be Jesus' most difficult, measurable command to carry out: "Do unto others"—the "Golden Rule." In our greedy, ladder-climbing society, many of us are afraid we'll get stepped on trying to live out Jesus' ultimatum. We've all heard the twentieth-century "golden rule": "He who has the gold makes the rule."

Jesus' idea is not unique to Christianity. Later Judaism tells the story of a non-Jew approaching the great teacher Hillel with the challenge that he'd become a proselyte (follower) if Hillel could teach him the whole Law while he stood on one leg. Hillel responded: "What you do not like, do not to your neighbor. That is the entire Law, and all the rest is commentary."

But Jesus takes this idea and states it in the positive: "Do for others just what you want them to do for you" (GNB). A simple concept, but almost impossible to enact. I imagine that Jesus knew this difficulty; therefore, he provided some examples of what he intended when he stated, "Do for others. . . . "

I. *Do not judge others.* We create many English words from the Greek word *krino* used here to mean "judge." All of our words built off "critic" come from this same idea. Jesus is saying, "Don't criticize." Don't nit-pick, looking for the worst in others. If you do, God will treat you in the same way.

II. *Do not condemn others.* Condemnation involves putting yourself in the position of judge over someone else. You decide in your own heart the punishment someone deserves for a "crime" against you. Jesus warns against this type of thinking and reminds us that none of our pasts or presents are devoid of all wrongdoing.

III. Forgive—a most difficult command to carry out. When someone hits you with the harsh jab of anger or scorn, turn the other cheek, Jesus says. When an aggressor wants to steal your security, give him far more than even he asks. Now, he adds, on top of all that, forgive! Forgiveness represents the exact opposite of the condemnation mentioned above. Jesus commands his disciples to release (in every way, including in their hearts) from any punishment those who have wronged them. Disciples do not respond in kind to those who abuse them.

IV. Give. Again Jesus addresses a very sensitive issue with no tact whatsoever. In times when money isn't particularly plentiful, every penny is squeezed for all it's worth. Jesus' audience understood what it meant to be poor. Yet, Jesus commanded them to give to anyone who asks and *not* to ask for anything in return— quite a reversal of thinking for an individualistic society that regarded money as a private matter and no one else's business.

Disciples live in a different economy. A coin or piece of paper with numbers on it does not hold the same value for disciples as for others. Disciples give their money *away,* knowing that Jesus has promised that God will pour out blessings of all kinds in return. In kitchen talk, Jesus says that for every level teaspoon you give, you will receive a heaping teaspoon in return—a teaspoon that overflows onto your counter-top.

The final reminder, which neatly sums up this passage, also involves measures. The measure you use for others is the one that God will use for you—in judgment, in condemnation, in forgiveness, and in generosity. Do unto others what you would have *God* do unto you, Jesus says. Difficult yes, but still the rule for the untarnished disciple's life. (Blake Harwell)

FEBRUARY 26, 1995

❧

Eighth Sunday After Epiphany

Worship Theme: Even in the dark days of our lives, God's presence with us provides hope.

Readings: Isaiah 55:10-13; 1 Corinthians 15:51-58; Luke 6:39-49

Call to Worship (Psalm 92:1-2, 4):
It is good to give thanks to the LORD,
    to sing praises to your name, O Most High;
to declare your steadfast love in the morning,
    and your faithfulness by night,

....

For you, O LORD, have made me glad by your work;
    at the works of your hands I sing for joy.

Pastoral Prayer:
    Lord God, we gather as your people searching for guidance, hope, and fulfillment in our lives. Lead us by your Holy Spirit to the true fellowship and joy found in Jesus Christ. We are anxious, Lord. Anxious about our future, about our society, about our families. Help us to see that we can be truly relaxed in the confidence of your love and sovereignty over our troubled world. Help us as a community of faith to minister to those who need a friend, a kind word, or a prayer on their behalf. Strengthen us, lead us, and help us mature in our faith in you. Amen. (Steven R. Fleming)

SERMON BRIEFS

WE HAVE GOD'S WORD ON IT!

ISAIAH 55:10-13

The penetrating question on the lips of God's people who have been carried into exile in Babylonia is, "How can we sing to the

Lord a new song in a foreign land?" With the Temple destroyed and the land of promise stripped from them, the people struggle to keep their trust in God alive. The prophet Isaiah prophesied toward the end of this Babylonian exile. The text today is the proclamation of God, word from the Lord whereby the people of God will be restored.

The images in the passage dare to declare, even in exile, that God is at work to return God's people to their homeland. This passage offers words of hope to those who seek the Lord. Seeing the Lord in good times is one thing. Seeking the Lord in exile is something quite different. Isaiah offers God's hope even in the face of exile.

This is a liberating word for us to hear, for anyone who has experienced life understands that it is both valleys and mountaintops. Isaiah dared to proclaim that God is present with us, even in the exiles of our lives. Through the prophet Isaiah, God sought to empower the people with a promise of hope and restoration.

Ken Callahan, in his book *Twelve Keys to an Effective Church,* talks about how one's perspective determines one's behavior, which, in turn, determines one's destiny. Isaiah reminded God's people that they must, even in exile, continue to seek the Lord, which would affect their behavior, which would in turn determine their destiny.

The passage today reflects Isaiah's own understanding of God's faithfulness even in the midst of exile. God is trustworthy in that God works out his will in the history and lives of the people. God seeks to restore, to bring life through his Word, and to offer hope in the face of struggle.

There is a story of a young boy who was terribly afraid of the dark. As he came through the kitchen one day from play, his mother was cooking supper. As he entered the kitchen, she asked him to please go into the basement to get her a can of corn. He went to the basement door, opened it, and turned on the light switch. The light bulb burst. The basement was dark. He told his mother the light went out and that he was afraid to go into the darkened basement. The mother assured him that God would be with him in the darkness and to please hurry and get the corn. The boy looked down the long, dark stairway and was afraid. Just then, he had an idea! He yelled into the darkness, "God, if you're down there, could you pitch me a can of corn?"

Isaiah proclaimed that God is in our darkness, offering light and hope. God is speaking his Word, and it will not return empty but will accomplish God's purposes. God is here, and God is leading—yes, even in the darkened exiles of our lives. We are called to go out in joy and to be led in peace, because God's Word will empower life to the point that even the mountains and hills will break forth singing and the trees of the field shall rejoice. How can we not trust the word of such power and hope? After all, we have God's word on it! (Travis Franklin)

THE VICTORY WE SHARE

1 CORINTHIANS 15:51-58

Elizabeth Kubler-Ross tells of asking an eight-year-old boy, dying of cancer, to express his feelings. He drew a tiny figure holding a "Stop" sign standing in front of an army tank. Feel the helplessness of that image. Feel the despair of Shakespeare's Claudio, "Death is a fearful thing. To die and to go we know not where."

Earlier in chapter 15, Paul asks us to envision the hopelessness of a world without Easter. Now, he declares for us to replace that hopelessness with the word *victory!* Christ lives! "Death has been swallowed up in victory" (v. 54).

I. Christ's Victory Over Death Means That Everything in Us That Needs Changing Will Be Changed

How this happens is a mystery (v. 51). This happens not because of understanding but because of faith. We do not understand electricity, but we do not sit in the dark until we do. Because of Jesus' faith, God raised him from the dead. Because of our faith, God raises us to new life.

At the Second Coming or through the entrance of death for the Christian, everything wrong will be made right; everything mortal will be made immortal, everything perishable will be made imperishable, and everything dead will be made alive.

Our tired, worn-out bodies, full of aches and pains, will be transformed to new and energized bodies, just like Jesus' body. Everything we have allowed sin and death to do to us will be reversed by love and grace.

II. Christ's Victory Over Death Means
That We Can Stand Firm

Stand firm in what? We can stand firm in our convictions that Jesus was everything he said he was, did everything he said he would do, and nothing can separate us from God's love. We can stand firm in our conviction that goodness is greater than evil. Evil did its best when it crucified Jesus, but Jesus conquered death. Everything that seemed so strong and indestructible—hatred, violence, and force—became temporary. Everything that seemed so fragile—love, forgiveness, and hope—was revealed to be eternal. The little figure with the "Stop" sign stops the tank.

John Claypool tells a story of the boot-camp experience of a young recruit from Georgia. Each evening the recruit would pray by the side of his bed to the irritation and eventual furor of the drill sergeant. The sergeant lost no opportunity to mistreat, embarrass, or abuse the recruit. Always, however, the recruit returned good for evil.

As the sergeant returned to the barracks, in a drunken state, from a rainy night on the town, he became infuriated by again seeing the recruit kneeling in prayer. He threw both muddy boots at the recruit, striking him, and then collapsed in his bunk. As the sergeant awoke, he saw hanging above him his boots, now cleaned and beautifully polished. He went to the young man, "I tried everything to break you. I failed. You have something I don't have, and I want it." Goodness is greater than evil.

III. Christ's Victory Over Death Means That We Can Give
Ourselves Fully to God's Work Because
Our Labor Is Not in Vain

We can continue to love, encourage, forgive, and sacrifice because God not only recognizes but rewards and multiplies our efforts thirty, sixty, and one hundred fold. Even a cup of cold water is noticed.

Someone said of a favorite teacher, "He made us feel as if tomorrow had already happened." With Jesus' resurrection from the dead and our faith response to it, Christ already had begun his life-giving work in us. There is an Easter, and there is hope for all who embrace the risen Christ in faith. (Gary L. Carver)

BUILDING A LIFE THAT LASTS

LUKE 6:39-49

Have you ever been frustrated about some product you purchased, only to learn that it was poorly constructed and didn't last? From cars to electronics, too often it seems that insufficient care goes into the manufacture of the things we use.

Sadly, that also seems true of many lives. From broken homes to broken relationships to broken spirits, all too many people are experiencing lives like the house described in Jesus' parable—built on an inadequate foundation and easily washed away when adversity arrives.

In a series of word pictures, Jesus encourages us to build a life that lasts. How is that done?

I. A Life That Lasts Begins with Dependence on God

In an era when we stubbornly insist on our autonomy and independence, it seems out of place to build a meaningful life on a foundation of dependence. Yet, apart from a recognition that we are ultimately dependent on God for all we have and are, we'll never build a life that lasts.

We imagine ourselves worthy judges of the flaws and faults of those around us, but the truth is that we share the sin and weakness of others. Once recognized in ourselves, what appears to be a tiny speck in the eyes of others is seen as a giant plank in our own eye. The reality is that we all are blind, and left to our own devices we will lead one another into the pit. We need help from beyond ourselves—help that can come only from God.

II. A Life That Lasts Is Constructed Through Obedience

One of the things that characterizes good furniture is the material out of which it is constructed. Good furniture is made of quality woods and hardware and finishes. Sacrifice the quality of the materials, and you reduce the value of the final product.

A life that lasts is built with obedience and the commitment to serve Christ and follow his direction in our lives. A life rooted in obedience is reflected in good fruit, which grows out of an obedient heart. Indeed, Jesus says that obedient lives produce a reservoir, a storehouse of good in our hearts.

III. A Life That Lasts Survives the Storms

A glance at the daily newspaper any day reveals the stories of countless lives that were built on weak, shifting foundations— lives based on financial security that can be wiped out with a job loss or recession; lives based on social position that can shift as easily as the styles of the day; lives based on a desire for immediate sensual gratification that can result in addiction, disease, even death.

The well-built house, the one rooted in faith and constructed with obedience, is able to withstand the storms that threaten us. Christ's presence and power in your life provides a secure foundation on which you can build a life that lasts. (Michael Duduit)

MARCH

❧

Replenishing the Well

Repent in Expectation

Lent is a time of reflection and repentance. It is a season when we prepare ourselves in expectation of the events of Holy Week and Easter. This exercise assists in Lenten reflection, repentance, and preparation for the Easter season.

Time: 2 hours.

Materials: A Bible, your journal, a pen or pencil, an icon or other personal object symbolizing the presence of Christ. As usual, you will need a quiet, private room. You will also need access to a public park or garden.

Exercise:
Today you will spend two hours in the wilderness. For today, the wilderness is any place that removes you from your ordinary schedule, takes you away for two hours from the people you see each day. However, you don't go into the wilderness alone. Christ is your companion.

In preparation for entering the wilderness, find an icon or picture of Jesus to take with you. If an icon is not available, take along an object that symbolizes the presence of Christ for you, like a cross or crucifix, a small statue, prayer beads, a pin, a chalice, a piece of sacred jewelry—anything that reminds you of Jesus. Once you have chosen your icon or object, go to the place you have designated for your day in the wilderness.

Select a mealtime during which to do this exercise. You will fast during this two-hour period in imitation of Jesus' sojourn in the wilderness.

Begin by placing your icon where you can easily see it. Read Luke 4:1-13. Now close your eyes and imagine you and Jesus are walking in the wilderness. The surrounding country is barren.

Suddenly, the devil springs out from behind a rock, but you are not afraid because Christ is with you. The devil begins to whisper temptations to you, and you listen to him.

Open your eyes and open your journal. Write in your journal what the devil said to you.

Close your journal. Get up and put it behind your chair, symbolically turning from temptation in repentance toward Christ. Be seated again and let your eyes rest on your icon or object. Meditate on this portion of the Lord's Prayer for about fifteen minutes, repeating it over and over to yourself, your eyes fixed on the icon or object: "Lord, lead me not into temptation, but deliver me from evil." Then retrieve and open your journal and write, "Blessed are you, O Christ, who forgives all my sins, who strengthens me against temptation, who walks with me and guides me on this Lenten journey."

Spend the remaining portion of these two hours walking and praying in a park or garden. (Harriet Crosby)

MARCH 5, 1995

❧

First Sunday in Lent

Worship Theme: Confession of sin and faith in Christ produce in us a new life in Christ.

Readings: Deuteronomy 26:1-11; Romans 10:8*b*-13; Luke 4:1-13

Call to Worship (Psalm 91:14-16):
Those who love me, I will deliver;
  I will protect those who know my name.
When they call to me, I will answer them;
  I will be with them in trouble,
  I will rescue them and honor them.
With long life I will satisfy them,
  and show them my salvation.

Pastoral Prayer:
  Lord, mark us, if you will, with ash. The Holy Season has begun. The cross and tomb draw near. Please mark us, Lord. We want to worship you as one we would be like; not merely like, but joined to. We beg a union with you, Lord. You looked and saw the cross and kept on walking toward it. You knew exactly why you had come.
  We want to walk toward our destiny as firmly as you walked. Were you afraid? We are. You saw your cross so clearly. Our crosses hide themselves. They look for us and lie in wait to take us by surprise. This uncertainty leaves us so in doubt and so in need. Please, Lord, mark us with ash and walk with us, until we are no longer afraid of crosses we can see. Amen. (Calvin Miller)

SERMON BRIEFS

HOW TO RECEIVE A GIFT!

DEUTERONOMY 26:1-11

  Herbert Brokering tells this parable in his book *I Opener*: "Once there was a man who was given a beautiful empty bag as

96

a gift. All he had to do was to fill it with anything he liked. He thought he didn't have time to do this, so he gave back the bag."

The people of God have received the beautiful gift of the land. This gift is the end result of many generations of patient waiting. The promise has now come true, and the people of God are ready to receive this most precious gift from God. In this time of receiving, Moses instructs the people of God as to their liturgical response in receiving this gift. The response is our focus today.

This is a historical moment in the lives of God's people as they lay claim to God's promise. They represent a long history of generations of Hebrew people who have kept alive this idea of a promised land. This passage makes it clear that God's good gifts to us are received only when we respond and acknowledge such giving through our own sense of gratitude, symbolized in the sharing of first fruits. It is not enough just to have the gift given, as in the opening parable. Such giving demands some kind of response from us that we have received the gift with appreciation and joy.

This ancient story is strange reading in a culture like ours. Far too often we have allowed the attitude of getting something for nothing permeate who we are in terms of receiving gifts. Such an attitude mocks the story we read today by trying to manipulate both the giving and the receiving. Bingo, state lotteries, slot machines, horse racing, gambling, sales gimmicks of all kinds seem to reinforce this whole idea of trying to get rich quick with little or no investment. It is certainly the easy way and, many times, prostitutes both the gift and the giver. The attitude of something for nothing is prevalent in our culture, and it is in direct conflict with the biblical tradition of giving and receiving, as witnessed in this story.

God, through Moses, wanted those receiving the gift of the land to understand that such an exchange between God and humankind is a sacred moment. Such an event in people's lives demands a response of thanksgiving, joy, celebration, and a very real sense of the power of receiving a gift. To receive such a gift, as did the man in the opening parable, and then to do nothing with it demeans the gift, the giver of the gift, and certainly the one for whom the gift was given. The sharing of first fruits as a remembrance of the history of the sacred relationship to past generations centering on this promise of God is a most appropriate response by the people as a way of expressing joy, thanks, as well as responsibility, for this most cherished gift of the land.

We would do well to listen to this story today. The heart, soul, and power of such a story is discovered in realizing that there is no such thing as a "free" gift. Any gift given freely ultimately implies a decision as to how one will respond to the gift being shared. While it is fine in the church today to help persons understand that God's motivation for giving is free from any condition or expectation, we must also be honest in saying that any gift given must be received. Even the man in the parable had to decide that he would not to do anything with the gift of the empty bag.

This rich story shares with us some valuable insights as to what it means to receive God's good gifts in our lives. Thanksgiving, joy, community, memory, celebration, and the sharing of first fruits become a standard by which we are to receive and respond to the sacred gifts that are given to us by God. Such liturgy reminds us of the powerful interchange between God and humankind as God shares the good and bountiful gifts that bring such meaning to life. Somehow, doing nothing with those gifts falls short of realizing why such gifts were given in the first place. What are we doing today with what God has given us? Maybe it is time we did something! Rejoice, celebrate, receive, be thankful, remember, and offer God some sense that you are allowing his most sacred gifts of life to find root and growth in who you are and how you live! We are finally learning how to receive a gift! (Travis Franklin)

HOW ARE YOU PREPARING FOR EASTER?

ROMANS 10:8*b*-13

Karl Barth, the great German theologian, once stated, " 'Yes' is what the Christian life is all about." In raising Christ from the dead, God has said yes to our yearning for life and hope; our need for forgiveness and grace. God already has said yes to you. What are you doing to say yes to him in preparation for the celebration of Easter?

I. Easter Begins with God

William Willimon has said that 90 percent of the sermons he has preached or heard went something like: "You have a problem! Jesus is the answer! Repent!" While that certainly is true, it may begin from the wrong perspective. It begins with our needs and problems. In reality, the scheme of salvation begins with God, not with us. God's grace and forgiveness are possible because God first sent Jesus to live, die, and be raised from the dead. The initiative was God's.

"The word is near you," Paul says (v. 8), not vice versa. God does not offer a quick fix to endless problems. Rather, God offers an eternal relationship. We can only respond by saying yes to God's gracious overture of love and relationship. In this "yes" we are preparing for Easter.

II. Easter Is Attainable Now

The resurrection life, both now and forever, is attained when we "confess with [our] lips . . . and believe in [our] heart" (v. 9).

To confess means to say the same—to say the same about our sin that God says about our sin. Why, then, when we confess our sin do we tell God something God already knows? Frederick Buechner reminds us that we confess our sins because our sins cause a separation to occur in our relationship with God. Our confession becomes the bridge over this relational gap. Both marriage partners may know of an unfaithfulness, but the relationship can never be whole again until confession and forgiveness take place.

To believe means to trust in God's saving act in Christ. By believing, we accept his punishment as our punishment and we accept the life he offers. Believing means approaching God with an openness for all God offers. Believing means yielding to all God has for us to do. Believing means we trust that God has raised Jesus and that God will raise us. Believing means to say yes to Christ's lordship over every aspect of our lives. By believing, we are preparing for Easter.

III. Easter Is Available to Everyone

There is no difference between Jew or Gentile, rich or poor. Everyone or anyone who says yes to God in confession and belief can know life abundant and eternal.

The worship service was over, and the offering plate filled with money was lying on the Communion Table. A five-year-old boy took five dollars from the plate while, unknown to him, the pastor watched. Quietly the pastor said, "Peter, don't you think you want to put that money back?" "Please, *please* don't tell my daddy!" the boy said. "He'll kill me!"

Knowing the punishment would not be quite that severe, the pastor did tell the father, who immediately responded, "I'm going to kill that kid!" The pastor said, "Now, before you act in haste, you might remember that possibly there was a time in your life when you stole also." "Come to think of it, you are right," responded the father.

Later, in talking to his son, the father related the story of how he, too, had stolen a dozen eggs. In a mutual moment of love, they hugged each other, and the boy exclaimed, "Oh, Daddy, I'm so happy! We're both thieves!"

And so are we all sinners! The realization of that may be a first step in saying yes to God, through believing. Easter is coming—how are you preparing?
(Craig M. Watts)

WHERE TEMPTATION STRIKES
LUKE 4:1-13

Have you ever given in to temptation? We all have, though we are tempted in different ways. Some are tempted when they sit down to figure their income taxes, while others are tempted when they set their time priorities. If only we could choose when and where our temptations come, it would be easy. Unfortunately, temptations invariably find us when we are least prepared for them and where we are most vulnerable.

Jesus faced the same situation. Following his baptism, Jesus spent forty days in the desert in a time of prayer and fasting, preparing himself spiritually for the challenges he was about to confront. During that time alone, Jesus faced significant temptations that could have scuttled his ministry and changed the course of human history. Those temptations came in the context of three potential areas of weakness, just as they often do for us. Yet in each event, Jesus demonstrated how to overcome the temptations we all face.

I. We Can Overcome Physical Temptations

After a time of fasting, Jesus was in a weakened physical state, so Satan attacked him at the point of physical need: hunger.

Perhaps your physical need is a different one. Maybe you are tempted in the area of sexual desire, or financial resources, or some other area. Whatever it is, you know what it's like to have temptation threaten to devastate your relationship with God.

Jesus faced such a situation as this, but it is important for us to notice that in this and the other areas of temptation he encountered, Jesus confronted the temptation through the use of God's Word. A knowledge of the Bible provides a strong weapon in confronting the temptations that would destroy us. Bible memorization is not encouraged and practiced as much as it once was; perhaps that is one of the reasons why young people are often less well equipped to stand up to the temptations they experience. They lack one of the essential weapons of spiritual warfare.

Jesus pointed out that although our physical needs are important, they are not primary. A proper sense of priorities helps us to keep our physical needs in balance and in perspective, and that helps in overcoming temptation. When our primary allegiance is to God and not our own physical desires, temptation is unable to take root in our lives.

II. We Can Overcome Emotional Temptations

Next Jesus was confronted at the point of emotional need: ego. "Just worship me and it will all be yours," urged the devil. It was an offer of a quick fix, a shortcut. Why spend three years of difficult ministry and end up hanging from a cross when you can have it all and more—all the glory, all the authority, all the splendor right away, here and now?

Again, Scripture provides the front line of defense. Only God is worthy of worship, and only in obedience to his will can we find ultimate peace and satisfaction. Anything else that bypasses God's will is illusory and will ultimately lead to defeat and disillusionment. Jesus' true authority could come only through submission to the Father's purpose and direction in his life.

101

III. We Can Overcome Spiritual Temptations

The third temptation was perhaps the toughest, because Satan even used Scripture to suggest to Jesus another way to achieve his purpose. Why not a grand public display of Jesus' faith before all the people of Jerusalem? Surely God will not let his Messiah come to harm! And once the people see this demonstration, they will recognize who Jesus is and clamor to become part of his following. It is a good reminder that Scripture can be improperly used, and we must be cautious in listening to others who would abuse its teaching.

As Jesus pointed out, however, what was being suggested was an effort to force God's hand, to jump ahead of God's timing. The obedient servant, as Jesus observes, does not try to put God to the test in this way.

One of the most common spiritual temptations Christians face today is the idea propounded by some "health and wealth" teachers that by praying in faith, God is virtually required to provide whatever we ask for, from divine healing to a new Cadillac! Such a philosophy turns God into little more than a magic box who works at our disposal, turning him into our servant. If Jesus knew better than to be so presumptuous by testing God in such a way, how can we be so foolish?

Jesus was prepared to face this time of temptation because he had been spending time with God in prayer and in the Word. As in so many ways, he is our model if we wish to be successful in overcoming temptation. (Michael Duduit)

MARCH 12, 1995

❧

Second Sunday in Lent

Worship Theme: Authentic faith is the key to a new relationship with God.

Readings: Genesis 15:1-12, 17-18; Philippians 3:17–4:1; Luke 13:31-35

Call to Worship (Psalm 27:1-4, 13-14):

Leader: The LORD is my light and my salvation; whom shall I fear?

People: The LORD is the stronghold of my life; of whom shall I be afraid?

Leader: When evildoers assail me to devour my flesh—my adversaries and foes—they shall stumble and fall.

People: Though an army encamp against me, my heart shall not fear; though war rise up against me, yet I will be confident.

Leader: One thing I asked of the LORD, that will I seek after:

People: to live in the house of the LORD all the days of my life, to behold the beauty of the LORD, and to inquire in his temple. . . .

Leader: I believe that I shall see the goodness of the LORD in the land of the living.

People: Wait for the LORD; be strong, and let your heart take courage; wait for the LORD!

Pastoral Prayer:
Lord, life can be certain but only for a while. Death is how every hopeful future ends. You looked and seemed to know exactly where your life would end. You knew the boundary of

103

death that could not paralyze the reason you had come to be. You knew that you would die, and yet you laughed and went to parties. They called you a glutton and a tippler. They criticized your love of good times. I marvel that the crossly shadow never loomed above your life with any darkness that could steal your joy. Your coming sacrifice never frayed your lent with insecurity, for joy crowned your days.

How well you taught us. Crosses hurt, but they must never be allowed to shadow the sunny days with gloom. There will be time for dying when it's time to die. Help us to live and laugh today, for before you showed us how to die you showed us how to live. Lord, help us to number all our days that we may apply our hearts to wisdom. As Lent progresses, may our own undaunted joy be the gift of our obedience to you. Help us to live and laugh and count the days. Amen. (Calvin Miller)

SERMON BRIEFS

THE GOSPEL IN GENESIS

GENESIS 15:1-12, 17-18

Many Christians largely ignore the Old Testament. Genesis 15:1-18 gives an excellent reason not to pass over the Old Testament in preaching and study. Here, one discovers the "gospel" centuries before Christ's ministry on earth. Walter R. Bowie (*The Interpreter's Bible,* vol. I, p. 600) reminds Christians of Paul's words: "walk in the steps of that faith of our father Abraham" (Rom. 4:12). Bowie continues: "The heart of the whole gospel that Paul preached is beating here [Genesis 15] . . . that it is not what a man is, but what a man trusts God to do that saves him."

Abram, later renamed Abraham, is a key figure in the Old Testament; his story fills sixteen chapters (12–25) in Genesis. He is obedient to God from the time he leaves his home (Genesis 12) to his willingness to sacrifice his precious son (Genesis 22). Nevertheless, he has moments of doubt and uncertainty. Genesis 15:1-3 suggests that Abram worried about his very survival. Perhaps he worried about retaliation for his rescue of Lot (chap. 14).

It is more likely his concern stemmed from the fact that he had no male child to pass on his lineage and possessions.

After God responded (vv. 4-5), the next verse might be called the "gospel" in Genesis. "Abram believed the LORD, and [God] credited it to [Abram] as righteousness" (v. 6 NIV). Centuries before Christ, here is outlined the way of salvation. Gerhard Von Rad, in his book *Genesis,* suggests three words are key to understanding this passage: *believed, reckoned,* and *righteousness.*

I. Believed

Abram believed that God would fulfill his promises. Regardless of our status, circumstances, or opportunities, our relationship with God must begin with *belief.* To believe is an act of trust, a willingness to put oneself under God's plans in history. Von Rad reminds us that such belief "refers as a rule to God's future saving act." Belief has always been a question of personal choice. It is up to individuals to choose whether to put their lives within the framework of God's plan.

II. Credited, or "Reckoned"

Abram's belief was judged by God to be acceptable. This concept has parallels in that the priests (as shown in Lev. 7:18 and Num. 18:27) would judge the acceptability of offerings. There is clear personal responsibility here. Our deeds of faithfulness or faithlessness are "credited" or "reckoned" to us. The image that comes to mind in modern times is the accountant's ledger (balance) sheet. Debits and credits are recorded. Abram's belief was credited as a spiritual asset on God's "balance sheet" for Abram's life—a valuable asset at that!

III. Righteousness

Biblical righteousness is not so much right behavior as it is a just and proper relationship. This can be a right relationship between persons, or between a person and God. Once Abram believes, and his belief is judged acceptable by God, he enters into a new and "right" relationship with God. It will be many years until we see this message of salvation personified in Jesus.

Indeed, for those troubled by what happened to those faithful people who lived before Christ was born, this passage seems to suggest that a way of salvation and right relationship with God has been possible from the earliest days of biblical history. (Steven R. Fleming)

GENUINE IMITATIONS

PHILIPPIANS 3:17–4:1

Imitation is not a word that inspires confidence or announces quality. An imitation is second best, cut rate. It's what you end up with when the real thing is unavailable or too costly. Imitation diamond: cut glass by another name. Imitation ice cream: cold and sweet, but it doesn't quite hit the spot. Imitation wood: fiberboard covered with wood grain wallpaper sure to dissolve in water. If we had our preference, most of us would rather not accept an imitation of anything.

How would you like to be an imitation? Chances are you don't find that a particularly appealing prospect. Every once in a while someone will say to one of my children, "You look just like your dad." They don't take the comment as a compliment, particularly my daughter. "I look just like myself," I've heard her say. We think of ourselves as one-of-a-kind originals, genuine articles, not imitations.

An imitation is not a bad thing. In fact, without imitation we couldn't even communicate. Learning to talk is all about imitation. To the toddler you say, "Put your tongue behind your front teeth and say, 'Thank you,' not 'Hank you.' Now, let's try it again." Without imitation, it's impossible. Carpenters learn by imitation. Imitation plays an important role in the education of doctors, lawyers, and pastors as well.

That's what the Apostle Paul said to the church of ancient Philippi. "Brothers and sisters, join in imitating me, and observe those who live according to the example you have in us" (v. 17). No one ever accused Paul of excessive modesty. It took some kind of conceit for him to tell people to use his life as a model.

In their extensive study *The Day America Told the Truth*, the researchers found that 70 percent of Americans believe there are no living heroes today and that children have no meaningful role models. What we lack in heroes, we make up for in celebrities.

Unfortunately, these are not usually individuals known for their moral integrity and spiritual depth.

Paul faced tough competition in the first century. Even in the church there were examples of behavior that was a long way from Christlike. Paul warned of people whose "god is the belly; and their glory is in their shame; their minds are set on earthly things" (v. 19). Evidently, some folks believed that Christian freedom from burdensome legalism set them free to be self-indulgent. They prided themselves in their ability to drink others under the table. They boasted of their sensual conquests. They were preoccupied with what they could get and enjoy in this world. They paid little attention to the heavenly. They weren't much different from the pagan majority.

Paul set himself up as an alternative and said, "Join in imitating me." I suspect that we are disinclined to set ourselves up as models of behavior, not just because we are so humble. Being models demands an uncomfortable amount of accountability. If we dare to invite others to imitate us, that means they will end up looking over our shoulders. We'll have to be awfully careful or we'll lead them into something that might not be so good.

As a frequently cited statement puts it, "Christianity is more caught than taught." It's not enough to offer people guidelines for living. The most lasting lessons of faith are not passed on in a classroom. They are conveyed in what we see in living, moving bodies.

Knowing that others have an eye on us can have a way of calling us back on track. It can make us aware of our own sloppiness of faith and shabbiness of dedication. If there's a chance that someone might imitate me, I'd better get my act together. I don't want to be responsible for any bad products. I need to remember the best examples of Christianity that I know and imitate them. Then, perhaps, I'll be able to offer others a model worth copying. (Craig M. Watts)

ODD COMMENTS ON THE ROAD TO JERUSALEM

LUKE 13:31-35

Luke put today's Scripture in the middle of a travel setting; from chapter 9 until chapter 19, Jesus is traveling through the villages on the way to Jerusalem, to the cross. Because some of the same comments are mentioned in other Gospels in connection with the entry into Jerusalem, perhaps these comments were made as Jesus passed through the lower part of Samaria or near Jericho. They seem to be separate statements strung, as in the manner of pearls, on verse numbers. We see two possible themes in this passage; on one hand it is a collection of odd comments that are noteworthy in that light, and on the other hand we have the theme of the inexorable will of God being done in the ministry of Jesus. Let us consider these verses in the honest light of their oddity.

I. An Odd Request

It is quite astonishing, when we stop to consider it, that a group of Pharisees came to Jesus to warn him of Herod's wrath. Our usual picture of Pharisees is that they were the ones who measured and counted every bean on their plate in order to tithe it, yet stole widows' houses. They were the ones who prayed on street corners to be seen by others; they were the ones who traversed land and sea to make one convert, and when he was converted, made him into a twofold son of hell. The Pharisees were like whitewashed tombs with all manner of uncleanness inside, like filthy cups all polished up on the outside. But here we see a group of Pharisees coming to do something good! Were they serious?

Perhaps this verse speaks to our tendency to lump all folks of a particular group together and judge them all alike, paint them all with the same brush. We do that in race relations; we do that in our discrimination against the elderly and those with handicapping conditions. No doubt we all identified with the above picture of the Pharisee; yet we know of at least two Pharisees in the Bible who were very different: Nicodemus and Joseph of Arimathea. There is so much good in the worst of us, and so much evil in the best of us, that it behooves us all to be careful in judging others.

II. An Odd Epithet

But verse 32 gives a needed corrective to the stance of being so nonjudgmental that we turn a blind eye and a deaf ear to obvious evil. There is no virtue in a hypocritical and simplistic refusal to see the devil at work! Jesus, you remember, said we will be known by our fruits. It is possible to be so "open minded" that, as someone put it, "our brains fall out." In this verse, it appears that Jesus did not believe their sincerity, or at least felt they were being, at best, dupes of Herod: "Go and tell that fox . . . " (v. 32). As to whether this was a clever scheme hatched up between the Pharisees and Herod to get Jesus out of their area and on down into Jerusalem, we cannot know. But we can clearly see that Jesus was not ambivalent about Herod. If I were to call a church member a "fox" in the tone and setting that Jesus used that word here, there would be no misunderstanding of what I meant! And there was no misunderstanding about Jesus' use here. The term *fox* signified craftiness and deceit. So in this verse, with its odd epithet for Herod, we see that there are times when the Christian needs to respond boldly and openly to the schemes of the evil one. Jesus' reply to their request indicates that he will continue his work of healing for the present. "Today and tomorrow" seem to mean that Jesus will keep to his pace and plan for the near future, and that at a definite point—"the third day"—his work would be completed.

III. An Odd Saying

The Herods of this world, the puppets of the devil, come and go, but the plan of God marches on. That is the message of verse 33. Notice the word *nevertheless* in the King James Version. It is a marvelous word as it is used in the Scriptures. Here Jesus uses it in regard to God's plan. Herod can scheme, the Pharisees can beg, the devil can pull strings; *nevertheless* Jesus "sets his face like a flint" and continues his steady pace toward Jerusalem. The cardinal thundered, "The Pope's little finger is stronger than all Germany. Do you expect your princes to take up arms to defend you—a wretched worm like you? I tell you, No! And where will you be then?" "Then, as now," cried Luther, "I shall be in the hands of God!" And so he stood, against all odds, realizing the powers arrayed against him—*Nevertheless* here I stand, so help me God!

Now notice the odd little saying in this verse: "It is impossible for a prophet to be killed outside of Jerusalem." Now obviously some prophets literally were, but the point of this saying is that Jerusalem is the focus of the hope of Israel in looking for the Messiah; it is the focus of the prophetic message of repentance; it is the seat of the religious establishment, which so often missed the essence of God's will. Jerusalem is where the dead past of religion and the lively prophetic hope come head to head—and so often the prophet perishes. In this saying Jesus was identifying himself with that long line of spokesmen for God. Consider the parable of the vineyard in Luke 20:9-16 in this light.

IV. An Odd Image

The theme of the rejection of the prophets is continued in verse 34, but here Jesus rises above the prophets to speak of himself as the one—the only one—who can really bless and comfort Jerusalem. The image he uses to describe his desire in regard to Jerusalem is striking—a mother hen. Who has not seen the little chicks—biddies, we called them—running to the old mother hen in response to her clucking, to take shelter under her spread wings? But most people would never think of this image for God! It is too feminine. Here we see the motherliness of the Savior. We do not need to change the biblical use of the masculine gender of God in order to acknowledge the wonderful and powerful feminine characteristics of God. After all, where do we think the fine attributes of womanhood come from, if not from God? He was like that long before any woman was like that! Here Jesus, in the presence of the Pharisees sent from Herod, seeing in his mind's eye the long, bitter trek to Jerusalem to die in rejection, still has a heart filled with a mother's love and tenderness toward those who would murder him.

V. An Odd Blessing

What a sad scene is pictured in Jesus' words in verse 35. He is still talking with the Pharisees who have come to him from Herod. Their house—Jerusalem with its Temple and all its religious system—is going to be left to them desolate with the "exodus" of Jesus. The idea here is not that of the parable of the empty house with its devil tenants (Matt. 12:43-45), but rather of a house in which a death has occurred, a tragedy has taken place.

Desolation is emptiness with loneliness and sorrow trailing along in its wake. Now notice the odd blessing in this verse; it is not a blessing bestowed by Jesus but by the those who inhabit this desolate "house." Jesus says he is leaving—that's what the Pharisees came to urge him to do. He is leaving their territory, their nation, their city, their Temple. And the point is that they will find that living without the presence of God is worse than living with his judgmental presence! One day they will be glad to see a prophet, glad to hear the message of God. The blessing here is one that the desolate people will bestow on him who comes in the name of the Lord.

This is an odd passage of Scripture, with its odd request, its odd epithet, its odd saying, its odd image, and its odd blessing. But then the gospel itself is odd, is it not? Why would God love this rebellious world so much that he just refuses to give up on us? Why would he choose a servant nation to spread the good news of his love? How odd of God to choose a cross, the instrument of execution in that day, to demonstrate his love. But then, we're odd people, aren't we? Odd in our perverse love of sin, but also odd, in the eyes of the world, in the way some of us respond when we finally see the light of God's love—remember the extravagant pouring out of the perfume by Mary? Do something odd today! (Earl C. Davis)

MARCH 19, 1995

❧

Third Sunday in Lent

Worship Theme: Genuine repentance is the gateway to new life in Christ.

Readings: Isaiah 55:1-9; 1 Corinthians 10:1-13; Luke 13:1-9

Call to Worship (Psalm 63:1-4):

O God, you are my God, I seek you,
  my soul thirsts for you;
my flesh faints for you,
  as in a dry and weary land
    where there is no water.
So I have looked upon you in the sanctuary,
  beholding your power and glory.
Because your steadfast love is better than life,
  my lips will praise you.
So I will bless you as long as I live;
  I will lift up my hands and call on your name.

Pastoral Prayer:

Lord, Lent should teach us to sacrifice. By giving up those things you help us to remember your sacrifice. Shall we diet to recall that others starve, or refrain from shopping sprees to remember universal poverty and shivering children? Yet you forbid true sacrifice. You baptize us in the abundance of such love that we've forgotten what sacrifice really is. Our confessions have been paid for by our hidden denials. Lord, help us to release our grip on trinkets that we esteem. And while our poor, supposed treasure falls, our empty lives will be filled with grace, and we will know the meaning of Paul's benediction: You do supply our every need according to your riches in glory in Christ Jesus. Amen. (Calvin Miller)

SERMON BRIEFS

THE SEARCH FOR CONTENTMENT

ISAIAH 55:1-9

USA Today (March 24, 1993) tells the story of a man and his forty-nine credit cards. His debts total $25,000. He uses cash advances from one card to pay another. When he "maxes out" a card, most companies simply raise his credit limit. Even though unemployed, he continues to receive even more offers of credit! It seems that companies are happy to help him spend his money in his search for the "American dream."

This search for contentment by the acquiring of possessions is an age-old problem. Isaiah speaks against the "consumer mentality" of his people when he says: "Why spend money on what is not bread / and your labor on what does not satisfy?" (v. 2a NIV). Reflecting on the fact that the attempts of our selfish contemporary to buy happiness, security, and power have failed, we see that Isaiah's question is one more Christians are trying to answer. There is a growing realization that life's most important values—happiness, a sense of security, meaningful relationships, a purpose in life—cannot be bought at any price. How timely is Isaiah's call to "listen to me, and eat what is good, / and your soul will delight in the richest of fare" (v. 2b). Isaiah called the people of Israel, now in bondage in Babylon, to return to their ancient faith in God, where true happiness and security are found. How?

I. Seek the Lord

There is only one way to find the happiness, security, and meaning in life that every person desires. You find it in relationship with God. The people of Old Testament Israel needed to be reminded that the covenant still exists. The love of God, once promised to David, is still available. They are called to rediscover their "roots" both as a people and as a religious community. Indeed, they were not only to seek out God, but they must do so "while he may be found; / call on him while he is near" (v. 6 NIV).

II. Turn Away from Sin to the Lord

We must leave behind our sinful ways and our evil thoughts. Although doing so is not easy, God "will have mercy on him, . . . for he will freely pardon" (v. 7*b*). We can see the parallel between Isaiah's message of salvation and that of Jesus. Indeed, there are so many parallels between Isaiah's message and Jesus' message that F. B. Meyer wrote a whole book entitled *Christ in Isaiah*. Those dismissing the Old Testament as irrelevant miss the richness, power, and unity of the Scriptures that comes only by careful study and reflection on the entire canon.

III. Lift Your Sights to God's Plans

Verses 8-9 may have a double meaning. On the one hand, "my thoughts are not your thoughts, / neither are your ways my way" (v. 8*a*) draws the prophetic contrast between God's perfection and the imperfect Israelites, who had fallen so short of God's intent. But these verses can also challenge us to seek a better, higher way, something like this: "My thoughts, ways, and even heaven are far beyond your limited understanding. To acknowledge that fact does not condemn us but is the key to ultimate redemption. If you want to get out of Babylon (symbolic of both physical and spiritual bondage), look *up* to my thoughts and my ways."

Isaiah is clear that God's ways and plans are higher than anything mortals can conceive. Would we want it any other way? No! Only the God whose message and truth surpass that of our finite beings can be the One in whom we will find true happiness and contentment. (Steven R. Fleming)

EXAMPLES TO AVOID

1 CORINTHIANS 10:1-13

My parents were raised on farms in East Tennessee. As I was growing up, they would tell me how things were when they were my age. Frankly, I couldn't relate to a lot of it. They told me of traveling to church by horse and wagon. They spoke of their one-room school house. They told me of how they would often get up

114

before daylight to milk cows, feed animals, and prepare to work in the fields.

In contrast, I was born and raised in one of the largest metropolitan areas in the country. My high school graduating class numbered over 600. I grew up with TV and rock and roll. The only animal I ever had to care for was my dog. The only chores I had were cleaning my bedroom and washing dishes—which I hated. When my parents occasionally tried to teach me some lesson by pointing to an incident or experience in their youth, I'd sometimes retort, "So what does that have to do with me?"

That was then; this is now, some say. They try to cut the ties with the past. They regard it as irrelevant. They refuse to see how the events of yesterday can be lessons for today. Things have changed. The world is so different from what it was in days gone by. We're so much more advanced now, so much more sophisticated. We're not so weak, gullible, or backward. Our world is unlike anything before. We have to pave our own way, blaze our own trail, trust our own instincts.

While every age is unique, many qualities seem to be with us always. The dynamics of foolishness and wisdom, greed and generosity, cruelty and compassion can be found wherever and whenever humans live. If we open our eyes and hearts, we can learn some crucial lessons from the experiences of those who have gone before us.

Apparently, the Apostle Paul believed as much. In the city of Corinth, he was confronted by a group who were confident of their spirituality.

In their confidence, they were careless. That can happen to us as well. A bright student becomes overconfident and doesn't study enough for a test and gets an unpleasant surprise when the grades come out. A man takes his wife for granted, neglects the small acts of consideration and tenderness, and he's shocked when she walks off with another man.

Some of the Corinthians were so confident that they were spiritually secure that they weren't cautious about how they lived. Sure, they performed certain rituals. They had been baptized. They partook of communion. They had a theology that made them feel nice and safe and self-satisfied. What they didn't do, however, was consider the Scriptures and learn from the downfall of many biblical characters. Paul calls the attention of the prideful Corinthians to their rebellious forebears who were destroyed.

Paul went on to say that despite their religious experience, they still fell away from God and met an unfortunate end. The apostle then wrote, "These things happened to them to serve as an example, and they were written down to instruct us. . . . So if you think you are standing, watch out that you do not fall" (vv. 11-12). In other words, don't forget the blunders of the spiritually cock-sure people of the past. Don't follow in their steps, or you are liable to fall on your face just as they did.

It is crucial that we pay attention to the spiritual warning that we are given in the Scriptures. Sometimes we simply need to change course in order to find God and live faithfully. God is faithful, Scripture tells us. The same cannot always be said of us. But we can become more faithful if we pay attention to the examples God provides. (Craig M. Watts)

THE PARABLE OF THE EXTRA YEAR

LUKE 13:1-9

If something dreadful were to happen to you today, would it mean you are a bigger sinner than the others sitting on your pew? Jesus deals with such questions in our Scripture passage today, and uncovers even deeper concerns we ought to be worried about as he tells the parable of the extra year.

In the preceding chapter, Jesus accuses the crowd of ignoring the signs of moral crisis, even though they could read the evening sky. In verses 58-59 Jesus urges a pragmatic approach to such spiritual hypocrisy—hasten to repent! So this much is clear from these verses: Hypocrisy leads to moral crisis, to willful spiritual ignorance, to a day of reckoning. But let us continue on as if there were no chapter break to the first verses of chapter 13. There were some folks in that crowd listening to Jesus—or perhaps they rushed up just then to the edge of the crowd and caught the last words—who assumed Jesus was speaking of very wicked people who richly deserve God's punishment in full strength. Thinking to have Jesus' confirmation on their view, they related the latest news: Pilate had slaughtered some Galileans who were in Jerusalem. On what pretext this slaughter was done is unknown, but he "mingled" their blood with the blood of their sacrifices (v. 1). And the tellers of the tale must have been eyewitnesses to the carnage. But surely these were exceptionally wicked men.

Jesus replied, "Do you think that because these Galileans suffered in this way, they were worse sinners than all other Galileans? No, I tell you; but unless you repent, you will all perish as they did" (vv. 2-3). He then brought up an incident sometime past: "Or those eighteen who were killed when the tower of Siloam fell on them—do you think that they were worse offenders than all the others living in Jerusalem? No, I tell you; but unless you repent, you will all perish just as they did!" (vv. 4-5). Mark it down, right here, that Jesus rejects the idea that terrible tragedy is a measure of punishment for sin; these men were no more wicked than the rest.

Jesus then went directly on to tell them the parable of the extra year. An open-ended story, it begins with the owner of a vineyard coming to check on a fig tree he has planted in a corner of the vineyard. This is the third year since it should have been bearing fruit, and yet it has none. The owner is furious, and tells the vineyard worker to cut it down! The vineyard worker proposes that he dig around it and fertilize it for one more year and see if it will bear fruit—if not, then cut it down! And that's the end of the parable.

What is the message of this scripture passage? What is the connection of this business about telling when it will rain, Pilate's slaughter of the Galileans, the tragedy of the eighteen men on whom the tower fell, and this open-ended parable? What did it say to that crowd? What does it say to us today?

I. The Danger of Spiritual Barrenness

Consider the charge of deliberate, hypocritical spiritual barrenness. That is a devastating charge; yet Jesus, as well as the earlier Old Testament prophets, clearly accused the Jewish nation of rejecting its calling. Many scholars think Jesus deliberately refused in this parable to use the image of a vine, though that would be the natural image since he dealt with a vineyard. Rather, he chose to scorn the common idea of Israel being the chosen vineyard of God by speaking of Israel as a fig tree planted

117

in a vineyard. So it is the nation that has become a hypocrite, morally unwilling to read the sky.

If Jesus said their failure to acknowledge and respond to him as Messiah put them in a danger far more urgent than worrying about being killed by a falling tower, what would he say about our time? About us as we go to great extremes to legitimize homosexuality and AIDS; as we make excuses for those who put drugs and alcohol into their mouths to steal away their brains; as churches become merely havens of memories or hives of entertainment rather than troops in a war against the prince of evil?

The parable of the barren fig tree, the parable of the extra year, is given for each of us as well as the first-century crowd around Jesus. The Bible says that every Christian is saved to serve God; it teaches that we are to be spiritually fruitful. Is it possible to be spiritually fruitful if we deliberately turn a blind eye and a deaf ear to God? Hypocrisy is willing self-deception. As individuals and as a church we must not deceive ourselves about the purpose of our existence and our part in the great plan of God.

II. The Certainty of Judgment

The second theme of this passage is judgment. Now, Jesus' comments on the slaughter of Pilate and the unfortunate ones killed in the fall of the tower tell us that we are all rushing toward judgment—some just get there quicker. He read in the fate of a few the doom of the entire nation. Those who perished are reminders of our own unworthiness. If we are spared, it is by grace, and we should not presume, but repent. Our tendency toward hypocrisy makes it hard for us to see our unworthiness.

Our hypocrisy makes us excuse ourselves when we are less than we should be, and our nature makes us seek a way out of judgment if it must come. The story is told of W. C. Fields on his death bed reading it. A friend noticed the Bible and asked why Fields was reading it. "Oh, just looking for loopholes," said Fields. But there are no loopholes, according to this passage. Judgment on sin, like the slaughter by Pilate and the falling of the tower, is severe and fatal and inescapable—unless we repent.

III. The Everlasting Mercy—Almost

And that brings us to the third theme in this passage, the mercy of God. In fact, some folks say the parable emphasizes the mercy of God rather than the coming judgment. It does both, and it points up the patience, the forbearance of God. So long as time shall last, God stands with arms outstretched, like that old rugged cross on the hill, willing to receive all who will repent. And in that light, this parable holds out hope for every sinner— give him one more year!

Let us ask some relevant questions for us all: If you knew you had one more year to live, what changes would you make in your life? Would your values suddenly change? Would you begin to think about spiritual things? Would you turn to Jesus for salvation? If, as a Christian, you knew you had one more year to bear spiritual fruit, where would you begin? If, as a church, we knew we had but one more year to get serious about serving God, where would we start? These are not just idle questions; none of us knows how much time we have left. There are limits to the patience, the mercy of even God. And in this parable we see both mercy and its limits in the phrase "one more year." Jesus preached an eminent day of reckoning; indeed, even if he does not come back soon, all of us will, in less than a century, go to him. Are we ready? Are we living as people who are ready? (Earl C. Davis)

MARCH 26, 1995

❧

Fourth Sunday in Lent

Worship Theme: Though we are lost, our loving God searches us out to bring us home.

Readings: Joshua 5:9-12; 2 Corinthians 5:16-21; Luke 15:1-3, 11*b*-32

Call to Worship (Psalm 32:11):
Be glad in the LORD and rejoice, O righteous,
   and shout for joy, all you upright in heart.

Pastoral Prayer:
   Lord, did Mary Magdalene's tears seem overdone? She cried so readily! Was her hair clean when she used it as a towel to dry your feet? Most people think she overdid it. Her brokenness seems pretty showy to our hiding hearts. But then we're petrified inside. We cry more eagerly in movies than we do at altars. We only list our sins inside the flaps of self-esteem books. We'd like to repent but, basically, you know, we're okay. The world's okay, and that's *okay.*
   Lord, does it seem that faces are a little hard this year? Does it seem that sin smiles out through unconfessing lips? It's Easter-tide, and nobody's crying this time around. Nobody's standing by with costly nard to dump it on you, Lord. The church seems chilly, doesn't it? Were Mary Magdalene's tears overdone? Why won't our own tears come? Amen. (Calvin Miller)

SERMON BRIEFS

FROM DEPENDENCE TO INTERDEPENDENCE

JOSHUA 5:9-12

   Steven Covey's *The Seven Habits of Highly Effective People* is a best-seller in the field of personal growth and change. Although not written for a "religious" audience, Covey's book contains the key teaching that the development of one's spiritual life is necessary to achieve the ultimate goal of interdependence. Today's text shows how God led the Israelites from dependence to interdependence. Symbolic of this transition is the moment in Joshua 5:12 when their supply of heaven-sent manna ends.

I. Dependence as a Fact of Life

God has ordained creation in such a way that there is a normal progression from dependence to independence to interdependence. Newborn babies are very dependent for their survival; children and youth need a nurturing environment in which to develop and mature; adults who are sick or infirm depend on the care and support of others. There is nothing inherently wrong with being dependent in the appropriate circumstances. When the people complain to Moses about possible starvation in Exodus 16, they were recognizing their almost total dependence upon God to provide for the people as they left Egypt for the forbidding desert wilderness. Christians must also recognize our appropriate dependence upon others and God.

II. The Search for Independence

Although some dependency is appropriate, people naturally seek independence. The people of Israel wish to "cut the apron strings." Such transitions from dependence to independence are difficult—as any parent of teenagers or young adults will tell you! As the people of Israel strain to find their own identity and establish a degree of independence, the inevitable tension appears between reliance upon their own devices and an ongoing reliance upon God. We see in the early biblical narratives much striving to become a people with their own identity. The struggle often leads them to turn away from their vital relationship with God with severe consequences. Scripture warns that if our search for independence leaves God behind, we'd better watch out!

III. The Goal: Interdependence

But God's plan is for us to remain neither totally dependent nor totally independent. God wants people to discover their *inter*dependence. Our identity is found when we recognize our "connectedness" to God. This blends both dependence and independence appropriately. This movement to *inter*dependence is shown as the people cross the Jordan to the Promised Land (Joshua 3) and reassert their religious and national identity by circumcision in Joshua 5:1-8. God announces the rolling "away from you the disgrace of Egypt" (v. 9). The Passover celebration (vv. 10-11) recalls the Source of their independence (vv. 10-11). Eating the "produce of the land" (v. 12) is symbolic of their ability to provide for essential physical needs while depending on God for the conditions that make crops grow. It is at this point that the manna stops. This is a sign of achieving interdependence.

The next event, the battle of Jericho (Josh. 5:13ff.), demonstrates this newfound interdependence. Victory requires the cooperation of the Israelites *and* their God. Indeed, one might read the history of Israel as a constant moving back and forth from dependence to independence to interdependence. Only when they work together in concert with God (true scriptural *inter*dependence) do the people of Israel realize their full potential. The same is true for believers today. (Steven R. Fleming)

A NEW POINT OF VIEW

2 CORINTHIANS 5:16-21

In Stephen Covey's book *The Seven Habits of Highly Effective People* are three rough sketches. One of them is a profile of an attractive young woman. Another is of a very large-nosed older woman. Covey said he first saw the pictures in a class he had at Harvard Business School years earlier. Half the class was shown the first picture, while the other half was shown the second picture. Then the entire class was presented with a third sketch of a woman.

Strangely, the members of the class did not see the same thing. Those who had first seen the picture of the attractive young woman could see her once again in this third picture. The portion of the class that had started out by looking at the picture of the large-nosed elderly woman saw her image in the third picture. When the professor called on the class members to describe what they saw, an argument began to rage. The various students saw the final sketch from different frames of reference and found it nearly impossible to make sense of the point of view of those who saw it in a contrasting way. In fact, the lines in the picture could be seen in both ways. The sketch incorporated the images of both the elderly woman and the younger woman.

A new point of view is hard won. But the Apostle Paul said that Christians have been given precisely that. "We regard no one from a human point of view," he said (v. 16). We once did, but no longer. What is a human point of view? When the people we gravitate toward are the ones who are the most physically attractive, then we see from a human point of view. When we neglect people who don't amuse us or help us "get ahead," then we see from a human point of view. When we treat with respect only people who have prominent positions, then we see from a human point of view. When we assume the worst of people who are unlike us, then we see from a human point of view.

But Paul said, "We no longer regard anyone from a human point of view." Sounds odd, doesn't it? After all, what other point of view can we have? I remember a commercial I saw on television a while back for some kind of dog food. It began by showing a woman pouring the chunky nuggets into the pet's dish. She then stepped out onto a porch to call her dog. Then the TV screen gave us a picture of the world from the pup's perspective. As though through the dog's eyes, down close to the ground, we were given a sense of the animal running, charging up a path. Crashing through the weeds, grass slapping at the field of vision. Up and over small hills. Splashing through a stream. Dodging trees. Bounding up the porch steps and, finally, the food dish fills the screen. Ah! Canine satisfaction!

But, of course, the Apostle Paul didn't have the animal alternative in mind when he said, "We no longer regard anyone from a human point of view." It was not a perspective lower than ours that he suggested, but one much higher. The Divine perspective. Now that we recognize that, in Christ, God suffered and died for all people, we cannot look at anyone in a demeaning way. We cannot devalue any person. We cannot see people as objects to be used or as annoyances to be eliminated. Because of the cross and the resurrection, we come to see the high value God places on us all. We are given God's point of view. When we see from

God's point of view, we recognize that there are no disposable people.

The love of Christ controls us, and that changes everything about how we look at others and live with them. What we experience is nothing less than "a new creation: everything old has passed away; see, everything has become new!" (v. 17). (Craig M. Watts)

THE TRIPLE TRAGEDY

LUKE 15:1-3, 11*b*-32

It has been called the greatest short story in the world. Truly, when other books crumble into dust and the world has waxed old like a garment, this story will be young and fresh. Yet this remarkable story, which we call the parable of the prodigal son, is but one of three connected stories the Master told and that Luke has recorded in the fifteenth chapter of his Gospel: the tragedies of the lost sheep, the lost coin, and the lost boy.

For you and me to feel the heart of these stories, we must try to recreate the scene when Jesus first told them to people just like us. They were told when opposition to Jesus had hardened. He was on his way to the cross, and the chosen people had rejected their calling—"He came unto his own, and his own received him not." Picture a day like that one when a paralyzed man was let down through the roof to be healed by Jesus, and the scribes and Pharisees began to gripe and grumble. Or the day when Levi, a notorious sinner and tax collector, walked away from his old life to follow the Master, and threw a grand feast to celebrate—and Jesus came, of course! The scribes and Pharisees? They merely muttered and complained that a religious teacher would stoop to eating with such a sinner!

I. The Tragedy of the Cold Ones

And so the first of the three tragedies of our text has to do with the attitude of the religious folks toward God's wonderful work of grace. In verses 1-3 we see the tragedy of the cold people of God: "And the Pharisees and the scribes were grumbling and saying, 'This fellow welcomes sinners and eats with them.' So he told them this parable. . . . " Now the climax to the three stories, the shadow behind them, is the portrait of the elder brother in the prodigal son parable. He is clearly a picture of how Jesus feels about church people who claim they know God, want to be like him, and yet turn away from the poor and the outcast, the misfits who would come from the darkness of sin into the circle of fellowship and love of the church, if we would only welcome them! No church can have revival if it is filled with "elder brothers"— and sisters!

Look further at the mirror of the elder brother in verse 28, when the ragged prodigal comes and the rejoicing begins. The elder brother hears the merrymaking while still in the field and calls a servant to explain. Upon hearing the "good" news "he became angry and refused to go in. His father came out and began to plead with him." Can you see it? He boiled over with anger at his father's taking the prodigal back. His thoughts were on himself. "I have never disobeyed . . . you have never given me . . . But when this son. . . . " See him sulking in the hot afternoon out behind the house!

What an unattractive character the elder brother is! I would hate to be cooped up with him all day in a bass boat or have to spend the morning with him in a duck blind or under the same tree at a dove shoot! He may well have been the reason the prodigal left home! He makes the committed Christian rethink the list of most serious sins, for the repentant prodigal was welcomed with a kiss by the father, who most surely represents God in this eternal portrait, while the scribes and Pharisees, who are just as clearly the elder brother, are definitely a disappointment to God.

II. The Tragedy of the Lost Ones

The second of the three tragedies is that of our lost condition. There is a haunting emphasis in all three parables on lostness. The sheep became lost through its own curiosity, wandering away, following its own foolish notion. Never bothering itself with cautions, never looking up to get its bearings, merely munching its way on to confusion, danger, and destruction.

The situation of the coin is different from that of the sheep, yet just as deadly. Through no fault of its own, the cherished coin—

no doubt part of the cherished symbolism of the married state worn by Jewish women much as we wear our wedding rings—rolled away. And I can see, in the images our Master used here, the pitiful condition of little children who, because of circumstance, parental neglect, environment, or lack of concern by Christians, roll off as human coins and fall unnoticed into the dark corners of life. The third picture of lostness is of yet another kind—that of the deliberately rebellious boy. This boy deliberately became lost; home was tedious to him; it fretted and chafed him; he wanted his "freedom." And so Jesus portrays in this parable the illusion of liberty without responsibility.

Jesus saw every soul as lost—like the sheep through thoughtlessness; like the coin through common participation in the web of sin that surrounds us all; like the boy who embraced a deliberate rebellion against his father. And Jesus saw the inevitable course of sin in our lives and projected it into the sad conclusion of the prodigal son's adventure: an inner disintegration, outer misery, and total ruin. Such is the message of the picture, so abhorrent to the Jew, of the boy sitting by the pig trough.

III. The Tragedy of the Searching One

The third of the triple tragedies is that of the sorrowful and searching Father. While it is truly the tragedy of the sorrowing Father so long as we turn from his love and care, there is a striking emphasis on the persistent, patiently searching Father. God is as concerned for his children as any shepherd ever was for a lost lamb; as concerned as any new bride ever was over the loss of the marriage headband coin. I just wonder if the father did not ask the elder brother to go look for his prodigal brother, and he refused. Just so the Pharisees never dreamed of God searching for persons! Yet it is clear as we listen to Jesus telling these stories that we have misnamed them all! It is not the story of the lost sheep but rather of the good shepherd. It is not the story of the lost coin but rather of the searching wife. It is not the story of the lost boy but rather of the loving father. And in each case, the final emphasis is on the joy of finding the thing that was lost.

Let us add to the lost condition of every person, and the everlasting picture of the searching God, the possibility of repentance—going home again, in every life. I can imagine that as

Jesus told these stories those whom the Pharisees condemned him for associating with, the outcasts and prostitutes and publicans, felt hope alight like a dove in their hearts. The possibility of coming home, of being accepted and forgiven and having peace with God, brought tears to their sin-ravaged faces. (Earl C. Davis)

APRIL

❧

Replenishing the Well

Expecting Holy Week

We began the year with the sacrament of baptism. As in baptism, the sacrament of the Lord's Supper is a meal filled with expectation—we celebrate the Lord's Supper *until he comes again.*

. The following exercise prepares our hearts in expectation of the events of Holy Week.

Time: 2 hours during the evening.

Materials: Bibles and ingredients for a simple soup supper, bread, wine or other beverage; access to a kitchen to prepare the meal. Or, if possible, a service of Holy Communion.

Exercise:

The sacrament of the Lord's Supper is the centerpiece of congregational spiritual life, especially during Holy Week. It is appropriate, therefore, to share a simple meal or celebrate the Lord's Supper at the beginning of Holy Week in expectation of the events to follow. The setting should be kept as informal as possible. And the meal should be planned for sometime just *prior* to Palm Sunday.

Hand out Bibles to three people willing to read aloud to the group. Before the meal, the first person reads Luke 19:28-40, Palm Sunday. Midway through the meal the second person reads Luke 22:14-53, the evening of the Last Supper. At the conclusion of the meal, the third person reads John 18:12–19:30, the Passion story.

Should you decide to celebrate the sacrament of Holy Communion, you may insert the readings where appropriate.

Whether sharing a simple meal or celebrating Communion, direct all participants to leave in silent expectation of the week to come. (Harriet Crosby)

APRIL 2, 1995

❧

Fifth Sunday in Lent

Worship Theme: Spiritual power comes from a mind and heart focused on Jesus Christ.

Readings: Isaiah 43:16-21; Philippians 3:4*b*-14; John 12:1-8

Call to Worship (Psalm 126:3, 5-6):

>   The LORD has done great things for us,
>   and we rejoiced.
>   ....
>   May those who sow in tears
>   reap with shouts of joy.
>   Those who go out weeping,
>   bearing the seed for sowing,
>   shall come home with shouts of joy,
>   carrying their sheaves.

Pastoral Prayer:

Lord, as we journey toward Easter we cannot ignore the powerful memory of the obstacles our Savior faced as he journeyed toward Jerusalem, toward betrayal, toward death. We stand in awe of love so awesome that it led to a cross. Now we pause from a week of pressures and details that seemed so important a few moments ago, until they were enfolded by the shadow of that terrible, wonderful cross. May that cross become a measuring rod by which we determine our priorities, understand your will, and recognize your love. We pray in the name of the One who gave himself for us that we might have new life and new power. Amen. (Michael Duduit)

SERMON BRIEFS

THE POWER OF RETELLING THE STORY

ISAIAH 43:16-21

Many Christians are anxious and troubled. A fragile economy, the breakdown of the family, the decline in moral and ethical values, the seeming inability of government to act to resolve pressing social problems—all these lead to a growing feeling of uncertainty and unease. How can Christians deal with such feelings? Our text from Isaiah suggests an answer: As we hear and learn more of the Word of God, we are less likely to be troubled by such feelings of apprehension and worry. In God's Word is great power. Isaiah retells one of the great past experiences of God's people as a way of injecting hope and renewed confidence into the present difficulties.

I. A Story Retold Can Give Hope and Courage

At the time Isaiah wrote, his audience was in despair and apparent hopelessness as a result of tremendous changes in their world. He reminded his listeners that they, even though now in bondage in Babylon, might have hope because of their past release from the bondage of Egypt in the Exodus. Isaiah retells (vv. 16-17) the story of God's actions on behalf of "his" people to give them hope.

Retelling stories of the faith is powerful. This is one reason why regular worship is so crucial to people of faith. The community of faith gathers to hear the Word of God as retold in Scripture, sermon, prayer, and song. Whatever worries or bothers us as Christians, we can find hope in what Isaiah says. His message? Since God has helped his people before, we can rest on God's promises that he will act again. This is the God, Isaiah tells us, who "makes a way in the sea, / a path in the mighty waters" and makes "rivers in the desert" (Isaiah 43:16, 19). Our hope rests in the God who stands by his people.

II. God Can Free People from Personal Captivity

There is a certain sense in which many people today live in some form of personal captivity. An undercurrent of pervasive hopelessness and pain leads many to seek a way of escape from these personal prisons. All too often they seek that relief in their own strength and by their own means. Christians need not be caught in such futile searches for self-salvation. If we would listen, we would know that God is already calling to us with words of hope, encouragement, and ultimate salvation. We will not find the joy and purpose of life we so desperately seek outside of a relationship with the Creator God, who made us and sent his Son to find and save us. Augustine said it well: "Our hearts are restless until we find our rest in Thee."

When Isaiah proclaimed the message that God is doing a new thing, "I will make a way in the wilderness / and rivers in the desert" (v. 19), he gave hope to all who find life closing in on them in some way. The season of Lent is often portrayed as a personal journey of faith. One aspect of that journey is to escape those self-made prisons in our lives by hearing the life-giving truths that come from God. Such a journey begins with listening once more to the marvelous story of Scripture.

Therefore, take courage. Those who put their trust in the Lord won't be abandoned. Although we may not know what's ahead, God does. He provides "water in the wilderness, rivers in the desert, / to give drink to my chosen people" (v. 20b). So keep going. Keep trusting that God will lead you into the future. That was the ancient message of Isaiah to the people in Babylonian captivity. This message is still true today. (Steven R. Fleming)

BECOMING A CHRISTIAN

PHILIPPIANS 3:4b-14

Despite appearances, no one is perfect. Those who imagine themselves nearest to perfection are often the furthest from it. Sometimes we end up defending ourselves from both the omnicompetent and the overconfident by listing our own strengths. In a way, the Apostle Paul did something like this when he wrote to the church of Philippi. Evidently some teachers who came on the scene claimed to be superior to Paul. They pointed to their pedigree and called on people to accept their version of salvation by good works.

Paul was not about to be intimidated by other people's claims. He responded by pulling out his credentials. While he urged the people not to put their trust in the flesh, he went on to say, "If anyone else has reason to be confident in the flesh, I have more" (v. 4b). As a faithful child of God, Paul was a true Jew. His credentials were impeccable.

Of course, all this sounds a bit like a bragging contest. But in our own ways, we do it as well, if perhaps, more subtly. Naturally we sound a little different from Paul. What is the nature of our confidence in the flesh? As to nationality an American, of the people of whatever state; as to politics, a member of a particular party; as to zeal, a fan of our own favorite team; as to righteousness, a part of a respected, well-paying profession. These things give us confidence that we count for something in the world.

No sooner had Paul laid out his credentials than he placed them, not in the assets column of his life, but with the deficits. "I regard everything as loss," he said (v. 8). Speaking even more strongly, he declared, "I regard them as rubbish," or as some translations put it, "I count them as dung." Why? Paul's answer was this: "That I may gain Christ . . . having a righteousness . . . that comes through faith in Christ, the righteousness from God based on faith. I want to know Christ and the power of his resurrection . . . becoming like him" (vv. 9-10).

Strange, isn't it? It is not the blemishes of evil, but the badges of virtue; not the acts of shame, but the points of pride that Paul calls dung and throws aside for the sake of being close to Christ. Are you prepared to do that with your heritage or accomplishments?

Confidence about the good things in our life can keep us from being all God wants us to be just as much as blatant evil can. We can list our good points, declare these good enough, and rest contented, reasonably satisfied with ourselves.

Few things are more hazardous to the spiritual life than complacency. If you are satisfied with your spiritual life, chances are it's in bad shape. One of the signs of spiritual health is the pained awareness of being a long way from where you need to be. Our land is awash in what one person called "decaffeinated Christianity"—Christianity that won't keep you up at night.

The rightful goal of a follower of Jesus Christ is to be like Christ. That's a tall order. In the face of it, the Apostle Paul said, "Not that I have already obtained this or have already reached the goal; but I press on to make it my own, because Christ Jesus has made me his own . . . forgetting what lies behind and straining forward to what lies ahead, I press on toward the goal for the prize of the heavenly call of God in Christ Jesus" (vv. 12-14). How can we share in this same journey Paul describes?

First, recognize your strengths and virtues, but resist complacency. There is nothing positive in thinking yourself devoid of good. But there is danger in being satisfied with the degree of goodness and closeness with God we have today. God can make us more like Christ than we are right now.

Second, accept the need to struggle and work spiritually. Salvation is a free gift. But a vital, intimate relationship with God does not come effortlessly. No relationship does. No marriage relationship develops in a healthy way without time and attention being devoted to it. The same can be said of friendship. There are bumpy spots in every relationship. This is true in our relationship with God as well. Struggle is a spiritual necessity.

Third, study the Bible, and especially the Gospels. We can't be like Christ if we don't really know what he was like. Sure, there are some variations in the pictures of Jesus given to us in the different Gospels, but there is more unity than diversity. Meditate on how the Scriptures show Jesus dealing with life. Pay attention to his priorities, to his conflicts, to his actions, and to his teachings. Let these things be used by God to challenge your life.

Fourth, continue in prayer. Confess your failings and open your life to the transforming power of God. Get away from the daily routines that keep you in the old patterns and lay your life before God, who can move you along new paths of life. In prayer, face the reality of whose you are and learn to submit yourself to God's purpose for you.

Fifth, don't fear change. Change is disruptive and sometimes painful. But ultimately when God evokes a change we can be assured that it's for our good. To resist is to deny ourselves the experience of living the adventure and wonder God wants for us. Recently I heard someone point out, "There is an 'ow' in the middle of growth."

A Christian life doesn't pop into existence full and complete. It is constructed over time, piece by piece, behavior by behavior, attitude by attitude. Wholesale, top to bottom change is not normally what happens when a person becomes a Christian.

Yet, bit by bit, we hand ourselves over to God, the only rightful ruler of our lives. We are remade, with Jesus Christ at the center of our new self. And as we are remade, we discover that we enjoy our relationship with God and our daily lives more than ever before. (Craig M. Watts)

A DYNAMIC SPIRITUAL LIFE

JOHN 12:1-8

Read the amazing story of the spilt perfume and notice the question of the scene: "Why was this not sold and the money given to the poor?" Never mind that Judas framed the question; it still needs an answer. It seems to me that in this passage we are stepping into the middle of a story, and the answer to Judas's question is found in what Paul Harvey calls "the rest of the story."

Most of us are acquainted with Mary and Martha from Luke's Gospel, where Jesus is a guest in their home (10:38-42). In that scene, as in our text, Martha hurried around either preparing or serving a meal. And Mary? She didn't have a domestic bone in her body! In Luke's scene, to borrow the characters of one of Luke's parables, Martha sounds like an elder sister carping about a prodigal daughter! Is there perhaps a story between the lines? Is it possible that Simon (leper or Pharisee) in whose house the anointing took place in Matthew, Mark, and Luke, is Martha's husband, as in some legends, or even the father of these two girls? Could it be that the unnamed woman in the anointing accounts of Matthew, Mark, and Luke is Mary, anointing Jesus in her own home? Could she have broken her father's heart and lived a life of sin and shame in Galilee earlier? Is this Mary the one called Magdalene, from whose life Jesus cast seven devils? Such a Mary is listed as following Jesus from Galilee all the way to Jerusalem, to the cross! (All four Gospels say that Mary Magdalene stood by the cross.) Was this a homecoming for Mary, a prodigal daughter returning to the fold?

In the anointing accounts in Matthew, Mark, and John, Mary is said to be showing her concern for the anointing of Jesus' body for burial, and it is she who goes before dawn on Easter morning, according to all four Gospels, to anoint Jesus' body. And it is to Mary that Jesus first appears on resurrection morning. Perhaps Martha's sister and the Mary who anointed Jesus and the Mary who was rescued from a life of slavery to seven devils is one and the same Mary. And the truth is that she didn't sell the perfume and give the money to the poor because her mind and heart were fixed on Jesus, not on the poor, at that moment. On other days and through other years, she would doubtless feed the poor, but just now she was experiencing one of the four essential elements in a dynamic spiritual life.

I. A Great Sense of Need

Think first about the realization of a great need. A firm conviction from the beginning of the Bible is that we are sinners and need Christ. "All have sinned and come short of the glory of God." Each of us has a great need to surrender our crooked will to God, to be saved, to come home again. No one ever really comes to Jesus without a sense of a great need to be made right with God. Sometimes we become aware of our need for Jesus when we realize we cannot stand up to the demands of life; we cannot tame and conquer, mold and shape life to our selfish dreams. That's what happened in Mary's life. She had a great need—a need to be set free of those seven devils destroying her life. And like that publican who went up to the Temple to pray, filled with a great sense of failure and sin, there came a cry from the heart: "O God, be merciful to me, a sinner." Without that heart-cry, without that sense of helplessness and need, there is no help, no great salvation for Mary, or for you and me.

II. A Great Salvation

But God hears the cry of the sinner's heart and draws near the repentant heart with a great salvation. Not in vain did the angel tell Joseph in a dream, "You are to name him Jesus, for he will save his people from their sins" (Matt. 1:21) nor the prophet say, "They shall call his name Emmanuel, God with us." For the great deliverance, the salvation God gives us, comes through the death and resurrection of Jesus. Remember that conversation of Jesus with Nicodemus one night. There Jesus spoke of the great need of every person, and how his being lifted up as Moses lifted up the brazen serpent would bring salvation (John 3:14-16). By Jesus' death we are set free—Mary from her seven devils and Paul from the albatross of vain works and empty morality, this man from alcohol and that woman from the fear of death; this youth from envy and peer pressure, and that youth from drugs. We are set free from ourselves and from the treadmill of empty and twisted lives. The Bible urges us not to neglect so great a salvation, a peace within and a peace with God. Jesus said that he came to seek and to save the lost. There can be no great spiritual life until we seize that great salvation God offers through the blood of Christ.

III. A Spirit of Great Gratitude

The sense of need that reaches up to receive so great a salvation overflows in a spirit of gratitude toward God. I think that's why Mary gladly, joyfully poured out a year's wages of perfume on Jesus' head and feet. She had experienced a great salvation! And God kept on blessing her, for at the same table sat her brother, Lazarus, who a few weeks before lay cold and dead in the tomb. No wonder she wept tears of joy and thanksgiving!

The hallmark of Christianity is gratitude. The New Testament rings with praises to God for his goodness, from the pen of Paul to the angels who cry holy, holy, holy and the saints who fling their golden crowns before his throne in the book of Revelation. In the early church, what we call the Lord's Supper or Holy Communion was called the Eucharist, the thanksgiving. The only great Christian lives are those lived out of a depth of gratitude to Jesus for what he's done for us! The Christian who thinks life has cheated him, who thinks it owes her something, who is always criticizing and griping about life, family, church will live no great spiritual life and will be no great blessing to others. Only that Christian who—like Mary, like Zacchaeus, like Paul—feels he or she can never repay God can be fully used of God. The only great spiritual life is a life overflowing with gratitude, which shows in your material giving, your love for others, your daily witness. I can hear Mary say as the fragrance of the perfume drifts through the house, past the voices of criticism, "Were the whole realm of nature mine, that were a present far too small; love so amazing, so divine, demands—yes, shall have—my soul, my life, my all."

IV. A Great Compulsion

Once more we'll ask: *Why was not that perfume sold for 300 denarii and given to the poor?* Because Mary was filled with a great gratitude and seized by a great compulsion to express her love for Jesus, to honor and serve him in this matter, as she had done those last months in traveling in his company. A truly genuine and dynamic spiritual life is an expression of a great compulsion, a conviction, that God has laid hold on our life, putting us, like King Hezekiah's vow to "walk softly all the days of his life" in response to God's healing, under a divine compulsion to live for Jesus, to act for Jesus. In Philippians 3:7-14 Paul said he pressed on to *lay hold on* that glory for which Christ had *laid hold of him.* Mary had a divine compulsion to pour that perfume; Zacchaeus had a divine compulsion to give away half his fortune; Paul had a divine compulsion to preach the gospel to the Gentiles. That same compulsion ought to lead you to walk worthy of Jesus, to give your best in his service.

We find in Mary's life the realization of a great need, the acceptance of a great salvation, the pouring out of a great gratitude, and the living in the grip of a great compulsion. There is no great, deep, satisfying, blessed life of faith without these four elements. Much spiritual unrest, much shallow and self-serving religion of our time is due to our failure to understand and develop these four essential elements of a dynamic spiritual life.

(Earl C. Davis)

APRIL 9, 1995

❧

Palm/Passion Sunday (Sixth Sunday of Lent)

Worship Theme: Authentic praise involves not only the enthusiasm of the moment but also the commitment of a lifetime.

Readings: Isaiah 50:4-9*a*; Philippians 2:5-11; Luke 19:28-40; 22:14–23:56

Call to Worship (Psalm 118:1-2, 19-24):

Leader: O give thanks to the LORD, for he is good; his steadfast love endures forever!

People: Let Israel say, "His steadfast love endures forever." . . .

Leader: Open to me the gates of righteousness, that I may enter through them and give thanks to the LORD.

People: This is the gate of the LORD; the righteous shall enter through it.

Leader: I thank you that you have answered me and have become my salvation.

People: The stone that the builders rejected has become the chief cornerstone.

All: This is the day that the LORD has made; let us rejoice and be glad in it.

Pastoral Prayer:

Lord, hosannah! Blessed is the King of Israel who comes in the name of the Lord! Lord, we lay our palms to pave your way into our lives. Do not enter into Jerusalem but come into our busy world. Do not enter into that old and long-forgotten Temple where money changers need rebuke. Enter instead into our stony hearts where money matters matter far too much and occupy our anxious days. Don't empty out that nest of Temple robbers. Start with that nest of secret sins that make our own small hearts the dens of thieves. And if their voices stop the cry of our disinterested hosannahs, then let the stones cry out, for our hearts are petrified. They need some litany of joy.

Lord, we lay our palms down. It's easy and expected. Help us, rather, to lay down our lives. That's harder work. But unless we yield to it, God cannot come to us. Our own hosannahs will then stick in our throats. Joy will then give way to business as usual. And that's a mockery for those who carry palms. Lord, blessed are you. Come in the name of the Lord. Amen. (Calvin Miller)

SERMON BRIEFS

THE CALL TO STEADFASTNESS

ISAIAH 50:4-9*a*

A German general, imprisoned and later martyred for his opposition to Hitler, wrote to his son: "To our last breath we all remain upstanding men, as we were taught to be from childhood and in our soldierly discipline. Come what may, we fear only the wrath of God that will fall upon us if we are not clear and decent and do our duty" (from *To the Bitter End,* by Richard Winston and Clark Winston).

Our text for this Palm Sunday is a reminder of the cost of faithfulness. On the very day we celebrate Jesus' triumphant entry into Jerusalem, we cannot overlook the fact that this week will end on the cross. Long before the coming of the Messiah, the prophet Isaiah proclaimed a word from the Lord that foreshadows these sad events. One of the key points here is the importance of steadfast faithfulness that comes from a disciplined life. The obvious parallel between the Servant here in Isaiah and the life of Christ only serves to magnify the power of this passage as we begin the observance of Holy Week.

I. We Are Called to Daily Faithfulness

The Sovereign Lord gives "an instructed tongue, / to know the word that sustains the weary" (v. 4*a* NIV). This instruction comes to the Servant who has been faithful-wakened each day by the Lord, willing to listen "like one being taught" (v. 4b). The image is of a student who desires to learn more daily of the truth of God. Many Christians are unable to stand fast when difficulties come because they have no daily devotional life, no regular time to "listen" to God's instruction and thereby be strengthened.

II. We Are Called to Stand Firm

The truth of God is often difficult to hear. The people to whom this message was originally spoken—the people of Israel enslaved in Babylon—were weary and defeated. Many had given up their religious and national roots. Others held on tenuously. Only a faithful remnant, symbolized by the Servant, keeps the truth alive. Isaiah calls the others to open their ears and draw closer—not "draw back" (v. 5b) from their God. Indeed, even though it is difficult to remain faithful when under intense strain or pressure, we are called to do just that. God's people are called to stand firm even in the face of potential personal persecution symbolized by beating, pulling the beard, mocking, spitting (v. 6).

III. We Can Stand Firm Because the Lord Helps Us

In the face of humiliation of bondage and personal persecution, there is always hope. Why? Because "the Sovereign LORD helps [us]" (v. 7a). One who stands up for what is right will "not be disgraced." Indeed, we can have such confidence in God that in the most difficult situations we may set our faces "like flint" (v. 7b) because the One "who vindicates me is near" (v. 8a). When the public and private attacks on the message and validity of the Christian faith grow, the knowledge that "it is the Sovereign LORD who helps me" (v. 9a) undergirds the faithful. Robert Louis Stevenson reminds us in his poem "If This Were Faith":

> To go on forever and fail and go on again,
> And be mauled to the earth and arise,
> And contend for the shade of a word
> and a thing not seen with the eyes;
> With the half of a broken hope for a pillow at night

That somehow the right is the right
And the smooth shall bloom from the rough.
(Steven R. Fleming)

OUR GREATEST MODEL
PHILIPPIANS 2:5-11

One of the childhood memories I recall with great fondness is putting together model airplanes. I would save up my dimes and nickels until, with great eagerness, I could go to Woolworth's or another dime store and purchase a new model. As I recall, they usually cost just under a dollar.

I was one of those who carefully looked over the instructions and proceeded step-by-step in assembling the model; some of my friends were a bit more devil-may-care in their assembly. Their models didn't always come out quite the way they looked on the box, but then nobody's model looked as good as the one on the box. It was wonderful fun to put together a model airplane—a fighter plane or a bomber or even an old-fashioned biplane—and then imagine yourself as the pilot of one of the real things.

In the earlier portion of his letter to the Philippians, Paul encouraged these young Christians to behave in a manner appropriate to the gospel they claimed to believe. Now, in this text, Paul helps them understand what it means to live the Christian life as he points to Christ as the ultimate model for our lives. Some scholars believe this may have even been an early Christian hymn that Paul inserted at this point. Whether that is so or if perhaps Paul himself wrote this wonderful poetry about Christ does not matter; what matters is that it demonstrates the model of humility Christ provided for us, a model that we can follow to find God's victory in our own lives.

I. We Are Called to Humility of Attitude

Although himself of divine nature, Jesus "did not regard equality with God as something to be exploited, but emptied himself" (vv. 6-7). He demonstrated an attitude of humility. He didn't dwell on his own status or position; he didn't try to grasp at everything that was due him.

141

It has been said that far more could be accomplished if no one was concerned about who got the credit. It's in our nature to be credit-claimers, isn't it? We want to be sure we get our fair share of the glory for any achievement, although we're perfectly happy to let someone else get the full share of blame when something goes wrong!

The remarkable thing is what resulted from Christ's humility of attitude: God "highly exalted him" (v. 9). Because Jesus was not concerned about exalting himself, God was able to honor him even more highly. Is there a lesson there for us?

II. We Are Called to Humility of Action

Although Jesus was God incarnate, he was willing to take on "the form of a slave" (v. 7).

What is the nature of a servant? A servant is focused on helping others, not himself or herself. Use a contemporary example of customer service: What makes a good waitress or waiter? Is it someone who hangs around the kitchen visiting with friends, or ignores the wishes of the customers, or is sloppy in handling food? Of course not; the good server is focused on the customer's needs and interests, and personal concerns become secondary.

Through his actions, Jesus demonstrated humility, a "servant's heart." He focused on the needs and hurts of others; he listened to them, showed compassion for them, loved them. And he provides a model for us to allow God to build in us an attitude of service.

What was the result of Christ's humility of action? The very esteem for which he showed no concern was given to him by God (v. 10). The one who made himself a servant will one day be recognized by all of creation, when "every knee will bow" (v. 10).

III. We Are Called to Humility of Abdication

Earlier in this century, Great Britain was shaken when the king abdicated his throne—gave it up so that he could marry a divorced American woman; "the woman I love," he said.

Jesus made a far greater sacrifice, for he gave his own life so that he could save the people he loved, the Bride of Christ, the church. In humility, he accepted death, "even death on a cross"

(v. 8). He abdicated, gave up the rights to his own life, in order to obey the will of God.

What are we willing to abdicate? What are we willing to sacrifice, in order to be obedient to God? Are we willing to yield the rights to our financial resources, to our time, to our carefully planned career paths? Are we willing to humble ourselves to the point of handing over the rights to some things that are very precious to us?

Jesus gave his life on a cross, yet that was not the end of the story. Three days later, the morning sun of that first Easter shone on a stone that had been rolled away to reveal an empty tomb. The one who abdicated his own rights on our behalf had been resurrected, vindicated, and is even now Lord (v. 11).

What you cling to, you ultimately lose. What you give to Christ, you ultimately have in even greater measure. It is in humility, modeled for us by Christ, that we find the greatest glory of all. (Michael Duduit)

REALITIES OF THE PASSION

LUKE 19:28-40 (PALM); 22:14–23:56 (PASSION)

The Passion narrative, which is our Scripture for this Sunday, flashes with the realities of a cosmic struggle between the dragon and God, between good and evil, darkness and light. Let us examine just a few of the powerful realities.

I. The Master Needs Him

After telling of the approach to the top of the Mount of Olives, the writer relates how Jesus borrowed a donkey on which to ride, as a fulfillment of prophecy (19:29-34). In this incident, there is significance in both the question of the bystanders as they see the disciples making away with somebody's transportation (it was equivalent to watching someone steal a car these days) and the response of the disciples. The folks standing around asked: "Who are you? What do you think you're doing? Why are you doing that?" That is the question the world always asks the disciple. That's the question put to Albert Schweitzer, to Mother Teresa, to the church ministering to the poor around it and proclaiming the gospel. Now notice the answer the disciples gave: "The Lord needs it" (v. 34).

What a profound statement! Does God need *anything?* Doesn't God have everything he wants? No, the clear teaching of the Bible is that God *needs us.* If every disciple of Christ could internalize the answer the disciples gave that day, what a difference it would make to every church, to the ministry of the body of Christ. Every one of us is needed in the work of God. Every Christian has a gift, which if unused, cripples the work of the church and his spiritual growth. If Jesus needed that little donkey, how much more does he need us!

II. There Must Be Praise

Now consider the actual entrance into the city (19:35-40). Most kings rode into the cities they conquered on horses or in chariots. But Jesus rode on a donkey. Notice the crowds. It is a *very great* multitude, a crowd of "disciples," an enthusiastic crowd from the area around Jerusalem. John says many of these folks were with Jesus when he raised Lazarus from the grave only a couple of miles away in Bethany, and because of this they met him with hosannas. The crowd was apparently divided into two large groups, one going before Jesus, putting their outer garments in the path in a sort of "red-carpet" welcome, cutting branches and strewing the road (interestingly, only John's Gospel speaks of these palm branches), while the other crowd follows.

Some scholars think these two groups were a sort of antiphonal choir, singing and chanting responsively some of the "Ascent Psalms"—what we know as Psalms 112–118—customary when approaching Jerusalem for the Passover. The Gospel writers remembered the people shouting things like "Hosanna to the Son of David! Blessed be the kingdom of our father David! Blessed is the king who comes in the name of the Lord! Blessed is the king of Israel." Heady stuff, those shouts and praises! Luke says that some of the Pharisees in the crowd—they are always among the crowd, but seldom believe—told Jesus he ought to stop such dangerous talk from his disciples; those chants could be considered treason! To which Jesus gave a memorable reply: "If these were silent, the stones would shout out" (v. 40). There must be praise! I wonder whether you and I have adequately understood this in our lives. So often the work, the joy, the privilege of praise of God is pushed to the background in our lives.

III. The Relentless Evil One

In addition to the Master's need of us and the inevitable nature of praise for our Creator and Redeemer, consider the reality of the evil one. At the Last Supper Jesus made several remarks that glow in the darkness of that evening. In the midst of their fellowship, he said, "See, the one who betrays me is with me, and his hand is on the table" (22:21). A little later Jesus announced that the devil had earnestly desired to take possession of Peter (22:31-32). The shadow of the evil one was over all that evening; the disciples could sense it. Their hearts were heavy; that is the background for the account in John's Gospel of Jesus saying, "Let not your hearts be troubled."

Evil has drawn near, even to the very table of the memorial of sacrifice. Surely the great lesson for us is that the devil is tenacious and that he is not afraid of any of us. If he had the audacity to oppose Jesus right on up to the Passion, and if he had the boldness to sit there at the table in the form of the traitor Judas, and if he clawed and clutched at Peter even in that hour, how foolish to think he will not attack us! Peter's only hope and our only hope is in the fact, the marvelous fact, that Jesus is praying for us! What a refuge, what a strength, what an assurance of final victory over evil!

IV. The Reality of Heaven

But among the heaviness of the Last Supper scene is to be found the most comforting and beautiful expression of the reality of heaven that the Bible affords (22:28-30). We are accustomed to thinking of heaven in terms that do not really speak to modern persons—golden streets, pearly gates, mansions. These are symbols drawn from the book of Revelation. But in Luke's account of the Last Supper there is imagery about heaven to which modern people, alienated and hungry for fellowship, can relate. Jesus, in these verses, first expresses his appreciation of the camaraderie of the eleven. It is true that they have not been models of faith— "How long must I put up with you?" "O ye of little faith!" "Will you also go away?" "Get thee behind me, Satan!"—but they stubbornly trudged along with him, learning as they went. Next Jesus tells them the Father has given him a kingdom, and he now gives them a kingdom, too. And like all good comrades, they shall sit down together and eat and drink and talk together. Then it begins to get clearer—both his and their kingdoms are on the other side of this experience of the cross, on the other side of this world, this eon. Heaven, Jesus was saying, is expressed in the idea of friends who sit down together for food and fellowship. More than that, Jesus was here saying clearly that he himself will sit down, on the other side, with these same eleven men, frail and sinful though they be, and they will talk about old days when they trudged through Galilee. What a beautiful picture of the reality of heaven!

As we approach the Passion of our Lord, let us gladly, joyfully give ourselves in whatever way he has need of us. Let us resolve that our lives will be songs of praise to God. Let us always keep in mind the reality of the evil one, and let us keep our hearts fixed on the fellowship of heaven. (Earl C. Davis)

APRIL 14, 1995

❧

Good Friday

Worship Theme: The cross of Christ is the gateway to new life.

Readings: Isaiah 52:13–53:12; Hebrews 10:16-25; John 18:1–19:42

Call to Worship (Psalm 22:26-31)

Leader: Those who seek him shall praise the LORD. May your hearts live forever!

People: All the ends of the earth shall remember and turn to the LORD; and all the families of the nations shall worship before him.

Leader: For dominion belongs to the LORD, and he rules over the nations.

People: To him, indeed, shall all who sleep in the earth bow down;

Leader: before him shall bow all who go down to the dust, and I shall live for him.

People: Posterity will serve him;

Leader: future generations will be told about the LORD, and proclaim his deliverance to a people yet unborn,

All: saying that he has done it.

Pastoral Prayer:

Eternal God, the sound of hammer against nail still rings in our ears through the centuries. This Friday is not good, for it is the day your Son made the ultimate and final sacrifice, shedding precious blood for scoundrels and thieves, murderers and adulterers, unloving and unfaithful—sinners like us.

Remind us anew that as your love was demonstrated on a cross, so was your power demonstrated when the stone was rolled away and all could see that he is risen, making it a good Friday after all. In the name of the One who transforms tragedy into victory, amen. (Michael Duduit)

SERMON BRIEFS

DYING TO FORGIVE

HEBREWS 10:16-25

God loves us so much that he'd just die for us. And he did. God in Jesus was dying to forgive us on that first Good Friday.

I. Jesus Saves Us

The good news of Christianity isn't how good we are but how good he is. God doesn't love us because of who we are and what we do. God loves us in spite of it all. Though we are stained with sin, God loves us anyway.

God proved his love in Jesus by washing away the stain of our sin with his own blood. That's what it means to say, "We're washed in the blood." Jesus poured out his blood—*dying to forgive*—as the price of paying the debt of our sin. By sacrificing himself on the cross, God in Jesus wiped the slate clean (v. 17) and restored holy communion (v. 18*a*). Jesus is enough to ensure our salvation from what existentially and eternally separates us from God (v. 18*b*).

Having enabled our salvation through the sacrifice of Jesus on the cross, our Lord's covenant of love with us was completed (vv. 16, 19-21). Or, as Jesus said on the cross, "It is finished."

Eccentric evangelist Alexander Wooten was asked, "What must I do to be saved?" He replied, "It's too late! It's already been done!"

II. Jesus Sacrificed Himself for Us on the Cross

It's hard for us to understand crucifixion. We buy gold and gem-studded crosses as gifts. But if we had told people back in the first century that the cross would become a symbol of hope and joy, they'd have thought we were drinking more than grape juice.

Back in the time of Jesus, crucifixion was one of the government's favorite forms of capital punishment. It was knocking off people with an attitude. It wasn't enough to kill the convicted. They had to suffer. Crucifixion let them know they had really ticked off a lot of people.

Jesus had ticked off a lot of people. He upset convention with his agape love ethic. And his self-awareness was too divine for a lot of people.

So this is what they did to our Lord: They stripped and whipped him. Loaded with pieces of bone and lead, the whip shredded his back, chest, and face. A mocking crown of thorns was pressed onto his head. The thorns ripped open the flesh of his head like razors. They made him carry his own cross from prison to Calvary. And *then* he got nailed. Blood streamed from his head, hands, side, and feet. He sacrificed himself for us (vv. 18-21). He was dying to forgive.

III. Jesus Shares His Saving Sacrifice with Us

Certainly, we wouldn't celebrate Easter if the story ended on Good Friday (see Acts 2:23-24). Christianity is more about an empty tomb than a cross.

And yet our religion does include a cross. Jesus died on one to pay off the debt of our sin. And part of identifying ourselves with him includes cross-bearing (see Matt. 16:21-28). Cross-bearing means showing our Lord how much we love him by suffering for him as we identify ourselves with him regardless of the cost. As Bonhoeffer said, the cross is laid on every Christian. Whatever separates us from our Lord must be sacrificed.

It may not sound like a good marketing pitch, but, knowing we're going to live a lot longer with Jesus than anybody else, it makes sense to follow him through the cross to the crown (see Matt. 16:25; Rom. 8:18).

God loves us so much that he'd just die for us. That's what Good Friday is all about. He was dying to forgive. We love him so much that we will worship him, work for him, and witness to him (vv. 21-25). We'll live and die for him. And then we'll live again happily ever after. (Robert R. Kopp)

IT IS FINISHED

JOHN 18:1–19:42

The climax of Evelyn Waugh's novel *Brideshead Revisited* is a deathbed scene. Lord Marchmain has come home to die after years of estrangement from his family, his country, and his church. Although he isn't one of the central characters in the story, his repentance as he faces death irrevocably changes the lives of all who stand or kneel around his bed.

I. Learning from Last Words

The church has always been interested in—even fascinated by—the death of its saints. Beginning with the martyrdom of Polycarp, Bishop of Smyrna, who met his fate with the words, "Eighty-six years have I served Christ and he has done me no wrong. How can I blaspheme this King of mine who saved me?" the church has collected last words of those who have "made a good death." From the martyrs of the Middle Ages to the testimonies of Fletcher, Bonhoeffer, and King, Christians have drawn inspiration from contemplating last words and events in the lives of the faithful. Isn't it strange, then, how little the Gospels say about the actual death of Jesus? Only thirteen verses in John, and these say more about other people who were present than the suffering of our Lord. We hear about Pilate's argument, soldiers throwing dice, who stood at the foot of the cross. Two criminals, and Jesus' words to those he loved. He thirsted. He bowed his head and died.

II. What We Are Not Told About Jesus' Death

If the passion, death, and resurrection of Jesus Christ are central to Christian faith, why is so little detail given about our Redeemer's death? It may be that early Christians who heard the text being read knew all too well what crucifixion was like. They had seen many, and knew it was an utterly offensive execution, inviting the sadism and creativity of the executioners. Spitting, flogging, and then nailing to the cross were common practice. John notes the few aspects of Jesus' death that were unusual: He

150

died after only a few hours, sooner than Pilate expected. Joseph of Arimathea was allowed to remove Jesus' body from the cross after death, contrary to the custom of leaving the corpse to be eaten by scavengers. Other possible reasons for the brevity of the crucifixion scene were respect for the Savior, a desire to glorify the risen Lord, or the writers' desire to tell only enough to establish the fact that Jesus died the physical death common to all humanity.

III. What We Are Told

These things may account for the spare brush strokes with which the text paints the crucifixion scene. But looking at these verses in the light of the whole Gospel, we perceive the narrative in a new way. Two theological motifs in the death scene reflect larger themes in John's Gospel: Jesus as King and Jesus as Good Shepherd who gives his life. The sign struck above the cross echoed what was said about Jesus when he fed the multitude, and when he was acclaimed by crowds on Palm Sunday. This king, unlike any monarch in history, was lifted up on a cross to conquer sin and death, and to reign in majesty forever.

Jesus' giving of himself, expressed in the phrase "he bowed his head and gave up his spirit" (v. 30), resonates with the self-giving love manifested elsewhere in the Gospel. The Savior who said, "I am the good shepherd, and I lay down my life for the sheep . . . of my own accord" and "the bread which I shall give for the life of the word is my flesh" is the Redeemer who completed all the Father had given him to do, and now announced his work was finished. Small wonder that John did not dwell on what was done *to* the Good Shepherd; his point is that our Lord suffered death on the cross voluntarily, of his own free will. Few words are needed to say what Jesus' entire life and ministry proclaimed. The Gospel writer reminds us, "These [things] are written so that you may come to believe that Jesus is the Messiah, the Son of God, and that through believing you may have life in his name" (20:31). (Carol M. Norén)

APRIL 16, 1995

❧

Easter Day

Worship Theme: Christ's resurrection is the guarantee of eternal life for those who follow him.

Readings: Isaiah 65:17-25; 1 Corinthians 15:19-26; John 20:1-18

Call to Worship (Psalm 118:14-15, 19-24):

Leader: The LORD is my strength and my might; he has become my salvation. There are glad songs of victory in the tents of the righteous: "The right hand of the LORD does valiantly." . . .

People: Open to me the gates of righteousness, that I may enter through them and give thanks to the LORD.

Leader: This is the gate of the LORD; the righteous shall enter through it.

People: I thank you that you have answered me and have become my salvation.

Leader: The stone that the builders rejected has become the chief cornerstone.

People: This is the LORD's doing; it is marvelous in our eyes.

Leader: This is the day that the LORD has made;

All: let us rejoice and be glad in it.

Pastoral Prayer:
Good morning, Lord! It's Easter! When you arose had the sun, itself, risen? We praise you for the spin you put on this poor planet, for, because the world spins, the sun is always rising somewhere. This spinning is the metaphor of life that defines our days. For life is always coming on each horizon's edge! And

Easter rides the centuries like that near star we call our sun, which never has known darkness.

Good morning, Lord. It's Easter. Your two-day wounds are scabbed with joy. You've conquered tears with laughter. We owned your grace the moment angels awakened you and you walked out of that dank graveyard and shook the earth with seismic joy. And morning spun a glorious sunrise to wash our old despair away.

Lord, Mary saw you in the garden, and then the disciples ate with you by Galilee. After Peter caught you fish and built a fire beside the sea, he boldly owned your right to rule his life. And so we've come to rake the ashes of that fire. Yes, there's still a flame there. And in that fire we, too, have seen you, as one born out of due time. Amen. (Calvin Miller)

SERMON BRIEFS

WHEN WE ALL GET TO HEAVEN
ISAIAH 65:17-25

There's a favorite old gospel hymn called "When We All Get to Heaven." Have you ever sung it? The chorus goes: "When we all get to heaven, what a day of rejoicing that will be! When we all see Jesus, we'll sing and shout the victory."

Easter Sunday is a day of victory, a day of overcoming and Resurrection power. Because of Easter, we can look with confidence to a future with God. Whatever heaven will be like—and we can only imagine its glories—it will be wonderful primarily because we will be in the presence of the God who loves us and the Savior who died for us.

The prophet Isaiah, in a beautiful poetic passage, shares what that future age will be like.

I. It Will Be Filled with Joy (vv. 17-19)

One reason the "new heavens and new earth" will be joyful is because "the former things will not be remembered." How much pain we carry around with us, how many burdens we willingly endure, because we are unwilling to lay aside the past and move on into the future. Isaiah says that someday God will wipe away every tear and take away every painful memory.

Another source of joy will be the presence of God, which will prompt great gladness and rejoicing. What a wonderful day it will be, when we can share the presence of God directly and fully.

It makes us wonder why we do so little to enter God's presence in the present! Why do we willingly sacrifice the joy that comes from being with God in prayer and in the Word?

II. It Will Be Filled with Satisfaction (vv. 20-23)

The life of average men and women in Isaiah's day was difficult. Hard labor and minimal medical care meant that life was short and hard; indeed, many infants died during or shortly after birth. So the picture Isaiah paints here is of a different kind of world—one in which life is not brief and hard but expansive and filled with satisfaction.

Notice that it isn't a world with no work! But it's not a "take-this-job-and-shove-it" kind of vocation; instead, it is a time when satisfaction and pleasure come from receiving the fruits of one's labors.

III. It Will Be Filled with Peace (vv. 24-25)

In a world filled with conflict and war, it is wonderful to know that a day is coming when relationships between people will be marked by peace and harmony. What will be the cause of such a new spirit? The pervasive presence of God will reshape hearts and minds, replacing conflict with cooperation. The joy and satisfaction that fill that day will produce peace.

The irony of all this is that Isaiah is not simply talking about heaven, but about life within the Kingdom of God here and now. We can begin to experience a foretaste of the glories to come even now as we walk with Christ. (Michael Duduit)

RISING TO THE OCCASION

1 CORINTHIANS 15:19-26

Life is like a roller coaster—it's filled with ups, downs, twists, and turns. There are days when babies are born and baptized, wedding bells ring, and anniversaries are celebrated. But there are also days when children bring home bad grades, divorces are decreed, cancer is diagnosed, and mourning more than dancing fills the hours.

No one is immune to the cycle of life. Everyone rides the roller coaster. And the most terrifying moment comes when we reach that downward twist signaling mortality. We're going to die to this life. Someday everybody will return from the cemetery but you or me.

Surviving the roller coaster depends on a resurrected view of life. It's the only way to rise above it all. The people who don't survive look at life through the eyes of what is. Christians survive because they look at life through the eyes of what is to come. Christians rise to the occasion because of Jesus.

I. Looking at Life Through the Eyes of What Is

Too many people are chained to the changing circumstances of life. They are flushed, rushed, and razzle-dazzled by the ups, downs, twists, turns, ins, outs, and roundabouts of life.

It isn't a smooth ride. When your life is focused on what is, what is determines your experience of wholeness, happiness, joy, and security. And if you believe what is is all there is, death becomes the end of the ride.

For people who look at life through the eyes of what is, death is an obsession. Mortality is a constant worry. It controls thoughts, actions, and attractions to every kind of snake oil salesperson promising longer life through drugs, diets, and celebrity exercise tapes.

It's ultimately pointless and pathetic because no one can avoid a trip to the mortician. Such people caused Paul to write, "If for this life only we have hoped in Christ, we are of all people most to be pitied" (v. 19). Assuming that what is is all there is, they spend more time counting their moments than experiencing the blessings within them. The joy and fun of the ride are lost in the belief that it will end sooner than later.

II. Looking at Life Through the Eyes of What Is to Come

Because "Christ has been raised from the dead" (v. 20), Christians know that what is is not all there is. Or as David Redding wrote, "Anyone who feels sorry for a dead Christian, as though the poor chap were missing something, is himself missing the transfiguring promotion involved" (*Getting Through the Night*).

Though our Lord created his life, declared it good, and invited us to share in his blessings through it, the good news of Christianity is our eternal life through faith in Jesus. "The last enemy," concluded Paul, "to be destroyed is death" (v. 26). When faced with death, Jesus beat it through his resurrection. And through faith in him, we beat it too.

Knowing we will live forever inspires us to rise above all of the occasions of this life. The Gaithers taught us to sing, "Because He lives, I can face tomorrow. Because He lives, all fear is gone." As we ride the roller coaster, we can hear him whispering into our ears through every up, down, twist, and turn, "I am with you always."

As my Grandfather Hayden was dying to this life, he called from the hospital. "Grandpa," I said, "I'll get on a plane and come to see you as soon as I can." "That's not necessary," he assured me. "When I die," he said with a resurrected view of life, "you will preside at my memorial service. And then I'll see you later."

Christians rise to the occasion because of Jesus. (Robert R. Kopp)

EVIDENCE AND ENCOUNTER

JOHN 20:1-18

People come to worship for a variety of reasons. Some remember with nostalgia other years and Easter celebrations. Some because another family member didn't want to come alone. And still others because of a longing, perhaps unvoiced, a hunger for the reassurance that the story told on Easter is true. Christ is risen indeed. And because he lives, the chains of death and hell are broken; we may live with him now and forever.

I. Mary Magdalene's Evidence

It was different, that first Easter morning. No friends and acquaintances gathered together in their best clothes. There was no glorious music or anticipation of a festive meal later in the day. Mary Magdalene went to the tomb early, while it was still dark, with spices and balm to anoint the body of Jesus. Grief and hopelessness filled her. Someone she loved very much was dead. The future looked empty. We are familiar with what she encountered, but consider, for a few moments, how Mary perceived the evidence before her. The stone was rolled away: a huge, heavy stone beyond the strength of one mortal to move. She assumed a group had come and stolen the body. Peter and John investigated the tomb, but this did not transform her grief. She saw two angels, and they spoke to her—but she didn't stop weeping. Outside the cave she saw our Lord himself, and didn't recognize him. The garden, the stone, expert opinion, heavenly messengers, the sight of the Savior—none of these touched her sorrow.

II. Mary Magdalene's Encounter

Only when Jesus spoke to Mary by name did what was real become real for her. Being addressed by the risen Christ, listening to him, doing as he commanded—these gave her the assurance and joy of the resurrection. Only at that point could she hurry to the upper room and proclaim, "I have seen the Lord!" (v. 18). In the same way the male disciples could not believe and confess the risen Christ until he spoke to them. And then they knew the truth: He is risen from the dead.

III. Evidence Today

We know what happened on Easter morning. There isn't the same suspense that Mary Magdalene and the other disciples knew. But there is the same longing to know that God's promises can be trusted, to have the blessed assurance that because he lives, we shall live also. The resurrection story in John suggests that what the world calls evidence or proof will not give us the peace and knowledge we seek. From time to time the Shroud of Turin controversy makes the news. I've read many stories over the years about the pattern of bloodstains or other data, but I've never seen anyone acknowledge that Peter and John were not convinced by examining that grave cloth on Easter morning. Why should we expect more of it today? Biblical and archaeological scholars have published volumes on the size and weight of the stone at the tomb entrance, first-century beliefs about angels, and so on. But Mary Magdalene wasn't convinced by the position of the stone, and she was there! Whatever she believed about angels did not enable her to receive their comfort. Intellect and evidence do not add up to resurrection faith.

IV. Encounter Today

Faith in the Redeemer who conquered sin and death is not induced by evidence handed to a jury. It doesn't come from scholarly opinion or even from signs and wonders. Faith comes from a personal encounter with the Lord, who knows and calls each by name at our baptism and throughout our lives. Listen to his voice this morning. In his holy Word, read aloud in worship; in quiet moments spent in prayer; in his Holy Spirit speaking through your brothers and sisters in Christ. Hear the Lord of love speak to you. Confess your faith in him. And go, with joy, to tell others he is risen indeed. (Carol M. Norén)

APRIL 23, 1995

❧

Second Sunday of Easter

Worship Theme: Faith overcomes the fear that would steal our joy in Christ.

Readings: Acts 5:27-32; Revelation 1:4-8; John 20:19-31

Call to Worship (Psalm 118:14, 29):
The LORD is my strength and my might;
  he has become my salvation.

....

O give thanks to the LORD, for he is good,
  for his steadfast love endures forever.

Pastoral Prayer:

Lord God, in spite of our many troubles and concerns, we take these moments to give thanks for all your good gifts to us. How often we forget the great blessings all around us: green trees, abundant water, the warmth of the sun, the miracle of growing crops and productive animals. We so easily become self-centered that we ignore your gifts of other people: the touch of caring family members, the love of friends, the services rendered to us daily by hundreds of merchants, workers, and businesspeople. Thank you, Lord, for making our lives so full.

Gracious God, help those of us who prosper not to forget that many are less fortunate. There are persons out of work today, families where one parent struggles to provide a home. We remember there are places where the crops will not grow and the livestock are dying. There are many for whom this day is one of physical pain, suffering, or mental and emotional anguish. Grant all who struggle courage and vision to face an uncertain future, trusting you to supply their needs. Touch them with your peace which passes all understanding, and grant to them your healing presence. Let us not pass by such persons but enable those of us

159

who can to speak and act kindly, compassionately, and warmly to all those we meet this week. Lord, into your hands we must ultimately place our lives and our future. Help us to be trusting and open to your guidance, and lead us ever onward to your heavenly home. We ask in humble obedience and faith. Amen. (Steven R. Fleming)

SERMON BRIEFS

WHAT DOES IT TAKE?

ACTS 5:27-32

The early church had to overcome many obstacles as it sought to make Christ's name known in the world. In this passage, we find the disciples warned again to keep their ideas about Jesus to themselves. What was it about these disciples that made them willing to suffer and even die if necessary for the sake of Christ?

I. They Had Courage

The instructions of the Sanhedrin had been very clear in the fourth chapter of Acts. The disciples were no longer to speak or teach at all in the name of Jesus (4:18). However, when they escaped from prison, the first place the disciples went was back to the Temple, where they continued to preach the good news. They could have left town, or laid low for a while, but God told them to return to the Temple and preach (4:20). They knew what would happen, but they were still obedient to God's call.

Today, society pressures us to ignore God's direction for our lives. Teenagers face a kind of peer pressure that says, "You want to be accepted, don't you?" Adults live in a world where compromise makes good business sense. After all, everyone else is doing it. The apostles teach us to be courageous in the light of enormous pressure. With Martin Luther, we can say, "Here I stand. I can do no other. God help me."

II. They Had Character

Peter, John, and the other apostles were consistent in their lives. They lived by a guiding principle that said, "we must obey God rather than any human authority" (v. 29). Their first thought was not "Is this expedient for me?" Rather, they focused first on what God wanted for their lives.

III. They Had a Calling

The apostles knew that Christ had called them to be witnesses. Jesus' last command in the Gospels was for his disciples to go into the world and share the good news. At the beginning of Acts (1:8), Jesus' command to be witnesses is recorded once more. To bear witness was not simply something they did; it was who they were. Their lives were a testimony to the power of what God could do. The testimony of a witness in a court of law has impact because that witness has seen something. These disciples had seen something as well. More than that, they had experienced something—the life-changing power of Christ. They were called to bear witness to the risen Christ. When confronted by the Sanhedrin, Peter didn't seek to justify his actions, but rather he used the occasion to proclaim once more the saving grace of God in Jesus Christ (vv. 30-32).

Just as the disciples, you and I are called to bear witness to Christ today. Although we have not looked upon Jesus with our eyes, we know in our experience and minds the life-changing power of Christ. If you were to find a cure for AIDS and told no one, that would be tragic because of the number of lives lost to this disease. However, as Christians, we have found the way to eternal life. How will we be judged for our silence? (Greg Barr)

THE IDENTITY AND INTENTION OF JESUS

REVELATION 1:4-8

Revelation has been called "words of encouragement in code." John was inspired to use highly symbolic language to herald the identity and intention of Jesus. He is our loving Lord from beginning (alpha) to end (omega).

161

I. The Identity of Jesus

When the resurrected Jesus identified himself as " 'the Alpha and the Omega' . . . who is and who was and who is to come" (v. 8, see v. 4) and John ascribed to him the adulation that is reserved for God, "To Him be glory and dominion forever and ever" (v. 6b), the Lordship of Jesus was revealed (see John 1:1-18; Col. 1:15-23; Heb. 1:1-4).

Jesus was not like God. Jesus *was* God. He was, as Karl Barth wrote, "God in person." Emmanuel. God-with-us. The Incarnate One. The enfleshment of God. Or as one child exclaimed, "Jesus was God with skin on." Hence, the earliest confession of the church concisely declared, "Jesus Christ is Lord." Continuing along with Father and Holy Spirit to be one of the three ways through whom our Lord has made himself known to us, Jesus was, is, and will always be Lord (vv. 4, 8). At one with Father and Holy Spirit, Jesus is Lord from beginning to end.

There has always been some confusion about the deity or *Godness* of Jesus because of the many references to him as the Son of God. Unfortunately, some interpret that as a kind of bio-logical sonship. But the biblical, confessional, and traditio-histor-ical meaning of Son of God is substance of God. To say that Jesus is the Son of God is to say that he is substantially God. Jesus is the Son of or same substance as God. That's why the Council of Nicaea used the word *homoöusion* (ομοοψσιονξτ)— "of the same substance of being"—to describe the relationship between God the Father and God the Son. Jesus the Son is the same substance as God the Father. He is Lord from beginning to end.

II. The Intention of Jesus

Confessing the Godness of Jesus and that knowing God is love (1 John 4:8), the intention of Jesus is to love us from beginning to end. Jesus exemplified the *agape* love that has always distin-guished his disciples from others. The highest expression of his love for us was his sacrifice on the cross (v. 5b). And that experi-ence, which freed us from our sins, of his unconditional love— We didn't earn it! We'll never deserve it! It's free and unmer-ited!—encourages our confidence in his eternal (alpha to omega) benediction. Because he is our loving Lord, we receive grace and peace through faith in him (vv. 4-5).

Grace is the free and unmerited favor of God. We can look at it in two ways. It's either getting what we don't deserve (his existential and eternal love) or not getting what we deserve (his condemnation).

Two men were quarreling at a congregational meeting about who deserved to be elected chairman of the board. Finally, an older man stood up and said, "I'm tired of hearing about what you think you deserve. If you really got what you deserve, you'd both be on your way to hell." It's like R. C. Sproul tells students, "Pray for mercy but don't pray for justice because you may get it."

Peace is living in holy communion with our Lord from beginning to end. It's like the terminally ill child who was told by a nurse, "God made you. God loves you. God came in Jesus to save you. And now God wants you to come home with him." The little boy said, "Tell God, 'Thank You!' "

Jesus is our loving (intention) Lord (identity) from beginning to end. And through faith in him, grace and peace are a part of our existential (here and now) and eternal (hereafter) reality. (Robert R. Kopp)

LOCKED DOORS

JOHN 20:19-31

Security systems are big business in our culture. Although many Americans grew up in an age when the back door was never locked, dead bolts, chains, alarms, and guard dogs are the rule rather than the exception today. Barricaded doors are an outward sign of inner fears.

I. The Price of Fear

The reading from the Gospel begins with an incident involving a locked door. The disciples were back in the upper room and had the door locked for "fear of the Jews" (v. 19)—and their fears were understandable. Only a few days earlier they had seen their Master die. Simon Peter and the others were afraid of guilt by association. Furthermore, the apocryphal Gospel of Peter reveals that someone had started a rumor that the disciples had tried to burn down the Temple. So they locked the door to avoid persecution from former friends. And surely they were anxious when the women returned from the empty tomb, saying that Jesus had risen from the dead. Was it true? What did it mean? What would happen next?

Fear protected them from their enemies, but also cut them off from the joy and fellowship and mission Jesus had given them. There was no more preaching, no teaching, no healing, no witness to the resurrection. They might as well have been dead.

Centuries have passed, but fear still locks the door on Christian lives and threatens to snuff out the mission of the church. We fear a world increasingly antagonistic toward Christianity—not just church vandalism and theft, but also in the way Christians are depicted in the media, and the extremes to which separation of church and state is interpreted. We may fear tension at home with those who do not share our beliefs, and therefore keep a low profile about Jesus Christ and what he means to us. Ultimately, however, we are afraid of losing control of our own lives to the Holy Spirit. We bear the name of Jesus Christ, but lock the door and close the book after the resurrection, afraid of God's future and what it may have to do with us.

II. Christ's Spirit Sets People Free

But God does not leave us alone behind the barricades erected in his name. In writing about his conversion, Kierkegaard said, "God came in through locked doors." Jesus did not force his way into the upper room with a battering ram. He appeared in the disciples' midst, and his first words were, "Peace be with you" (v. 19). And then, "As the Father has sent me, so I send you. . . . Receive the Holy Spirit" (vv. 21-22). The invitation to receive the Spirit came right after their marching orders, for it is impossible to do one without the other. It was Christ's Spirit, breathed upon them, that set them free from the safe and stagnant upper room to go out and start being the church. They witnessed, they healed, they exhorted, and they did wonders in the name of the risen Lord, and the church increased daily. They knew the security and freedom of being under God's control.

We gather today as disciples of the Christ who conquered death. Our Lord promises that where two or three are gathered in his name, he is there. And his words to us are the same: "Peace be with you. As the Father has sent me, even so I send you. Receive the Holy Spirit." Some say yes daily to God's gracious invitation, and it shows in their words and actions. Others said yes and meant it sometime in the past, but the fear or love of this present world have gradually shut the door on the Spirit, and that, too, shows. And some of us have understood what it means to be used and filled by the Spirit—but God's Word is the same to all. Receive the Holy Ghost, and he'll replace your fear of those outside the upper room with the power to transform them. Christ will turn your fear of being conspicuous into winsomeness and joy. Receive the Holy Spirit, and you shall be witnesses to the resurrection unto the ends of the earth. Which will we choose: the closed doors of an upper room, or hearts open to the gifts of the Spirit? Suffocating in our own defenses, or drawing the breath of life from God? Will our lives be spent making disciples or making excuses? Greet the risen Christ with joy. Receive the peace that comes from him. And go forward in the power of his Spirit to love and serve the Lord. (Carol M. Norén)

APRIL 30, 1993

❧

Third Sunday of Easter

Worship Theme: Worship is essential because it brings us into right relationship with God.

Readings: Acts 9:1-6, (7-20); Revelation 5:11-14; John 21:1-19

Call to Worship (Psalm 30:4-5):

Leader: Sing praises to the LORD, O you his faithful ones, and give thanks to his holy name.

People: For his anger is but for a moment; his favor is for a lifetime.

All: Weeping may linger for the night, but joy comes with the morning.

Pastoral Prayer:
Father, we are ashamed to confess that not everything we do in your name and in this sacred place is always for you! Sometimes habit motivates us. We rarely go out of our way or put ourselves out for you. Sometimes we delude ourselves into thinking that you are grateful for whatever we do because you need us so much—as if your church would not thrive and your kingdom could not expand without us and what we do. Forgive us, God, for forgetting that we can do nothing without you. Let this day be a turning point in our relationship with you. Reveal yourself to us in powerful, unexpected ways. Most of all, change our lives and our ways so that our hearts might truly be filled with love for you, and that our love might be the reason we serve and worship you, through Jesus Christ our Lord. Amen. (Gary C. Redding)

SERMON BRIEFS

CAUGHT BY SURPRISE

ACTS 9:1-6, (7-20)

As a teenager, I lamented that my testimony was not very exciting. I didn't have the same kind of radical conversion story others had. In Acts 9, we find one of the most remarkable conversion stories of all. In fact, the conversion of Saul was so remarkable—so surprising—that it is told three times in the book of Acts alone (9:1-6; 22:3-21; 26:2-23). It is an incredible story, one expected on tabloid headlines, one filled with surprises.

I. Surprised by God's Choice

The choice of Saul as missionary to the Gentiles has to be one of God's greatest surprises in the Bible. If you were to poll early Christians as to who would have the longest-lasting impact on the Christian world (other than Jesus), Saul's name wouldn't even be on the list. After all, he was one of the greatest persecutors the early Christians had known.

Verses 1-2 paint a vivid picture of Saul's life before Christ. Saul's goal was to stamp out this new Christian movement, and he was relentless in this pursuit. In Acts 8:1, we learn that Saul had been present at the death of Stephen, and soon after had conducted a house-to-house search of Jerusalem for Christians to be shipped off to prison. Apparently, some had slipped away to Damascus, and Saul soon followed them, hoping to arrest and bring them back to Jerusalem. There was no way in the world that God could use someone like Saul! What we discover in the story, however, is that God has a way of taking the Sauls of this world, cleaning them up, and using them for incredible things.

II. Surprised by God's Timing

Saul met up with Jesus on the road outside Damascus. Saul was not in church. He was not reading his Bible or having a time of prayer. There is no indication that Saul was looking for God at

167

all. However, in the middle of this day, at an unexpected place, Christ broke in, and nothing was the same again.

James Cox has written a book entitled *Surprised by God*. If Saul had written an autobiography, that might be a fitting name for it. Have you ever been surprised by God? Surprised by God's goodness and grace? Surprised by the unexpected things God can do in and through you? Saul's story reminds us that God can break into our lives unexpectedly, and do amazing things.

III. Surprised by God's Impact

When Saul met up with the risen Christ on the road to Damascus, everything about his life changed. Acts 9 emphasizes the complete transformation of Saul from the persecutor of the church to the one persecuted for Christ's sake. Saul, who just days before had been "breathing threats and murder against the disciples of the Lord" (v. 1), now fell before Christ and responded in faithful obedience. The once proud Saul was led to Damascus by the hand, because he had lost his sight (v. 8). When his eyes were opened three days later, he had a new vision. Letting go of his terrible past, and focusing on what God had in store for his future, he became God's spokesman.

Some of us may be able to identify with Saul's experience of Christ's presence in a blinding light. More of us, however, have heard God's still, small voice as it pricks our conscience and convicts us of sin. Would we respond as Paul this day? "God, if you can forgive me, then for the rest of my life, I will gladly serve you. Whatever that means, wherever you lead, I will go." (Greg Barr)

HEADED IN HIS DIRECTION

REVELATION 5:11-14

Worship "is what we say and what we do when we stand together before God, realizing in high degree who he is and who we are" (Richard Davidson). Worship "is the outcome of belief in a God who has done something 'for us men and for our salvation'" in Jesus (Donald Macleod). God has acted on our behalf as Creator (Father), Redeemer (Jesus), and Sustainer (Holy Spirit), and we respond by ascribing ultimate worth to him (vv. 12-14). That's why worship is our response to God's gracious acts. Or, as an older pastor told me many years ago, "We worship God because God is to be worshiped." I think of worship as being headed in his direction.

I. Worship Includes Looking to Our Lord

There is a story about a church that laid a cement sidewalk in the front of its doors over twenty years ago. A woman asked if she could stand her baby on the wet cement. Her request was granted. And when people pass by that church today, they can still see two baby footprints with the toes pointed toward the church. That's the story of a mother who wanted her child to be headed in God's direction.

When we are headed in God's direction (see Heb. 12:2), we are looking to the only lasting source of wholeness, happiness, joy, and eternal security. While ascribing to our Lord the ultimate worth due to him (v. 12), our looking to him keeps us headed in his direction, which is always the right direction for our lives.

II. Worship Includes Listening to Our Lord

It is said that a woman approached Tony Campolo and complained, "I don't like the way that you pray in public." He reportedly replied, "I wasn't talking to you." Unfortunately, too many worship services and personal prayers are more like performances than Holy Communion. Worship must be real communication, really expressing our thanks to God for his love, and really asking his direction for our lives in real language. And it is absolutely imperative to remember that communication includes listening. In other words, if we don't stop talking to God, we'll never hear what he has to say to us.

I'll never forget a conversation I had with Brother Daniel, a Trappist monk at Assumption Abbey in Ava, Missouri. While monking around (i.e., doing what monks do, which in his case meant packaging incense), he meditated on the Psalms. On this particular day, he was meditating on Psalm 91. Having studied it under Bernhard Anderson at Princeton, I thought I'd enlighten him. While and after I talked, he seemed thoroughly under-whelmed. So I asked him what he thought it meant. As he spoke, I felt as if the heavens were opening and God's voice was speaking through this simple monk to me. After he finished, I asked him how he knew so much about it without the benefit of Dr. Anderson and Hebrew lessons. He said, "I asked God what it means."

A man called and said, "I'm terribly unhappy. What can I do?" I told him what I have repeated so often, "Invite Jesus into your heart as Lord and Savior. Then worship, pray, read your Bible, and hang out with Christians. You'll be fine." He did, and he is.

William Barclay once commented on this text: "Here is the truth that heaven and earth and all that is within them is designed for the praise of Jesus Christ." Augustine so poignantly confessed, "You made us for Yourself, and our hearts are restless until they rest in You." Donald Macleod put it this way, "Worship is the only indispensable activity of the Church." That's because it gets us headed in the right direction—his direction! (Robert R. Kopp)

BAD NEWS, GOOD NEWS
JOHN 21:1-19

"Bad news travels fast," wrote Plutarch, and he was right. The newspaper headlines are evidence of the perversity of human nature; we're much more inclined to report and believe bad news than good. Even so, it seems strange that it was so hard for the disciples to accept the good news that Jesus had risen from the dead. Simon Peter and the beloved disciple had inspected the empty tomb on Easter morning. Mary Magdalene saw angels; the resurrected Christ addressed her by name. Jesus appeared to the apostles in the upper room that night, and again eight days later to doubting Thomas. In sights and sounds and invitations to touch, the good news was proclaimed, "Christ is risen indeed!"

I. Getting the Message Across

But good news takes a while to sink in, as evidenced by today's text. It was sometime after Easter. Several of the disciples were sitting around when Simon Peter announced, "I am going fishing" (v. 3). This wasn't a casual outing; the verb used implied Peter was going back to his former life's work—back to business as usual—as though the last three years with Jesus had never happened. The other disciples went with him, but they caught nothing.

As day was breaking, they saw a figure standing on the shore. You'd think by now they'd recognize Jesus, but they were so caught up in the bad news of poor fishing that they didn't recognize the good news when it stared them in the face. Jesus called to them: "Children, you have no fish, have you?" (v. 5). No one but the Savior called them "children," but they still didn't know him. Peter explained the problem (or what he thought was the problem!) and Jesus said, "Cast the net to the right side of the boat, and you will find some" (v. 6). His authority in giving this promise should have revealed his identity, but it didn't. Finally, when the net was filled, one person on board got the point, and John cried out, "It is the Lord!" (v. 7). Peter, seeing the evidence and hearing the testimony of John, also realized the truth, and he swam to the shore to greet the Master. By the time the other disciples reached land, and Jesus invited them to have breakfast, there was no need to ask, "Who is this, and what does this mean?" They knew. What they believed in their hearts was confirmed by sense and sight. They'd finally heard the good news.

II. Hearing and Sharing the News Today

It is safe to say that we who worship God today in this upper room belong to one of two parties: those who have heard and believed the good news that Christ is risen, and those who, for one reason or another, have not. Within this text is a message for both groups. First, for those who have heard and believed: You know your faith puts you in the minority, at least outside this place. Like the beloved disciple, you may be the only one in your boat who sees the truth. When everyone around is looking elsewhere for answers, it's hard to maintain what you know in your heart is real. To you the text says, "Don't give up. In whatever way you can, keep on proclaiming the truth that Christ is risen indeed." And if, like Peter, you were slower to hear the good news, don't let your witness be hindered by comparing yourself with Christians who may be more mature in the faith or articulate in testimony. The Holy Spirit can use your witness, faulty and foolish though it may seem to you.

This text is also a message of hope for the other group: those who have listened to confessions of faith, and sung the hymns, and wish the words were real and true in their own experience. God offers hope and comfort; the action in this story demonstrates that our Lord doesn't give up on people, even when they're not as quick to understand and believe. God won't give up on you. Through miracles, through other Christians, through the convicting work of the Holy Spirit—whatever it takes and as long as it takes—the good news invites you to faith. Sin may impair our hearing of the message; doubt tries to discredit it; fear begets reluctance. But the good news remains the same: The Lord of Life is risen indeed. Thanks be to God. (Carol M. Norén)

MAY

◆

Replenishing the Well

Expecting the Holy Spirit: A Personal Easter

Of course, Easter is the most important occasion in the life of the church. It is a great communal celebration of the resurrected Lord, returned to his church from the dead. In expectation of Easter, we are going to focus this month on a more personal Easter. We will listen to the voice of the risen Lord through the Holy Spirit.

Time: 30 minutes a week for four weeks.

Materials: A Bible, your journal (optional).

Exercise:
Read John 14:23-29. Now reread verses 26-28 and focus on this portion of verse 28, "You heard me say to you 'I am going away, and I am coming to you.' "

The spiritual discipline of silence has been practiced for centuries by the church. In silence, one waits in expectation for the voice of God, the Holy Spirit. Once a week during this month, choose a time when you can spend thirty minutes alone, listening for God.

Follow these directions for each weekly, thirty-minute session:

During the first ten minutes reread John 14:23-29 and sit quietly, letting your thoughts and concerns drift away.

During the next ten minutes, sit in silence, listening for the voice of the Holy Spirit. God may not speak to you in words but in feelings or in images. Hear the risen Lord speak to you through the Holy Spirit. Should nothing come during this time, that's okay—this is an exercise that takes practice. We have spent noisy years drowning out the voice of God, and it may be difficult to hear his voice at first.

The final ten minutes should be spent in prayer, responding to whatever the voice of the Holy Spirit has said to you during your silent time.

At the conclusion of the half hour, you may, if you wish, record your experience in your journal. Write down whatever God spoke to you or draw pictures of the images God sent. (Harriet Crosby)

MAY 7, 1993

⌁

Fourth Sunday of Easter

Worship Theme: Our faithful obedience to Christ gives evidence that we have experienced his saving grace.

Readings: Acts 9:36-43; Revelation 7:9-17; John 10:22-30

Call to Worship (Psalm 23 KJV):

Leader: The LORD is my shepherd; I shall not want.

People: He maketh me to lie down in green pastures:

Leader: he leadeth me beside the still waters. He restoreth my soul:

People: he leadeth me in the paths of righteousness for his name's sake.

Leader: Yea, though I walk through the valley of the shadow of death, I will fear no evil:

People: for thou art with me; thy rod and thy staff they comfort me.

Leader: Thou preparest a table before me in the presence of mine enemies:

People: thou anointest my head with oil; my cup runneth over.

Leader: Surely goodness and mercy shall follow me all the days of my life:

All: and I will dwell in the house of the LORD for ever.

Pastoral Prayer:

O Holy God, we would worship and adore you. Pardon our sins so that we may come into close and loving fellowship with you this day. We cannot hope to fully comprehend you, for

175

your nature is so vast and our minds are so slow and small. We cannot always understand your ways with us. Sometimes we are bewildered, confused, frightened. Evil seems so strong, misery so widespread, and pain so universal. Have mercy on us, O Lord, for you know our weakness. Have pity on our groping minds and aching hearts. Draw us close so that we may be like little children, content to look up into our Father's face, certain of your loving care for us. O God, who has made the heavens and the earth and all that is lovely and good in them, and who has shown us through Jesus Christ that the secret of joy is a heart free from selfish desires, help us to find delight in simple things and ever to rejoice in the riches of your goodness. Through Jesus Christ our Lord. Amen. (John Bishop)

SERMON BRIEFS

LESSONS FOR LIFE

ACTS 9:36-43

Some of the best lessons in my life have been learned from observing others. At times, I have learned from people's mistakes, but more often they have taught me by setting a good example. From my parents I learned values. Sunday school teachers and pastors taught me to appreciate the Scripture. Let's look to the life of Dorcas, and see if we can find lessons for our lives. This is the only time Dorcas, or Tabitha, is mentioned in the Bible, but in this brief picture of her life, we can find an excellent model for living.

I. Disciples Are Called to Service

The first lesson we can learn from Dorcas is that when we make a decision to give our lives to Jesus, we are also making a commitment to follow him in service and love. Dorcas models in her life what it means to be a servant. "She was devoted to good works and acts of charity" (v. 36). When Peter arrived in Joppa (v. 39), the widows showed him all the garments Dorcas had made for them. When they thought of Dorcas, they thought of her as a loving servant. How would you like to be remembered?

What is seen in too many churches today is a struggle for power rather than servitude. Like the disciples, we can become preoccupied with who gets a position of authority (Matt. 20:20-28). Jesus reminded them, and us, that "whoever wishes to be first among you must be your [servant]" (Matt. 20:27). Jesus taught that authority comes from service.

II. Death Is Inevitable

Rabbi Harold Kushner's famous book asks *Why Do Bad Things Happen to Good People?* Dorcas and her friends discovered that bad things happen, even to wonderful people. Although Dorcas was a beautiful person, who served the Lord with all her heart, she was unable to escape death. It has been said that the only two sure things in life are death and taxes. Physicians can prolong life. Exercise and a good diet can make you live longer. Seat belts and air bags can save lives. But someday we will all die. Hebrews 9:27 says, "It is appointed for mortals to die once." There is no escape. The question for us is this: Are we prepared to die? Dorcas was. She had devoted all of her life to following Christ, and she could face death's door with confidence.

III. Death Has Been Defeated

The final thing Dorcas teaches us is that death does not have to be the end. There is something more. In the story of Dorcas, this is illustrated in an unusual way. After Dorcas died, her friends and family laid her in an upper room for three days. This was a Jewish custom that allowed an adequate period of time to ensure death had taken place. Peter came and was met by those who had been touched by Dorcas's service. After clearing the room, Peter prayed, and then said, "Tabitha, get up" (v. 40). Dorcas awoke, and her life was restored.

We look at these types of events and sit in awe of the miracle. We must understand, however, that what happened to Dorcas was a resuscitation. She would eventually die again. God offers something greater for those of us who have trusted Jesus Christ. Disciples can face death with assurance, knowing that Christ defeated death on the third day. At death's door, we can say with Paul, "Where, O death, is your victory? Where, O death, is your sting?" (1 Cor. 15:55). (Greg Barr)

WHERE'S THE TIE THAT BINDS?

REVELATION 7:9-17

Heavenly worship includes everybody who loves our Lord (v. 9). Looking at each other through the eyes of Jesus, we realize that he loves us no more and no less than he loves everybody else. He loves the world (see John 3:16). That includes you, me, and *them*. Jesus is the tie that binds.

I. Worldly Worship

While studying in Heidelberg, Germany, in the early seventies, I often crossed the Neckar River from the university to the "Philosophers' Walk," which snaked up Saints' Mountain (Heiligenberg). Near the top was an amphitheater (Thingstätte). I was told youths gathered there to celebrate their *Germanness*. Remembering my German roots, I thought it seemed like a harmless expression of ethnic pride until I discovered it was started in 1935 by the Nazis to link their doctrines to *Germanness*.

That discovery set off my spiritual alarm clock. I began to understand why Pope John XXIII concluded, "Nationalism belongs to the wastebasket of history." Or as one little boy said to a friend, "My mommy said I can't go with you to church because we belong to different abominations."

I began to understand why our Lord doesn't play favorites (see Rom. 2:11). And while remaining fiercely patriotic to my country, I began to understand that being a Christian is an ultimately more important and *eternal* identity than being an American. And while remaining loyal to my part of the Kingdom (i.e., denomination), I began to understand that the Kingdom is more important and *eternal* than any one particular part of it. I began to understand that God's people come from all colors, cultures, countries, and classes (v. 9). And what keeps them *(us!)* together is common worship of our Lord (vv. 10-12). Jesus is the tie that binds.

II. Heavenly Worship

Can you imagine meeting Jesus in heaven and saying, "You know, Lord, I was a Presbyterian"? Wouldn't he be impressed? How do you think he feels when he looks at the people for whom he died on the cross and sees them observing the most segregated hour of the week? Doesn't it strike you as spiritually sick for Christians to separate themselves from each other over ethnicity, nationalism, or even forms of church government and yet so sanctimoniously sing, "Blest be the tie that binds"?

Heavenly worship includes everybody who loves our Lord (v. 9). Everybody who loves him comes together through him. Heavenly worship is the saints' response to our Lord's prayer that "they may all be one" (see John 17; Gal. 3:28). In heavenly worship, people of all kinds come together and see each other through the eyes of Jesus.

Jesus expected believers to get along with each other. Jesus expected believers to be bonded together through common faith in him. He expected the unity of believers to be among the most persuasive witnesses to his saving Lordship. Jesus expected the world to look at his church and exclaim, "See how they love each other!" Together in him, Christians can experience the full blessings of unity (vv. 13-17; see also Ps. 133).

But if we take Jesus out of the equation, there is no hope for unity. Take Jesus out of the equation, and there is no tie to bind.

There is a way to bring the world, families, and churches together. That way is through the tie that binds—*Jesus!* (Robert R. Kopp)

WHO WANTS TO KNOW?

JOHN 10:22-30

"None so blind as those that will not see," wrote Mathew Henry (1662–1714). He could have been describing the critics of Jesus, as depicted in this section of John's Gospel. The Jews who watched our Lord heal the man born blind, who overheard the discussion about the identity of the Messiah, who heard Jesus' gracious words, or who simply stood in his presence surely ought to have recognized him as God's anointed. Their demand "If you are the Messiah, tell us plainly" (v. 24) reveals as much about the identity of those posing the question as the one being asked. Twenty centuries later, the same question reveals who we are in relationship to Christ.

I. Why Didn't These Critics Know Jesus Was the Christ?

The demand for a disclosure of messianic identity could not have taken the Messiah by surprise. Throughout Jesus' ministry there was an undercurrent of tension with the scribes and Pharisees, who criticized his acts of mercy and challenged his authority to forgive sins. The words and deeds of Jesus already gave them the answer to their question. All the signs pointed to the Lordship of Christ. But as Jesus indicated after healing the man born blind, the Pharisees were blinded by unbelief. Furthermore, their questions were intended to trap Jesus rather than to satisfy their longing for the coming of God's Messiah. Perhaps it would be more accurate to say that they did not know Jesus as the Christ; their sin and pride prevented them from apprehending grace incarnate. Paul said in his first letter to the church at Corinth, "Jews demand signs and Greeks desire wisdom, but we proclaim Christ crucified, a stumbling block to Jews and foolishness to Gentiles, but to those who are the called, both Jews and Greeks, Christ the power of God and the wisdom of God" (1 Cor. 1:22-23).

II. How Do We Know Jesus Is the Christ?

No one in Jesus' day or in ours is born with faith in Christ. In the healing depicted before this incident in Solomon's portico, the Gospel writer shows the progression of a person from unbelief to belief. Asked who had restored his sight, the man first said, "I do not know," then "he is a prophet" (9:24-34). In subsequent conversation, his faith grew until he was able to confess to Jesus, "Lord, I believe." Jesus' words in verses 27-28 suggest that knowing him for who he is happens the same way to all who are "in his flock." The works that Jesus did, recorded in the Gospels, bear witness to him as Christ. His relationship to the Father and his fulfillment of prophecy point to him as the Son of God. His care for "his sheep," even to laying down his life for the flock, reveals his identity as Savior.

III. How Do We Know We Are Christ's?

This is the implicit question in Jesus' response to the Jews. Among those who have come to confess Christ as Lord, the question reflects the desire for assurance in the faith—the "witness of the Spirit" Paul writes of in Romans 8:16. John Wesley's longing for certainty that he was part of the Good Shepherd's flock culminated in the famous "Aldersgate experience." The same verses that confirm Jesus' messianic identity present the marks by which disciples may know they are Christ's. Jesus said, "My sheep hear my voice" (v. 27); their ears are always eager to hear what the Shepherd says. "They follow me" (v. 27); disciples strive to conform to the will of God as revealed in the Word. "They will never perish" (v. 28); they enjoy fellowship with Christ through the power of the Spirit, a foretaste of the bliss of the life to come. And their reliance is not on their own merits, intellect, or resourcefulness, but on divine goodness: the God who can "satisfy every need . . . according to his riches in glory in Christ Jesus" (Phil. 4:19). (Carol M. Norén)

MAY 14, 1995

❧

Fifth Sunday of Easter

Worship Theme: The new age inaugurated by Christ's resurrection calls God's people to new challenges and new avenues of service.

Readings: Acts 11:1-8; Revelation 21:1-6; John 13:31-35

Call to Worship (Psalm 148:1-5*a*):
Praise the LORD!
Praise the LORD from the heavens;
   praise him in the heights!
Praise him, all his angels;
   praise him, all his host!
Praise him, sun and moon;
   praise him, all you shining stars!
Praise him, you highest heavesn,
   and you waters above the heavens!
Let them praise the name of the LORD.

Pastoral Prayer:
   Through Jesus, O God, you bring people together. Common faith in him overcomes everything that separates us. But sometimes, we confess, we allow little things to become wedges in our relationships. Forgive us, O God, for the sins of separation. Remind us through your example of Jesus, the Bible, and the movement of your Holy Spirit that separation from other people signals separation from you. Help us to see each other through the eyes of Jesus. By your mercy, strengthen the unity of our church with your church to the glory of Jesus Christ, in whose name we pray. Amen. (Robert R. Kopp)

SERMON BRIEFS

NEW FAITH INSIDE AND OUT

ACTS 11:1-18

   "God shows no partiality" (Acts 10:34) is a wonderful dictum—noble and generous and grand. But what about when it gets applied to real life? What happens, for instance, when people start coming into the church who live in ways the church has never condoned? Maybe they have been touched by God, but do they really know what it means to be a "true" Christian?

I. No Laughing Matter

"Why did you go to uncircumcised men and eat with them?" (v. 3) was not just a friendly jibe, teasing Peter about his taste in dining companions. It was an utterly serious accusation, and one of fundamental religious importance. It had to do with what it meant to be a true Christian. As we know, Peter was forbidden by the religion on which he cut his eye teeth from sharing a meal with a non-Jew. His circumcision was an indelible reminder of that injunction. To be circumcised was to be set apart; it was to mark the lines clearly between God's people and the Gentile world. To lose that separation was to lose one's identity as belonging to the people of God.

II. And What About Us?

Is that threat any less real today? On an institutional level, when newcomers with life-styles different from our own begin to get involved in the church, we risk losing the church as we have always known it. Eventually, the whole congregation may look, feel, and act—even believe—differently than ever before.

On a theological level, the entrance of such people into our community shakes the very foundations of our faith. Catalogues of virtues and vices, drawn right from Scripture, have guided us for years, generations, centuries. Are they to be cast off for the sake of sharing the table with strangers, sharing the faith with outsiders whose life-styles do not accord with our traditional understanding of the Christian life?

What Peter did by his action was to bring the walls of the traditional moral code crashing down upon the whole church, like Samson in the house of the Philistines. This one move on his part was to create more dispute and dissension within the church than anything else in the whole book of Acts, all in the name of acceptance and openness. Surely Peter didn't realize what he'd done!

III. What God Wants, God Gets

But Peter was no reed shaken by the wind, no docile pushover. For sheer strength of will and resistance, none could have matched "the rock." We all know that. On this one matter, however, even the rock says, "Who was I that I could hinder God?" (v. 17).

That was, apparently, an answer his critics couldn't argue with: "When they heard this, they were silenced" (v. 18). They had figured it out, at least for the moment: "Then God has given even to the Gentiles the repentance that leads to life" (v. 18).

IV. Faith Beyond, Faith Within

"God shows no partiality" is more than just a grand maxim; it is God's modus operandi for bringing the good news to the world, no holds barred. It just so happens that at times that modus operandi closely resembles a wrecking ball, set to make powder of some of our best-loved, most well-maintained walls of self-preservation and self-definition. To be sure, dispute and dissension resulted from Peter's bold action; but also, dynamic new faith, fervent and deep, not just in those who heard the gospel, but also in those who shared it! (Paul L. Escamilla)

A NEW DAY

REVELATION 21:1-6

I live in an old historic community where many of the dated buildings are being restored to an original likeness. John relates that there will be a time when God makes all things new. The Greek word John uses for "new" does not suggest an absolutely new creation but a restoration of the original creation—new in relation to the original, the renewal of something that had previously existed. This is the regeneration of the earth, which Jesus spoke of in Matthew 19:28.

Biblical writers anticipated a new creation (see Isa. 65:17; 66:22; 2 Cor. 5:17; Gal. 6:15; Eph. 2:15; 4:24; 2 Pet. 3:10). Many apocryphal writers were also convinced that God would make a new heaven and a new earth (see 2 Bar. 32:6; 44:12; 48:50; 51:3;

1 Enoch 91:16; 2 Esd. 7:30). The new creation indicated a great moral and spiritual revolution by which the people of God would be freed from their imperfections and distress.

John opened Revelation 21 with a seer's usual introduction of a new vision. However, looking beyond the agony of human history (Revelation 20), what he saw was anything but ordinary! A new age had dawned, and the contrast of the new experience with the life his readers had known was immediately recognized.

A new day contrasts a restored wholeness with a dispelled evil. God himself is with the people. It is not a mediated nor partial presence but his full, personal, abiding presence. In the Garden of Eden, God walked with the man and woman until God withdrew at the entrance of sin. God dwelled with humanity in the transient tabernacle and later in the Temple. But God was always separated from humans by a veil. Jesus tabernacled among us (John. 1:14), but was removed to glory at the ascension. In the new age, the church, as a bride, will be reunited with God. The relationship between God and humans will be restored to its original state, whole and complete.

The restoration will eliminate the rubble of life left in sin's path. The first heaven and earth will be destroyed. The sea, which represents danger, fear, and isolation, will also be gone. Just as created life began in a garden, so also the new age will be located in a garden-like city in contrast to the wilderness exile of sin.

A new day also contrasts the awesome power of God with his demonstration of tenderness (v. 3). The judgment of God is seen as severe. "A great voice" introduced the Creator's greater presence. However, the judgment will be finished and God will wipe away the tears of his people. There will be no more death or mourning. No more weeping. No more pain. In place of negative experience of life God offers a thirsty people—"the fountain of the water of life freely."

A new day contrasts the experience of mortality with an experience of God (vv. 4-6). Sin limits life to a temporary experience. God will banish all that shadows and saddens humankind in the present. Isolation and loneliness, death and sorrow, crying and tears do not exist in the new creation. The plural use of the word *people* emphasizes the inclusive nature of God's redemption.

God will establish his dwelling with his people. The thought "and he will dwell with them" is repeated to avoid any misunderstanding. The earthly, transitory nature of life will yield to an eternal reality. What will remain will be unmarred fellowship between Creator and creation. The Apostle Paul's words in Romans 8:36ff. are representative of the shared hope of God's people, which becomes a reality in the new age, insisting that no experience in life can separate Christians from God's love and purpose in redemption.

"It is done," declared the one on the throne. On the cross Jesus said, "It is finished," with reference to God's provision of redemption. When the new age dawns, however, the act of redeeming the creation will be complete. (Barry J. Beames)

STRANGE GLORY

JOHN 13:31-35

Three things about this text stand out. It is important that we take account of all three in order for the text to find its way into our lives.

First, there is its setting in the Gospel of John. Jesus gathered with his disciples in preparation for the Passover, and this text comes from the earliest of five chapters in which John remembers that gathering. In that strikingly beautiful symbol of humble hospitality, Jesus washed the feet of his disciples, thereby declaring to them that he, their master and teacher, characterized his lordship in terms of servanthood.

Immediately following this act of humility, Jesus foretold his betrayal, and he gave the bread, which he dips into the wine, to Judas as a sign of Judas's treachery. Judas, his action as yet not understood by the other disciples, slipped out into the night.

After this comes today's text. The setting in the Gospel is significant. Jesus ate his last meal with his disciples. He performed an act of servant lordship. Might we say that Jesus gave to his betrayer the food that became sacramental? Even here is a foreshadowing of a grace that we yet find overwhelming!

Then, in the second place, there is the setting of this text in the calendar of the Christian year. Though it is a Holy Week setting in the Gospel of John, it is an Easter setting in the lectionary: the fifth Sunday of Easter. It is one thing to consider the text in its setting in the Gospel, as preparation for the Passover. In that setting, the disciples did not understand what Jesus said or did. It is an altogether different thing, however, to consider the text from the point of view of Easter, post-resurrection. From this point of view we know, as it were, the rest of the story. We know that victory belongs not to treachery and betrayal but to humility and grace, not to violence and ulterior scheming but to self-giving and love.

All of which brings us to the third thing about the text: its content. Foreshadowed before the crucifixion and vindicated after the resurrection is this strange glory about which Jesus spoke. It is so different from what the world calls glory. Sometimes the world is simply silly in its attribution of glory, as in the automobile I once saw advertised as "resplendent in its glory." Then again, the world is sometimes tragically mistaken in its understanding of glory, as in ways throughout history we have glorified selfish power, narrow nationalism, or the exclusivism of prejudice.

Standing between those extremes, still paradoxically being accorded center stage each year at Easter, and called to our minds' eyes again in this season of Easter, is this One whose glory is forever a paradox: the glory of self-sacrifice, the glory of cross lifted high and stone rolled away, the glory of giving that takes precedence over receiving—all of which is, finally, the glory of love.

That is the glory we behold in the Gospel, on this fifth Sunday of Easter, in this paradoxical text.

> In the cross of Christ I glory,
> Towering o'er the wrecks of time;
> All the light of sacred story
> Gathers round its head sublime.

It is the glory that saves us. It is the glory in which we hold and care for one another as his disciples. (J. Lawrence McCleskey)

MAY 21, 1995

෴

Sixth Sunday of Easter

Worship Theme: Christian discipleship is motivated by love.

Readings: Acts 16:9-15; Revelation 21:10, 22–22:5; John 14:23-29

Call to Worship (Psalm 67:1-5):

Leader: May God be gracious to us and bless us and make his face to shine upon us,

People: that your way may be known upon earth, your saving power among all nations.

Leader: Let the peoples praise you, O God; let all the peoples praise you.

People: Let the nations be glad and sing for joy,

Leader: for you judge the peoples with equity and guide the nations upon earth.

All: Let the peoples praise you, O God; let all the peoples praise you.

Pastoral Prayer:

Almighty God, we bring our praise and thanksgiving to you for all the wonderful blessings you have given to us in life. How wonderful is your creation! We also give thanks for the friendships and loving relationships that have made life so rich in the past, and that keep us from terrible loneliness in the present. We are thankful for the opportunity to worship with other Christians within your sanctuary, and to share in the ministry you have entrusted to us: a ministry of sharing good news with others.

Yet, Lord, we also think of those less fortunate than ourselves, for whom thanksgiving may be more difficult. Touch them with a sense of your presence, and continually hold them in special relationship with you. Lord, in all things, you *do* work for good through those who love you. Use us, teach us, lead us in your work, which needs to be done this day and throughout our lives. Help us to love as you love. Amen. (Steven R. Fleming)

SERMON BRIEFS

THE THIRST WE ALL LIVE BY

ACTS 16:9-15

They couldn't have been more different. She was from the Northwest, he from the Middle East. She was well-established; he was a venturer. She had a stable home; he was a migrant. She had family; he, none to speak of.

She bore a name drawn from generations, the proud name her homeland bore centuries earlier under a rich and distinguished king named Croesus; he went by a name he had received just a few years before. She worked a luxurious and sophisticated trade in fine purple linens; he peddled a story about a crucified Jewish person who claimed to point the way to God.

They couldn't have been more different, these two. But Lydia and Paul had one thing in common: a desire that, once they met, was to link them inseparably.

I. Insiders and Outsiders

Such encounters between "insiders" like Paul and "outsiders" like Lydia are what this strange and marvelous book of Acts is made of. The "insiders"—that is, the gospel-tellers—share their message with "outsiders"—that is, whoever hasn't yet heard or believed. In chapter 2, "insiders" were given Pentecostal tongues—but to speak to whom? Devout Jews who hadn't a clue as to what was behind all this nonsense. And many of these "outsiders" believed. In chapter 10, Peter, by now the ultimate insider, was told to go to a Gentile's house! Talk about an outsider! And the Holy Spirit fell upon all in that household who heard the Word.

The gaps get bigger! So far everybody who has encountered the gospel has been either a Jew or a "God-fearer," already a believer in the one God of Israel. But in Athens (Acts 17), Paul tried to win over some people who were way, way out. They were not Jews or even God-fearing Gentiles. They were into popular philosophy. They sarcastically referred to Paul's message as "babbling" on the subject of "foreign divinities." We're talking worlds apart! But after that remarkable encounter, "some of them joined him and became believers."

II. Our Deepest Yearning

It could be said that the book of Acts is the story of one person or group after another, each more far-flung and far-fetched than the one before, being introduced to the gospel based on the bold conviction that one inner human yearning is more basic than any other; more basic than the desire for security, for wealth, for intimacy or self-fulfillment; more basic than the urge to know truth or beauty or love or wisdom. The conviction of the book of Acts is this: Our most basic yearning in life, no matter who we are, is to know God.

You may have the urge to share your faith with a neighbor or co-worker or friend or study partner, and yet they are as different from you as night from day, as Mercury from Pluto, as Paul from Lydia. By the power of the Holy Spirit, differences are dissolved when that common yearning to meet God is shared. It has happened again and again in history, over and over in Acts, over and over since.

"If your heart is with my heart," John Wesley once said, "give me your hand." Acts would have us take that bold and open-hearted invitation one step further, to the point some might even call presumptuous: "Because we are both human, your heart *is* with my heart; we both thirst to know God. Will you give me your hand?" (Paul L. Escamilla)

AN ORIENTATION FOR HEAVEN
REVELATION 21:10, 22–22:5

Upon receiving my travel plan packet from the auto club, I discovered some unexpected, but helpful, information. Included in the material were suggestions of things I should not expect to find upon my arrival, and things I should expect to find at my destination. John viewed the new city from a mountain as God punctuated life as it has been and revealed his new creation as it can be expected.

As you prepare for your experience in heaven, there are some things you should not to expect to find and some things you should anticipate. From John's view of the beginning of the future, we find that four commonplace and ordinary elements of life, as we know it, are unmistakably absent.

First, you should not expect to find a church (21:22). Jerusalem's exiled pastor naturally looked for a church. But he "saw no temple therein." There was no need for a temple, for God himself dwells there and directs unmediated communion.

Neither should you expect light from the sun or moon (21:23-24). Light was created to dispel the darkness (Gen. 1:3-4). In the new creation, the glorious splendor of God's brilliance provides inextinguishable illumination. Unsurpassable glory radiates from God, eliminating the necessity of created light by extinguishing the dark (22:5).

Further, you should not expect to find the city secured (21:25). Twelve open gates are never closed. The gates do not prohibit entrance. Rather, they provide abundant accessibility to the city. In ancient times, city gates were closed at night and during enemy attacks for the security of the inhabitants. To be caught outside the city when the gates were closed meant probable disaster. The new city will be absolutely safe, secure.

Finally, in heaven you should not expect to find anything evil (21:27). Nothing that has a defiling or deteriorating quality can infiltrate the city. There will be no one who practices immorality or nothing that resembles untruth. The only ones who will have entrance into the city are those whose names are written in the Lamb's book of life.

John's orientation also reveals some things that you can expect. The character of heaven eventuates from the very nature of God. What can you expect? John perceived that God provided every essential for eternal life.

Life requires water, and in heaven you will find a river of life (22:1). Crystal clear, the source of the river is God. In the Garden of Eden there were four rivers. In the new city there is one river. Greater than the river that flows from the Temple in Ezekiel 47, this river flows from the throne of God—a source that never runs dry.

You can also expect to find food (22:2). On either side of the street you will find the tree of life. Unlike the tree of the knowledge of good and evil in Genesis 2:17, there is no prohibition against eating this fruit. Twelve kinds of fruit, completely accessible, provide for the residents' needs. At creation, to eat the fruit of the tree of knowledge was to incur death. To eat of the fruit of the tree of life was to experience life.

You can also expect to experience God. Inhabitants of the new city will be completely possessed by God. The predominant character of heaven will be eternal life, provided by the eternal experience of God. You will see his face and be identified with his name written on your forehead. The normal activity in heaven will be to serve God. The expected result is that you will reign forever with the Savior.

Filled with hope, Christians not only anticipate heaven accurately but are also enabled to live without despair in the present age. (Barry J. Beames)

A DIVINE DWELLING PLACE?

JOHN 14:23-29

A child in my second parish used to ask where God lives. He concluded that God lived in the big brick house that was up the road from the church and sat several hundred yards off the road, at the end of a long, tree-lined driveway. Such a conclusion is not as inappropriate as it might seem at first glance. The house was large. It was far enough off the road that most passers-by never drove up that driveway; so it was, in a sense, a removed, mysterious, unknown, somewhat awesome place. In the three years I drove by it on the way to the church, I never approached it either! I knew the name of the man who lived there, but I never met him. He was, so far as I knew, real. He existed. But I had no dealings with him. I knew that he was "other" than my congregation and I.

Something of that distance often characterizes our relationship with God. Sometimes God seems so mysterious, removed, distant from us, that God might as well live in the big house at the end of the driveway up which we never dare to drive. While there is theological validity in a concept of God as "wholly other," transcendent, majestic, and awesome, if that dimension is all we ever know of God we remain separated from God as portrayed by Jesus in this passage from John's Gospel.

Look especially at verse 23, the first verse of the text. Jesus responds to a question: "Lord, how is it that you will reveal yourself to us and not to the world?" (v. 22). Jesus' answer bespeaks an intimacy with his disciples that is unique: "Those who love me will keep my word, and my Father will love them, and we will come to them and make our home with them" (v. 23). Notice three things.

First, the relationship is based on love—in this case, the love of a disciple for the Lord. It is one thing to respect and admire Jesus, to appreciate his teaching and emulate his moral example. But one can try to follow Jesus' example for behavior with little or no personal, emotional, or spiritual connection with Jesus. The disciple is not simply one who tries to follow an example. The disciple is one bound to the Teacher by bonds of *agape*—by love returned in gratitude for love received.

In the second place, notice that obedience to Jesus is ultimately motivated by love. There is a difference between compliance with a course of action and obedience to a freely chosen way of life. Compliance to a course of action can be coerced, demanded, prescribed by law or power. But obedience to a freely chosen way of life grows out of a relationship of love. A contract can require certain behavior. A covenant assumes certain behavior because of a prior commitment.

In the third place, there comes from Jesus a promise that disciples whose way of life is motivated by love will experience God in an intensely personal dimension: "We," says Jesus, my Father and I, "will come to them and make our home with them." Far from a God who is distant and unapproachable, this God manifest in Jesus Christ actually abides with us! Augustine once said, "Thou hast made us for thyself, O God, and our hearts are restless until they rest in thee." This text gives that reality a distinct twist, as expressed in a bit of poetry:

My spirit longs for Thee
Within my troubled breast,
Though I unworthy be
Of so divine a Guest.
Of so divine a Guest
Unworthy though I be,
Yet has my heart no rest
Unless it comes from Thee.

(J. Lawrence McCleskey)

MAY 28, 1995

❧

Ascension of the Lord

Worship Theme: Christ has given the church the responsibility of carrying on his work in the world.

Readings: Acts 1:1-11; Ephesians 1:15-23; Luke 24:44-53

Call to Worship (Psalm 47:1-2, 6):

Leader: Clap your hands, all you peoples;

People: shout to God with loud songs of joy.

Leader: For the LORD, the Most High, is awesome,

People: a great king over all the earth. . . .

Leader: Sing praises to God, sing praises;

All: sing praises to our King, sing praises.

Pastoral Prayer:

Lord, ascend! And shatter that dull gravity that drags us down toward the center of our little selves. Fly to our waiting Father. Tell him we're still down here, earthbound and in need of a Comforter. We cannot get off the ground. We'd like to, but we can't. Lord, you're the author and finisher of our faith—the Archegos, the first goer. You die before we die. You rose again before we will. You gave gravity the day off and left the earth in white to disappear against the burning blue. Now you're seated in the heavenlies and making constant intercession for our sin. Tell our Father for us our prayers are very weak; there's still a lot of need down here. There's also quite a lot of pain, but then there's joy down here as well. And while we're waiting for you to come again in that same way you left, we'd like to know you're still up there telling our Father that we're still down here. Heal us from your heaven. Give us joy while we wait. Amen. (Calvin Miller)

195

SERMON BRIEFS

THE BOOK THAT BEARS OUR NAME

ACTS 1:1-11

"In the first book, Theophilus, I wrote about all that Jesus did and taught" (v. 1). The Gospel of Luke was all about Jesus. And what is this "second book" by Luke to be about? Luke doesn't say. But then he does, too.

This second book is not about Jesus directly. It is about the followers of Jesus. And the introduction, the text for today, is already making that clear. It has more to say about the disciples than about Jesus. In fact, it would have been as accurate to call this text "the commissioning of the apostles" as to call it "the ascension of Jesus."

I. Changing the Subject

Don't misunderstand; Jesus' departure is prominent in the first chapter of Acts. But it is those who don't depart who quickly move to center stage. Jesus makes sure of that. Listen for the direction of the discourse. Disciples: "Lord, is this the time when *you* will restore the kingdom to Israel?" Jesus: "It is not for *you* to know. . . . But *you* will receive power when the Holy Spirit has come upon *you*; and *you* will be my witnesses" (vv. 6-7, emphasis added). And then he's gone.

All of a sudden the subject has shifted from Jesus to the disciples. Why couldn't Luke devote a few more pages to Jesus here to really get the book of Acts off to a good start? Perhaps an imaginative gloss about Jesus' ascended life in the great beyond? Chapter 1 could be "The Ascent," chapter 2, "The Arrival," chapter 3, "Getting Settled In," and so on. The reader could sit back and enjoy the quaint descriptions, holding on to the idea of still being, in a certain ethereal way, in Jesus' audience, rather than on God's stage.

II. Jesus of Nazareth Is Gone

But the fact of the matter is that Jesus of Nazareth is gone. It's time to wash the spare linens and put the picture books away;

time to go on about our day, and carry on with our lives. And yet as hard as we try to stay busy, the house seems so quiet now, and empty. We know what it is we're already lonesome for—the friend who left only this morning.

Jesus is gone, and we would do well to linger for a time with that familiar emotion of goodbye—sadness. For a time, but not forever. Jesus is gone, but the Spirit is near, very near. The promise-language of Pentecost stirs the air of this ascension text like a fresh breeze on a sultry day: "power," "the Holy Spirit," "witnesses," "the ends of the earth." And we can feel ourselves turning toward that breeze with heightening anticipation.

III. Dust in the Air Suspended

T. S. Eliot once wrote that "dust in the air suspended marks the place where the story ended." "The first book" is history now, and the story of Jesus of Nazareth has ended. But by no means has the dust settled. The adventure has really only begun. "The second book" began to describe the "Acts of the Apostles," but its story hasn't ended at all. On the contrary, it's still being written, and in a marvelous sort of way, it's about us. This is a book that bears our name. (Paul L. Escamilla)

THE POWER CHRIST GIVES

EPHESIANS 1:15-23

Would you like to pray a prayer that you know God will answer? Then pray the text for today. This prayer for spiritual perception (vv. 15-19a) and spiritual power (vv. 19b-23) for God's people coincides with God's will for his people. That Christians may know "what is the immeasurable greatness of his power" (19a) constitutes the last petition related to spiritual perception. The remainder of the prayer states the source of that great power: the resurrection and ascension of the Lord Jesus Christ (v. 20). We generally fail to realize the "immeasurable greatness" of the power available to us as the people of God. In verses 21-23 of our text, we are reminded of the extent of that power.

I. Christ's Power Extends Over All Other Authority

Our ascended Lord's power is both universal and timeless. "Far above all rule and authority and power and dominion, and above every name that is named" (v. 21), it endures over this age and the age to come.

The apostle stated this truth in another letter, writing that God exalted Jesus on high

> and gave him the name
> that is above every name,
> so that at the name of Jesus
> every knee should bend,
> in heaven and on earth and
> under the earth,
> and every tongue should confess
> that Jesus Christ is Lord,
> to the glory of God the Father. (Phil. 2:9-11)

Absolutely every created being must bow before him. Through the resurrection and ascension of Jesus, God has crowned his Son with sovereign majesty.

Therefore, Christians need not be overwhelmed either by such forces as the evil in the structures of unredeemed society or disease or wicked individuals who may oppress us or the awesome struggle with temptation. Our Lord ultimately controls such forces and turns them to divine purposes.

II. Christ's Power Extends Over the Church

Our exalted Savior is not only Lord of all creation (v. 22a), "the head of every ruler and authority" (Col. 2:10), but he is also head of the church. The expression "head over all things to the church" means supreme head of the church.

When Jesus died on the cross, he submitted himself to us in order to deliver us from sin. This is the gift of the gospel. Because of his suffering for us and his subsequent resurrection and ascension, he calls us to submission to him so that he may live through us. This is the demand of the gospel.

A church's submission to Christ as Lord should be strikingly evident in the life of the church and the lives of its members.

Christ's presence in a church submitted to him will be manifest both in the character of the members and the ministries of the church.

III. Christ's Power Extends Through the Church

The victorious Lord not only has power over the church, but his power also permeates the church. In the analogy, Christ is the head and the church is the body. Of course, the head and the body are one; therefore, the other parts of the body derive life and power from the head. The church receives life and power from the Lord Jesus.

Variant translations of verse 23 reflect different opinions concerning the meaning of "fullness" in this particular context. I prefer the rendering of the Revised English Bible, which states that the church "is his body and as such holds within it the fullness of him who himself receives the entire fullness of God." The church has the mandate to live out the life of Christ because he has authority over us. But we also have the opportunity to live out the life of Christ because his power infuses us. The great victory provided to the church by the ascension is that the living Lord enables his church to practice his principles and perform his ministries.

On one occasion, Jonathan, son of Saul, went with only his armor bearer to check out a Philistine garrison. When they approached an outpost of some twenty men, Jonathan proposed to his armor bearer that the two of them attack because the Lord would give them victory. The young armor bearer's reply was essentially, "Go ahead! I'll be right at your side." God has put into the hearts of his people a confidence that he will be with us to give us the victory. We can almost hear him say, "Go ahead! I'll be right at your side!" (Jerry E. Oswalt)

WAITING FOR THE POWER

LUKE 24:44-53

Waiting! It is not always easy to wait. In fact, it can actually be quite difficult to do. And one can wait with so many different attitudes and in such a variety of circumstances.

In the hospital "waiting room" we sit anxiously as we await word about surgery. The person out of work waits both eagerly and uneasily as one more résumé goes through the application process. The candidate for public office waits for the votes to be tallied. The student who has taken a difficult exam waits for the professor to post the grades. Expectant parents-to-be wait for a birth. And someday the child, in a reversal of roles, may well be waiting for a death.

It is not always easy to wait! Nor was it, I suspect, easy for those disciples to wait. As Luke tells it, the two who had encountered the risen Christ on the road to Emmaus returned to Jerusalem as soon as they realized who the stranger was, and they told the eleven disciples and others gathered with them that the Lord was risen. Suddenly Jesus was among them, interpreting to them the promises of Scripture. Then he led them out of Jerusalem to Bethany, where he left them for the last time, and they returned to Jerusalem to wait. Before he led them out to Bethany, Jesus had told them to wait "in the city until you have been clothed with power from on high" (v. 49). Now, that is an interesting kind of waiting—a waiting for "power from on high." How does one wait for that power?

Much of our waiting is passive. We wait for news over which we have little or no control. We wait for results of actions taken by someone else. We wait for the conclusion of events that, once set in motion by us, run their course finally without us. We wait for results in which our effort is at the mercy of someone else's judgment. Much of our waiting is passive.

This text, however, suggests a different kind of waiting—an active waiting, a waiting in which one can actually pursue some activity that will contribute to the desired result. The result is not totally of the disciples' doing, for they are to be clothed with power from on high. But they do have some input into the process of waiting. "They were continually in the temple blessing God" (v. 53). That is to say, they worshiped. They availed themselves of time with God's people, time to remember and to be receptive of God's direction, time to prepare mind and heart for the indwelling spirit of God.

Luke wrote this Gospel, which ends with Christ's taking leave of his disciples, with the admonition that they wait. Luke also wrote the book of the Acts of the Apostles, which begins with the presence of the Holy Spirit, empowering these disciples for their mission. They must have waited proactively, with faith and hope.

"If you build it, he will come" is the famous line from the movie *Field of Dreams.* Is not the same true for disciples? "If you wait, you will be clothed with power from on high." (J. Lawrence McCleskey)

JUNE

❧

Replenishing the Well

Expecting the Power of God

Pentecost is the birthday of the church, when God empowered his people to proclaim to others the good news of the risen Lord. This exercise will help you to identify and to ask for the power of God at work through your church.

Time: 30 minutes.

Materials: A Bible; a photo album or collection of photographs of your church. If you don't have a photo album recording the life of your church, borrow as many photographs as you can from your parishioners.

Exercise:

Read John 14:8-17. When Jesus' disciples asked to see the Father, Jesus indicated that they take a look at him. And then he told them to take a look at anyone who believes in Jesus. When we want proof of the Father, we must look first to Jesus, then to the church doing the work of God.

Now, open the photo album and thumb through the photographs. As you look at the photos, ask yourself, "Where and in whom have I seen the power of God at work here?"

Next, go back through the photos and select ones where you would like to see the power of God touch the lives of individuals and groups of people. Arrange those photos on your desk or somewhere in your office where you can see them easily.

Each week during this month, spend twenty minutes in prayer, asking the power of God to touch the lives of the persons in these photographs. You may ask for blessings of healing, talent, strength, vision, courage, and the like. Remember, "I will do whatever you ask in my name, so that the Father may be glorified in the Son." (Harriet Crosby)

JUNE 4, 1995

❧

Pentecost Sunday

Worship Theme: Through the Holy Spirit, God saves and empowers us.

Readings: Genesis 11:1-9; Acts 2:1-21; John 14:8-17 (25-27)

Call to Worship (Psalm 104:33-35):
I will sing to the LORD as long as I live;
   I will sing praise to my God
      while I have being.
May my meditation be pleasing to him,
   for I rejoice in the LORD.

....

Bless the LORD, O my soul.
Praise the LORD!

Pastoral Prayer:
   Lord, we thank you for the wind and flame. Wind is mysterious as the spirit—the breath of Yahweh, the wind of promise, the gale of Pentecost. Lord, this wind roars, and your presence gathers round us in church. And yet above the roar we hear a still, small voice, almost inaudible unless we really listen. We perceive your flame above each person's head, burning to confirm that everyone has dignity and worth. Every person can now be a dwelling place of the Spirit. Your fire, O God, anoints your entire church. Now, like a thoughtful parent, you give to none of your children a gift unless you give that gift to all.
   Lord, have we not somehow mixed our seasons? Is Pentecost not our May Noel? Does not your Spirit come and dump this gift beneath that six-week tree where Jesus died? Lord, we bless you! We were once poor, lost children, but now we are made rich, enfranchised all at once, our gifts are all triune: simple wind, sim-

203

ple flame, simple joy, and your clear call to export grace throughout the world. Amen. (Calvin Miller)

SERMON BRIEFS

LET US LET GOD

GENESIS 11:1-9

So far in Genesis, things aren't turning out so well for the human venture. We've seen Adam and Eve fall into the wrong; then with Cain and Abel, rage and murder left deep and dreadful marks. From there we move to Noah, the (more or less) righteous remnant who engineered creation's survival of the great flood, only to drown himself in drunkenness.

And so we arrive at Genesis chapter 11, bewildered, perhaps angered, largely ashamed by these stories of the failed human enterprise. And what does today's text hand us? Another story of the failed human enterprise. With the very first words of the story, we can almost feel something about to go wrong. "Let us make bricks," the story begins, and we already hear the echoes of what has come before: "Let's eat the fruit"; "Let's get even"; "Let's get drunk."

I. Making a Name

"Let us make bricks," the settlers said. Why? So they could build a city. Why? So they could build a tower. Why? So they could make a name for themselves. And by verse 4 we know the motive for this, the latest human enterprise: to "make a name for ourselves."

There are certainly less noble enterprises. Many a monument, many a building carries one name or another into relative immortality, but while so doing it benefits art, science, medicine, or religion. Every city has its share of streets, buildings, parks, museums, churches, and fountains bearing name after name in perpetuity. But people travel those streets, work in those buildings, play in those parks, worship in those churches. Among the various and sundry "Let us" enterprises, surely "Let us make bricks" doesn't belong at the bottom of the moral heap.

But God saw matters differently. Basically, God seemed to reason, one "Let us" would lead to another (v. 6). And so, perhaps tongue in cheek, God said, "Let us . . . " (v. 7). And the rest is history.

Are buildings bad? Monuments, cities all evil? Of course not, in themselves. Human arrogance, not architecture, was the principal problem with Babel. Ambition, territorial conquest, and national self-exaltation were the direction Babel's tower seemed to be leaning.

II. Building as a Backdrop

A few thousand years or so after Babel, a group of people would be standing around in an extraordinary building, named for its chief builder, Herod, when a most incredible, history-making, earth-shaking event would occur. What's funny is that this magnificent monolith of a building would only be a minor prop in the whole deal, a mere backdrop to this cataclysmic event. What was to happen would not be about bricks and mortar, but about flesh and blood and new tongues and warmed hearts and the Spirit of God (Acts 2:1-13).

From the first "Let us . . . " to the very last, whenever that occurs, God will likely be on hand to nudge us with judgment at once gentle and severe, tenderly driving us from gardens, carefully marking our foreheads for our own banished protection, discreetly covering our nakedness, sweeping down to gingerly scatter whole cities to distant locations and languages. "Let us . . . " we will have said. And God will answer, nudging us the way only God can, "I would teach you a new language: 'Let God through us. . . . ' " (Paul L. Escamilla)

WHAT THE SPIRIT DOES IN US

ACTS 2:1-21

There is a hymn that pleads, "Send the old time power, the Pentecostal power. . . ." This plea is really unnecessary, because the power of the Holy Spirit came into the church once and for all on the day of Pentecost, immediately following the resurrection and ascension of Jesus Christ. What the Holy Spirit began that day as an extension of his work among God's people in fulfillment of Jesus' promise (John 14–16) will continue in the church until Jesus returns. Notice the items involved in that extended work.

I. The Holy Spirit Identifies the Church as the Special Place of God's Presence

The disciples gathered together in Jerusalem and waited as the Lord instructed. They prayerfully awaited the coming of the Holy Spirit into their lives (1:4-8, 12-14).

The experience the church had with the Holy Spirit was unique. Never before had he infused people as his permanent dwelling. The coming of the Spirit was accompanied by physical phenomena that were intended to point out the uniqueness of the occasion. The description of the phenomena reminds us of the spectacular events that God used to convince his people of his presence in the tabernacle in the wilderness at the time of its completion. A cloud by day and a pillar of fire by night represented God's presence in the tabernacle. On Pentecost the sound of a mighty rushing wind and the sight of tongues of fire convinced the disciples of the presence of the Holy Spirit in their lives.

The fruits of the Spirit (Gal. 5:22-25) and the exercising of Spirit-given ministries (1 Cor. 12:4-11) in the lives of Christians prove the church to be the special dwelling place of the Holy Spirit today.

II. The Holy Spirit Enables the Church to Do God's Work

The main business of the church is evangelism. Jesus said that this primary mission of the church would begin in Jerusalem. Pentecost was the strategic time for the church to begin evangelism, because thousands of pilgrims (Jews and God-fearers) from other countries were in Jerusalem to celebrate Pentecost. Many of them would believe the gospel and take the message back to their homelands as far away as Rome and northern Africa. In order for that to happen, the Holy Spirit enabled the Christians to speak spontaneously the languages of all the people gathered in Jerusalem. Clearly, the tongues they used were known languages (vv. 6-11).

So the Holy Spirit enabled the church to do on that occasion what needed to be done to carry out its evangelistic mission. The same Holy Spirit continues to enable Christians to perform deeds that must be performed to reach our world with the gospel.

A poor, unemployed, homeless man was an agnostic. He broke his leg in an accident. A church paid his medical bills, and one family took him into their home and nursed him back to health. As a result, the agnostic became open to the gospel and was saved. The Holy Spirit gave the church love and hospitality, which were much more effective with the agnostic than a miracle of language.

III. The Holy Spirit Guides the Church to Understand Scripture

In an effort to clarify for the bewildered masses what was happening, Peter referred to a passage from the prophet Joel. He interpreted the events on the day of Pentecost to be the fulfillment of Joel 2:28-32. Joel foretold the coming of the Holy Spirit upon both young and old to join generations together in a mighty spiritual movement during the end time. The implication is that the Holy Spirit gave Peter that insight.

The most essential ingredient for correct interpretation of Scripture is the illumination provided by the Holy Spirit (John 16:13). Other guidelines for proper interpretation contribute significantly to the understanding of a passage. It is helpful to know author, date, occasion, and so on, but it is absolutely necessary to have the illumination of the Holy Spirit.

When the Holy Spirit came to abide with believers on Pentecost nearly 2,000 years ago, he identified the church as the place of his special presence, enabled the church to accomplish Christ's work, and guided the church to understand Scripture. He continues those exciting actions in the church today. (Jerry E. Oswalt)

THE PRESENCE IN THE ABSENCE

JOHN 14:8-17 (25-27)

The day is Pentecost, a major celebration in the life of the church. However, many of us mainline religious types are not very comfortable with the emphasis we are supposed to place on the Holy Spirit on Pentecost. Not wanting to be given to spiritual excess, we are at a loss for other understandings of the day.

If that were not enough, Pentecost follows Ascension Day, the day we remember that Jesus left his disciples and ascended into heaven. And in our postmodern world, where we long ago abandoned a three-story universe, we just are not sure what to do with this account of the ascension of Jesus.

So the day is Pentecost, a major celebration in the life of the church. But we are not at all sure what to do with the day.

Then there is the text from the Gospel of John. At least it leaves us a bit more comfortable, for it comes from an account of some words Jesus spoke while he was still with his disciples. So they are a bit more real. But they come from what are called the "Farewell Discourses" in John's Gospel. Jesus spoke these words to his disciples in anticipation of leaving them. In this text, he actually talks about the time when he will no longer physically be present with them. He sheds important light on this matter of Pentecost, this matter of the departure of Christ and the meaning of a new Presence: "If you love me, you will keep my commandments. And I will ask the Father, and he will give you another Advocate, to be with you forever. This is the Spirit of truth, whom the world cannot receive, because it neither sees him nor knows him. You know him, because he abides with you, and he will be in you" (14:15-17).

This text confronts us with a theological issue: the presence in the absence. At least one of the things the Ascension and Pentecost mean is that when the risen Christ was no longer visibly present with the disciples, they became aware that he was present in a new way. He was present through the Spirit. That may sometimes seem difficult to express, but it is a genuine presence. This presence could be experienced only after Jesus was visibly absent. Ascension and Pentecost, then, are symbols for the transition to a new experience of Christ's presence, a presence that reaches across the years from then to now, from Jerusalem to today.

My grandfather died two decades ago. When the extended family gathered for his funeral, he was so noticeably and undeniably absent that it left an immense void, for he had been a person whose presence filled the entire room. In another sense, however, he had never been more present. He was in every conversation, every memory. Everyone knew that the entire family had gathered because of him. And there are ways in which, throughout those two decades, he has remained with us, and he always will.

If such is true of that relationship, how much more is it true of the presence of Christ in the Holy Spirit, who does abide with us forever! (J. Lawrence McCleskey)

JUNE 11, 1995

❧

Trinity Sunday

Worship Theme: We experience God as three in one: Father, Son, and Spirit.

Readings: Proverbs 8:1-4, 22-31; Romans 5:1-5; John 16:12-15

Call to Worship (Psalm 8):

Leader: O LORD, our Sovereign, how majestic is your name in all the earth!

People: You have set your glory above the heavens.

Leader: Out of the mouths of babes and infants you have founded a bulwark because of your foes, to silence the enemy and the avenger.

People: When I look at your heavens, the work of your fingers, the moon and the stars that you have established;

Leader: what are human beings that you are mindful of them,

People: mortals that you care for them?

Leader: Yet you have made them a little lower than God,

People: and crowned them with glory and honor.

Leader: You have given them dominion over the works of your hands;

People: you have put all things under their feet,

Leader: all sheep and oxen, and also the beasts of the field, the birds of the air, and the fish of the sea, whatever passes along the paths of the sea.

All: O LORD, our Sovereign, how majestic is your name in all the earth!

Pastoral Prayer:

O Lord, we marvel at the world of mystery in which you have placed us. It seems the more we learn, the more questions we have. As children, our questions were simple: Why is the sky blue? Why is the grass green? As we grew older, our questions took on a different cast: Why am I here? What meaning can my life have? The older we become, the deeper and more profound become the mysteries we face. Even your very nature, three in One, single yet plural, is a mystery to us.

And yet, Lord, in the midst of mystery that we may never understand in this life you bring comfort, strength, assurance. Although we may not understand all of life's questions, we see your loving hand sheltering us in the face of the worst life can bring. Although we may never understand your nature fully until we gather around your throne, yet we see you manifest yourself to us as One in three—as Creator, as Savior, as Indwelling Presence. Thank you, Lord, that even though we now see darkly, you give us all the light we need to find our way to you. Amen. (Michael Duduit)

SERMON BRIEFS

DELIGHTFUL THINGS OF US ARE SPOKEN

PROVERBS 8:1-4, 22-31

Hear Wisdom as she speaks:

> "And I was daily [God's] delight,
>   rejoicing before [God] always,
>   rejoicing in [God's] inhabited world
>   and delighting in the human race." (vv. 30-31)

Did we hear that right? Delighting in the human race? Hasn't Wisdom overlooked something? Like the fact that humans are often corrupt, sinister, devious, selfish, and foolish, among other things? Has Wisdom been skipping the morning paper and napping during the evening news? Has she been wearing rose-colored glasses to school and work and church and on the freeway and even at home?

I. Soberest of the Sober

Not a chance. If Wisdom were speaking from a book of love poems about "counting the ways I love thee," maybe we could say she was under the influence of romance. If she were singing a rock song about "every heartbeat belonging to you," maybe we could assume she had merely gotten swept away by the beat. But this is Proverbs. And nobody knows better than the writer of Proverbs the frailty of the human character. On that one point alone, Proverbs is about as sober and stodgy as they come. A quick scan of the book gives a convincing array of descriptions of human nature and behavior: foolish, wicked, adulterer, evildoer, stupid, scoffer, crooked, and (my favorite) lazybones (see 6:6). If you want to see praise for the human species carried too far, don't look here.

II. Wisdom's Children

Yet, if you want a fair and balanced assessment of human character and potential, then this is your book. Proverbs isn't exactly carried away with confidence in the human species, but neither is it completely negative. Amid all these other less flattering names, its most common label for its listeners is "my child." And this is not just another slight on the human character. This is a tender, hope-filled name. A child can learn; a child can be taught, shaped, molded, raised. For Proverbs to call its listener "my child" is not pejorative; it is utterly hopeful.

III. What's Wise About Proverbs?

What is wise about the Proverbs is that they know the delicately intertwined labyrinth of good and ill within the human soul. "Nothing human's not a broth of false and true," Buechner's Godric has observed. And Wisdom and the Proverbs know how true it is. In this proverb, Wisdom assumes human ignorance (vv. 1-5), but then proceeds to inform it (vv. 5ff.), assured of what the human heart and mind and soul are truly capable of: delightful things!

In one of Miguel de Cervantes's novels, the wiser, elder man repeatedly hounds his younger apprentice with the exclamation,

"Necio, aprende!" (literally, "One-who-knows-nothing, learn!") In the divine order of things, the bereft can be made whole, the child can be raised, the fool can become wise, the one who knows nothing can learn.

Wisdom has it right: Human behavior as a race is, potentially, delightful—creative, compassionate, humble, and pure, good-humored, just, honorable, and good. Ah, delightful! But this is not a given, not an automatic profile of humanness; it is, rather, something that can be learned, heard, studied, heeded, practiced, and lived. Delightful things of us are spoken because, by the divine instruction of Wisdom, delightful things in us can come to be. (Paul L. Escamilla)

KNOWING GOD IN THREE WAYS

ROMANS 5:1-5

James Stewart once said that the doctrine of the Trinity is both the most controversial and the most unassailable doctrine of the Christian faith. He stated further that the reason the concept of the Trinity is unassailable is that Christians from the time of the early church have found no other way to express what God means to us than to say "Father, Son, and Holy Spirit." Today's text demonstrates this fact. The apostle expressed it in another letter when he wrote, "The grace of the Lord Jesus Christ, the love of God, and the communion of the Holy Spirit be with all of you" (2 Cor. 13:14).

Our experience of God can be adequately stated only in Trinitarian terminology. We can't explain the Trinity, but we must affirm with Christians across the ages that God is our Father in heaven; our Savior, the Son of God who died for our sins; and our Holy Spirit, the Spirit of the living Lord who dwells within us and interacts with our spirits.

I. We Experience God as Father

Dante, the great poet of the Renaissance, when exiled from his home in Florence and cast down by the cruel turn of fate, determined to walk from Italy to Paris where he could study philosophy in an effort to find a clue to the riddle of human destiny. In his travels, Dante found himself a weary pilgrim, forced to knock at the door of Santa Croce Monastery to find refuge from the night. A surly brother within was finally aroused, came to the door, flung it open, and in a gruff voice asked, "What do you want?" Dante answered in a single word, "Peace."

Until we know God as Father, we experience a deep sense of restlessness in our lives. The uneasiness is there because we have alienated ourselves from the One who created us in his image to have fellowship with him. Just as rebellious sons and daughters destroy relationships with parents, so also we break our relationship with God through sin. We have no peace until we know God as Father again. The word translated "peace" is derived from a verb that means to bind together that which has been separated. Christians have a profound sense of peace because we are bound together with our heavenly Father.

II. We Experience God as Son, the Savior

It is through our Lord Jesus Christ that we have peace with God, because it is by him that we gain access to the "grace in which we stand" (v. 2). Actually, our experience of God as the Savior-Son is the beginning point of our knowledge of the Trinity.

Verses 6-10 of Romans 5 delineate the work of salvation from sin completed by Jesus Christ through his substitutionary death on the cross. "But God proves his love for us in that while we still were sinners Christ died for us . . . we were reconciled to God through the death of his Son." Thus we discover peace with God through faith in Jesus Christ.

When Paul gave his Trinitarian benediction (2 Cor. 13:14), he began with "The grace of the Lord Jesus Christ." This was because of his own personal experience. He did not personally know the God he supposedly served as Saul the Pharisee until he was beaten down by a blinding light outside Damascus. At that moment he met Jesus and trusted him as Savior. Then he found peace with Father-God.

III. We Experience God as Holy Spirit

The immediate presence of God in our lives is through the Holy Spirit. Actually, the Spirit is the main player in the whole matter of our personal experience of God. The Spirit teaches us, illumines our minds, and authenticates to us the reality of God as Savior and as Father.

He delivers to our lives the salvation experience from beginning to end. He enacts the new birth (John 3:3-8). He gives us assurance that we are God's children (8:16), works through our tribulations to teach us patience, and through our patience to transform our character, and through the experience of proven character to enhance our hope in the glory of God. Meanwhile, he also infuses our lives with God's love. Finally, he will raise us from the dead (8:11).

Christians can't say "God" without thinking "Father, Son, and Holy Spirit." To think of him simultaneously as three in one is as natural as breathing. May God enrich our experience of him so that increasingly our spirits will cry, "Father, Father," our souls will rejoice in the grace of our Lord Jesus Christ, and our hearts will know more of the love of God through the presence of the Holy Spirit. (Jerry E. Oswalt)

MYSTERY AND PRACTICALITY

JOHN 16:12-15

One of the interesting phenomena of the religious world in America during the past decade has been the revival of the controversy between so-called fundamentalists and moderates. But if you think today's religious controversies are intense, you will do well to remember an ancient religious controversy that began in the early fourth century and came to its first fairly clear conclusion in A.D. 451. What was at stake? The doctrine of the Trinity. The Nicene Creed, which was the result of the controversy, established the Orthodox Christian affirmation of a triune God, God in three persons, or three manifestations, three expressions: Father, Son, and Holy Spirit.

I want to make two affirmations about the doctrine of the Trinity. First, the doctrine of the Trinity expresses a mystery. It tells us that the church has experienced God in three distinct forms of revelation, but still there is mystery in the being of God.

There is God beyond us, God transcendent, God whose name was regarded as so sacred by the ancient Hebrews that they would not speak it and substituted an Aramaic word whenever they encountered the sacred name in Scripture. This God beyond us we have referred to as Father, Creator of heaven and earth.

There is God among us, the Word become flesh, the very revelation of God in human form, Jesus Christ the Son, who redeems us from sin.

And there is God within us as individual Christians and within the community that is the church: God the Holy Spirit, who sustains us personally and corporately. You and I have not seen the risen Christ, but we have experienced the presence of God within us and the church.

These three ways of speaking about God affirm a mystery. We cannot exhaust the nature of God. We cannot fully explain it. We can only speak of how we have experienced God, and the doctrine of the Trinity helps us to do so.

Then there is the second affirmation. Although the doctrine of the Trinity expresses a mystery, there is also a practicality to this doctrine which the church needs to recall. The church did not originally develop this doctrine simply for utilitarian purposes. It was a theological issue at the heart of the church's faith. But there is a practical effect of the doctrine that is very important in today's church. The doctrine of the Trinity acts as a kind of theological system of checks and balances. The text for today discusses God's three manifestations as if they are interrelated, which suggests something important for the church.

Test your understanding of God by whether it reflects God's fullness. Test your interpretations of the spirit life of the church by whether it reflects God's fullness. Do you believe that God's Spirit has spoken to you? Test the call of that word by how it measures up to the Creator's intentions for creation, by how it measures up to the Son's command to love. It is not too strong to say, "Beware the person who talks too much about either Father or Son or Holy Spirit, and ignores the other two persons of the Trinity."

The doctrine of the Trinity expresses a mystery that eludes our total comprehension, and it reminds us that we are to believe and live out of a whole concept of God. (J. Lawrence McCleskey)

JUNE 18, 1995

❧

Second Sunday After Pentecost

Worship Theme: Joyful worship emerges from a sense of God's forgiveness.

Readings: 1 Kings 21:1-10, (11-14), 15-21*a*; Galatians 2:15-21; Luke 7:36–8:3

Call to Worship (Psalm 5:1-2, 8):
Give ear to my words, O LORD;
   give heed to my sighing.
Listen to the sound of my cry,
   my King and my God,
   for to you I pray.

....

Lead me, O Lord, in your righteousness
   because of my enemies;
   make your way straight before me.

Pastoral Prayer:
   O God, who has put an eternal silence at the heart of all our clamor and who speaks with eternal wisdom when we are willing to be silent, we praise you for this morning and all its special qualities—the singing birds, the flowers at our doorsteps, the smell of bacon frying in the pan or coffee brewing in the pot, church bells ringing, the joy of being alive. Teach us to hold this joy as a special treasure and never surrender it.
   Show us how to live with one another and to care for ourselves and to be such lively stewards of grace that the world will be a finer and better place for our having been here. Enable us, amid all our singing and speaking and celebrating, to remember the poor and suffering of the world, and to be aware of both the silence and the voice of your eternal presence, challenging us, changing us, lifting us above all difficulties and divisions, for you

are our God, our Rock, and our Salvation, and we are the people of your handiwork, through Jesus Christ. Amen. (John Killinger)

SERMON BRIEFS

DIVINE JUSTICE

1 KINGS 21:1-10, (11-14), 15-21*a*

The story of Naboth and his vineyard reads like the plot of an intriguing novel. A good man is the target of injustice and murder. What was rightfully his is taken from him by someone of wealth, influence, and power. It is only after his death that the truth comes to light. The guilty parties (King Ahab and Queen Jezebel) are confronted and called to account for their actions.

This story has universal appeal, for it points to the injustice of this world and the evil consequences of corrupt power. Most of us have been the target of injustice at some point in our lives, which leaves us crying out for vindication.

Today's text reminds us of three important lessons:

1. Faith in God does not spare the righteous from the evil of this world. Good and righteous people are not inoculated against injustice, hurt, and wickedness. Envy, jealousy, and greed can be terribly destructive. Human sinfulness at its worst can decimate the lives of all it touches. Naboth kept God's law, displayed fidelity to his ancestry, and was apparently a model citizen of his community. Despite all of this, he was killed because of the treachery of others.

Crime, disease, and famine do not examine the values of their victims. They are common to all nations, all races, and persons of every religious tradition. Belief in God does not make one immune from the heartache of life's journey. Faith opens our eyes to realize that we do not make the journey alone.

2. Power without accountability leads to sin and injustice. Jezebel knew how to manipulate power (her own and the power of Ahab's throne) to achieve her evil desires. Justice was ignored because the king was accountable to no other person. Elijah, God's prophet and messenger of the divine Word, reminded Ahab that all people, even kings, are accountable to God.

One of the blessings of our system of government is the many checks and balances built into our democracy. Individuals within any branch of government can attain power, but ultimately all are subject to the scrutiny of the other branches of the system as well as the public. History, both contemporary and ancient, is replete with examples of governments gone awry due to power without accountability. The Hitlers of this world stand as testimony to the destructive consequences of unlimited power.

3. *God is not mocked.* Divine justice cannot be circumvented or ignored. Our own life experience may appear otherwise, but this truth is absolute.

While on vacation in the Texas hill country, my wife and I received an urgent message to return home. An older lady in our congregation, a very gentle and gracious woman of the faith, had been kidnapped from her home, sexually molested, and brutally murdered. I was to officiate at her funeral.

The family was simultaneously outraged and in shock. It seemed inconceivable that such a gentle soul in such a quiet community could be the victim of so vicious a crime. After a brief investigation, a suspect was identified and an arrest made.

Years went by before the man who killed her, her neighbor, was brought to trial. He was convicted and given a sentence that will result in his release from prison in a few short years.

As Christians, we are called to live lives of peace and justice. Yet, as in the case of Naboth or the lady in my congregation, doing so is no guarantee of justice in our lifetime. The Apostle Paul warned, "Do not be deceived; God is not mocked, for you reap whatever you sow" (Gal. 6:7).

When the forces of injustice wreak havoc in our world, we must remember that God is with us. We are *not* alone. God still has the last word! (Gary G. Kindley)

LIVING WITH CHRIST

GALATIANS 2:15-21

The verses preceding the text (Gal. 2:11-14) indicate that a conflict between Peter and Paul, Christ's apostles, has arisen. Peter, who had been the first to preach and welcome Gentiles into the fellowship of believers (Acts 10), and who lived like one of them (Gal. 2:14) fell under peer pressure from the Jewish Christians. He refused to sit down at the Lord's Table and participate in Communion with these Gentile brothers. What a contradiction! What hypocrisy! Paul could not accept it any longer and proceeded to tongue-lash Peter for such alienation. Paul felt it was his job to convince the Jewish Christians and remind Peter that the experience of salvation was for all—Jews and Gentiles alike.

The universality of the gospel crumbles prejudice and snobbishness, and opens the door for all to come in and abide with Christ forever. How is that accomplished? Paul declares that being crucified with Christ, we no longer live with Satan as our partner, but Christ and his followers live together.

I. Living with Christ Means Life, Not Death

We have died to our trespasses and sins, which opens the possibility of spiritual life through Christ. We can now experience genuine living. Someone wrote that "life is that childhood of immortality." Real living includes:

- *Liberty*—freedom from bad habits, an immoral life-style, false guilt, despair, discouragement and a host of others.
- *Joy*—a twinkle in the eye like a Spurgeon or a Graham.
- *Encouragement*—Charles Swindoll wrote in *Seasons of Life:* "Is there some soul known to you in need of financial encouragement? A student off at school, a divorcee struggling to gain back self-acceptance, a forgotten servant of God laboring in an obscene and difficult ministry? Encourage generously!"
- *Grace*—God's unmerited favor released to repentant sinners.

II. Living with Christ Means Faith, Not Law

Faith simply means trust. It begins with conviction, a knowledge that our righteousness does not meet God's standard. The law helps us to discover this reality. Faith is not blind. It builds on authentic biblical facts, so it is not mere speculation. We stake our lives on the outcome. Faith is trusting Christ to prove his promise.

James Boice says of verse 16 that it means we have literally "believed *into* Christ. That implies a personal commitment, not just assenting to the facts concerning Jesus. We actually run to Him for refuge and seek mercy."

When that embracement of Jesus occurs, there is a turning away from the old life-styles as we can honestly sing, "Every Bridge Is Burned Behind Me."

Law pushes open the door of salvation. Faith enters through the door. Have you walked by faith through the doorway of God?

The Westminster Catechism states, "Faith in Jesus Christ is saving grace, whereby we receive and rest upon Him alone for salvation, as He offered to us in the gospel."

III. Living with Christ Means Present, Not Past

Past experiences are the building blocks of the present. We learn from our mistakes as we let God build us today. Living in past glories stops our hearts from advancing to the present-day's tasks.

Christ is in the present tense of life. He speaks boldly today through his Word, circumstances of life, prayer, his Spirit, and others. Don't throw away your greatest opportunity to live in the present. To do that requires living in Christ! (Derl G. Keefer)

LOVING WORSHIP

LUKE 7:36–8:3

The Dutch have a saying when a sudden silence falls on a group: "The preacher walked by." Can you imagine the silence that must have fallen on the Pharisee's dinner party when a former prostitute stole across the room, anointed the feet of Jesus, and wiped his feet with her hair? This was extravagant love. In this woman's act of devotion, we discover how we may show our love to Christ through adoration and worship.

I. Loving Worship Is Unembarrassed

When this woman came to Christ as he was reclined at the table, she stood behind him, weeping. The other guests watched with mouths open. But she loved Christ. She did not care what others thought of her. She trusted her reputation to Christ.

Chuck Colson, a former White House adviser to President Nixon during the Watergate scandal, was converted to Christ. Many people were skeptical. Was he merely one more example of a "foxhole" conversion? Yet, Colson showed his loyalty to Christ by beginning a prison ministry, writing his own conversion story, and becoming a recognized Christian leader.

Other people are watching us, too. We can show our loving worship to Christ through unembarrassed loyalty to him at dinner parties, at a civic club, at work, or on prom night. First John 4:18 says, "Perfect love casts out fear"—including the fear of what others think of us. Have we given our reputation to Christ?

II. Loving Worship Is Extravagant

Jesus said of this woman, "She has shown great love" (v. 47). Can any praise from the lips of Jesus be greater? She spent one year's wages (the cost of the fragrant oil) in one act of worship.

A church in the Midwest had saved over $500,000 for its new building. The church heard about a special missions project where the need to minister to others challenged the church's priorities. The church gave everything it had to missions.

Jesus watched the people as they put money in an offering plate. Wealthy people gave liberally. Then a poor widow gave less than a penny. Jesus said, "This poor widow has put in more than all" (Mark 12:43 NKJV). The measure of our gift to Christ is not the size of the gift, but what we have left over after we've given.

Is what *we* give to Christ the measure of *our* love? Is there some act of extravagance by which we may show our love to Christ? Our gift may not be some possession; rather, we may give our time, energy, and talents in the worship of Christ.

III. Loving Worship Is Self-giving

Jesus said this woman loved much because she had been forgiven much (v. 47). When she realized what she had been, and what Christ had done for her, she gave Christ herself.

A congregation was at worship in the jungles of Africa. The offering plates were merely large baskets. The worshipers dropped fruit, vegetables, or other gifts into the baskets. A little boy watched everyone offer something to Christ. He had nothing to give. When the basket was held out to him, he climbed into it.

The greatest act of loving worship is still to give ourselves to Christ. Whether we are sitting in a worship service, working on a community project, preparing a meal for our families, or teaching in a public school, the heart of loving worship is giving our heart. Jesus said, "Inasmuch as you did it to one of the least of these . . . you did it to Me" (Matt. 25:40 NKJV).

The key to this woman's loving worship was recognition of her need, and an awareness of the forgiveness of Christ. When we know we're forgiven, our worship of Christ becomes unembarrassed, extravagant, and self-giving. (E. Langston Haygood)

JUNE 25, 1995

❧

Third Sunday After Pentecost

Worship Theme: Faith opens the door to God's great provision.

Readings: 1 Kings 19:1-4, (5-7), 8-15*a*; Galatians 3:23-29; Luke 8:26-39

Call to Worship (Psalm 42:1-2, 8, 11):
As a deer longs for flowing streams,
    so my soul longs for you, O God.
My soul thirsts for God,
    for the living God.
When shall I come and behold
    the face of God?

....

By day the LORD commands his steadfast love,
    and at night his song is with me,
    a prayer to the God of my life.

....

Why are you cast down, O my soul,
    and why are you disquieted within me?
Hope in God; for I shall again praise him,
    my help and my God.

Pastoral Prayer:
    We praise you, O God, that into this troubled world you came as our Redeemer and Savior. We praise you that you joined yourself with this human family, wearing our painstricken flesh to know the worries and cares of a human being. O God, when life is hard and burdensome, when the prospects are gray and cheerless, when we lose faith and give way to despair, when our feet are lead and songs die on our lips, comfort us with the knowledge

that you will never leave us or forsake us. Help us to put our trust in you and to spend our strength in your service. From Jesus Christ we learn that the secret of joy is a heart free from selfish desires. May we find delight in simple things and ever rejoice in the riches of your grace, through Jesus Christ our Lord. Amen. (John Bishop)

SERMON BRIEFS

IS YOUR NAME ELIJAH?

1 KINGS 19:1-4, (5-7), 8-15*a*

If you believe that faith in God is a means of avoiding life's difficulties, this text is for you. If you expect appreciation as a response to faithful service, this text is for you. In today's passage, Elijah demonstrates faith as a prophet of God and rises up against the worship of the false god, Baal. Elijah's *faith* leads him to *action,* which gets him into *difficulty.* Through the experience of Elijah, this marvelous Scripture passage reveals three important truths about faith and following God.

1. Difficulty and obedience to God go hand-in-hand. We may not think that faith in God would lead us into difficulty. In reality, if we choose to live our lives firmly rooted in the faith, we can be certain that conflict will soon be at our doorstep.

Elijah faithfully represented God in the face of the prophets of Baal. He faithfully demonstrated the power of Yahweh and denounced the pagan worship of idols, only to discover that he was now the target of Jezebel's wrath.

Elijah discovered (as we must if we are to grow) that serving the Lord brings *both* joy and challenges. Someone once wrote, "The mystery of life is not a problem to be solved but a reality to be experienced." It is when we fully participate in life's challenges by throwing ourselves headlong into the journey that we discover fulfillment and joy.

For contemporary Christians, it is no different. Obedience to Christ leaves no room to equivocate in the face of injustice. Jesus' words and actions to the Pharisees, money-changers, young lawyer, and even his own disciple Peter are direct and plain.

Christian discipleship is demanding. We are called to count the cost and then choose whom we shall serve.

2. *Faith in God is a call to action.* When we make decisions of faith that call us to action and lead us into difficulty, we must always rely on our faith if we are to cope with the difficulty at hand. *It is a cycle, not a one-way equation!* Faith calls believers to act, which may cause us to encounter difficulty, which must be met with faith.

When we make decisions based on fear, we often get ourselves into trouble. When we make faith decisions and our faith does not endure, we can also get ourselves into trouble. Elijah acted boldly on faith and then shriveled in the face of Jezebel's threats. Ultimately, when Elijah realized God's presence once again, Elijah made an important discovery.

3. *Elijah discovered that God will provide.* Elijah's life was on the line, and he was overcome by fear. Was his reward for fidelity to Yahweh to be hunted down and killed by the followers of Baal?

God did not forget Elijah. God instructed Elijah to continue on his journey and carry out another task for God. Elijah still had work to do, and purposeful work is always better than worry. God had a plan. Elijah need only be faithful and follow. As he did for Elijah, God provides for our needs, especially when we encounter difficulties along life's journey.

Is your name Elijah? Is your faith and Christian action stymied when difficulties arise? Is the two-headed monster called doubt and fear stalking you? Faith in God naturally calls us to act on that faith. God's grace merits a response of loving service and joyous, generous living. Like Elijah, we must remember that hardship is to be expected on a faith journey. It is also vital to remember that God *will* provide! (Gary G. Kindley)

LIVING BY FAITH

GALATIANS 3:23-29

Fritz Reidenour wrote, "Faith is, after all, surrendering to what you know is right." Faith is letting go of the wrong things, people, and objects and hooking on to Jesus, who directs us in the right way.

Several years ago a house caught fire in a residential part of a certain city. All of the family members got out but one. A young boy of about seven years was asleep upstairs when the flames started. The family members assumed he was out of the house when suddenly they heard his cries and call for "Daddy" from the upstairs window. He could be seen by the glow of the fire in his room; however, because of the thick black smoke he could not see the family or the neighbors below. He heard voices and he shouted out, "Daddy, save me!" His frantic father beneath the window cried out, "Frankie, just jump down in my arms and I'll catch you!" Frankie crept out of the window, but clung to it because he was so high off the ground. "Frankie, you must jump, son," came the plea of the concerned father. The boy screamed out, "I can't see you, Daddy! I can't jump. I'm scared!" His family and neighbors started hollering up to him, "Let go, don't be afraid. Your father will catch you." Frankie felt the heat of the flames and realized if he stayed much longer he would be burned. He knew his father was strong and that he loved him, and that he was waiting to save him. He closed his eyes, let go, and fell down to his father's waiting arms.

Paul explained to the church in Galatia that he had been held prisoner by Satan's fiery flames and was afraid to jump into the arms of God (v. 22). He let go of pride, tradition, sin, and his outward show of religion, and fell into the loving arms of God. The Lord redeemed him from the fire of the law. In that moment he realized, like the prophet Habakkuk, "The righteous live by their faith" (Hab. 2:4).

I. Faith Unites Persons with God

When Alan Paton was translating the New Testament into an island dialect, he found it difficult to find the right word for "faith." He struggled with the word until one day a native teacher wearily came into his room and sat down on a cane chair. Bringing another cane chair close, he placed his feet on it and used a word in his native language that meant "I am resting my whole weight here." Automatically Paton had his word for faith. The indigenous people of that island learned that the act of faith was to rest the whole weight of mind and heart on Jesus!

James Boice in the *Expositors' Bible Commentary* stated that faith is primarily "acceptance of the gospel message concerning Jesus Christ and the committal of one's self into him or God as revealed in him." Jesus must be the object of faith. He alone united people with the Father.

II. Faith Grasps God's Promises

The law defines sin; however, it defies curing sin as well. God promises forgiveness, but the law fails to produce it.

Legally, an agreement depends on both sides keeping that agreement. The law placed that boundary on all who depended on it for salvation. Break the law, and the whole agreement was shattered.

A promise focuses on one person and is not altered by another person's action. God offers salvation. We may sin, stray, or reject Jehovah's promise, but nothing wrecks the promised offer of redemption.

Grab hold of that promise, and salvation will translate to assurance. We can be forgiven and cleansed by a loving God of promise.

III. Faith in Christ Delivers Righteousness

A missionary was talking to an old Indian about what it was like to be a Christian. The old chief said that it was like two dogs fighting inside him. There was the evil dog (sin) and the good dog (righteousness).

"Which is winning?" The missionary asked.

"The one I feed the most," answered the Indian.

Which dog are you feeding the most? Faith in God feeds righteousness. (Derl G. Keefer)

CHRIST'S POWER

LUKE 8:26-39

A nineteenth-century Scottish preacher, Thomas Chalmers, once preached a sermon titled "The Expulsive Power of a New Affection." The Gadarene demoniac had lost the power to control himself, and no one else could help him. But when Jesus came, he expelled the demons, delivered the Gadarene, and gave him a new affection. This story vividly portrays how Christ's power extends over the visible and invisible worlds. He can change even the most hopeless individual. But when he changes a person, he may not want that person to change everything.

I. Christ's Power Over the Invisible World

A popular theme in movies portrays the power of good against the power of evil. In the *Star Wars* trilogy, the dark side, Darth Vader, opposes the young and noble Luke. *The Exorcist* was one of the first movies in a long line of films emphasizing the struggle for supremacy between God and demons. The trouble with most of these popular treatments is that they attribute an equal amount of power to evil as they do to God.

Yet in the New Testament, there is no comparison between the power of the devil and the power of Christ. Christ's power is complete. It extends over all worlds—visible and invisible. When Christ appeared to the Gadarene, there was no fight to the finish for supremacy. Christ's power is incomparable and complete. The demons recognized the Lord from Glory, and they trembled.

Someone once said, "Hell is close, but God is closer." The Christian does not need to fear the unseen world. We may live our lives in full confidence that Christ's power extends over the invisible world and that no power is able to overwhelm us. John said, "He who is in you is greater than he who is in the world" (1 John 4:4 NKJV).

II. Christ's Power upon Our Inward Spirit

By the time he was fifty, John D. Rockefeller had become the wealthiest man in America. Yet he lived under such stress that his diet included a bland combination of milk and crackers. He lost the hair on his body, and one reporter said that Rockefeller would be dead in a few months. But Rockefeller changed from the inside out—and even lived into his nineties.

Before Christ came into his life, the Gadarene demoniac had no power over his own life. He could not change himself. Many people today are searching for cures that will help them change and improve their lives. But no amount of external influence—

good health, money, fame, personal influence, or success—can put a person *in his or her right mind* (v. 35). These things may help, but Christ's power changes a person's heart.

III. Christ's Power in Our Personal Choices

One of the natural outcomes of experiencing the life-changing power of Christ is that we discover we are set free to follow Christ. The Gadarene demoniac was ready to leave everything for Christ.

Christ calls some of us to mission fields or some other special ministry, but more often than not, what he really wants us to do is this: Stay where you are, use what you have, and be a witness to Christ's life-changing power in your life. Whether we are teachers, auto-workers, or students, the world needs to see Christ's power in our lives right where we live. (E. Langston Haygood)

JULY

❧

Replenishing the Well

Expect Trouble

Trouble is always a part of the life of faith. Trouble follows us not in spite of the fact that we are Christians, but because we are Christians. As today's Bible reading shows, we follow a Lord who "sets his face" toward trouble. This month's exercise will help to ease the troubles we face because of our faith.

Time: 60 minutes once a week for the next four weeks.

Materials: A Bible; a fellow clergyperson or a Christian friend who is *not* part of the congregation.

Exercise:
Read Luke 9:51-62. Especially note the statement "his face was set toward Jerusalem." Jerusalem, of course, is where passion and death awaited Jesus—and perhaps anyone else too closely allied with him. Jesus tries to tell people exploring a life of discipleship that it is a miserable, possibly dangerous business. A life of discipleship, that of following in the footsteps of Christ, naturally brings trouble.

All God's children got trouble, the saying goes. And so do you. No church runs like clockwork. Personal doubts and professional anxieties come with the territory. But none of us is meant to carry these burdens alone.

Arrange to meet with a fellow clergyperson or a Christian friend who does not attend your congregation for an hour once a week for the next four weeks. Spend the first forty minutes sharing, as honestly as you can, your troubles with each other. The closing twenty minutes should be spent in prayer asking God for strength, healing, courage, or whatever it takes to continue on toward Jerusalem with Jesus. (Harriet Crosby)

JULY 2, 1995

Fourth Sunday After Pentecost

Worship Theme: Commitment to God's direction and purpose for our lives is the only way to true fulfillment.

Readings: 2 Kings 2:1-2, 6-14; Galatians 5:1, 13-25; Luke 9:51-62

Call to Worship (Psalm 77:11-13):

Leader: I will call to mind the deeds of the LORD; I will remember your wonders of old.

People: I will meditate on all your work, and muse on your mighty deeds.

Leader: Your way, O God, is holy.

All: What god is so great as our God?

Pastoral Prayer:

God, we are gathered in your house to worship and adore you. We are thanks-filled people today, for we look around us and see others who have experienced your power in their lives. In this church and in churches everywhere, you are working to change the lives of people, to make them whole, to bring them into relationship with you through your Son, Jesus Christ. Help each one of us here today to feel your presence and power within that we might share the excitement of the gospel with others. O Lord, let this church be an instrument of your love, and may we be instruments of your peace!

We are thankful for our nation. What a great blessing our country has been and should be into the future. Yet, sadly, we pervert our national ideals and our religious foundations each new day. Help us, and our country, to regain a sense of direction. Have mercy on us for our violence and prideful living, our obsession with things, our disregard for the importance of other per-

232

sons and the value of nature and beauty. Help us, Lord, to be the kind of Christian citizens who will honor you. Amen. (Steven R. Fleming)

SERMON BRIEFS

CHANGE, GRIEF, AND GOD
2 KINGS 2:1-2, 6-14

Life is filled with change and transition. From birth to death, the human body is in a state of constant change. If that were not enough, we are also undergoing changes intellectually, emotionally, and spiritually throughout our life experience. Today's passage is about the fear of change and the constancy of God.

Elisha was afraid of change. Elisha considered Elijah his mentor, prophet, teacher, and father-in-the-faith. The younger Elisha clung to his mentor-friend, for he was fearful of the future that change can bring. Three times Elijah instructed his protégé to remain behind (vv. 2, 4, and 6), but Elisha refused.

It is not difficult to see ourselves in the character of Elisha. It is human tendency to cling to the past or to familiar traditions. Faced with the reality of an uncertain future, aging parents, growing children, or an ever-changing business environment, it is no wonder that life's transitions can be overwhelming at times.

Fear is a human response, but faith is a Christlike response. Faith does not deny fear but rises above it. Faith looks ahead in courage rather than back in fear. Faith always looks toward hope rather than to despair.

Elisha felt the despair of grief. Life is full of significant losses. We say goodbye to a lifetime of yesterdays, relationships, places, and situations. We say goodbye to countless opportunities every time we make choices. Grief is a part of the human existence.

We can choose to get bogged down in our despair, or we can discover that many of those same goodbyes are also associated with some significant hellos. Change may bring discomfort or even despair, but it also brings opportunity and promise.

One characteristic of most any crisis is that it often blinds us to the reality at hand. I find it significant that Elisha said in despair and loneliness, "Where is the LORD, the God of Elijah?" (v. 14). Immediately God gave a sign of the divine presence. The water of the Jordan parted to allow Elisha to cross back to his homeland.

It is as if God said, "I have never left you. Life goes on. Elijah's journey in this world may have ended, but your journey continues."

Elisha felt the fear of change and the despair of grief, but he also discovered the constancy of God. The same God who empowered and equipped Elijah was with Elisha as well. He was not alone. The good news is never are we! (Gary G. Kindley)

LIFE BY THE SPIRIT

GALATIANS 5:1, 13-25

Paul emphasizes theology, our understanding of God, and often dwells on theological premises. However, Paul never leaves it hanging there, for he puts his theology into practice as revealed in Galatians 5:13-25. William Barclay commented, "To Paul a theology was not of the slightest use unless it could be lived out in the world."

Life by the Spirit serves us well in the factory, behind the desk, in the school hallway, on the sports field, in the home, and everywhere! Why? It is the simple fact that life by the Spirit places God everywhere in life. How liberating!

I. Life by the Spirit Liberates Us to Love

Sinfulness, rebellion against God, perverts true love. It twists and turns love inward toward carnality. Self-centeredness overlooks the feelings, joys, and satisfactions of others as their importance dwindles to near zero levels.

A new attitude develops in a person when God enters the heart. Agape love implanted by the Holy Spirit binds the believer to God and to fellow Christians. There is generated a concern for others in material, physical, and spiritual realms.

Bishop William A. Quayle told of a woman sitting beside her sick husband. As she gazed at him lying in his bed, he asked in a feeble voice, "What are you doing?" She replied, "Just loving you."

Bishop Quayle told his audience that when God looks at us and asks, "What are you doing?" our answer should be, "Just loving you."

In these materialistic days, full of hustle and bustle, we must never forget the priceless value of cultivating the habit of loving God and others. It is not accomplished by just staring at him, but by doing something *for* him.

II. Life by the Spirit Liberates Us from Sin's Domination

Maxie Dunnam emphasizes that Paul was not concerned with human psychology, but the divine work of sanctification—the Spirit shaping and reshaping the individual into the kind of person who can overcome the desires of the flesh or carnal nature.

Sin misdirects physical desire in the area of sex. Sin misguides faith in the realm of religion. Sin violates love through society and the church. Sin accesses self through indulgences.

Outward sin results from the inner sin of carnality. Death to sin's grip comes through the Spirit's controlling force.

Paul wrote earlier in Galatians: "I have been crucified with Christ; it is no longer I who live, but Christ lives in me; and the life which I now live in the flesh I live by faith in the Son of God, who loved me and gave Himself for me" (Gal. 2:20 NKJV).

III. Life by the Spirit Liberates Us to Listen to the Spirit

Many years ago in England there lived the most famous elephant in the world. He was a gentle, loving animal until one day unexpectedly he turned absolutely wild. Nothing seemed to quiet the huge elephant. His owner concluded that Bozo must be killed. It was a difficult decision, not only because he loved him, but Bozo was the only elephant he had, and Bozo was imported from India.

The desperate owner struck upon an idea to sell tickets to Bozo's execution to recoup some of the money he was about to lose. The story spread, tickets sold, and the place jammed. Bozo was put in his cage with three men with high-powered rifles.

Just as the signal was about to be given to shoot, a small chunky man with a brown derby called out to stop the execution. The owner was furious and asked why the man had interrupted the show. The man explained that Bozo was not a bad elephant and asked to be let into the cage with him for two minutes. It was finally and reluctantly agreed upon, and a legal document absolving the owner of all damages if the man was hurt or killed was signed.

As the man entered the cage the elephant raised his head and was ready to charge. Before Bozo could charge, the man began talking to him, looking him straight in the eye. People up close could hear the man talking to the elephant in a strange language. As Bozo heard the words, he began to tremble, whine, and wave his head back and forth. The stranger walked up, patted the elephant, and was tenderly picked up by the mammoth beast. Everyone applauded.

The man diagnosed the problem as homesickness. The elephant was homesick to hear his native Indian language—one he could recognize. The stranger suggested to the owner that he find someone who could speak eastern Indian. If there was any trouble the owner was to let him know at the address he wrote down, along with his name—Rudyard Kipling.

God understands each of us—our hurts, frustrations, disappointments. He knows our language. He can turn defeat into victory, as we live close to the Spirit! (Derl G. Keefer)

FACING THE MUSIC

LUKE 9:51-62

Rabbi Bernard Raskas tells the story of a pious Jew who was having a dialogue with God. "Dear God," he asked, "in your infinite wisdom, what is a million years?" The voice from above replied, "In my infinite wisdom, a million years is like one minute."

The rabbi persisted, "Lord of the universe, in your infinite goodness, what is a million dollars?" The voice replied, "In my infinite goodness, a million dollars is like one penny."

"If that is true, O Mighty One," responded the man, "in your infinite generosity, could you grant me one of your pennies?" The voice from above answered, "Just a minute."

Everybody wants a shortcut in life. None of us wants to work hard for our money and earn it. We would like to have God, or someone else, give it to us.

A lot of people in life have trouble facing the music. They know what they should be doing, how they should behave, what their responsibilities are, but they just can't face the music. They just won't take responsibility for their own behavior and the consequences of it.

How can we "face the music" when the consequences may be difficult? Jesus faced the same problem, and our text makes it clear how he handled it.

I. He Recognized That Life Has a Purpose

Jesus knew his days were numbered (9:51). He had come from God—Jesus' presence on earth was part of God's plan—and would soon be going back to God. Hence, he was eager to "be about his Father's work." Jesus was here for a purpose.

Everything I just said about Jesus is not unique; it could be said about every life that God places on this earth. You have come from God for a purpose, and you are also returning to God. Your presence here is part of God's plan for this universe. It is God's plan to work his purpose through us every day that we are here.

II. He Recognized That Life Requires Commitment

Jesus "set his face" firmly (v. 51). The Bible makes it clear that Jesus was a person of commitment. He stood for the best in a world that accepted what was good enough to get by. He stood for excellence in a world that settled for the acceptable. He challenges us to reach our full potential in a world that wallows in compromise.

III. He Recognized That Life Has a Goal

"Jesus set his face to go to Jerusalem" (v. 51). "Facing the music" in life means accepting a goal, doing what God wills for us.

"Jerusalem" meant a painful, humiliating death. In this passage, it is a code word for the cross. Jesus knew that he must do with his life what God wanted, and if it meant the cross, so be it. Life is too short not to do with it what it was created for.

What is your Jerusalem? Is it a family burden? Is it children returning home after they have grown? Is it the slow, lingering illness of a loved one? Is it a cancer in your own body, ticking away? Is it worry over your young children, growing up in an immoral world?

Life does play some strange tunes that make it difficult for us to face the music. But face it we must, and with God's help, face it we can. (C. Thomas Hilton)

JULY 9, 1995

❧

Fifth Sunday After Pentecost

Worship Theme: We are called to encourage and support one another in Christ.

Readings: 2 Kings 5:1-14; Galatians 6:(1-6), 7-16; Luke 10:1-11, 16-20

Call to Worship (Psalm 30:4-5, 12*b*):

Leader: Sing praises to the LORD, O you his faithful ones, and give thanks to his holy name.

People: For his anger is but for a moment; his favor is for a lifetime.

Leader: Weeping may linger for the night, but joy comes with the morning. . . .

All: O LORD my God, I will give thanks to you forever.

Pastoral Prayer:

Our Father, who reaches out to us in the midst of our sin and rebellion and draws us into your love and forgiveness, we marvel at your transforming grace, which changes darkness to light, bitterness to compassion, stubbornness into obedience. Thank you for your persistent love, which would not let us go but drew our souls until they found peace and purpose in your presence.

Lord, may we become tools of your grace in the lives of others. As you have given love to us, help us to love others; as you have forgiven our sins, help us to forgive our brothers and sisters; as you have encouraged and sustained us in joys and sorrows, make us encouragers for those around us. Let others see your love in our actions, motivated by the One in whose name we pray. Amen. (Michael Duduit)

SERMON BRIEFS

THE SURPRISE OF OBEDIENCE

2 KINGS 5:1-14

When I was a boy, I wanted God to give me a miraculous, divine sign so that I could be certain about an important decision that I had to make. Of course, the sign never came, and eventually I got over it. Thinking back, I now realize that God did offer many signs of the divine presence. God still does. The problem is that I often looked in the wrong places. Perhaps I still do. I suppose that some things never change.

This passage offers two important insights about obedience to God.

1. Like the king of Israel, we often try to solve life's problems by ourselves. The king grieved for what he believed would be the loss of his kingdom. He mistakenly thought that it was personally up to him to heal Naaman. The king feared the possible consequences if this famous military leader did not receive the healing that he sought. Elisha hears of the king's worries and sends him the message that he can heal the commander. Elisha sees this as an opportunity to demonstrate the power of the God of Israel.

The king thought that he had to solve his dilemma by himself. The Hebrew Bible and the New Testament both demonstrate that God intends for us to work together in life. In Genesis 2 the partnership of Adam and Eve is established to overcome loneliness and isolation. In Exodus 18, Moses' wise father-in-law, Jethro, admonishes Moses for personally taking on too much responsibility. In Acts 4, the new Christian community pools its resources for the welfare of all.

Clearly the biblical narrative offers the message that life's burdens and bounty are meant to be shared. Different people have differing gifts for various tasks. We are obedient to God when we realize that we need one another and work to help each other. Elisha confidently sends for Naaman, realizing his opportunity at winning a convert from a pagan culture. So Naaman's entourage of horses, chariots, slaves, and gifts arrived at Elisha's door with great expectations. What Naaman received is not exactly what he expected.

2. Like Naaman, we often want God to respond to our needs in marvelous, miraculous ways. Sometimes God's response, like Elisha's to Naaman, simply calls us to *obey* and *follow.* We go looking for the power of God in dazzling displays of miracles. Our surprise is in discovering the power of faithful obedience to God.

Naaman had traveled a long and arduous journey with lavish gifts and a royal blessing just to be made well. The purpose of his quest, the restoration of his health, would be fulfilled if only he followed the simple instructions of one man. Naaman balked at the idea because it seemed absurdly simple.

We, too, can be stymied by the complexities of life so that we overlook the power of simple faith, humble obedience, and righteous living. God answered Naaman's desire through the prophet Elisha, who humbled himself and obeyed God.

Repeatedly, the biblical story reveals the power of obedience to God, who equips those whom God calls. We choose whether to respond to God's grace and mercy. When we listen and obey, we discover the miracle of God's presence through the lives of the people God sends our way. (Gary G. Kindley)

STRENGTHENING ONE ANOTHER

GALATIANS 6:(1-6), 7-16

Our word for "strength" stems from a word that means "twisted together." It is a comforting thought to realize that God strengthens or twists himself with humankind to help us bear life's load. His Spirit intertwines with our spirit and demands we strengthen others at their lowest times. Paul expressed that idea as he penned the text for today. Prison, chains, torture, inquisitions, and questioning played significantly upon Paul's mind. Thank God for a Barnabas, a Silas, and a Luke who strengthened him at his spirit's inner depth.

I. Supporting One Another Through a Fall

Moral failure robs a person of a relationship with God. Nothing hurts a pastor more than to know a parishioner has tumbled from grace. A temptation overtook them in their journey. A pastor listens to accusations flying rapidly through the air as one spouse spits out venom of disappointment at the other for an adulterous affair, or knows that the lies of another led to mistrust, or gossip has destroyed the reputation of another, and the result has devastated the individual.

How do we deal with a brother or sister overcome by sin? Paul answers the question: with gentleness. C. Norman Bartlett, in his book *Galatians: Freedom for Modern Man,* wrote, "[Gentleness] is spontaneous overflow of love in the heart. We need to cultivate resourcefulness in kindliness, to gain proficiency in the artistry of applying Christian love to the hearts and lives of those with whom we come in contact in the multitudinous activities and relationships in life."

If we correct someone, it must stem from the atmosphere of a healing, rather than a punishment. Who do you know needs a cure rather than an accusing finger today?

II. Supporting One Another Through a Difficulty

In some parts of the country in my denomination, people refer to friends as "Brother" or "Sister" instead of "Mr." or "Mrs." This implies a sense of fellowship, especially when going through a crisis.

Two brothers in Switzerland went out to join their father, having to cross a frozen lake. Their mother anxiously peered out the window, watching every move. After a few minutes, she could hear the cracking of ice and watched the ice move about a foot wide at the spot where the boys were walking. Her heart skipped a beat as she thought the oldest could make it over, but the youngest would try to make it and fall in. They were out of earshot to hear her call. As she watched in agonizing fear she saw the oldest get down on the ice, his feet on one side of the crack and his hands on the other, like a bridge, to let his little brother creep over him to the other side.

May we bridge some burdens, dangerous difficulties, and shaky grounds for our brothers and sisters who belong to the Father.

III. Supporting One Another Through Sharing

James Boice in *The Expositor's Bible Commentary* writes, "The reference points to a class of paid teachers at a surprisingly early date. . . . To support the Lord's servants is not, however, a grim duty, though some congregations seem to treat it as such. Instead, Paul speaks of it as sharing; it is a 'fellowship' or 'partnership.' As the teacher shows the good things of the word, so the congregation is to share all things with the teacher."

These servants of God need financial support, but they, like any other Christian, need spiritual support through prayer, encouragement, emotional support, smiles, and love. All are essential in true sharing.

A friend was with eighty-five-year-old Albert Schweitzer in his jungle hospital at Lambarene. As they walked in the equatorial sun that beat down mercilessly, Dr. Schweitzer suddenly left the group and crossed the slope of a hill to a place where an African woman was struggling upward with a huge load of wood for her cook fire. Dr. Schweitzer took the entire load and carried it up the hill. When he returned to the group, one in the party asked him why he did things that way, implying that at his age he should not. Schweitzer looked him in the eye, then pointed to that woman and simply said, "No one should ever have to carry a burden like that alone."

People in our congregations dare to carry sins, burdens, and need. We must come alongside to strengthen their lives with loving correction, encouragement, and support. (Derl G. Keefer)

HAPPY IN CHRIST'S SERVICE
LUKE 10:1-11, 16-20

What is the key to happiness in our service for Christ? As Christians we want to know whether what we're doing makes some measurable difference. Often, our own happiness is tied to the degree of the results we see in our work. Sometimes we try so hard, see little results, and experience burnout, discouragement, and weariness. Yet Christ shows us how to avoid burnout by being happy in his service.

I. Our Lord's Commission to All Christians

The first commission Christ gave to his church was to pray. Oswald Chambers said, "Prayer is not preparation for the work of

Christ; it is the work of Christ." And a missionary once stated, "You can do more for Christ after you've prayed, but you cannot do more for Christ until you have prayed."

Prayer is to the work of Christ what electricity is to a power outlet. Jesus said, "Without Me you can do nothing" (John 15:5 NKJV); the first step in realizing Christ's presence and power in our hearts and work is to pray.

The second commission Christ gave was this: Go. Announce the good news. Before *going* there is *praying*, but after praying, there must be going. The first leads to the latter. Not all of us are called to mission service, but all of us are called to *go*. Going may simply be remaining where you are—in your neighborhood, at your job, or at school. The goal is still that we are ambassadors for Christ (2 Cor. 5:20).

II. The Perils of Serving Christ

A fifteen-year-old girl was asked to participate in a class debate on the issue of sex before marriage. The girl related that her view was based on Scripture and that sex was only for marriage. Some of her peers rolled their eyes and even gave her piercing looks.

One of the most devastating disappointments in serving Christ is when we have been faithful but experience scorn, rejection, or indifference. Jesus warned the disciples that despite the fact that they were representing the Kingdom of God, not everyone would be interested or tolerant.

Similarly, another pitfall to serving Christ is to equate our worthiness with the results we see. But that attitude leads to discouragement—if we do not see results—or to pride—if we do.

III. The Key to Happiness in the Work of Christ

The seventy disciples experienced remarkable effectiveness, and full of happiness they told Jesus the good news. But what if they had not been as successful? It is not inevitable that every effort we make for Christ will be a great success; on the other hand, it is inevitable that Christ's Kingdom will finally triumph. Even our apparently unsuccessful attempts will work out to promote Christ's final Kingdom (Rom. 8:28).

If success is not what we should focus on to give us happiness, then what is? A survey was taken in New York City that involved business executives who changed jobs. It was discovered that these highly successful leaders who dropped out of their high-paying positions said they were not looking for mere financial success, but for meaning, purpose, and happiness.

The source of true happiness in Christ's service is not to buy into the principle of measurable results as the standard for success. Rather, the source of true happiness is to know that eternal life in Christ is ours. If we know that, then that perspective will carry us through the lean times. Our eternal reward is secure. That makes a difference in our happiness today. (E. Langston Haygood)

JULY 16, 1995

❧

Sixth Sunday After Pentecost

Worship Theme: God calls on us to love without limits, just as he loves us.

Readings: Amos 7:7-17; Colossians 1:1-14; Luke 10:25-37

Call to Worship (Psalm 82:2-4, 8):

Leader: "How long will you judge unjustly and show partiality to the wicked?

People: Give justice to the weak and the orphan; maintain the right of the lowly and the destitute.

Leader: Rescue the weak and the needy; deliver them from the hand of the wicked. . . ."

All: Rise up, O God, judge the earth; for all the nations belong to you!

Pastoral Prayer:

In this quiet moment of prayer, O Lord, we sincerely reach up to you. Help us to find that you are also reaching down to us. Remind us that we often deny ourselves your blessing by bringing all our plans and schemes to you and having the nerve to ask you to bless them. We know that some of the things we want and are tempted to do, you will never bless. Remind us that your aim is not to make life easier by giving everything we want. Your aim is to change us to make us different. So, Father, begin changing us now by shaping our desires so that you may truly bless us in all we pursue.

Forgive us that we so often give our best to the wrong things. At times, we are far more enthusiastic about the thought and effort required by our trivial pursuits than we are about our daily work, our worship, and our service in your kingdom. Help us to know what is important and what is unimportant, so that we will never forget the things that truly matter, and never allow the things that don't matter to matter too much. Through Jesus Christ our Lord, we pray. Amen. (Gary C. Redding)

SERMON BRIEFS

CONFRONTED BY GOD

AMOS 7:7-17

Prophetic passages of Scripture are often difficult to understand and, even worse, uncomfortable to apply. The prophets reveal more than history; they reveal something about ourselves and our human weaknesses. Today's passage from the prophet Amos is no exception.

Writing at a time in Israel's history when Israel was prosperous and the people too comfortable, Amos denounced the obsession with military strength and the false piety of the people. Today's text reveals Amos's strong words of denouncement, his banishment from the king's sanctuary by Jeroboam's priest, and Amos's warning of the consequences for failing to heed God's warning.

Consider these important ideas from this urgent prophecy:

1. *God's "plumb line" helps us to see how far we have strayed.* Every person, every community, every society, every nation needs some moral standard by which to gauge human behavior. Left to our own devices, human sinfulness would destroy us all. Through the voice of the prophet, we are given the opportunity to reflect upon our life, our behavior, and our morality.

Amos, speaking for the Lord, confronted the immorality, injustice, self-righteousness, and arrogance of the people of Israel. In this confrontation, we can see ourselves and our society. The warning has a frighteningly familiar sound. The marvel of good prophetic literature is how contemporary the ancient text sounds in describing our present societal problems.

The divine warning carries even greater weight for us today. We know how Amos's prophecy for Israel came to be. We know about the exile, the destruction of the cities, and the scattering of the people. Our knowledge of history makes this text all the more urgent for our consideration.

2. *The Word of the Lord cannot be squelched by any earthly authority.* Amos is censured by Amaziah, the priest of Bethel, where King Jeroboam worships. Accused of treason against the king and Israel, Amos is banished from the royal sanctuary and sent to Judah.

Undaunted, Amos responded forcefully to Amaziah's criticism. Amos reminded the priest that God called Amos from the shepherd's field. Amos was no professional prophet. He had no salary or pulpit to protect, no budget to be concerned over, no building fund to oversee. His call was simply to preach the Word of the Lord.

He predicted the continued moral decay of the people, even the destruction of the priest's own family, and Amaziah's death in "an unclean land" (v. 17). There the confrontation ends. We can only assume what happened to Amos. His message survives because it is an urgent message of God.

3. *If the church fails to be obedient by proclaiming God's Word, God will use others as channels of the message.* Amos reminded Amaziah that he was not a professional prophet. Amos came from outside the established religious community. He was not of the priestly order, but he listened to God and was willing to proclaim the divine Word. He left behind his flocks to take on the task of shepherding a defiant Israel.

It might be easy for the church to dismiss such prophecy as pertinent only to the time in which it was written. It *might* be easy, were it not for the prophecy's haunting relevance to our time. It might be easy for the church to dismiss contemporary prophets who "rock the boat" and shake us from our complacency. Instead, we would be wise to listen intently and to test their words for the divine message. The prophetic task is not in vain if it causes us to consider where we are headed as individuals, as a church, and as a human family. (Gary G. Kindley)

THE PEOPLE OF GOD

COLOSSIANS 1:1-14

Paul's purpose in writing Colossians grew out of his personal interest in the people, to warn them against reverting to their old pattern of heathenism and to refute false teaching that was threatening the church. As A. T. Robertson says, it is Paul's "full length portrait of Christ."

We who claim Christ must "lead lives worthy of the Lord" (Col. 1:10). The truth of this verse for first-century Christians holds true for twentieth-century Christians as well!

I. The Christian's Camaraderie

The camaraderie includes service. William Barclay relates a story of E. F. Brown of the Oxford Mission in Calcutta, India. Barclay says that Brown was every man's friend, "but he was specifically the friend of the hackney carriage drivers, the carters, the tram conductors, the menial servants, and the hundreds of street boys. . . . It was his brotherliness which brought men to his Master."

The camaraderie includes fellowship. If we live as Christians, it cannot be with a style of snobbishness,but, rather, as one who associates with all sorts of people. Barclay wrote, "As Paul grew older he came more and more to see that what matters is individual people. The church is people. The church is not a kind of vague abstract entity; it is individual men and women and children and as the years went on Paul began to think less and less of the church as a whole, and more and more of the church as individual men and women."

Do we see people through dollar signs in our eyes, responsibilities to carry, teachers to conduct classes, programs to promote? Do we know the names of those who worship with us? We must become familiar with individual men and women who are brothers and sisters in Christ.

II. The Christian's Thankfulness

Someone once told of a sick and elderly woman who lived in abject poverty. She was asked for what she had to be thankful. Looking at the shabby walls in her room she replied, "For the sunshine through the cracks." Somehow God's love sifts in through the open cracks of our lives.

What do we have to be thankful for as Christians? God's love (v. 3), Jesus as Lord (v. 3), reliance on him (v. 4), hope (v. 5), the gospel (v. 5), and faithfulness (v. 7). How wonderful and glorious is the God of the Christian!

III. The Christian's Prayer

Paul begins this section sharing his prayer of intercession for the people of Colossae. Sensitivity to God's will forms his first agenda item in his prayer of intercession.

God has a plan for the universe and for our lives. Maxie Dunnam wrote, "Discerning God's will is our task, and it is not easy. It is surrender of our identity as human beings and a blasphemy against God to give in to the pain, hopelessness, and helplessness we feel, the gnawing doubts that haunt us by passing through our struggles, conflict, pain, disillusionment, and despair with the superficial affirmation, 'It's God's will.' "

Then Dunnam adds a powerful thought, "The will of God is often enshrouded in darkness, clouded in ambiguity; silence as well as speaking marks His communication with us. In prayer we struggle to discern God's will. We talk. We listen. We ponder scripture. We reflect. We wait, and graciously the response comes. Not according to our timetable . . . but in God's timing and in His way."

Are we attempting to discern God's will today?

Paul's second agenda item of prayer petition demands the Colossian Christians (all Christians) to walk worthy of Christ. That means that holiness unto the Lord becomes both our watchword and song.

His third item on the prayer petition agenda is for us to be equipped by God (v. 11). The Christian is equipped with prayer. H. Dermot McDonald states: "The participle translated, 'May you be strengthened' is present tense, thus denoting the empowering is continuous."

What will happen to Christians who are equipped with awesome power? They will be fortified against evil, sin, Satan, and hell, and fitted for service.

We are equipped with *endurance*, able to carry out as Christians to the end of life. We are equipped with *patience*, holding on for life, not giving up. We are equipped with *joy*, the inner satisfaction that knows God.

When was the last time you prayed for others and yourself using Paul's prayer model? (Derl G. Keefer)

CLENCHED FISTS OR OPEN ARMS?

LUKE 10:25-37

It is a common practice for a pastor to escort a needy person to our church's Thrift Shop when he or she is in need of clothes. Recently, I was asked how long it takes to talk with the person, escort him or her across the street, wait until the person finds what is needed, and escort him out of the Thrift Shop. Having answered that it takes as much as twenty minutes for the whole process, the person with whom I spoke expressed concern for the routine "taking me away from better things" I had to do. I thought nothing of it until later, when I had to ask myself, "What better things?"

I think you and I need to reread with great care this parable which Jesus shared with the lawyer, who asks the question "What shall I do to inherit eternal life?" The dialogue leads to the question "Who is my neighbor?" Jesus answered him with this parable.

Jesus returned the lawyer's question in a different form: not who *was* the neighbor, but who *acted* as a neighbor to this unfortunate victim? The question cannot be "Who is worthy of my love?" because to ask that is to place limitations on love. It is like going through life with one's fists clenched, unwilling to be open to opportunities and new possibilities.

A farmer, sitting on the steps of his home, was approached by a stranger in search of a drink of water. "How's your wheat coming along?" asked the stranger. "Didn't plant none," said the farmer.

"Really?" the stranger returned. "I thought this was good wheat country." The farmer said, "Afraid it wouldn't rain."

"Oh, well, how's your corn crop?" "Ain't got none. Afraid of corn blight."

"Well, how about potatoes?" "Didn't plant any. Potato bugs would probably take 'em."

"Didn't you plant anything?" asked the stranger.

"Nope," the farmer replied. "I like to play it safe."

If we go through life playing it safe all the time, we have no hope of inheriting eternal life. If we are to inherit this eternal life, we must practice the art of *being the church.* And we cannot be the church if we go through life clenching our fists, refusing to help the hungry and the homeless.

Albert Schweitzer was once asked to name the greatest person in the world. The good doctor replied, "The greatest person in the world is some unknown individual in some obscure corner of the earth who at this very hour has gone in love to be with another person in need."

To inherit eternal life, to live in the eternal glory of God's forgiving and mysterious love for us, we must first say to others, "Here is a place where love is," and we must begin making this love felt here and now.

What better things? There is nothing better than to meet life with open, outstretched arms to hold and comfort, arms that reach out in love, arms that open one to giving and receiving. (Eric Killinger)

JULY 23, 1995

❧

Seventh Sunday After Pentecost

Worship Theme: Doing good things must not be allowed to get in the way of the most important thing: spending time with Jesus.

Readings: Amos 8:1-12; Colossians 1:15-28; Luke 10:38-42

Call to Worship (Psalm 52:8b-9):
I trust in the steadfast love of God
    forever and ever.
I will thank you forever,
    because of what you have done.
In the presence of the faithful
    I will proclaim your name, for it is good.

Pastoral Prayer:
    You have acted, O God, for us and for our salvation through Jesus. Through worship we respond to your grace, your free and unmerited invitation to eternal life and confident living through Jesus Christ. In worship, we praise you as Sovereign and thank you as Savior. Yet we confess that there are times we have excused ourselves from worship, pretending there are more important things to do. And when we forget you, O God, when we withhold the worship you deserve we cheat ourselves of the holy communion with you, which ensures personal peace and joy and eternal security. Father, forgive us for forgetting you. By the persuasion of your Spirit, help us to make worshiping you the first priority of our lives, to the glory of Jesus in whose name we pray. Amen. (Robert R. Kopp)

SERMON BRIEFS

BEYOND UTILITY

AMOS 8:1-12

    I don't suppose there is a pastor today who hasn't heard someone say, "Well, preacher, I'd like to come to church, but I'm too busy. You know how it is. I have to put bread on the table. So don't look for me at church. I have to work, but I'll be there in spirit."

I. Rotting Fruit Leaves Little to Desire

Amos's basket of summer fruit is an interesting image. We all know the way of fruit. For a few days, it looks appealing, but after sitting out in the summer heat, it decays quickly. Evidently, this is how Israel looked to Yahweh. Perhaps, Israel had looked winsome to Yahweh, but now in questionable faith, their outward appearance is depreciating. The words are devastating:

> "The songs of the temple shall
>   become wailings in that day,"
>   says the Lord GOD;
> "the dead bodies shall be many,
>   cast out in every place. Be silent!" (v. 3)

II. Yahweh's First Complaint

Yahweh's displeasure is twofold. First, those for whom the nation of Israel should be looking out—the needy and poor—are actually ones who are trampled by those wanting to feather their nests and line their pockets. There had commonly been a concern for the poor, the widow, the orphan, and the sojourner in Israel. When the people of Israel were instructed in how to harvest a grain field, they were told to leave a fringe around the field's borders, so the needy would have something to eat. Obviously, Israel's faith tradition was being ignored by those who "practice deceit with false balances, / buying the poor for silver/ and the needy for a pair of sandals, / and selling the sweepings of the wheat."

III. Yahweh's Second Complaint

Yahweh's second complaint was that there seemed to be those for whom the Sabbath was an inconvenience for doing business. They were so busy buying and selling that the Sabbath had become an annoyance. Originally, Sabbath had a double intention. First, it was to be a day celebrating creation and ceasing normal endeavors—a day set off from other days, relishing the goodness of God's created order.

Second of all, Sabbath was a day of rest. People could attend religious observances as well as use Sabbath as a day of recreation. Obviously, the line of demarcation between both intentions of Sabbath converge. Yahweh's complaint is against those who see Sabbath as an impediment to more important pursuits—essentially the making of money.

IV. What Is Coming

In Amos's prophecy is the warning that difficult days are coming for Israel. When people lose touch with the things that give life meaning and purpose, then what good are the material things gained? These material things thus assume the status of idols. Jesus suggested something like this, saying, "What does it profit them if they gain the whole world, but lose or forfeit themselves?" (Luke 9:25). Good question!

Worship, for many people today as in Amos's time, does not seem to fulfill our idol of utility. Often we hear folks say that they don't get anything out of worship and, therefore, conclude it is a waste of time. If the truth were acknowledged, people were created for much more than simply "making hay while the sun shines." We were created for relationship with God and each other. There exists no more noble pursuit.

Those truly in touch with themselves and God know that the worship gathering, confession, hearing the reiteration of God's promises, and the recovenanting to be servants of the living God are so important that life is not the same without them. All of us need moments of reflection and praise afforded us in weekly—and daily—worship of God. Our friends who say, "I have to work, but I'll be there in spirit," never know much of the life they missed. The task of prophetic people is to remind them that "people do not live by bread alone, but by every word that comes from the mouth of God." This is negatively what Amos says: "They shall run to and fro, seeking the word of the Lord, but they shall not find it." (David Neil Mosser)

TO TELL THE TRUTH

COLOSSIANS 1:15-28

When I was growing up, one of my favorite shows on television was "To Tell the Truth." The game was played with a four-member celebrity panel and three contestants. The panel's goal was to find which one of the contestants was telling the truth. One by one, the panel asked the contestants questions. Two of the contestants would lie in an attempt to fool the panel. One contestant, and only one, was telling the truth.

The game began with the contestants introducing themselves. Then Gary Moore, the host, would say something like, "Each of these contestants is claiming to be John Doe, a certified parachuting instructor. Panel, start the questioning." The panel posed questions that a parachuting instructor probably could answer. Based on the perceived veracity of the answers given by the contestants, the panel had to decide which one of the three was telling the truth and who were the two impostors. Often the impostors were so clever with their answers that the panel had to rely on other clues to determine the truth teller—for example, which one of the contestants *looked like* a parachuting instructor. After the questioning ended, Gary Moore would say, "Will the real parachuting instructor please stand up." The panel was often totally stumped—the most unlikely looking of the three turned out to be the instructor. The panel's preconceived ideas swayed their judgment.

People often misunderstand the nature of God, what God is like, how God works in the world. In his book *Your God Is Too Small,* J. B. Phillips decries the inadequacy of many modern images of God, images created by our presuppositions about how God is supposed to work and relate to the world. Phillips lists some of the images as "God as grand old man" and "the God in a box." He urges Christians to realize that God is so much bigger than any image our finite minds can conjure. We limit God by limiting him to our preconceived notions.

In today's Scripture lesson, Paul presents a christologic hymn to describe the nature of Jesus Christ—what Christ is like, how Christ relates to the world. To begin with, Jesus Christ is the image of the invisible God. When we want to know what God is like, how God works, how God relates to the world, we should look to Jesus Christ.

Paul provides the Colossians with a picture of salvation not as an escape from the world, but as a process of redeeming the world. We are saved in the world to transform the world, because in Christ all things in heaven and on earth were created. Christ is the firstborn of creation; his work of salvation is to redeem not only individuals, but the entire created order. He is God's reconciling agent in the world. He is also the head of the church. And in him, God dwelled and reconciled all things to himself through Christ's death on the cross.

Paul wanted to make sure that the Colossians had a crystal-clear image of Christ and how Christ related to the world. We modern Christians must be careful about the image we paint of Christ. In a world in which religions are often shaped into the image of the beholders, we strive to proclaim a clear biblical image of Jesus Christ.

What picture comes to mind when you think of Jesus Christ? What image do you conjure? Will the real Jesus please stand up! (Craig A. Loscalzo)

THE BEST PART OF LIFE

LUKE 10:38-42

A group of soldiers was released from prison camp at the end of World War II. Because transportation was limited and bad weather threatened to cut off the port, the remaining soldiers who were to board the last boat were told they could bring only one piece of luggage. Two soldiers had been together throughout the war and had looked out for each other. When one was selected to go and the other was forced to stay behind and wait for a later boat, the first man turned over his duffel bag, spilling out all his personal possessions onto the ground, then told his friend to step into the bag. He then strenuously lifted the bag onto his back and carried his most important item of luggage onto the ship. There are certain moments in our lives that reveal where our true priorities lie. For the believer, what is most important in life is time spent alone with God.

I. Our Lives Have Many Distractions

This text is found here out of chronological order. The reason Luke put it here after the seventy were sent out and the parable of the good Samaritan is to show that doing things for God is not all that is important. We find two characters in our story who are sisters, Martha and Mary. They lived in Bethany, about two miles outside Jerusalem, and it was to their house that Jesus came. Martha was very busy working to serve Jesus in whatever way she could. Mary, on the other hand, seated at Jesus' feet, listened to his every word. Martha was bothered by this situation, and she asked the Lord to tell Mary to help her.

Many times we can be busy doing good things that are really distracting us from what is most important. Responsibilities of work, family, and church can get in the way of the best part of the Christian life. It is a strange irony that we can be pulled away from the Lord while we are ministering in his name.

II. Our Lives Must Have One Attraction

Jesus responded to what Martha said and repeated her name twice for emphasis. She was worried and bothered about so many things, when only one thing is really important. What is necessary is called by Jesus the good part. Sitting at the feet of Jesus, talking to him, listening to him, worshiping him—that is the good part, the best part of life. This intimacy with Christ is always available to the believer if he or she will make it a priority.

One night a father was going by his little boy's bedroom when he saw the boy kneeling beside his bed, head bowed, repeating the alphabet. "What are you doing?" the dad asked. The son said, "I'm saying my prayers, but I couldn't think of just what I wanted to say. So I'm just saying all the letters, and God can put them together however he thinks best." God wants us to come to him and not worry about what to say, just spend time with him.

The Christian needs to value intimacy with God as a primary goal of life. This requires setting aside time to pursue knowing God above all else. (Rick McDaniel)

JULY 30, 1995

❧

Eighth Sunday After Pentecost

Worship Theme: True joy is found as we live our lives "in Christ."

Readings: Hosea 1:2-10; Colossians 2:6-15, (16-19); Luke 11:1-13

Call to Worship (Psalm 85:7, 9):

Leader: Show us your steadfast love, O LORD,

People: and grant us your salvation. . . .

Leader: Surely his salvation is at hand for those who fear him,

All: that his glory may dwell in our land.

Pastoral Prayer:

Eternal God, is it possible we live on just one of hundreds of millions of planets? We scan the night sky and see there the evidence of your majesty and glory. What an incredible and wondrous creation! Help us to see that our rightful place in that creation is to be one of your faithful peoples. In the infinite mercy and plan you have for our world, we are placed side by side with many other races and nations. Help us always to be loving and accepting of those peoples as we put aside our disagreements and prejudices.

Lord God, we pray for our church—such a tiny place in the midst of a great universe. Use it to draw men and women, boys and girls, young and old to faith in you. And in that wonderful day of the future when you come again to claim your creation in person, may you claim us as well. For we believe that nothing can separate us from the love of God, through faith in his Son, Jesus Christ. Amen.

(Steven R. Fleming)

SERMON BRIEFS

WHAT'S IN A NAME?

HOSEA 1:2-10

About a month ago, I held a funeral for a man who had a penchant for giving nicknames to people he deemed worthy of his friendship. He was an unusual man, but a decent one. Those who were closest to him could measure the depth of their relationship by hearing themselves called by a "term of endearment." People often give nicknames to others or objects they value. At our house, naming a family dog is taken with utmost seriousness.

I. What's in a Name?

In our text today, the method of reversal is at work. Generally, a time of naming a child is one of rejoicing and jubilation. In Hosea 1:2-10, however, it is a time announcing Yahweh's judgment against Israel. The prophet is told: "Go, take for yourself a wife of whoredom and have children of whoredom, for the land commits great whoredom by forsaking the LORD" (v. 2). Undoubtedly, when Hosea assumed the prophetic mantle, this was not anticipated in the job description.

II. Baby Boy: Jezreel

If we look at the children's names, we can see the content of the prophecy Hosea delivered to Israel. The first son was to be named Jezreel, which means "God sows or plants." Jezreel had been the location of several bloody incidents in the history of Israel; the kings of both Israel and Judah had been killed there by Jehu. It was also in Jezreel that "when the letter reached them, they took the king's sons and killed them, seventy persons; they put their heads in baskets and sent them to him at Jezreel" (2 Kings 10:7). Thus for a child to receive this name was indeed a foreboding message to Israel in the extreme.

III. Baby Girl: Lo-ruhamah

The second child, a daughter, was to be named Lo-ruhamah, meaning "no mercy" or "no pity." For Israel, this symbolized the reversal of God's abiding mercy, which had been with them from ancestral days. This certainly was received as an ominous word from the Lord. To live without Yahweh's mercy would have been almost unthinkable, for the Lord had delivered Israel from their enemies again and again.

IV. Baby Boy: Lo-ammi

The third child was a boy, receiving the prophetic name Lo-ammi, which means "not my people." Israel saw this as a final straw, so to speak, for God had cut himself off from the people. They will not be saved, they will have no divine mercy, and they are not the chosen people anymore—all because of their waywardness toward Yahweh.

V. Naming as Gift and Obligation

When one gives or receives a name, certain implications are inherent in this relationship. A parent has absolute responsibility for a child: food, shelter, education, and nurture. Yahweh's reneging on such implicit relationships indicates the Lord's loss of patience with the people. When God, in the garden of perfection, named the man and the woman, it was a covenant-sign in paradise. Yet, time and time again, Yahweh called the people back, while the people failed to respond. God's discipline, seen in this prophecy, is to show no mercy and cut off the relationship with the people, which had been an essential element in the religious lives of the people for centuries.

The question before us is this: Do we appear to be faithful people before the Lord, or do our religious observances call for a desire on the part of our God to cut the cords of the divine-human relationship today? Perhaps it is not a question we often entertain. Then again, was it a question that Israel took seriously enough? (David Neil Mosser)

CLAIM YOUR NAME

COLOSSIANS 2:6-15, (16-19)

A man was visiting a city on a business trip. One evening, while walking to a restaurant, he passed by a shop that had a sign in the window. The sign reminded him of an errand he needed to run. It said "Chinese Laundry." The next morning, he gathered up his soiled laundry, and on his way to a meeting in town, he stopped by the shop. He walked in and placed his laundry on the counter. The clerk behind the counter said, "May I help you?" The man said, "Yes, I'd like to drop off my laundry. Light starch in the shirts. Can I have them back by five this afternoon?" The shop-keeper looked a bit puzzled and queried, "Pardon me? What exactly do you want me to do?" A bit flustered, the customer repeated his request, only this time more abruptly: "I just want my shirts laundered and these slacks cleaned and pressed. I'll pick them up this afternoon." The puzzled look on the clerk's face bristled the customer even more: "Look," he said, "I saw your sign in the window. It says 'Chinese Laundry.' Can you please do my laundry?" At which point, a wave of understanding came over the clerk. "Oh," he said, "but you don't understand. This isn't a Chinese laundry. It's a *sign* shop!"

Signs can often be misleading. Names don't always describe the real essence of persons or things. What message does it communicate to those around us when we call ourselves *Christians?* Do they look at us and see compassion and understanding? Do they see a community that really loves one another? Do they see in us the characteristics of the One whose name we carry? Do they look at us and see Christ? What do they think when they read the "sign" that says "I am a Christian"?

Paul encouraged the Colossians to *live* up to their name. "As you therefore have received Christ Jesus the Lord," Paul says, "continue to live your lives in him" (v. 6). The apostle unfolded the picture by telling the Colossians to remember that they are planted firmly in Christ. Christ is the foundation of their faith. Their lives should reflect their Lord.

Having said this, he charged them not to become captive to the vain philosophies and teachings of their culture. They were to remain rooted in Christ because he is not just another good teacher or philosopher. Christ is God dwelling in human form. And they, through their baptism, had identified themselves with God, who raised Christ from the dead. God forgave their sins by nailing them to the cross. Paul implied that these facts should motivate a behavior, an ethic of living up to their name!

In our modern culture, people often misunderstand when they hear us call ourselves "Christians." In Ireland, Catholics and Protestants, both claiming the name "Christian," have murdered each other for years. In Bosnia, atrocities have been committed by those claiming the name "Christian." In 1993, in Waco, Texas, a cult leader and many of his followers, claiming to be "Christian," died a fiery death. Crosses are still burned as a sign of warning and threat to certain groups of people. These examples are tragic instances of abusing the name of Christ.

Paul's encouragement to the Colossians is a word the modern church needs to hear. Because we have received Christ, we must live our lives in him. Our actions speak louder than our words. Our practices are seen more than our beliefs are understood. It's time to claim our name! (Craig A. Loscalzo)

SERPENT FOR A FISH

LUKE 11:1-13

Some things just never go away. Sometimes you see something, and you can never forget it. It doesn't always have to be dramatic, important, or emotional. One of those documentary-type programs on TV featured the problem of the persistent lover. The problem was that the person being loved did not want to be loved by the lover. The feature explored the problems of having a lover who would not take no for an answer. The suitor was relentless. Phone calls and notes, flowers and cards, candy and gifts. They came all the time. The suitor created problems for the person at home, within the family life, in the desire to develop relationships with other people. The one being pursued had told the suitor no in every way possible. The person had tried changing the phone number, changing jobs, moving to another state, even a court order to prohibit contact, but still the suitor came on. How do you stop such behavior?

Most of the attention and most of the concern from this kind

263

of situation is the problem of the one being pursued. Talk about struggle between freedoms and rights to privacy! Don't we have a right to prevent people from bothering us all the time? The one being harassed has our allegiance. We want to help her or him find a way to get free from the persistent lover.

And yet my first thoughts and my loyalties and sympathies go to the one who is knocking at the door in the parable Jesus tells about a man going to his neighbor's house at midnight in order to get bread for unexpected company. Reading this story, I find myself on the side of the one who is persistent, who bangs on the door of the neighbor's house until everybody is awake; the neighbor might as well get up and give the man what he wants, because all the possible damage has been done—the dog is awake, the children are crying, and nobody can get any rest now.

This is a parable about prayer, and while I am troubled about a persistent lover tormenting one who does not want that love, I am troubled more in this story by the notion that God might not want to respond to my every request. God is the neighbor who wishes I would go away so that he and his family might go back to sleep. And only by my persistence will I be able to get what I need.

But as I reflect on this story I am driven to the realization that this story is precisely all about persistence. On the one hand, the biblical story tells of God as the persistent lover, always coming to us, always seeking us out, always calling men and women into relationship with him, "Jerusalem, Jerusalem. . . . How often have I desired to gather your children together as a hen gathers her brood under her wings, and you were not willing!" (Matt. 23:37). Jesus came to seek and to save the lost. God was in Christ reconciling the world to himself. The Light of the world came into the world, and the world received it not. The biblical story is the story of God as the persistent lover who is not accepted by the pursued.

And on the other side, the biblical story affirms that what God wants and desires from us is that we might seek his love and will with that same kind of persistence. "Strive first for the kingdom of God and his righteousness, and all these things will be given to you as well" (Matt. 6:33) "You shall love the Lord your God with all your heart, and with all your soul, and with all your mind. . . . You shall love your neighbor as yourself" (Matt. 22:37, 39). The parable does suggest that prayer, our conversation with God, is much like a conversation between a parent and a child, with the parent not wanting to get up from the chair, but the child wanting to go for a walk. The parent resists, and it is only by persistence that the child wins. Our children carry on so because they know that by single-minded devotion to what they want they have a much better chance of getting what they want. No, God is not going to answer and give us every little thing we happen to mention in prayer that we would like to have. God does not receive just any old little petition we happen to toss off like a wish list or a quick little prayer that we find a parking place. What the parable suggests is that by our persistence we reveal what is at the very heart of our lives. By our persistence, we reveal where our treasures are.

By his persistence, the man at night demonstrated that he knew that his commitment to his sudden visitor at midnight was crucial to standing in the community of people around him. He had as a member of that society a sacred duty to feed his sudden guest, and he would not be prevented from fulfilling that obligation. Prayer is our conversation with God, and what we will find being given to us is what we keep coming back to time and time again—that which is at the very heart and center of our lives. We may pray for a job for a couple of months, but what has been the nature of your prayer to God since you were a child?

Jesus seems to suggest that it is through our persistence that we reveal what is our heart's greatest desire and need, and even as we would not give to our children a snake when they needed a fish, God will not fail us where his persistent coming, seeking us, and our persistent asking, seeking, knocking, and banging, meet in the common desire for his Kingdom to come on earth, even as it is in heaven. (Rick Brand)

AUGUST

ᕉ

Replenishing the Well

God Comes Unexpectedly

Expect God to come unexpectedly. Our Lord is a mysterious visitor. As this month's Bible reading tells us, the Son of Man comes to us like a thief in the night. The following exercise, called a guided imagery, helps us to learn how prepared we are to meet God.

Time: 60 minutes.

Materials: A Bible, your journal, a pen or pencil.

Exercise:
Carefully read Luke 12:32-40. Now read it again and let the images sink into your imagination. Before beginning the next part of this exercise, read it thoroughly.

Sit in a comfortable position and close your eyes. Imagine you are at home. It is 2:00 in the morning and you are watching the late, late movie. The house is very quiet. Suddenly, you hear footsteps coming toward your front door. There is an imperious knock on the door. Frightened, you cautiously open the door.

A man stands before you, impeccably dressed in expensive evening clothes, a blood-red rose fixed in his boutonniere, an exquisite white silk opera scarf hanging casually around his neck. You look at his face. You gasp for air. You recognize this elegant man as Jesus and fall down on your knees. "How, out of the treasure in your heart, are you prepared to serve me?" he demands.

Now open your eyes slowly and open your journal. Write Jesus' question, "How, out of the treasure of your heart, are you prepared to serve me?" across the top of the page. Answer his question in your journal. Answers may include something like, "I am prepared to serve you by adhering to my ordination vows"; "I am prepared to serve you working with the homeless shelter in my neighborhood"; "I am prepared to serve you in meditation and prayer."

Once you have finished answering the question completely, close in prayer, asking God to bless your service and keep you ever watchful for the Christ. (Harriet Crosby)

AUGUST 6, 1995

❧

Ninth Sunday After Pentecost

Worship Theme: The wise person recognizes God's rightful place at the center of our lives.

Readings: Hosea 11:1-11; Colossians 3:1-11; Luke 12:13-21

Call to Worship (Psalm 107:1):

Leader: O give thanks to the LORD, for he is good;

People: for his steadfast love endures forever.

Pastoral Prayer:

Almighty and ever blessed God, you are waiting patiently to set your seal upon the hearts of those who love you. With songs of praise on our lips and eager expectations in our hearts, we turn our steps toward the place where your truth and honor dwell. We thank you today for open doors: for the open door of the sanctuary, through which we may enter and learn the true meaning of life; for the open door of confession, where we face up to our humanness and through which we can feel the reach of a hand that lifts us up; for the open door that music provides by which our worship is hallowed and our inner feelings are moved to express themselves in hymns of joy; for the open door of ministry by which your Word is declared. As we pass through the open door of worship into your presence, brighten the journey ahead with the vision of a better life for us and through us for others. May the radiance of victory in your face cause us never to be afraid. This we ask for the sake of Jesus Christ our Lord. Amen. (Robert R. Kopp)

SERMON BRIEFS

THE TRIALS OF YAHWEH'S PARENTING

HOSEA 11:1-11

As a campus minister, I remember hearing many students speak of their parents in different ways, depending on their age.

First-year students spoke of the freedom from their parent's rules and regulations, never mentioning the support money. Older students had learned to appreciate the trials their parents endured as adults. Hosea employed this parent-child image to describe the relationship between Yahweh and the people of Israel.

I. Out of Bondage

Hosea began his prophecy by addressing what Yahweh has done for the child Israel. There is a prominent contrast in the relationship, as one expects between a parent and a child. On the one side, Yahweh, as a parent, has been active: "I loved, I called, I taught, I took them up in my arms, I healed, and I led them." Doubtless, Yahweh takes the initiative, being a good parent. Yahweh has "bent down to them and fed them." No child could want more of a parent—every required need of a child, so it seems, has been attended to. But Israel has shown immaturity, being ungrateful, as children often are.

II. Into Bondage

Yahweh again speaks through Hosea's words. The people are to be returned to bondage. Using the symbols of Egypt and Assyria, Hosea declared that Israel's ingratitude would be manifested in a return to slavery. When the desperate situation made itself clear, the Lord would not rescue the people, for this was their choice.

III. Does God Change God's Mind?

Suddenly, the text displays divine anguish. Yahweh asks a series of rhetorical questions, calling into question the wisdom of God's judgments. Every parent knows this anguish. Several months ago, I disciplined my son by sending him up to his room. He had been performing dangerous tricks on his bicycle, to the amusement of the neighborhood children. I was upset because we live on a dangerous and busy street and he placed himself at critical risk.

Thirty minutes passed, and it was so quiet upstairs, I became suspicious. When I got to his room, I discovered he had slipped out the window and was standing on the roof of our house, twenty-five feet off the ground. In his punishment, he was doing something even more dangerous than the activity for which he was being punished in the first place. No punishment seemed to show itself to fit the new crime, so instead, I gave him a big hug. We had a long talk about what could happen if he were hit by a car or if he fell off the roof. Parents know the anguish of helping children understand the reasons for our demands—we love them.

IV. For the Love of God

Yahweh, this text says, is the ultimate optimist. In spite of contrary human evidence, Yahweh continues to hope for these people Israel, who often act like small children. This is the God we worship, One who never tires of chasing us and pursuing us. This God keeps coming for us, even when we reject our divine parent and run from the Holy.

Perhaps this, too, is Paul's message to the church: "If God is for us, who is against us? He who did not withhold his own Son, but gave him up for all of us, will he not with him also give us everything else? . . . Who will separate us from the love of Christ? Will hardship, or distress, or persecution, or famine, or nakedness, or peril, or sword?" (Rom. 8:31-35). *No!*

God loves God's people so much that they will never be abandoned, no matter how shamefully they treat the divine parent. This is the nature of love—as every parent worth the name knows. (David Neil Mosser)

A VIEW FROM ABOVE

COLOSSIANS 3:1-11

I remember listening to an old farmer joke about church people. He quipped: "Some people are so heavenly minded that they're no earthly good." In last week's lesson (Col. 2:6-15), Paul urged the Colossians to live up to their name. It was not enough for them merely to have mental assent of their faith; their faith should be put into practice. They should live up to their name. They should not be so heavenly minded that they're no earthly good.

In today's lesson, it almost sounds as though Paul is contradicting himself. Here he urges the Colossians to seek the things that are above, to set their minds on things that are above, not on things that are on the earth. It sounds as though Paul has taken the farmer's adage and flipped it around: "Some people are so *earthly* minded that they're no *heavenly* good."

Many modern Christians avoid talking about heaven, about the things that are above. Our contemporary society has little room for such transcendent things, and that sentiment has filtered into the church. Our culture is a "see it to believe it" society. We want the tangible. Let me hold it. Let me measure it. Let me examine it. Transcendence cannot be examined under the microscope. That makes us uneasy.

Yet, the church and our culture need the transcendent. We need to be able to speak of things that are above. It is there that we talk about hope that transcends material possessions, joy that moves beyond shallow happiness, faith that enables us to claim what we cannot see, and grace that loves us unconditionally. How can we voice eternal hope when our eyes fail to look up? We have become so earthly minded that we're no heavenly good.

Now, Paul is not speaking of a Pollyanna, escapist theology here. He still has an ethical motive in mind. He presumes a behavior based on a belief. When Christians seek the things that are above, they are able to transcend the things that are below. Paul exhorts the Colossians to get rid of the life-styles that they once followed with zeal. Their old ways are no longer appropriate. He provides a litany of his concerns: fornication, impurity, passion, evil desire, greed, anger, malice, slander, and abusive language. It is possible to change one's life-style, Paul notes. The believer is now clothed with a new self, a self not driven by earthly passions but with passions motivated by the One who is seated with God.

When we have our minds on things that are above, our viewpoint of the things that are on earth changes radically. Relationships are seen differently, and thus we no longer treat people the way we once did. Paul said it this way: "In that renewal there is no longer Greek and Jew, circumcised and uncircumcised, bar-

barian, Scythian, slave and free; but Christ is all and in all!" (v. 11).

Life is then lived differently when we realize how radically our viewpoint has changed in Christ. Because we are heavenly minded, with thoughts set on things that are above, we see things in a new light. People who are different are viewed with compassion instead of hate. The homeless are viewed with mercy instead of pity. The differences between race and gender and ethnic background are minimized. There are no second-class citizens in God's realm. Our earthly eyes did not notice that, but it is so obvious when we view things from above. (Craig A. Loscalzo)

FOOLISH ASSUMPTIONS

LUKE 12:13-21

A tough-minded CEO was touring his company's shipping department when he came upon a young man leaning against a file cabinet, humming a song and watching the action around him. The CEO went up to him and asked him how much he got paid. The young man said, "About two hundred a week." "Here's two weeks' pay," the CEO said, stuffing four one hundred dollar bills into the man's pocket. "Get out of here and don't ever come back." As soon as the young man had gone, the CEO turned to the department manager and shouted, "Who hired that loafer?" "We didn't hire him," the manager answered. "He was just here from the messenger service to pick up a package." You have to be careful about your assumptions; they can prove to be very costly sometimes. A wise person has correct, God-informed assumptions about the meaning of life.

I. What Is Ours for What Is God's

It is a foolish assumption to think that what we have is ours alone when it is not. The rich man had many goods and wondered how he would be able to store all his goods. He thought that what he had was his and did not acknowledge that it came from God. When we have much (most of us really do) we can think it came from us and our hard work. God owns everything, and we are simply his stewards with whom he has entrusted so much. The wise person is one whose goal is to be rich toward God. Our lives do not consist of what we have but how we can give to those in need.

II. The Body for the Soul

It is a foolish assumption to believe the body and the soul are the same. Life is made up of both the physical and the spiritual realms. The rich man's view of life was strictly physical with no spiritual dimension. The motto "eat, drink, and be merry" is not a wise way to live because it will do nothing for the soul. The rich man's emphasis was shown by his repetition of "I" and "my" three times, which indicates his distorted view of life. The wise person understands that the physical body is declining each day but the soul is being renewed day by day (2 Cor. 4:16).

III. Time for Eternity

It is a foolish assumption to think that physical life is not terminal. Jesus said, "This very night your life will be demanded from you." We never know when the last day of our physical life may be, but we do know we will live on for eternity. Every day we have 86,400 seconds before us to spend and invest. Each day the bank named Time opens a new account. It allows no balances, no overdrafts. If we fail to use the day's deposits, the loss is hours. We do not know what tomorrow will hold, and so we must live to the fullest today. It is foolish to believe you can plan and plan and never plan for eternity. The old saying holds true, "I never saw a hearse pulling a U-Haul."

Making wrong assumptions can cost us everything we think we have. Being a wise person means making informed choices about the quality and future of our lives. (Rick McDaniel)

AUGUST 13, 1995

☙

Tenth Sunday After Pentecost

Worship Theme: The life of faith changes our priorities and our perspective.

Readings: Isaiah 1:1, 10-20; Hebrews 11:1-3, 8-16; Luke 12:32-40

Call to Worship (Psalm 50:23):
"Those who bring thanksgiving as
    their sacrifice honor me;
  to those who go the right way
  I will show the salvation of God."

Pastoral Prayer:
    Father God, you are the same yesterday, today, and forever. We thank you and praise you for keeping your word and for honoring every promise you make. We bring to you today our many hurts, scars, and the painful, open wounds that have been caused by broken and unfulfilled promises of family, friends, and countless others on whom we depend. Heal our hurt and disappointment. Help us to forgive those who have failed to keep their promises, and forgive us for failing to always keep faith with our own promises—for the things we said that we would do but never did; for the things we promised we would never do but did anyway; for the things we denied doing, even when the responsibility was completely our own. Let truth, integrity, and peace rule our hearts and our homes, our places of work and worship, and all our relationships. In the name of Jesus, who never taught us anything that was not the truth and who never made a promise he is unable to keep. Amen. (Michael Duduit)

SERMON BRIEFS
WHAT DOES GOD REALLY WANT?
ISAIAH 1:1, 10-20

    Isaiah had a vision that was both gruesome and beautiful, depending on your point of view. From the first detail of Isaiah's prophecy (v. 1) we can see that Isaiah's career spanned the reigns of four Judean kings.

I. Worship Critique

Many pastors know the pain of enduring endless suggestions by the congregation about what is wrong with worship or how to improve it. The hymns are never right, and neither is the temperature. Most pastors tolerate these criticisms, for as a commonsense philosopher suggested: "Don't sweat the small stuff."

Unfortunately, when Isaiah measured Judah's worship, he said the Lord is grieved by more than the music and the temperature. The Lord questions the very heart and motive of the people, reflected in their practice of holy worship. To address the "rulers of Sodom! you people of Gomorrah!" is not to show anything but contempt. When the Lord says, "I do not delight in the blood of bulls, or of lambs, or of goats," this is total denunciation indeed.

II. The Outcome

Isaiah proceeds, telling the people that Yahweh does not want them trampling in the Temple courts anymore. For those in Judah, this is tantamount to being cut off from Yahweh. The tirade against their worship observances then begins anew. The people's offerings, solemn assemblies, and festival celebrations have burdened the Lord. Even their prayers reveal a people with bloody hands. Later this image will be used of Pilate with reference to Jesus' sentence of guilt. Is there any hope for the people?

III. The Way to Forgiveness

In utter despair, the people now listen intently to Isaiah's word from Yahweh. The escape from their apostasy is to begin anew. They are told to wash and make themselves clean. As a result of this cleansing, a new ethic will emerge to symbolize their repentance. They will cease doing evil and, instead, practice righteousness toward the oppressed, the orphan, and the widow.

True worship is reflected in people's outlook toward others. Isaiah reminds the people that one cannot be holy toward God and not be likewise righteous toward those who need defense. Our outward actions toward others reveal the inward state of our spiritual lives.

If the people change their sinful ways, then they will receive good, but if they refuse, they will reap the reward of their disobedient actions. Isaiah seals the Lord's word with a promise: "Though your sins are like scarlet, / they shall be like snow; / though they are red like crimson, / they shall become like wool" (v. 18).

As a pastor, one of the questions I am frequently asked is "Why do we pray the prayer of confession on most Sundays?" The people asking this question are like many folks in Judah. Often we presume we live good Christian lives by attending church and giving our offerings.

The truth, as Isaiah's text so powerfully reminds us, is that God is not as interested in our outward forms of worship as in the devotion and purity of our hearts. Those who truly worship God will be loving toward others as God is loving toward them. Jesus' words ring true for all who consider themselves righteous, when he said to those who trusted in their own righteousness: "Woe to you . . . hypocrites! For you tithe mint, dill, and cummin, and have neglected the weightier matters of the law: justice and mercy and faith. It is these you ought to have practiced without neglecting the others" (Matt. 23:23). These form the true essence of God's desire. (David Neil Mosser)

THE FAITH ADVENTURE

HEBREWS 11:1-3, 8-16

Who doesn't love a good adventure? We enjoy watching adventure stories on TV or in the movies; the bestseller lists demonstrate we enjoy reading a good adventure story. And with the advent of "virtual reality" devices, we will be able to simulate personal involvement in some adventure without, of course, actually putting ourselves in danger or getting dirty!

Yet it's not the same as actually being involved in a real-life adventure. Reading about white water rafting isn't the same as feeling the foam in your face. Watching a hot-air balloon rise into the sky can't match the feeling of climbing ever higher as you soar into the clouds. When it comes to adventures, there's no substitute for the real thing.

That is particularly true of the adventure called faith. You've never thought of faith as an adventure? Then you haven't learned from the models of those who have taken the path before us people, like Abraham, whose life is a case study of the power and purpose that come through this adventure of faith.

Faith has all the characteristics of a great adventure, as we see in these verses that tell us about Abraham's own faith journey.

I. Faith Involves Going Where We Can't Yet See (v. 8)

Imagine getting a phone call from your boss, instructing you to pack your goods, sell your home, take the kids out of school, then start traveling. Your destination? You won't know that until you get there! Your boss says, "I'll let you know when it's time to stop. Trust me!"

Abraham's faith adventure began with open-ended travel plans. Sometimes God leads us to begin a journey before we know where or how it will end. Faith is being willing to follow God's direction wherever it leads, even if we don't know where that will be during the journey itself.

Have you ever walked through the woods at night with just a flashlight? No moonlight—just that single beam shining ahead of you. You can see only as far as the light shines, but no farther. Yet you keep walking, knowing that as you proceed, the light will continue to move ahead of you, revealing a little more of the path ahead with each step you take.

That's part of the adventure of faith, trusting God to lead you to the best possible future, even though you don't yet know what that may be. Faith involves going where we can't yet see.

II. Faith Involves Living Where We Aren't Yet Home (v. 9)

Abraham's faith journey didn't lead directly from point *A* to point *B*; he had detoured along the way. Yet it was during these intermediate places, like Egypt, that God was able to teach Abraham some of the most valuable lessons he would ever learn.

As we move forward on our faith adventure, there may well be detours along the way; sometimes they may be brief, while other ones may seem so long and frustrating that we begin to wonder if our journey has ended. The key is to keep our eyes to God and his will for our lives, understanding that sometimes we will spend time in places that aren't our ultimate home. Use those detours as times of learning, allowing God to teach the lessons that will help us along the remainder of our faith adventure.

III. Faith Involves Accepting What We Don't Yet Have (vv. 11-12)

Can you imagine how Abraham and Sarah must have wondered about God's promise that they would produce a mighty nation when for decades they had not been blessed with even their first child? Nevertheless, Abraham clung to faith that the God who had led him through so many challenges would yet find a way to accomplish that promise. He accepted God's promise even though he didn't yet have it—even though it seemed impossible.

The faith adventure involves trusting God for our best future, even when it may seem distant or even impossible. God wants to do great things in your life; are you willing to trust him with your future and follow him in faith? (Michael Duduit)

THE UNEXPECTED HOUR

LUKE 12:32-40

Jesus talked to his disciples about life lived in faith, and in these three short parables Jesus pictured the way faith puts life out on the edges. Faith is that feeling of trust that moves us away from the comfortable and familiar, out toward the edges of life where it is not as predictable or routine.

I. Life on the Edges Changes the Way We View Security

On the edges is where our salvation comes. As Annie Dillard wrote in *Holy the Firm*, "A person who sees her life as satisfactorily defined by the society in which she lives will have no need to roam the border area which, while it does hold her salvation, also threatens her with madness." Faith puts life out on the edges so that redemption may be found.

Jesus pushed his disciples to move away from the economic security they so zealously guarded, and it is no less with us. Move out to the edges of life so that you can discover that the grace and power and love of God is what keeps and protects and defends you, not the full purse or tax-sheltered annuities.

II. Life on the Edges Changes the Way
We View Priorities

Jesus said that faith puts us out on the edges of life where we become concerned about all of life; where we become stewards and servants of the house and we want to make sure that everything is ready for the coming of the Master. We take care of all the little things, because there really are no little things.

Faith makes us responsible for the little things—the little people, the little injustices, the little immoralities, the little pollution, the little evils. On the edges we can see that the little things are really not so little. The little thing can be seen as the crack in the house's foundation that will lead to its collapse.

Mother Teresa began to do a little thing like care for the lost in India, the little people, the untouchables. In so doing, she has been able to bear a worldwide witness to the love of God. She has discovered that there are no little things.

III. Life on the Edges Changes the Way
We View Time

Faith puts life on the edges by making each hour, each minute of the day, a moment of possibility for encountering the living God. Faith makes each moment the one when God might open up time and history and show grace and mercy to us again. Every moment may be a moment when God's providence moves in our lives.

The stories suggest that faith in Jesus Christ will take us out of our normal paths. Faith will get us up and moving, out onto the edges of life where the questions of what we shall eat or wear are spiritual questions as well as material—where little questions cannot be distinguished from big ones, where every moment is an opportunity to bear witness to God's love and every moment is alive with the possibility of being encountered by the living God. (Rick Brand)

AUGUST 20, 1995

❧

Eleventh Sunday After Pentecost

Worship Theme: Christ's claim on our lives requires change.

Readings: Isaiah 5:1-7; Hebrews 11:29–12:2; Luke 12:49-56

Call to Worship (Psalm 80:19):

Leader: Restore us, O LORD God of hosts;

All: let your face shine, that we may be saved.

Pastoral Prayer:

Our Creator and Sustainer, as we examine the world you fashioned, we marvel at your creative power. You have placed us in a world that is constantly changing, as each season takes shape after the next. And you have given us bodies and minds that change through the years: from weakness to strength, and again to weakness. Yet in a world of changes all around us, how we resist the changes that come our way! We struggle to maintain our old assumptions and bigotries; we cling to our fears and insecurities.

Lord, we know you call us to change, for through your Son you have transformed us into new creatures in Christ. Help us not to be terrified of change, but to embrace it in the power of your Spirit. And help us not to scurry after change for its own sake, but to discern your will and to accept the changes that you bring so that Christ might be honored, for it is in his name we pray. Amen. (Michael Duduit)

SERMON BRIEFS

ON KEEPING THE GARDEN

ISAIAH 5:1-7

Our text today is "The Song of the Vineyard." It sounds like a song sung at the joy of harvest. In fact, it is a caricature of Yahweh's relationship with "the inhabitants of Jerusalem and the people of Judah."

I. The Song's Beginning

The song begins with promise. Isaiah sings of a vineyard to a merry-making audience, for, other than shower-singing, most songs are to be shared. Isaiah's song is of a wonderful vineyard given as a gift to the beloved. We hear of the vineyard's work of preparation:

> He dug it and cleared it of stones,
>   and planted it with choice vines;
> he built a watchtower in the midst of it,
>   and hewed out a wine vat in it;
> he expected it to yield grapes. (v. 2)

So far, so good. Everyone likes happy songs.

II. The Song's Sad Twist

Yahweh "expected it to yield grapes, but it yielded wild grapes" (v. 2) is another way of saying that Yahweh expected the vineyard gift to yield a righteous return, but the return was nil.

At this point in the song, as one might expect of this allegory of Yahweh and the chosen people, Isaiah sings of Yahweh's disappointment. The people are asked rhetorical questions:

> What more was there to do for my vineyard
>   that I have not done in it?
> When I expected it to yield grapes,
>   why did it yield wild grapes? (v. 4)

Judah is summoned to judge itself.

The prophetic story of confrontation between Nathan and David, over Bathsheba and Uriah, should be in the back of our minds. Could David answer other than he did, saying, "As the LORD lives, the man who has done this deserves to die" (2 Sam. 12:5)? Isaiah's Song of the Vineyard has similarly boxed in Judah's response—they are guilty!

III. The Song's Judgment

Judah must gird its loins, for Yahweh spells out exactly what the refusal of the vineyard gift will cost them. Yahweh will remove the vineyard's hedge and the vineyard will be devoured. It will be laid waste and become briars and thorns, with Yahweh withholding rain—a precious commodity in Judah. The perfection of the garden will turn back into the primeval chaos. The creation story has now been reversed in Isaiah's telling.

The final verse is a summary for those who have no musical inclination—in case they have missed the point of Isaiah's prophetic refrain. "For the vineyard of the LORD of hosts / is the house of Israel . . . he expected justice, / but saw bloodshed; / righteousness, but heard a cry!" (v. 7).

IV. To Sing a New Song

Once there was a good man who wanted to do good. One day he noticed the miserable condition in which a poor carpenter lived. The rich man called the carpenter and commissioned him to build a beautiful house. "I want this to be an ideal cottage. Use only the best materials, employ only the best workers, and spare no expense." He said that he was going on a journey and hoped the house would be completed when he returned.

The carpenter saw this as his great opportunity. Therefore, he skimped on materials, hired inferior workers at low wages, and covered their mistakes with paint. He cut corners wherever he could.

When the rich man returned, the carpenter brought him the keys and said: "I have followed your instructions and built your house as you told me to."

"I'm glad," said the rich man. Handing the keys back to the builder, he continued, "Here are the keys. They are yours. I had you build this house for yourself. You and your family are to have it as my gift" (William B. Silverman, *Rabbinic Stories for Christian Ministers and Teachers*). (David Neil Mosser)

IN THEIR STEPS

HEBREWS 11:29–12:2

Watching my nephews play the other day, I noticed how the younger ones would watch the older children, then imitate their actions. They learned from one another for good or ill!

That's how many of us learn things: by watching other people. When you start a new job, it's nice to have someone on hand to demonstrate how certain procedures are handled. When I'm learning a computer program, I hate to read the manual! I'd much rather have someone sit at the terminal with me and walk me through the steps.

In the faith adventure, we also learn by observing those who have gone before us. Most of us who are citizens of the Kingdom today came to faith in Christ because of the influence of a parent or sibling, a friend or teacher, someone who not only taught us about Jesus but modeled faith for us. Those who have walked before us in the adventure of faith offer us worthy models.

I. They Encourage Us by Their Example

The writer of Hebrews carries us through a litany of examples of faith put into action, from the crossing of the Red Sea to the bold obedience of the prophets. This "great cloud of witnesses" provides a model of faithfulness and commitment to encourage us in our own walk of faith.

II. They Challenge Us by Their Sacrifice

We live in a day when sacrifice is considered something we should make others do for our benefit. The thought of personal sacrifice is almost alien to our culture.

Yet as we walk down the corridors of this gallery of faith's heroes and heroines, we are impressed with the willingness of so many to endure persecution, withstand opposition, and remain faithful in the face of danger and even death. Their examples of sacrifice for their faith offer a model for us.

III. They Remind Us of Our Dependence on Christ

The hall of fame found in the eleventh chapter contains some of the greatest names of faith in all of history: Abraham, Isaac, Jacob, Joseph, Moses, and on the list goes. They were men and women who walked with God, and whose faithfulness is a model for us.

Yet that is not enough. As 11:39 notes, "They were all commended for their faith, yet none of them received what had been promised." Their personal obedience and sacrifice alone were not enough. What did they lack? "Jesus, the author and perfecter of our faith" (12:2). The most we can do on our own is not enough to earn our place in God's Kingdom; Christ alone can welcome us into God's presence.

In track and field competitions, the runners assemble on the track, the gun sounds, and they break for the finish line. One thing you don't see those sprinters do is gaze into the sky or look at people in the stands as they run; they keep their focus locked on to the tape that crosses the finish line. That's the goal, and they run toward it with all their energy and determination.

As we run the race of faith, our ultimate hope is in Christ. We are to keep our eyes focused on him. (Michael Duduit)

COSTLY CHANGE

LUKE 12:49-56

For many years the opening of "The Wide World of Sports" program has shown the agony of defeat with the painful ending of an attempted ski jump. The skier appears to be in good form as he heads down the jump, but then, for no apparent reason, he tumbles off the side of the jump, crashing into several other structures. What viewers don't know is that he chose to fall rather than finish the jump. Why? As he explained later, the jump surface had become too fast, and midway down he realized that if he completed the jump, he would land on level ground, beyond the safe landing area, which could have been fatal. As it was, the skier may have looked bad, but he suffered nothing more than a headache from the tumble. Change is sometimes painful, but it is better than a fatal ending. To come to Jesus means to respond to his costly call for change.

I. The Purpose of His Coming

Only Luke records for us this great heartburst of Jesus as he speaks in an atmosphere of excited crowds, hostile rulers, and perplexed disciples. He says that he has come to bring fire on the earth, which speaks of judgment. His purpose was to judge sin, to bring a clear separation between good and evil. The symbolism of fire denotes two things: Fire destroys the temporary, and it refines the permanent. There are times that demand radical change, and the coming of Jesus was the ultimate example.

II. The Passion of His Life

The passion of Jesus' life was to fulfill the Father's will. Jesus referred to a baptism he must undergo, which is symbolic of the work of the cross (Mark 10:38). The shadow of the cross hung over Jesus; he knew it was his purpose for coming. The heart of Jesus is shown when he says essentially, "I am burdened by this passion to go to the cross until it is finally accomplished." The death of Jesus is to be seen not as mere fate but as a destiny to be fulfilled.

III. The Process of His Work

This work that Jesus will do brings inner peace but outer division. Even families are divided by the message of the cross; it challenges us, and when some do not respond to this challenge, they criticize those who do. Jesus knew that the call for decision was a call for division. Division over God's call for change is evidence of the coming of the kingdom of God. As we look at our world today, it should never surprise us that the call for change that Jesus requires will upset the status quo.

In the novel *The Strange Life of Ivan Osokin,* by the Russian writer P. D. Ouspensky, there is the story of a man who wants to amend his mistakes by living life over again. Ivan goes to a magician, who reluctantly complies with his wishes but warns that nothing will be different. Ivan watches, as in a movie, how he makes the same mistakes over again, down to the smallest details. He cries out in desperation, "What am I to do, then?" The magician responds: "In order to change anything, you must first change yourself." Jesus calls us to make a change, a costly one that will result in division, but one that we must make. (Rick McDaniel)

AUGUST 27, 1995

❧

Twelfth Sunday After Pentecost

Worship Theme: Worship allows us to enter into a new and deeper relationship with God.

Readings: Jeremiah 4:1-10; Hebrews 12:18-29; Luke 13:10-17

Call to Worship (Psalm 71:1-6):

Leader: In you, O LORD, I take refuge; let me never be put to shame.

People: In your righteousness deliver me and rescue me; incline your ear to me and save me.

Leader: Be to me a rock of refuge, a strong fortress, to save me, for you are my rock and my fortress.

People: Rescue me, O my God, from the hand of the wicked, from the grasp of the unjust and cruel.

Leader: For you, O Lord, are my hope, my trust, O LORD, from my youth.

All: Upon you I have leaned from my birth; it was you who took me from my mother's womb. My praise is continually of you.

Pastoral Prayer:

O God our Father, we are grateful for another Sunday and pray that it may be a day of rest and gladness, a day of prayer and peace. May every evil thought be arrested, every faithless fear stilled, and give to all who worship this day a sense of your living presence. If any have come here hungry, Lord, feed them with the living bread and satisfy their longing souls. If any have come in a careless or indifferent spirit, clear away their spiritual blindness and make their hearts to burn within them as they receive the riches of your grace.

We thank you for every good gift, for the loving care with which you have watched over us all our days. We thank you for all who have helped us by their example, their words, and their prayers. Above all, we thank you for your greatest gift, your Son Jesus Christ, who though he was rich became poor for our sakes, who humbled himself that we might be exalted, and who was wounded for our transgressions and now makes intercession for us. Open our eyes that we may behold wondrous things out of your Word, and open our lips that we may show forth your glory, for the sake of Jesus Christ our Lord. Amen. (John Bishop)

SERMON BRIEFS

WHEN GOD CALLS

JEREMIAH 4:1-10

David Livingstone became a famous missionary to Africa— "Dr. Livingstone, I presume?"—but there was a time when the young Scot was called on to preach his first sermon in the village of Stanford Rivers. When the time came for the sermon, Livingstone slowly read his text, but by the end of it, the rest of his sermon had apparently evaporated right out of his head. He announced, "Friends, I have forgotten all I had to say," and with that he hurriedly left the chapel and went home!

Jeremiah must have felt some of the same terror that day as he encountered God and the challenge to be a prophet to his own people. Yet when God calls us to a task, we receive some divine promises to carry with us.

I. God Calls Us

If you compare Jeremiah's call to that of other spiritual leaders—like Moses, Samuel, Amos, Isaiah—one thing that is common to all is that the initiative is with God. These are not people who decided one day to take on a new work for God. Indeed, Jeremiah and Moses each struggled with God and sought to avoid his call. Each offered his lack of speaking ability as a reason to pass over him; to that, Jeremiah added the further reason of his youth (v. 6).

Yet God is not interested in our capabilities or gifts—after all, any talents we have are gifts he has given us. God is interested not in our ability but in our availability. Will we respond to God's call with a willingness to follow his will?

II. God Equips Us

God does not call us and then send us out empty-handed. God will provide whatever we need in order to fulfill his call in our lives.

Jeremiah believed he could not speak adequately to serve as a prophet, but God reached out and touched his mouth. It was not Jeremiah's words that would make the difference, but God's equipping and empowering hand upon the prophet's life.

Still wondering what God has called you to do? Perhaps one way to identify that is to look at the way God has equipped you already—what gifts has God already given you that may be used in his service?

III. God Works Through Us

Despite the awesome challenge God has given to the young prophet, Jeremiah can be assured of God's presence in his life. "I am with you" (v. 8), God tells Jeremiah. "I have put my words in your mouth" (v. 9). It was not Jeremiah the prophet who would play such an important role in the nation's life; it was God working through Jeremiah that would bring both judgment and hope to God's people.

Eight times in this chapter, Jeremiah uses the statement "The word of the LORD came to me." Jeremiah had no authority of his own; his sole authority came from God's work through the prophet.

God also calls us to serve him. The call may take a variety of forms, but it always carries with it the promise of God's presence and power. Even today, he wants to work through you and me to accomplish great things. Are we willing to respond to his call? (Michael Duduit)

NEW COVENANT WORSHIP

HEBREWS 12:18-29

We enter a sanctuary to worship and too often believe that what occurs during the worship time is routine and has no continuing existence after the benediction is prayed. However, we must realize that our worship is a reflection of the activity in a celestial unseen realm before the throne of God. Viewing our temporal worship from the eternal perspective stretches our spiritual commitment and results in growth as disciples.

I. Worship in the New Covenant Is Relationship

Verses 18 through 21 of our text remind us of Israel at Mount Sinai hearing Yahweh thundering his commands. It was a literal mountain that evoked paralyzing fear in the people. They wanted no communication from the God of that mountain and realized they could not bear the demanding standards of holiness.

This picture of worship lacks a relationship between the creation and the Creator. The fear of the people results from a lack of their knowledge of the God of the mountain. We cannot know someone with whom we have no relationship.

This picture of humanity's relationship with God is accentuated by the Pharisees and Sadducees in the day of Christ. While they taught legalistic and unbearable regulations, Jesus taught his disciples to pray openly, addressing God as "Father." The tearing of the veil in the Temple during the crucifixion was a vivid symbol of the open access to the Father, which Christ procured for humanity. Since Christ has opened the way, we can worship the Father in a relationship of grace and not out of fear.

II. Significance of New Covenant Worship

Worship in today's churches may seem to be simply songs and praises uttered for the congregation to hear one another. On the contrary, verses 22-24 note that there is greater significance to what we are doing when we gather together to worship. We are coming to the Mount Zion of the "heavenly" Jerusalem—that is, the throne room of our Creator—because we have access through the mediator of the new covenant, Jesus Christ.

In the book of Revelation, the aged apostle John was allowed a vision of the throne of God and found angelic hosts and elders worshiping continually around the throne. In this text we see that we come and join with those thousands of angels and righteous ones who worship at the throne. When we gather together to worship, our words are heard not only by those near us and then forgotten; no, there is another dimension to our acts of worship. We are joining with creation and worshiping God in the Spirit of truth.

III. Practical Implications of New Covenant Worship

Verse 25 encourages us first not to "refuse the one who is speaking." Since we now worship God, with whom we have a relationship, we can expect him to communicate to us. He speaks warnings and promises, sifting the eternal from the temporal (the "shaken" and that which "cannot be shaken"). Our worship is to be a response to his word. His word may give direction or promise, but our worship response is one in faith and trust with God as we are in relationship with him.

Verse 28 gives a second exhortation: Since we are receiving an eternal ("unshakable") kingdom, we are to "be thankful." Worship is not only a response to the Word of God, but it is a response with a proper perspective as well. Our worship response to God should be done out of a heart of gratitude and thankfulness.

Verse 28 also gives us a third directive: We should worship with reverence and awe. While we worship God in a relationship, we do not profane his name or his presence. While we do not come with fear and trembling, we do come before God reverently, awed by his acts, which are wondrous and merciful.

An example of proper balance between reverence and relationship is in the very image of addressing God as our "Father." How disrespectful we perceive it for young children to call their human parents by their first names or nicknames. Our feeling of disrespect stems from what we perceive as an improper relationship between the parent and the child. The child is not the parents' equal and needs the parents for guidance, direction, and love.

Likewise, we come to God as children in relationship to him, but still in need of his love, guidance, and direction. We gather around his throne with love and thanksgiving while reverencing his majestic authority unparalleled in the universe. We should, in fact, be overwhelmed with hearts of gratitude that this majestic one desires a relationship with us.

Our text shows us that New Covenant worship is more than gathering together for mutual human friendship. We gather with the eternal celestial host around the throne of God, worshiping as a response to his word, with thankful hearts and in reverence and awe. We worship the God who gave his Son that we may know him whom we are worshiping. (Joseph Byrd)

F-R-E-E

LUKE 13:10-17

The scene is forever etched in our minds: water being pumped out over Helen Keller's hand while Anne Sullivan spells w-a-t-e-r again and again on Helen's drenched palm. A new world opened up for Helen Keller. What a wonderful story, one that inspires us all!

But it hasn't always been so. The Gospels indicate that when Jesus healed people, not everyone was inspired. The woman in this account wasn't blind. but she might as well have been. For eighteen years she suffered from a severe curvature of the spine. She had seen only the sandals of others, not their eyes; only the mosaic floor of the synagogue, never the elaborate menorah; and during the prayers she raised her hands to the heavens, but never her eyes.

Still, she participated in the prayers, gave alms, and listened to the reading of Scripture and the interpretation that followed.

On this day the services had been stirred up by the presence of Jesus. She had seen his feet and had heard the rumors of healings. Could he heal her? Then suddenly, Jesus approached her, a woman in a man's world, and said, "Woman, you are set free from your ailment" (v. 12). What a wonderful story!

The synagogue official, however, didn't agree. Jesus was a guest. He shouldn't have done such a thing. The sabbath must be kept holy. The official cleared his throat and announced, "There are six days on which work ought to be done; come on those days and be cured" (v. 14).

Of course, healing was not the main concern for this ruler; rather, it was the keeping of rules. Jesus spoke up, "You hypocrites! Does not each of you on the sabbath untie his ox or his donkey from the manger, and lead it away to give it water? And ought not this woman . . . whom Satan bound for eighteen long years, be set free from this bondage on the sabbath day?" (vv. 15-16).

Jesus used the rabbinic technique of lesser to greater. If they will be kind to an animal on the sabbath, then why not to a person? The whole passage hinges on two key words, *bound* and *freed*. The woman is "freed" from her sickness. Everyone "frees" an animal for watering, then why not "free" this woman whom Satan had "bound"?

What a wonderful story! She heard those words, felt his touch, and looked up into the eyes of Jesus. She stood up "and began praising God" (v. 13). The Jewish position of prayer was to stand with hands and head lifted toward heaven. She had lifted her hands before. Now she lifted her head.

The synagogue religion involved being bound to rules. It's like William Blake's poem about a chapel in "The Garden of Love":

> And the gates of this chapel were shut,
> And "Thou shalt not" writ over the door;
> So I turned to the Garden of Love,
> That so many sweet flowers bore:
> And I saw it was filled with graves,
> And tombstones where flowers should be;
> And priests in black gowns were walking their rounds,
> And binding with briars my joys and desires.

The Pharisees of the synagogue had spent their lives binding others. Jesus came to set captives free from the oppressive religion of "Thou shalt not." Authentic Christianity is a permission to be free and live to the glory of God.

As the woman left, she couldn't help noticing that the ruler appeared to be bent over, bound to his traditions. It was the woman, this "daughter of Abraham," as Jesus called her, who went free. He might as well have written it out on her hand, "F-r-e-e-!" (Mike Graves)

SEPTEMBER

❧

Replenishing the Well

Expect to Be Found

Luke 15:1-10 contains the parables of the lost sheep and the lost coin. God seeks out those who are lost, finds them, and rejoices. Sometimes on our faith journey there are times when each of us feels lost. During those difficult times, we long to be found by God. If you have been feeling lost lately, this month's exercise may be helpful. It explores being found by God.

Time: 1 hour, 15 minutes.

Materials: A Bible, a good pair of walking shoes, a wrist watch.

Exercise:
Take ten minutes to read Luke 15:1-10 carefully. Notice that neither the coin nor the sheep did anything to attract the attention of the woman or the shepherd. In these parables, God does all the work of seeking, finding, and rejoicing.

Put on your walking shoes. Go to a park or neighborhood where you can walk at a leisurely pace for the next hour. This exercise is divided into four fifteen-minute segments. As you walk, you will open yourself up to God, who always seeks your company.

During the first fifteen minutes of your walk, concentrate on the simple experience of walking. Look at your feet. Focus on what your feet are doing. Feel the rhythm of putting one foot in front of the other. Walk at a leisurely pace—*do not hurry.* Let the world slip away as you look at your feet and concentrate on the rhythm of walking.

For the next fifteen minutes, raise your eyes to look straight ahead. Continue to feel the rhythm of walking, and begin to focus on your breathing. Take even, measured breaths. Feel the fresh air fill your lungs. Each breath you take is cleansing.

During the next fifteen minutes, look around you. Take in your surroundings while continuing to feel the rhythm of your feet, each breath. You don't need to think about anything—let any thoughts come and go. Simply open yourself to the sights and sounds around you as you walk.

The final fifteen minutes are a time of simply "being" before God, who seeks the pleasure of your company. Let God do the work of finding you. *You don't have to do anything.* Simply continue your walk. God knows where to find you. If you feel a need to pray, do so. But prayer is not necessary. God takes all of the initiative here—your job is to continue your walk, quietly expecting to be found by God.

After your walk, gently return to your schedule for the day. Repeat this exercise anytime you are feeling lost. (Harriet Crosby)

SEPTEMBER 3, 1995

❧

Thirteenth Sunday After Pentecost

Worship Theme: We are called to live out our Christian faith in our activities and our relationships.

Readings: Jeremiah 2:4-13; Hebrews 13:1-8, 15-16; Luke 14:1, 7-14

Call to Worship (Psalm 81:1):

Leader: Sing aloud to God our strength;

People: shout for joy to the God of Jacob.

Pastoral Prayer:

Creator God, we are blessed with fruits and vegetables that come from the land by your hand. All we have done is to provide the labor; you have given the sun and the earth, the rain and the other vital elements of growth. We praise your goodness as we eat sweet corn or enjoy fresh peaches. These are powerful reminders that we have much to be thankful for in the world!

As we give thanks for the harvest, we recall that many in this world have only parched lands and meager crops with which to feed their families. We remember that in many places in this world children are dying because they lack even the most basic foods. We remember that "those who have much must share much"; yet we too often turn away from mission work and food programs that bring hope to the desperately hungry. Change our hardened, calloused hearts. Open our closed hands and our selfish attitudes, and fill us with generosity. Call us to a new sense of love for others whose land is not as bountiful or beautiful or productive as our own. Transform us into those who care so much for others that our hearts are indeed enlarged in Christ, in whose name we pray. Amen. (Steven R. Fleming)

SERMON BRIEFS

GOOD DO-BE'S

JEREMIAH 2:4-13

You find them in the strangest places, those little gems that can be called "keepers." I found this one on a sign on a cash register at a golf course. There it was, an entire philosophical/psychological debate in three easy lines, the polar alternatives to the "chicken and egg" question of behavior and identity. What was printed on the sign was the following:

> **To be is to do. (Aristotle)**
> **To do is to be. (Sartre)**
> **Do be do be do. (Sinatra)**

That pretty much covers the options, as near as I can tell.

It could be that we act the way we do on account of identity and disposition (Aristotle). On the other hand, it could be that we develop authentic identity as a result of what we do (Sartre). It could also be that none of us really knows one way or the other, and we might as well make a little ditty out of the whole issue (Sinatra).

I am not one to existentialize Scripture; nonetheless it seems to me that if you were going to put Jeremiah in a camp, he would be camping out, as it were, with Jean-Paul Sartre. Note especially verse 5 in the lesson for today:

> What wrong did your ancestors find in me
> that they went far from me,
> and went after worthless things,
> and became worthless themselves?

And that last part—how their doing, that is, "going after worthless things"—changed their being, made them "worthless themselves."

This is a recurring theme in Scripture, and not just in the Old Testament. Paul, in a famous analysis in the first chapter of Romans, argues that when persons do foolish things they become fools. And, Paul says, such is essentially the case with all forms of idolatry, "[exchanging] the glory of the immortal God for images resembling a mortal human being or birds or four-footed animals or reptiles" (Rom. 1:22) causes an exchanging of the true nature and affections of people for a lesser nature and affections. In sum, those who worship animals become like animals.

Likewise, in 2 Kings 17, as the narrative recounts the reasons for the fall of Israel, verse 15 quite tellingly states, "They went after false idols and became false"—almost pure cause and effect, and especially as it relates to worship. It is as if to say worship well, acknowledging God and God's will, and you will grow in faith and knowledge and love of God and God's children; worship and serve other gods—whether they be idols of gold, positions of power, or lusts of the flesh—worship falsely, and you will become false.

The poignancy of this lection is found quite early, in verse 4, when God laments the waywardness of his people. A free paraphrase would read, "What did I do so wrong to make them act so wrongly?" Not just a few acted wrongly either, and not just these people—generations of priests, rulers, and prophets all went after worthless things and became worthless themselves (v. 8), even though God had acted mercifully, gracefully, in bringing the people out of Egypt.

God's very grace became the occasion for sin—as if the people had turned their backs on a fountain of good water, only to dig out a cracked cistern to hold no water at all (v. 13). It could hardly be sillier: Thirsting after other water, they became only parched.

And "Be appalled, O heavens, at this," God says (v. 12), "be shocked" and "utterly desolate" at the people's desolation. God will contend with the children of the sinners (v. 9*b*) and will call all heaven to witness the trial.

But God may yet prove graceful again, more worthy even than our worthlessness. (Thomas R. Steagald)

LIVING OUR FAITH

HEBREWS 13:1-8, 15,16

Christian faith is not simply a decision we can give only passing notice. In being Christian, we become open to the possibilities of

God's power in our lives. Christ called his disciples not only to agree with a theological point, but to a transformed life with new relationships and new priorities. The writer of Hebrews deals with how faith can make an impact on specific areas of our lives.

I. The Nature of Christian Faith

Christianity is based on a confession in the person and work of Jesus Christ. Our text states the confession in verse 8: "Jesus Christ is the same yesterday and today and forever." Great significance surges beneath these simple words. Jesus is not only changeless, but he is changeless in his character and nature. He is still the answer for the human problem of sin.

The proper human response to the encounter of the changeless Christ is a life-style of worship. Verse 15 notes that with the confession of the name of Christ, we are to offer God a sacrifice of praise. Verse 15 quickly adds that the life of worship includes not forgetting to do good and sharing with others. In short, those who confess an encounter with the changeless Christ worship with words of praise and life-styles that reflect his mercy and love.

II. Christian Relationships

Christianity is not individualistic. It begins in a relationship between the Redeemer and the redeemed. The relationship with Christ is to overflow into our relationships with other humans. In the first three verses of Hebrews 13, the writer notes that our relationships with others are of ultimate significance.

We are to love one another as brothers. True love of our brothers involves affirmation as well as confrontation. If we love one another in Christian love, Christ said, the world will know we are his disciples.

We are to treat strangers as invited guests. The writer notes that sometimes a Christian may entertain an angel, being unaware of his identity. Christian faith affects not only the way we treat brothers and sisters in Christ, but also how we treat those who do not claim our faith.

Verse 3 notes that we are to treat the imprisoned as fellow prisoners and the mistreated as fellow sufferers. This means we are to identify with the bondage and suffering of those around us. Christ's ministry was set forth in Luke 4:18 as a fulfillment of the prophecy to set the captive free and heal the broken hearted. His purpose is the purpose of his followers, and it has not changed; we are still to be setting people free and healing their suffering.

III. Christian Priorities

This text notes three Christian priorities that needed attention by his readers. The first is that marriage was to be honored. It is certainly unpopular to speak against sexual immorality in this day and age, but it is nevertheless condemned in Scripture. One must also speak in an honorable way about marriage and the necessity for the institution to be honored by us.

The second priority mentioned is the bondage of materialism. Believers are not to be bound by the accumulation of material wealth, but have an eternal perspective that was proclaimed by Christ. This issue speaks to the motivations of Christians and begs us to ask, "What motivates me to do certain actions?" Correct motives spring forth from our desire to please God; sinful motives result in pleasing ourselves.

The third priority mentioned in this text is honoring the leadership in the church (v. 7). This priority cuts both ways. While it is clear that believers should honor those who are spiritual leaders, it also speaks to the faithful life-style that is to be modeled by the leaders. This priority points us again to relationships among one another.

This text demonstrates that those transformed by the renewing power of Christ will live in a manner that bears the fruit of spiritual change. The spiritual fruit is a change in relationships and priorities in our lives. (Joseph Byrd)

R.S.V.P.

LUKE 14:1, 7-14

Picture this: A man in his fifties, distinguished and properly attired. He is a faithful husband and strict father. He is a respected businessman and, above all else, a deeply religious man. In a word, he is a Pharisee.

Surprised? Don't be. The Pharisees of Jesus' day were not bad people. They were highly respected merchants with a heart for God. In fact, it was with the Pharisees, as opposed to the Sadducees, that Jesus was most readily identified.

And it was in the home of one of these highly respected Pharisees that Jesus sat down to eat. Attention was given to the proper prayers and ritual cleansings. Everything had to be just so, and it was—until Jesus began to speak. Jesus had obviously never studied under Dale Carnegie. He was not the least bit concerned with winning friends and influencing people.

At the dinner, Jesus noticed how subtly but surely the guests made their way to the places of honor in the home. They were good people, and they simply wanted to be recognized as such. But Jesus saw it differently. He severely rebuked them for seeking out the places of honor. At stake in this passage is more than lessons on etiquette. After all, this is a parable, according to Luke (v. 7). People's actions reveal their hearts. The Pharisees saw themselves as more important than others. In the eyes of the Son of Man, that is a serious charge. Jesus calls for humility among religious leaders, not blowing their own horns and announcing their own importance.

The air was still. A few mumbled under their breath, "Who invited this guy?" No one smiled. It was an awkward moment. Surely it would pass.

Then Jesus continued, only this time he picked on the host. Not a smart move if he wanted to eat there again. In effect, he said, "Why do you invite only the beautiful people? What about the poor, the crippled, the lame, and the blind? What about them?"

Silly question. Good religious people know that there are standards to be upheld, reputations to consider. Besides, this was a Sabbath dinner.

Of course, that is Jesus' point exactly. The Sabbath is an institution of God, who loves and invites all to his table of fellowship. A Sabbath dinner is the perfect time and place to welcome all of God's children—the poor, those who can't even afford to invite you back; the crippled and lame, those who may even need to be carried inside; the blind, those who have to be led.

In this chapter of Luke it becomes increasingly clear that the religious leaders may be the blind ones. They can't see what

Jesus is saying about the kingdom and entrance into it. They assume it is the powerful who will inherit the earth, not the meek, and that the meek must be stepped on in the process.

Jesus says that religious leaders should see themselves more as servants than rulers and that the table of fellowship is open to all.

Have you ever seen a picture of that scene in heaven in which the artist depicts a table set with fine china and crystal? The places settings are immaculate. You can only imagine what the food will be like. The interesting thing is the size of the table: It stretches out for what seems like forever.

That's the idea here in Luke. All are welcome at this table, for it is the table of God. He is host. R.S.V.P. (Mike Graves)

SEPTEMBER 10, 1995

❧

Fourteenth Sunday After Pentecost

Worship Theme: Christians do not cling to "rights" but are motivated by love.

Readings: Jeremiah 18:1-11; Philemon 1-21; Luke 14:25-33

Call to Worship (Psalm 139:1-6, 13-14):

Leader: O LORD, you have searched me and known me. You know when I sit down and when I rise up; you discern my thoughts from far away.

People: You search out my path and my lying down, and are acquainted with all my ways.

Leader: Even before a word is on my tongue, O LORD, you know it completely. You hem me in, behind and before, and lay your hand upon me.

People: Such knowledge is too wonderful for me; it is so high that I cannot attain it. . . .

Leader: For it was you who formed my inward parts; you knit me together in my mother's womb.

All: I praise you, for I am fearfully and wonderfully made. Wonderful are your works.

Pastoral Prayer:

We thank you, Father, for showing us how to love through Jesus. Yet we confess the times we have disregarded the unconditional love of Jesus and placed conditions on too many of our relationships; offering love if others talk and walk as we expect, when you have taught and shown us how to love regardless of what others do. Father, we confess the times our passion for winning ignores your commanding call for loving like Jesus. We ask your forgiveness as we turn to you again and ask for the assistance of your Holy Spirit in making loving like Jesus the motivating and operating principle of our lives. We pray this for your honor in the name of Jesus. Amen. (Michael Duduit)

SERMON BRIEFS

HAVE THINE OWN WAY, LORD

JEREMIAH 18:1-11

Why is it, as Linda J. Clark says in *Carriers of Faith,* that "usually mild-mannered folk who inhabit Christian communities can become outrageously loud and outspoken when members of hymnal committees begin to meddle with their hymn books"? It may be because hymns are more than static words on a page; rather, hymns are near sacramental, something on the order of "icons." They are "carriers of faith" at the very least, and some are the very vehicles of God's grace.

As Linda J. Clark points out, "hymns provide the means through which people express their faith, and when people sing hymns their faith is formed by the experience. . . . A hymn is a highly complex set of images, both verbal and aural, set in motion through singing by a group of people who have intentionally gathered to worship God."

There's just something about the singing of the old hymns that brings God to us, something that takes us away. I have heard it said that crayons can take you places a starship could never go. It has been my experience that the old hymns can transport you to places no time machine can, for part of what these powerful "carriers of faith" carry is us.

"Have Thine Own Way, Lord" carries me away to a little church in Milton, Tennessee, where my dad served a little Baptist church. It sat on the side of a dusty road that bisected the white frame sanctuary and the cemetery where all the old-timers were buried. It had two doors on the front that, from a distance, looked like sad, spaniel eyes. Each door was for an aisle, and the women would stand in front of one, the men the other, until time to go in. To take the men's attendance on any given Sunday, you could follow the formula advanced by the late Grady Nutt—count the number of cigarette butts and divide by seven!

It was a wonderful place for forming faith. Now I am quite sure that on Sunday nights, driving down that long, lonely road back to Nashville and home and listening to the "Day of Decision" or "Old Time Gospel Hour," or some such, Dad dreamed of bigger churches, a greater ministry. And yet it seems to me, and especially now, that ministry could hardly get much bigger or greater than at that Baptist church. And that on account of Sunday nights.

On Sunday nights we sang the old hymns—all of them. "On Jordan's Stormy Banks I Stand," "Onward Christian Soldiers," "Rock of Ages," "I Will Sing the Wondrous Story"—all of them. And the singing of those old hymns did provide for us the "complex set of images" that formed our understanding of what it meant to be a Christian. The singing of those images set them in motion, set us in motion to be what we were singing.

"Have Thine Own Way, Lord," was one of my favorites, then and now. The images in that hymn come out of this text in Jeremiah 18. God tells the prophet to go down to the potter's house, there to hear God's further word. Jeremiah goes, and sees the potter working at his wheel. The potter is making a pot, but all at once the clay is spoiled, the pot ruined. But with the skill and perseverance by which good potters shape their work, he makes another pot. The former intent becomes a new actuality.

God uses this image as a sign of how the judgment he is forming may become something else—a blessing. The people at my dad's church were blessed to sing of how God was forming something new of them. I am pleased to think of it still, and still find myself praying, as if in song, have thine own way, Lord. (Thomas R. Steagald)

CHRISTIAN GRACE

PHILEMON 1-21

In asking for mercy upon Philemon's rebellious, now converted Christian, slave, Paul writes a letter that becomes a treatise of the "outflow" of grace in our lives as Christians. The details of his discussion demonstrate the relationships that should be found within the body of Christ.

I. Character of Christians

In verse 5, Paul notes that he gives thanks and prays for Philemon because of the reports he has heard about Philemon's faith and love. Faith is to be actively shared to increase our growth as Christians (v. 6). Love in the body of Christ gives joy, encouragement, and refreshes the hearts of believers (v. 7).

Christian character is to be shaped by our faith in God and our love for people. These are basic building blocks of a Christian life. Love also is a natural result of true faith in God. By building upon these two foundational areas of our lives, we find corresponding traits in terms of motives, attitude, and activity.

II. Christian Motives

The best example of Christian motivation is Paul's basis for appeal in verses 8 and 9. Paul is appealing to Philemon to be merciful to Onesimus on the basis of love. Paul has the "right" to demand Philemon do the right thing, but Paul desires him to be motivated by the right stimulus.

"Rights" are not important considerations in the New Testament's teachings about the Kingdom of God. In fact, as this text indicates, we lose certain rights of retaliation and are exhorted to forgive in the teaching of Jesus. The Kingdom of God seems to be more concerned with our responsibility. Jesus and Paul never tired of speaking about the Christian's role as a steward of the grace and blessings of God. Bypassing our right to respond in retaliation, Christians are to respond motivated by love.

III. Christian Attitude

A believer can do or fulfill the requirements that the motivations of love demand, but our true disposition is determined by our attitude toward those whom we are to bless and forgive. Paul exhorts Philemon in verse 16 to treat his returning slave, Onesimus, as a "dear brother." While the roles of subordinate and leader are still intact, the relationship of love is demonstrated in the attitude of Philemon (and Onesimus for that matter).

We may be in different stations in life, but we are all to treat brothers and sisters in Christ as "dear ones." Believing in someone and encouraging that person is the quality of relationship that we often overlook in the Body of Christ. If our motivation is love, our attitude toward one another will demonstrate that.

IV. Christian Actions

Motivated by love, equipped with an attitude of brotherhood, the Christian is to act in certain ways. Paul is clear in verse 17 as to the course of action Philemon is to take. Philemon is to welcome Onesimus as a partner; that translates into "forgiveness." Correct motives and proper attitudes culminate in one possible result: the act of forgiveness. Forgiveness is the cornerstone of Christianity. It is the way we enter into faith and the mode of operation in the family of God. The characteristics of our faith and love are realized in our ability to forgive. (Joseph Byrd)

EVERYONE LOVES A PARADE

LUKE 14:25-33

Everyone loves a parade, right? Sure! I remember my dad taking me downtown to see all the clowns and floats. I remember him lifting me up on his shoulders so I could see. Everyone loves a parade.

Even in Jesus' day that was true as well. Jesus' journey to Jerusalem in this passage seems more like a parade than anything else.

Luke tells us that great multitudes were going along with Jesus. We know that when they got to Jerusalem the streets were lined with onlookers, probably even youngsters on their dads' shoulders. So maybe a parade is the best way to describe this approach to Jerusalem.

It certainly wasn't a funeral procession. Not even the disciples understood that Jesus was going there to die. It's not a military march either. Luke doesn't say, "Now great throngs were *marching* to Jerusalem with him." It says, "Now great multitudes were *going along* with him"—just going along.

So there they were, having a parade when Jesus stopped and rained all over their parade. Three times he spoke of those who could not be his disciples—*disciple* is a word meaning "committed follower" (vv. 26, 27, 33).

He said they could not be his disciples if they did not hate their own families in comparison to their love for him. Not a vicious hate, but rather a priority placed on allegiance to Christ. Jesus' chosen twelve disciples had left family behind to follow him.

He said they could not be his disciples if they did not carry their own cross. A cross was not a piece of jewelry worn around the neck. It was Rome's cruelest means of execution. To follow Jesus meant to be prepared for death. Jesus certainly was.

He also said they could not be his disciples if they did not give up their own possessions. Jesus' twelve disciples had sacrificed their possessions to follow him.

These were hard words. They still are. But Jesus had his reasons for being so demanding. He knew that to follow him would be so demanding later, so he told them up front. And just to make sure they got it, he told them two crazy stories.

He said, "Can you imagine someone setting out to build a watch tower, drawing up the plans, selecting a site, and so forth, but never figuring whether they have enough money to buy all of the materials? If they didn't count the cost *ahead of time,* people would laugh every time they walked by that old, half-finished tower."

He also said, "Or can you imagine some great king going into battle with a neighboring kingdom, but never checking to make sure the other guys didn't have more troops and ammunition? If the king didn't count the cost *ahead of time,* people would remember that foolish old king every time they passed that memorial cemetery where his troops were buried."

I can appreciate those stories. I remember a few years back that a rich Texas oil man decided to build a house like no other. The fence around his property alone was going to cost somewhere in the neighborhood of $150,000. That fence was very impressive, but after a couple of years the whole thing became a big joke because a fence was all there was. He never did build that house. That was Jesus' point exactly.

Everyone loves a parade, except maybe those folks who were following Jesus that day. Jesus spoke of conflict—not the overthrow of Rome, but the overthrow of each follower's own desires. Following Jesus is no parade. (Mike Graves)

SEPTEMBER 17, 1995

∽

Fifteenth Sunday After Pentecost

Worship Theme: Sin inevitably results in judgment, but the promise of God's grace is available to bring forgiveness and new life.

Readings: Jeremiah 4:11-12, 22-28; 1 Timothy 1:12-17; Luke 15:1-10

Call to Worship (Psalm 14:2-5):

Leader: The LORD looks down from heaven on humankind to see if there are any who are wise, who seek after God.

People: They have all gone astray, they are all alike perverse; there is no one who does good, no, not one.

Leader: Have they no knowledge, all the evildoers who eat up my people as they eat bread, and do not call upon the LORD?

All: There they shall be in great terror, for God is with the company of the righteous.

Pastoral Prayer:

We thank you, Lord, that you are always nearby, watching over us even when our restlessness leads us away from you. We all wander away from time to time. Sometimes it takes entirely too long for us to realize what we've done and how far away we've strayed before we turn around. We are grateful that you patiently wait for us to come to our senses, that you never give up on us. You never stop loving us; you never stop longing for us to return no matter what we've done, where we've been, and how much we've tested your patience.

We want to honor you with our lives, Lord, but we confess that we've not yet learned to depend upon you to meet our needs. We've not yet learned to rely fully on your promises. Forgive us, Lord. Hear us as we pray for the freshness of your Spirit to renew our faith, to brighten our hopes, and to finish the work you have begun in us through the power and the blood of Jesus Christ our Lord, in whose name we pray. Amen. (Gary C. Redding)

SERMON BRIEFS

TRUTH AND CONSEQUENCES
JEREMIAH 4:11-12, 22-28

Call it truth *and* consequences, this passage, instead of truth *or* consequences, for the truth is that what is coming—a "scorching wind from the north" and destruction for the Holy City—is the consequence for the people's sin.

The wind that is coming, which is stronger than your average wind and serves for no comfort or cleansing—that "wind" is the armies of Nebuchadnezzar. The exact date of this oracle is unknown, but no matter. The invader's siege is inevitable, the destruction of Jerusalem unavoidable, its fate all but incredible. The people had always believed such a thing impossible—surely the Holy City of David, Zion, the home of God could never be destroyed. But the destruction is not only a possibility; it is an certainty. That's the truth. But why these consequences?

As we noted in an earlier lesson, 2 Kings 17 gives a chronicle of the reasons for the fall of Israel: "This occurred because the people of Israel had sinned against the LORD their God, who had brought them up out of the land of Egypt from under the hand of Pharaoh king of Egypt. They had worshiped other gods and walked in the customs of the nations . . . [And they] secretly did things that were not right" (2 Kings 17:7-9).

In this lection from Jeremiah 4 we read another "chronicle," an indictment against Judah and Jerusalem. It is not nearly as extensive as 2 Kings 17; it is, however, just as telling. Verse 22 of Jeremiah 4 reads:

> "For my people are foolish,
>   they do not know me;
> they are stupid children,
>   they have no understanding.
> They are skilled in doing evil,
>   but do not know how to do good."

311

It is a damning indictment, covering, as it were, a multitude of sins. Idolatries and injustice, infidelities and faithlessness—all are matters of foolishness, of not knowing God. And foolish as they are, it is no wonder that the people have refused to listen to the truth of God's prophet, that they should show genuine confusion as to why such a consequence should befall them.

Perhaps the last charge is the most poignant. God had called all the people of Israel, in the persons of their ancestors Abraham and Sarah, that they might both be blessed and become a blessing to all the nations of the earth. God called them to a new land, then brought them back to that land after their Egyptian sojourn. God set them and their land apart for good, and for the doing of good—for the benefit of the nations.

Here, however, is the announcement not of blessing, but of a curse, on the people and the land, as at least one of the nations turns against the would-be vessel of God's grace (vv. 23-27a).

The good that God had intended was about to come to an end, and all because the people had great knowledge of evil, but flunked when it came to the knowledge of good. They were industrious in doing the wrong, and slothful to do right. Such was the truth, and the blessing God intended became judgment instead, a terrible consequence to those who had foolishly forgotten their place, their history, and their call.

And yet: "I will not make a full end," said the Lord (v. 27). There is yet a glimmer of hope, that God, like a potter at the wheel, would take what was left of ruined Judah and start again, turning it to the right, turning it until God formed from the clay of his poor people one Son of Man who would be faith for the faithless, love for the loveless, hope for the hopeless, peace for the victims of war.

Judgment is coming, truth to tell. But there will come another consequence, another to fulfill the promise made to Abraham. (Thomas R. Steagald)

SONG OF A TRANSFORMED LIFE

1 TIMOTHY 1:12-17

We may look around at critics of Christianity and not sense a need to pray for them. We too easily perceive our loudest critics as enemies who can never be won. Christ taught us to pray for those we perceive as enemies, and the life of the apostle Paul demonstrates why that is so important. Our prayers for perceived enemies of the faith should be rooted in the knowledge of the transformation of our own lives and the hope that their lives will be transformed also.

I. The Present Faith

Paul wrote to a young pastor, Timothy, to encourage him in the ministry. No doubt, Timothy looked up to his mentor and colleague with great respect. Timothy also knew the problems and adversity faced in the "doing" of ministry. Paul's attitude, however, is that he was thankful for his appointment to serve in ministry (v. 12). He realized that it was truly a blessing to be part of the kingdom of God.

II. The Past Rebellion

Paul's stature in Christian ministry was not always so trusted. After his radical conversion, many believers were terrified of this former persecutor. Paul described himself prior to divine transformation as a "blasphemer," "violent," and "persecutor" (v. 13). Paul understood that in regard to sin, he was the "worst" among all sinners.

We can only imagine that Paul probably did not look at those who persecuted the church with the eyes of the other apostles. Paul knew the transforming power of Christian faith that changes violence to gentleness, the blasphemy to worship, and the persecutor to the apostle to the Gentiles. His life call was to share that power of Christian faith.

III. Transforming Grace

Verses 14-15 unfold the transforming power of God's grace. First, Paul describes the grace, love, and faith as being "poured out." This pouring is a divine act that is done even in human ignorance and unbelief. The mystery of grace is that Christ died for us while we were yet sinners.

Second, Paul notes that Christ came to save sinners. It was a single motive and goal that brought Christ to dwell among humanity. Paul's own conversion served as an example of the unlimited patience of God in accomplishing this divine goal. Christ was determined to atone for humanity and reconcile us to God.

IV. A New Song

After experiencing the transforming grace of Christ, there is but one proper response: worship. Paul breaks forth in a worship song of praise to the King, the author of our transformation. He is described as eternal, immortal, invisible, and the only God. To God, the giver of grace, we are to bestow honor and glory.

We worship for our transformation. We worship for the power of God to transform those around us and to make enemies our brothers and sisters—fellow pilgrims on the path on which God has placed us. We were created and newly transformed to worship; it is our highest calling. We truly sing a new song since encountering the grace of God. (Joseph Byrd)

GUESS WHO'S COMING TO DINNER

LUKE 15:1-10

It was a cinematic shocker in 1967—Sydney Poitier in *Guess Who's Coming to Dinner*. A good, respectable white girl courted by a black man (Are you ready for this?) brought him home to dinner. The shock of it all! You didn't do that in the sixties.

Apparently, you didn't do it in Jesus' time either. According to the Pharisees and scribes, Jesus was having fellowship with the wrong kind of people. You know, no-good sinners.

But don't be too hard on the Pharisees and scribes; after all, they had a point. I mean, there are some people who should be avoided. The Apostle Paul himself warned, "Bad company ruins good morals" (1 Cor. 15:33). So the Pharisees murmured among themselves, "Does he have to eat with them?"

Jesus' reply? "Let me tell you a story." So he did—three actually, two of which concern us today.

In the first story, Jesus says a man with a hundred sheep loses one. The obvious thing to do is to go looking, but who's going to watch the others? The old shepherd scratches his bearded chin a while and then decides it's worth the risk. He hikes his outer garment with one hand and walks with his staff in the other. He scours the countryside in search of the lost sheep. Everywhere he looks he finds nothing. Then suddenly he hears the lonely bleating. The sheep is caught in the brush, whimpering to be free. The shepherd balances the little thing on his shoulders and comes back whistling. All of his friends are ecstatic. They celebrate around the campfire.

All of the Pharisees nodded in agreement. What a wonderful feeling to find something that's been lost! When I was a boy, I had a dog named Sam. He was a great dog. Then one day he was gone. We searched everywhere, put up signs, you name it. Nothing. Then one day he showed up suddenly. My mom suggested a party—Sam was guest of honor.

Then Jesus told another story: A woman, looking through her coins one day, can't find one. Oh, some of them are there, most of them, in fact, but not all. One of her ten coins is missing. What a feeling of frustration. She pours some oil in her lamp and looks everywhere. But it's nowhere to be found. It's not under her bed roll or among any of the water pots. Just as she's about to give up hope, she finds it. She tells all her friends, and they throw her a party.

Again, all of the Pharisees nodded in agreement. What a wonderful feeling to find something that's been lost! An elderly couple returning from vacation suddenly discover the wife's purse is missing. They stopped to eat hours ago and probably left it there. At the next exit they pull over to call. She gets off the phone, "It's been found. Thank goodness." They feel like celebrating.

Of course, that is Jesus' whole point. When something has been lost, you look for it. These parables remind us that God diligently seeks the lost. And while he searches, it is, as C. S. Lewis puts it, a time when "the angels of God hold their breath" to see what will happen.

There's something else here as well. When something has been lost, you look for it, but when that something has been found, you celebrate. As Jesus says in verse 10, "Just so, I tell you, there is joy in the presence of the angels of God over one sinner who repents."

Joy over repenting sinners? That seems a bit much. Maybe so, but guess who's coming to dinner at God's table!. (Mike Graves)

SEPTEMBER 24, 1995

✑

Sixteenth Sunday After Pentecost

Worship Theme: We are called to be wise and faithful stewards of the possessions God has entrusted to us.

Readings: Jeremiah 8:18–9:1; 1 Timothy 2:1-7; Luke 16:1-13

Call to Worship (Psalm 79:9):

Leader: Help us, O God of our salvation, for the glory of your name;

All: deliver us, and forgive our sins, for your name's sake.

Pastoral Prayer:

O God, who has made us and all that is around us, we know that you are the owner of everything in this world—the land and the sea and every living thing. When we become proud of our possessions and material achievements, remind us, Lord, that they all belong to you; remind us that we are but stewards, managers entrusted with the care of our own little part of your world. Help us, Father, to be faithful with those things you have placed in our care, whether little or much, that we would honor you through material possessions and resources as well as in every other area of life. Help us that others would see your love at work in our attitude toward things, for we ask it in the name of our Lord and Savior, Jesus Christ. Amen. (Michael Duduit)

SERMON BRIEFS

MORE ELOQUENT THAN WORDS

JEREMIAH 8:18–9:1

John Patton, in his book *From Ministry to Theology,* relates the story of a rather green chaplaincy resident, naive to many of the pressures and pains of a teaching hospital. While on call one night, the intern was summoned to the room of a woman whose baby had been stillborn a few hours earlier. "We want our baby baptized," the young mother said, cradling her lifeless daughter, her husband at her side. "Her name is Nicole."

The intern didn't know what to do, but asked them to come to the chapel a few minutes later. In the meantime he tried to find another, more experienced chaplain to take over, but to no avail. He was on his own and quite unsure as to how to proceed. He had not only professional uncertainties about what he had been asked to do, but theological qualms as well. Still, he knew he had to meet with grieving parents. He sketched in his mind something to say, hoping it would be appropriate to the moment.

The young parents arrived at the appointed time, but the chaplain found he could not say what he had prepared. Instead, and almost without realizing what he was doing, he took a tissue, wiped at the tears in the eyes of the parents, then wiped his own tears and touched the tissue to the baby's head and said, "Nicole, I baptize you in the name of the Father, and of the Son, and of the Holy Spirit."

He said nothing else—the tears were more eloquent than words could have been.

Tears are quite often more eloquent than words. I think in this regard of President Jimmy Carter. Whatever you might have thought of the former president's politics, you could not fail to be moved by the shot of him on election day 1980 on the porch of the courthouse in Plains, Georgia. The latest polls showed him a full ten points behind soon-to-be president Ronald Reagan; Carter's staff had shown him the news, so that he had almost certain knowledge of his imminent defeat. He took a moment to speak through the gathered press to the American people and said that he hoped they knew he had done his best. And he cried. He bit his quivering bottom lip to keep from losing his composure.

He said nothing else—the tears were more eloquent than words could have been.

You have to think of the prophet Jeremiah in these terms, too. The "Weeping Prophet," he has been called, and mostly because of this passage:

> For the hurt of my poor people I am hurt,
>   I mourn, and dismay has taken hold of me.
> ....
> O that my head were a spring of water,
>   and my eyes a fountain of tears,
> so that I might weep day and night
>   for the slain of my poor people! (8:21; 9:1)

Jeremiah was moved to mourning and tears because of the certain destruction of Jerusalem. What God had intended for the people of Israel, what God had willed for Jerusalem and the Temple—all of it was about to fall before Nebuchadnezzar's swords and torches.

The people were beset on account of their sins. Whatever hope there was in the bright days of summer had ended; there was no hope of salvation, nothing to save them from their certain end. The Lord was not in Zion; the king was not in her. The people cried to God, but it was too late. There was no balm in Gilead, no slave equal to the wound; no doctor, even, to heal what ailed them. The poor people suffered, with none to help.

Jeremiah wept for the people and the city, for what should have been but wasn't; for what shouldn't have been but was. Jeremiah wept for the slain and for the living. It is a powerful passage, this recollection of his pain.

But there is another, perhaps even more profound, power in this text. For years it was read in the company of those who knew intimately of the fall of Jerusalem. The passage helped them frame their own sadness, helped them deal with their own sadness about the loss of everything. Jeremiah recollected the people's grief, gave them a way to share the pain and grief together. Such may have given them something of the focus they lost when they lost the Temple—a central meaning to life, a community of suffering.

One can easily imagine that when the passage was read, Jeremiah's weren't the only tears in evidence. Perhaps there were whimpers all around. No one had to say anything else—the tears were more eloquent than words could have been. (Thomas R. Steagald)

MINISTRY BEYOND THE CONGREGATION

1 TIMOTHY 2:1-7

Paul understood that one of Timothy's roles as a pastor was a responsibility for the worship in the church at Ephesus. Worship extended far beyond the walls of any building in which this first-century church met. The results of the worship were to be felt beyond the congregation. This extension of Christian worship is rooted deeply in the devotion of prayer.

I. The Directive to Pray

Our worship is to include the act of prayer in the form of "requests, prayers, intercession, and thanksgiving" as a priority ("first of all" in v. 1). These various descriptions for the act of communion with God indicate that we pray for our needs (requests); we are to pray publicly (prayers); make a time of intimate conversation with God (intercession); and take time to give thanks for the concern and hearing of God (thanksgiving).

II. The Objects of Our Prayers

Whom do we pray for? Verse 2 indicates that we are to reach beyond the needs of the congregation and offer prayers on behalf of those in authority. This may seem easily acceptable in a democratic society, but the authorities in first-century Ephesus were the enemies of the church. Paul urgently beseeched the Christians at Ephesus to pray for those who may in fact have been enemies.

What reason stands behind this directive? Paul notes that these prayers should be offered up in order that the Ephesian Christians might live their lives peacefully and quietly in godliness and holiness. Paul notes that such prayers and the results of such prayers please God (v. 3).

III. The Hope of Our Prayers

Verse 4 indicates that the prayers within our worship please God because he desires all humanity to be saved and come to a knowledge of the truth. In our acts of worshipful prayer, we truly become salt of the earth and light of the world. We become agents of God's plan for reconciliation.

We not only assist in completing the objective of God, but also we bear the nature of God as ministers of reconciliation. Verses 5-6 remind us that Christ's function was to mediate between God and humanity and that he even gave his life to accomplish this purpose. Our call to reconcile is no different in its nature.

This text makes us aware that we are not members of Christ's kingdom for our own sakes, but that we are his disciples that we might make other disciples. We often overlook the fact that we may make disciples by praying for those outside our congregation and being agents of reconciliation in nature. What a marvelous act of worship and ministry to pray for those outside of the church. (Joseph Byrd)

MAKING YOUR MONEY WORK FOR YOU

LUKE 16:1-13

This is an unusual text for, on the surface at least, it is a biblical story glorifying a scoundrel. We can hardly pretend the fellow is more. He has been a lazy, do-nothing steward, an accountant who has terribly neglected his master's business, so that it has cost the master a great deal of money. His master finally gets wind of what is going on and decides to fire him. "Turn in your books," he says, "you're finished with me."

The lazy fellow is shocked. He is too old to find another job. Besides, if word gets around that he was fired for being an inadequate steward, he doesn't stand much chance of finding employment anyway. So he gets busy to keep the job he has.

What he does is, by our standards, the most reprehensible part of the story. He goes out among all his master's debtors—people who owe him oil and wine and cheese and wheat—and strikes a quick bargain with each of them to pay off the debts at discount rates. Thus the steward makes instant friends of all the debtors so that they praise him to his master, and he pleases the master by suddenly swelling his storehouses with goods. The master knows he is a rascal, but he likes the ingenuity, the *chutzpah,* and reinstates the steward in his job with commendations for his uncommonly good sense.

You know, I never had a Sunday school teacher who dared touch that story. Jesus must have had fun telling it, for it doubtless shocked some people in his day. But what Jesus wanted to get across was the importance of using their money in clever ways that would greatly benefit them. "Make friends for yourselves by means of dishonest wealth so that when it is gone, they may welcome you into the eternal homes" (v. 9).

When it fails. That tells you what Jesus thought of money, doesn't it? I know people who have everything they want financially and are very unhappy. They cheat on their spouses, drink too much, work too hard; they are throwing their lives away because their money cannot make them happy.

It wasn't really *his* money, you're thinking. It was his master's money he was using, not his own. Jesus wanted to make the point that it is never our own money we are dealing with, it is always *God's* money. That's why the fellow in the story is a steward, a person who looks after someone else's property. We are all stewards; we are only caretakers, no matter how much or how little we have.

Some people forget about this, like that rich man Jesus talks about a little later in the same chapter of Luke. He thinks everything he has is really his, so he doesn't bother to share it with the poor man who lies at the gate begging alms. Then he wakes up in hell for misusing what was God's. His mistake, you see, was in not making his money work for him. A lot of it was lying around without doing any good, when it could have been taking care of the poor beggar at the gate.

The Gospel draws a vivid contrast between this foolish man and one wise woman, who appears in chapter 21. Jesus is at the Temple and sees a poor woman, her gnarled hands clutching two tiny copper coins, come and drop both of them into the treasury. "Truly I tell you," Jesus said, "this poor widow has put in more than anybody, for it was all she had" (see 21:1-4).

Talk about making your money work for you! Only two copper coins and they earned her a place in history. Here she was with her pittance, and she made it work for her as if it were millions of dollars!

It isn't how much you have in life, it's what you do with it that counts. Everything we have is a trust from God. And the important thing is to learn to use it wisely by sharing it and taking care of God's world. When we do this, we are making an investment in our own souls. (John Killinger)

OCTOBER

❧

Replenishing the Well

Expect Faith to Work

Faith works. Faith is active. God expects faith to work, to have an impact on our lives, our relationships, our world. This month's exercise helps to identify the results of a working faith.

Time: 30 minutes each week for four weeks.

Materials: A Bible, your journal, a pen or pencil.

Exercise:

WEEK 1

Read Luke 17:5-10. Open your journal and spend 25 minutes answering the following question:
• *How is faith expected to work in these parables?*
Each week, for the next three weeks, you will be asked to identify how your faith works.

WEEK 2

Read again Luke 17:5-10. Spend 15 minutes at the beginning of the week to identify in your journal one area of your inner, spiritual life where you expect faith to work this week. For example, "I expect to see my faith at work in my prayer life—that my prayers have some kind of transforming effect on my life, my relationship with God, or my church."

At the end of the week, open your journal and spend 15 minutes recording any results of your faith at work. For example, "I found my trust in God increased and my fears lessened as I prayed this week."

WEEK 3

Read again Luke 17:5-10. Spend 15 minutes at the beginning of the week to identify in your journal how you expect faith to work in your personal relationships this week. For example, "I believe that God will help me communicate better with my family this week."

At the end of the week, open your journal and spend 15 minutes recording any results of your faith at work. For example, "With God's help I was able to clear up a misunderstanding with my daughter."

WEEK 4

Read again Luke 17:5-10. Spend 15 minutes at the beginning of the week to identify in your journal how you expect your faith to work in your church or the world. For example, "I will put my faith to work by volunteering to work in a soup kitchen one day this week."

At the end of the week, spend 15 minutes recording any results of your faith at work. For example, "Working in the soup kitchen, I saw the eyes of Jesus in the faces of the men and women I served."

OCTOBER 1, 1995

◆

Seventeenth Sunday After Pentecost

Worship Theme: Ultimate security is not found in material possessions but through faith in Jesus Christ.

Readings: Jeremiah 32:1-3*a*, 6-15; 1 Timothy 6:6-19; Luke 16:19-31

Call to Worship (Psalm 91:14-16):

Leader: Those who love me, I will deliver; I will protect those who know my name.

People: When they call to me, I will answer them;

Leader: I will be with them in trouble, I will rescue them and honor them.

All: With long life I will satisfy them, and show them my salvation.

Pastoral Prayer:

Praise waits for you, O God, within this holy place, and with glowing hearts and cheerful songs we gather in your presence. In your image we were created, and from your hands we receive our daily bread. We thank you, Lord, for all your benefits to us and to all of humanity. We thank you for our country, our homes, our family and friends; for the opportunities that we have to work and to serve those in need. We thank you for our knowledge of you and your gospel of love and for the joy that comes from the knowledge of sins forgiven.

Bless this congregation of your people; strengthen every ministry that makes for the advance of your kingdom among them. Follow us with your favor, O Lord, when we leave the fellowship of this place. May those who came here under the burden of sin go out with a sense of release. May those for whom life has little meaning rejoice in having found the will to go on. May all who have found a renewed commitment to you rise to a higher level of living, where work and service are filled with purpose. Accept the words of our lips and the dedication of our hearts this day and forever. Amen. (John Bishop)

SERMON BRIEFS

HOPE IN THE MIDST OF THE DARK

JEREMIAH 32:1-3a, 6-15

Jeremiah is often called the "weeping prophet." If anyone had reason to cry, it was Jeremiah. God had promised so much; the people had such possibility. Now, they were surrounded by the Babylonians. There was no bright hope in their future. Jeremiah was in jail.

For most of us, that would have been a good time to give up, to call it quits, to throw in the towel. What did Jeremiah do? He sent word from jail that he was ready to buy some property, to purchase a field at Anathoth. The text interests us as it contains a clear picture of a land transaction during the Old Testament period. It is of interest to us because it illustrates how we can live with hope in the midst of darkness. Jeremiah affirmed his hope for the future in the purchase of land. He was saying, "I will be free again. Houses and land will again be built in our land. God will restore the devastation. Crops will again flourish. Families will return. Life will take precedent over tragedy and sorrow."

I. Hope Is Not Born from Our Circumstances, but from Our Faith

Jeremiah could not justify his hope from a single circumstance of his own or of God's people. Human reason and wisdom could only say, "Give up! Quit!" Jeremiah found his hope through faith in God. Years before God called Jeremiah, God gave him the tasks of witness and declaration. Jeremiah told of his faith and declared the love of God. God's love was not tied to external joys, but to inner peace.

William Least Heat Moon, in his book *Prairyerth,* tells of Blanche Schwilling. She lives in Bazaar, Kansas, which really isn't a town any longer. She was the postmistress for twenty-eight years, but the Postal Service closed the office. They took away her stamps, declaring that Bazaar was no longer a real place. All that is left are twelve citizens and a church, which was finally closed. A neighbor says of Blanche, "She holds things together with her own two hands." Every other week a preacher travels to Bazaar to have services. The rest of the time, Blanche conducts devotionals and rings the church bell every Sunday. She said, "No one hears it but those of us already there, but I guess that's who it's for."

II. Hope Is Expressed in Deeds, Not in Thoughts and Words

Jeremiah didn't shout his thoughts from behind the bars of the prison. He didn't send messages out to declare his thoughts. He bought a field. The children of God have the light of Christ to illumine the darkness that overwhelms us. We have light only where we are. We step to the outer limit of the light we know and see, and the light moves beyond us. We do not have to see all the way to the end of the road. We have only to see the one step that is before us.

There are fields of faith for sale in our world today. We can express hope rather than despair when we purchase the fields on which we can build tomorrows. (Harold C. Perdue)

APOSTOLIC ECONOMICS

1 TIMOTHY 6:6-19

The old television commercial would have everyone listen whenever E. F. Hutton would speak. There is reason to listen when the Bible speaks about money, for the Bible remains our greatest book, and money continues to be a powerful force in human life. The words of the older apostle to young Timothy offer insight into what we might call "apostolic economics."

327

I. Apostolic Economics Warns Us Against the Wrong Attitude About Money

Paul's warning speaks against making money an object of our love. What is wrong with loving money?

Money can become a rival god. Jesus made this point in his Sermon on the Mount, and it became the guideline for all New Testament thinking. The way Jesus defined the issue in Matthew 6:24, riches compete with God for our attention and devotion. We cannot love both God and money.

Money can destroy relationships. The heavy weight of greed can break the tight bond that ought to exist between brothers and sisters. Many of us know more than one case of siblings who no longer speak with each other because of the way their parents' material goods were divided.

Money can ruin our vision. What happens is that, when we love money inordinately, we begin to see everything through its green lens, which leads to distortion. If a monetary value is assigned to everything, then nothing is appreciated for its own sake or seen in its true light.

Money does not last. According to an old proverb, "There are no pockets in a shroud." Such a proverb reflects the apostle's word to Timothy: "We brought nothing into the world, so that we can take nothing out it" (v. 7). To love money with an ultimate allegiance is to love something that will ultimately fail.

II. Apostolic Economics Guides Us to the Right Attitude Toward Money

According to the apostle, money itself is not diabolical, only the love of it. There can be a healthy appreciation of money.

The right attitude toward money is to know its place in life. It is not money that gives life to all things or serves as the foundation of our hope. God alone rightly occupies that place in life. There can be no healthy appreciation of money until it is knocked out of life's center.

The right attitude toward money is to enjoy it as a gift from God. There is no sin in being rich. Material goods are not to be despised. Calvin believed that material possessions are part of God's creation and providence. He understood that they were created for our good rather than for our ruin. Yet, he stressed that material goods are not to be enjoyed immoderately, but reverently, always aware of and grateful to God the provider.

The right attitude toward money is also to use it as a tool in the service of God. This is what the apostle meant when he told Timothy to teach the rich that they are to "be rich in good works, generous and ready to share" (v. 18).

May the Lord help you handle your money according to the principles of apostolic economics. This may not lead to wealth in the eyes of the world, but it can keep your soul from being impoverished both in this world and the next. (Mark E. Yurs)

A COLD, COLD HEART

LUKE 16:19-31

A teenage girl was talking to her boyfriend about her parents one evening. "My mother is happy only when she's spending money," said the girl. "In fact, she went shopping every day until someone stole all her credit cards."

"Have the police caught the person who stole them?" asked her boyfriend. "Oh, no," said the girl. "Dad didn't even report it. Whoever stole them is spending less than my mother did."

If you had as much money as you would ever need—and more—how would you spend it? Would you live lavishly—and selfishly—like the rich man in the text, or are there other, more hopeful possibilities?

I. The Man Who Had Everything and Lost It

In a twist of irony, the rich man remained nameless in the story, even though traditionally he has become known as Dives. That's quite different from the way it normally is in the world. Most of us know the names of the people who have money in our towns. It's the poor, the homeless, the hungry, and the welfare recipients who are unknown to most of us.

In personal life-style, most of us are more like the rich man than the poor. The only reason you don't feel rich is that everyone around you is rich also. Still, in all fairness, there is nothing wrong with having fine clothes, good food, nice homes, and modern conveniences. It is by God's grace that we live in the most prosperous nation on earth.

However, numbness always seems to plague a satisfied soul. We grow less and less sensitive. Compassion takes a smaller and smaller place in our life. When we allow money and the stuff it buys to become idols, the first sacrifice we make to those idols is our compassion and mercy. So it was with the rich man in Jesus' story. He had everything and lost it simply because he hoarded everything in a vain attempt to keep it.

II. The Man Who Had Nothing but Gained Heaven

The poor man's name was Lazarus, which means "God is my helper." And it's a good thing because apparently no one else was going to help him. God was his only friend!

There are many Lazaruses walking the streets of our communities. They are the pathetic, dirty, and frightening forms we see climbing in and out of dumpsters, foraging for food. Lazarus is the name of every poor soul who sits at our door, needing our love and attention.

Both men died—and they died as differently as they lived. Why did each wind up where he did? It was not his poverty that carried Lazarus to Abraham's bosom. Neither was it his riches that condemned the rich man to hell. Neither is the issue the relative length of the lists of their good and bad deeds. Nothing at all meritorious is credited to Lazarus. And nothing damaging is charged against the rich man. He was never cruel or brutal—not even to the poor man at his doorstep. In fact, it was the leftovers from his table that kept Lazarus alive for as long as he survived.

The rich man's sin was unbelief. He had faith, but it was not placed in God. His security and comfort were based on this world's values. His heart was bound up with his treasure.

That is our sin also. Many Christians would like to be more generous in their giving, but they just can't! It's not that they don't have the resources. Neither is it because they are selfish. It's simply that they don't have enough faith to believe that God can take care of them on what they will have left. Their problem really isn't greed. It's unbelief!

Alexander the Great conquered the known world by the time he was thirty years old. It is said that just before he died a few years later, he requested that holes be cut in his coffin so that his arms could be extended outside. He wanted to be carried through the streets with his arms outstretched and his palms pointed upward to show the world that even the most powerful men leave the world empty-handed.

If you can't take it with you—and you won't—then why do you hold on to it so tightly? (Gary C. Redding)

OCTOBER 8, 1995

❧

Eighteenth Sunday After Pentecost

Worship Theme: Even in the midst of difficult times, we can live victoriously through the power of Jesus Christ in us.

Readings: Lamentations 1:1-6; 2 Timothy 1:1-14; Luke 17:5-10

Call to Worship (Psalm 37:1-4):

Leader: Do not fret because of the wicked; do not be envious of wrongdoers,

People: for they will soon fade like the grass, and wither like the green herb.

Leader: Trust in the LORD, and do good; so you will live in the land, and enjoy security.

People: Take delight in the LORD, and he will give you the desires of your heart.

Pastoral Prayer:

Great God in heaven, we come to you in this moment of prayer with thanksgiving in our hearts and with hopes and dreams for a future filled with wonderful things. We have experienced your blessings in so many ways, Lord. There is the quiet mystery of early morning dew; the commanding majesty of thunderstorms; the beginnings of autumn's splash of color, just now evident. We are surrounded by sights, sounds, and smells that are wondrous gifts from you. Help us to treasure these blessings!

Yet, heavenly Father, there are those for whom we must intercede this morning, asking yet more and crucial gifts from you to them. We think of those who have lost a close friend or loved one, and who quietly grieve their loss. May you grant comfort of heart and soul that eases the pain but erases not the memories. We bring before you those families in trouble: fathers and mothers in conflict with their children; husbands and wives who are

332

seeking to recapture the love they once shared. Your love can help them overcome, Lord. We bring these petitions and thanksgivings to you because you have promised that our prayers will not go unanswered, as we ask these things in Christ's name. Amen. (Steven R. Fleming)

SERMON BRIEFS

LESSONS FROM LIFE

LAMENTATIONS 1:1-6

Lamentations is one part of the Scripture that I have seldom used as the basis for a sermon, and I do not believe that I am alone in ignoring this book. The very name is a deterrent. We have enough sadness in our lives. We already know how to moan about our misfortune. We can feel sorry for ourselves and our circumstances without any help from this source.

Yet, there is more to this text than sadness and misfortune. There is a statement of faith here. In this text we find a statement of God's involvement in life when we think God is absent.

The people of Israel had been exiled. Babylonians had terrorized them, defeated them, exiled them. The issue is what were they to do in the low estate they were now in. There are two lessons detected in this Scripture.

I. We Must Learn the Lessons of the Past

Although such advice seems simple, this truth is more complex than it appears. When God is ignored, life tumbles in. When God is focused upon, life has meaning. In the Garden, with Adam and Eve, life was a joy when they walked with God. Forgetting God, they invited disaster. The brothers, Cain and Abel, could have lived in love and peace if God had been in them. Without God, it was death, destruction, and fear. Hunger drove Jacob's family to Egypt. Their eyes grew large looking at the bounty of Egypt, and soon they were in slavery.

Victory came when Israel depended on God in the promised land. Troubles and difficulties were the result of forgetting about

God. God added to one person is more than two. With God, defeat is brushed aside and victory is grasped.

In Estonia, there is a small United Methodist church pastored by Alexander Krums. He was ordered to disband his church and stop preaching. He refused and was imprisoned for five years. When Pastor Krums was released, he came back to a church that was five times larger than when he had first gone to prison. The leader could have known that jailing Peter and Paul didn't stop the early Christians. It won't work in our time either.

II. In Difficulty, We Can Learn to Retain Faith

Terry Anderson was one of the hostages detained in Lebanon for many years. After his release in 1992, he was interviewed by *Time* magazine. He was asked whether he held any bitterness toward the people who had held him so long. Terry Anderson replied, "I don't have time for it. I don't have any need for it. It is required of me as a Christian to put that aside, to forgive and to try to understand them. I pray for them. I wish them no ill in their lives. My life is very, very busy." Faith is retained when we focus on our Savior, not on our tormentors. Faith is retained when we respond to love, not hate. Faith is retained when we seek reconciliation, not spite. Faith is retained when we act in love, not in revenge. (Harold C. Perdue)

THE MINISTRY OF ENCOURAGEMENT
2 TIMOTHY 1:1-14

The spirit of 2 Timothy is that of an older worker who is writing to encourage a younger colleague. The apostolic ministry of encouragement is needed today in churches where workers may tire or flag in zeal. How can we offer support? Look to the ministry of encouragement as conducted by the author of 2 Timothy.

I. The Apostle Brought Encouragement by Voicing His Gratitude

Paul told his young friend that he was grateful to God for Timothy. To be appreciated, especially by someone one respects and admires, is a boost to hope and a boon to courage. The morale in many churches could be strengthened if more words of gratitude were spoken.

A certain woman was responsible for the flowers in her church for more years than she could remember. Her work of ordering and arranging flowers, seeing that they were there for worship or that they arrived in the hospital room, was her labor of love. She expected no thanks. Still, whenever her pastor or another parishioner did speak a word of gratitude, there was new joy in her heart and renewed incentive in her soul.

II. The Apostle Brings Encouragement by Pointing to the Community of Faith

A technique that doubt and disappointment seem to love is divide and conquer. If you feel alone in your work and with your problems, then courage can escape in a slow leak until nerve and joy are flattened. The apostle must have known that, for he reminded Timothy of the faith of his grandmother and mother.

Young Timothy was not alone. There was a community of faith, and thought of that community can plug the leak of courage. We build courage in others by making practical witness to the reality and vitality of the fellowship of believers.

III. The Apostle Brings Gratitude by Reminding of the Call of God

New strength comes from being reacquainted with the call of God, whether it be the call to become a Christian or the call to a particular work as a Christian. Thought of the call is strengthening because of all the doctrine of call implies, particularly the truth that God supplies all things needed for the realization of the call. So we build courage in others by helping them become reconnected with their call in life-affirming ways, for that new sense of call can send folks back to old labors with new power.

IV. The Apostle Brings Encouragement
by Stressing the Glory of Christ

In simple words packed with eternal meaning, Paul shared the gospel of Jesus Christ, which speaks of salvation, grace, victory over death, the light of life eternal, and the power of these truths for today. The apostle understood full well that true courage comes not when we look to ourselves, but when we look to Christ, who is able to do all things.

This is the testimony of former major league baseball player Dave Dravecky, who is coping with the loss of his pitching arm to cancer. He confesses, "I am not getting through the loss of my arm because I am a great coper. I'm getting through it because I have a Father in heaven who is a great giver."

We build courage in others when we lead them to think less of themselves in their weakness and more of Christ, of his divine and living power, which is both present and able.

In these ways let us mutually encourage one another, strengthening the souls of those whom we love and empowering our church with new vitality. (Mark E. Yurs)

YOUR CHRISTIAN DUTY

LUKE 17:5-10

Have you ever noticed how two different people can look at exactly the same scene and yet see two entirely different things? One of the best illustrations I know is taken from Mark Twain's *Life on the Mississippi.* Late one afternoon, the novice riverboat pilot and his friend are watching the sunset. The friend is waxing eloquently about the beauty of the river. But where he sees loveliness, the pilot-in-training sees something very different—and worrisome. The way the sky looks indicates there will be strong winds by morning. The floating log means the river is rising. The slanting mark on the water means that there is a dangerous reef just under the surface—one large enough to kill somebody's steamboat one of these nights. The ripples in the water warn of a changing channel, and the slight circles up ahead mean that there are troublesome shoals to be negotiated.

I. Two People Looked at Exactly the Same Thing and Saw It Entirely Differently

It happened frequently with Jesus and his disciples. The text records one of those occasions. Luke 17:1-10 contains four separate teachings of the Lord that have been woven together by the Gospel writer. The first two alternatives (vv. 1-2 and vv. 3-4) call for radical, responsible love within the fellowship of Christian disciples. Upon hearing the expectations of Jesus, the disciples say to him, "Increase our faith!" (v. 5)—the implication being that, in order to live as he expects them to live, much more faith than they currently possess will be required.

II. Only One Person's Perspective Matters

However, Jesus responded by affirming the faith they possess. "If you had faith . . . " (v. 6) is not a reprimand for the absence of faith but an invitation to live out of the full possibilities of their existent faith. As small as it may have been, their faith was sufficient to cancel the word *impossible* from their vocabulary. The disciples saw their primary need as deeper spiritual growth—that is, more faith. Jesus, however, understood that their most significant need was merely a willingness to obey.

The parable that forms verses 7-10 is a reminder that the first obligation of a servant is to obedience. A servant does not enjoy the prerogative of being able to decline the master's demands. No matter what the servant may have already accomplished for the master, the servant is still responsible for fulfilling every demand. With regard to Jesus' demand for radical, responsible love, his servants do not have the prerogative to "beg off," either on the basis of other worthy deeds or personal weakness or inability to perform what is demanded.

This story is an antidote for the dual dangers of self-pity and self-conceit. A Christian must always be prepared to endure the demands of the kingdom, even if he or she has already given a reasonable effort. That is what God expects. Furthermore, once a Christian has done everything that can be done, he or she must not retreat in pride and satisfaction. The Christian's only real comfort is in knowing that she or he has been faithful in performing the duty as the Lord's servant. (Gary C. Redding)

OCTOBER 15, 1995

❧

Nineteenth Sunday After Pentecost

Worship Theme: Joy comes from a grateful heart.

Readings: Jeremiah 29:1, 4-7; 2 Timothy 2:8-15; Luke 17:11-19

Call to Worship (Psalm 66:1-2):

Leader: Make a joyful noise to God, all the earth;

All: sing the glory of his name; give to him glorious praise.

Pastoral Prayer:

O God, giver of all good gifts, in whom are the springs of our life, we praise you for your lovingkindness and tender mercies. We thank you for your hand upon us in sickness and in health; for the comfort of friends and family; for the joys of home and country; for every precious gift of your providence. We thank you for every messenger of your love whom you have granted to us, and especially for him who from the height of heaven stooped to enter into our low estate. We bless you that our darkness has been illumined by the gracious words of Christ, that our burdens have been lightened by his tender sympathy, and that by his holy influence our feet have been guided into the right way. Above all, we thank you that through the sacrifice of himself upon the cross and his victory over the grave, he has redeemed us from sin and death and made us partakers of eternal life. Hear us, O Lord, for the sake of Jesus Christ our Savior. Amen. (John Bishop)

SERMON BRIEFS

TODAY'S LIVING IS TOMORROW'S LIFE

JEREMIAH 29:1, 4-7

Jeremiah remained in Jerusalem. It was a desolate city. The Babylonians were victorious. The leaders of Jerusalem had been deported. Jeremiah heard from the deportees about the prophetic messages given them. Popular prophets tell them the return is imminent. God will not desert them. They will not have to remain in this foreign land for long. Their salvation is near.

The weeping prophet wrote a letter to his friends in exile. It does not affirm their wishes, but challenges them to live for their God in the midst of an ungodly circumstance. His message for them can be God's message for us.

I. It Is Time to Be Realistic, Not Idealistic

Faith is not constructed on dreams. Life with God is built on understanding the circumstances in which we live. Today our churches struggle with their settings. A recent report told of a church located in a racially changing neighborhood. There were hundreds of potential members of another ethnic heritage. The Anglo membership continued to dwindle to about twenty members. They were given the opportunity to establish a program to reach out to those around them, but they refused. They would not accept the assistance of others to build a church that ministered to their community. They unrealistically believe that something will change to enable them to be large again.

II. We Cannot Live in the Past, Only in the Present

Faith is lived today, not yesterday. Erma Bombeck has written many humorous books. A recent one, *I Want to Grow Hair, I Want to Grow Up, I Want to Go to Boise,* grew out of experiences at a camp for children and young people battling cancer. Bert was five. He loved to draw. One day a visitor asked, without proper thought, "Bert, do you want to be an artist when you grow up?" Bert replied matter of factly, "I am an artist."

Life is not to be lived in the concept "I have been." Life is to be lived with the understanding "I am."

III. The Present Is the Doorway to the Future

It is through living today that we can live tomorrow. If we cannot relate to God, serve God, love other persons where we are, it is not likely that we can do so in the future. A realistic understanding of where we are enables us to be faithful both today and tomorrow.

Fred Rogers, whose TV show for children has been on public television since 1968, presented an address at Boston University in which he told about a young boy who wrote to him after watching his show. The boy told of a troubled and abusive childhood. He related how he would sneak into the living room to watch "Mr. Roger's Neighborhood" and that he wrote to Fred Rogers because the boy considered him his only friend. The boy is now fourteen, has been placed in a foster home, and is writing a book. He told Fred Rogers about his new parents, "My dad has shown me that if I can take care of the present, I can take care of forever at the same time."

Jeremiah wrote to his exiled friends that they should settle down to reality. Release was a long way off in the future. There is much to do today that prepares us for tomorrow. In the midst of any circumstance there is life to be lived, persons to help, reality to be viewed. (Harold C. Perdue)

THE UNFETTERED WORD

2 TIMOTHY 2:8-15

In a typical motel, the television and its remote control device are bolted down, but the Gideon Bible is free. It can go anywhere and influence anyone. With this image in mind, think about the unfettered word Paul talks about in 2 Timothy, focusing on its content, its liberty, and its servant.

I. The Content of the Word (v. 8)

The content of the unfettered Word is the good news of Jesus Christ. The apostle says, "Remember Jesus Christ, raised from the dead, a descendent of David—that is my gospel" (v. 8). From this point of view, the content of the Word is the life of Jesus, the death of Jesus, the resurrection of Jesus, and, crowning it all, the divinity of Jesus.

II. The Liberty of the Word (v. 9)

Paul stressed that this Word of God is not fettered, chained, or bound in any way. The Word is not bound by the physical limitations of the speaker, the practical limitations of the speaker's sur-roundings, or the attitudinal limitations of the speaker's world.

Paul himself is an example, showing that the Word is not bound by the physical limitations of the speaker. He wrote that the Corinthians talked about him saying, "His letters are weighty and strong, but his bodily presence is weak, and his speech con-temptible" (2 Cor. 10:9).

Confined as he was in prison, Paul also is an example, showing how the Word is not bound by the practical limitations of the speaker's surroundings. In this he is joined by John of Patmos and a host of others, including John Bunyan, Dietrich Bonhoef-fer, Corrie ten Boom, and Martin Luther King, Jr.

The Word is not bound by the attitudinal limitations of the speaker's world. Walter Brueggemann claims that contemporary Americans handle the Word either too trivially or too technically. The result, he says, is that the "gospel is thus a truth widely held, but a truth greatly reduced." Even so, among the last sentences of the book in which he discusses that issue, Brueggemann says, "We have only the word, but the word will do. It will do because it is true that the poem [i.e., the message] shakes the empire, that the poem heals and transforms and rescues, that the poem enters like a thief in the night and gives new life, fresh from the word and from nowhere else." The Word is not bound by the small attitudes of the world.

III. The Servant of the Word (vv. 10ff.)

The servant of the unfettered Word speaks for the sake of oth-ers. His or her aim is the salvation of the hearer. Evangelical the-ologian Donald G. Bloesch quotes John Bunyan as saying that, when he was preaching, he was "in real pain, travailing to bring forth children to God." That is in concert with Paul, who said, "I endure everything for the sake of the elect, so that they may also obtain the salvation that is in Christ Jesus"(v. 10).

The servant of the Word who speaks for the sake of others speaks courageously. The courage for today comes from one's hope and confidence about tomorrow. The servant relies with confidence on the sure promises of Christ.

The servant who speaks courageously for the sake of others is a constant student. Under God, he or she studies not only the

Word but also human life. In that way he or she seeks to interpret the truth of God for life today.

Let us come to this Word with reverence and serve it with faithfulness, all in the confidence that God will mightily use our efforts for the sake of the kingdom. (Mark E. Yurs)

WELL ENOUGH TO ENJOY THE BLESSINGS

LUKE 17:11-19

A mother and her small son were walking along the riverfront in one of our nation's large cities when the youngster fell into the water. The currents quickly swept the boy beyond his mother's reach. A businessman, at lunch in one of the nearby riverfront restaurants, heard her hysterical cries, jumped into the water, and rescued the child. When the mother and her son were reunited, she noticed that his baseball cap had come off while he was in the water. She spotted it many yards down river, floating rapidly away. Without hesitation, she pointed out to her son's rescuer that he had failed to retrieve the cap. Then she demanded that he go back into the water to get it. Can you believe it? Is there anything that galls you more than ingratitude?

This story represents a mood that seems to be sweeping across our land. This past Halloween, scores of children came to our door. Most were grateful for the treats they received. However, an alarming number wanted one of each kind of candy in the basket. In fact, many insisted on helping themselves—wanting to take handfuls, instead of small samplings. What I noticed was that the greedy ones were the ungrateful ones. Those who took what they were given without whining and complaint seemed genuinely sincere in their appreciation for the favors.

I. The Need for Healing

If the spirit of thankfulness troubles you, you can understand why Jesus was concerned about the nine ungrateful lepers. Leprosy was the worst thing life could do to a person. It was a hopeless disease, as hopeless as death. In fact, it was death—except that just a part of you died every day. There was simply no way to treat it.

Beyond the physical torment, lepers could not even count on the comfort, sympathy, or compassion of their friends and family. Leprosy was a highly contagious disease. So, for the good of everyone concerned, those afflicted with it were forced to suffer the most extreme forms of isolation and ostracism.

II. The Miracle of Healing

To be healed of leprosy, then, was to be healed of a terminal illness. Surely, all ten lepers realized that. How could they not be grateful? Yet only one returned to say "thank you"—ten requests for mercy to one expression of praise. Someone suggested that that is about par for prayer. When we get the things we ask for and are satisfied, many have no further need of God.

Gratitude is a rare phenomenon. It's more than common courtesy, politeness, or even civility. Genuine, heartfelt gratitude is a spirit, an attitude. It is based on a deliberate decision to appreciate the world instead of biting back at it or being greedily preoccupied with it. Gratitude is what overwhelms a person when she realizes that God is being too good to her.

III. From Healing to Health

In this incident, ten were healed but only one got well enough to truly enjoy the Lord's blessing. He was the only one to turn back in humble thanksgiving and praise. Perhaps the single most surprising thing about the story is that the one who went back is the one no one would have expected to go back. He was a Samaritan (v. 16); the rest were Jews.

Perhaps, however, that explains his gratitude. He had less to trust in, less to rely on, less to be proud of than the others, who probably felt that they deserved the healing. They certainly had not deserved the kind of sickness they had. The fact that they did not turn back even to say a simple word of gratitude indicates how sick they remained.

Thanks may be the most valuable word in any language. When Mark Twain was at the peak of his career, his writing was valued at five dollars per word. Some prankster wrote Twain a letter stating, "Dear Mr. Twain: Enclosed is $5. Please send me your best word." Shortly, a reply came. It read simply, "Thanks."

Someone once said that God has two dwelling places. One is in heaven and the other is in the thankful heart. The season approaches when we should remember to "give thanks in all circumstances; for this is the will of God in Christ Jesus for you" (1 Thess. 5:18). (Gary C. Redding)

OCTOBER 22, 1995

~

Twentieth Sunday After Pentecost

Worship Theme: Prayer is the support that can carry us through all of life's circumstances.

Readings: Jeremiah 31:27-34; 2 Timothy 3:14–4:5; Luke 18:1-8

Call to Worship (Psalm 121):
Oh, how I love your law!
  It is my meditation all day long.

....

How sweet are your words to my taste,
  sweeter than honey to my mouth!
Through your precepts I get understanding;
  therefore I hate every false way.

Pastoral Prayer:
  Lord, we marvel at the remarkable gift of prayer that you have given to your children. To be able to walk boldly into your very presence is a unique and precious gift that we do not always value as highly as we ought. Indeed, there are times, Lord, when we act as if prayer is more burden than privilege; more duty than treasure. Forgive us for our presumptuous attitudes, and help us to understand better the awesome power to be found in prayer. Help us to learn to come into your presence with petitions and burdens, but also with joy and thanksgiving; help us learn to intercede for the needs of others, and also to praise you for your love and grace. In a world that runs from bookstores to therapists to psychic phone lines seeking answers and direction for life, thank you for placing the ultimate truth as close to us as a whispered prayer. Thank you for the privilege of praying in the name of our Lord and Savior, Jesus Christ. Amen. (Michael Duduit)

SERMON BRIEFS

KNOWING WITHOUT HEARING

JEREMIAH 31:27-34

After many years of marriage, communication takes place whether you say a word or not. My wife and I have been married nearly forty years. In my work for the church, we often travel together. Someone asked us what we talk about during those long hours of travel. We don't talk. We communicate in few words.

Several years ago, I discovered a book in the library and took it to a seminary professor. He glanced at it and began to comment on what was written. I asked him, "When did you read this book?" He replied, "Oh, I've never read it. I know the author. I know how he thinks and what he would write. I don't have to read his book to know what he is saying." Knowing a person intimately allows us to know what that person would say before she or he says it.

God promised Jeremiah such communication in the future. The day would come when God and persons would communicate without words. God's will and purpose would be so much a part of the heart and nature of all persons that there would not have to be verbal discussion and debate. God and persons would agree. After Jesus' death, the disciples remembered these verses. The hope of a new covenant was realized. It is one of the most profound and moving passages in the entire Bible.

I. God Has Forgiven Our Iniquity and Set Aside Our Sin

God acted in Jesus Christ to forgive the past. No matter how terrible our failure, no matter how far we have wandered from him, no matter how severely we have rebelled, God acted on our behalf. Like a searching shepherd, God has come seeking us to return to his care.

As I reflect upon my life, I realize God has sought me out when I wasn't seeking him. I thought I had everything worked out. Everything was fine; life was going well. God came to me to bring new insights, new directions, new opportunities.

II. God Has Provided to Us His Holy Spirit

The reality of God is with us always. We are never alone. God is with us. All around us and within us are signs of his presence. In the words of Holy Scripture, in the feeling of our inner being, in the fellowship of God's people, in the moments of personal prayer, in the experience of public worship, in the sacrament of Holy Communion, we discover the signs of God's presence.

God has provided a new covenant. Jesus established that covenant with the giving of his body and his blood and in that sacramental meal in the Upper Room. We recreate that holy moment in the Holy Communion. God comes again in our midst and for our sakes when we kneel at his Holy Table. We receive from him, in silence, without words because he has established it in our hearts. Then, we rise to go forth with God alive in us, guiding us, supporting us, directing us. (Harold C. Perdue)

FINDING YOUR WAY IN A CONFUSING WORLD

2 TIMOTHY 3:14–4:5

As Paul wrote to Timothy he was not naive about the difficulties awaiting the next generation of believers. He foresaw that his younger colleagues would face a time during which the faithful would be persecuted and the faithless would become more notorious (vv. 12-13). These conditions will no doubt confuse believers and tempt them away from the faith. How will Christians be able to find their way through these challenging times? Paul suggested at least four answers.

I. You Can Find Your Way Through Confusing Times by Continuing in the Right as You Have Learned the Right

P. T. Forsyth taught ministers that, in their preaching, they are not to strive after originality or novelty simply for the sake of newness. He said, "The preacher is not there to astonish people with the unheard of; he is there to revive in them what they have long heard. He discovers a mine on the estate. The Church, by the preacher's aid, has to realize its own faith, and take home

347

anew its own Gospel." Those words are in the spirit of Paul, who told young Timothy in our text, "As for you, continue in what you have learned and firmly believed" (3:14).

The world is changing, to be sure, but do not seek the avant garde or the fashionable for its own sake. In spite of changing times, trust the truth you already believe and live the right you already know.

II. You Find Your Way Through Confusing Times by Thinking of Your Teachers and Using Them as Respected Examples

Paul encouraged Timothy to remember those from whom he had learned the faith he now held. Who were those teachers? We do not know for sure, but perhaps Paul had Eunice and Lois in mind as well as himself. Each one of them faced difficult circumstances and came out strong. Timothy's generation was not the first to confront a confusing and challenging world. Much can be learned from the example of respected elders.

III. You Find Your Way Through Confusing Times by Relying on the Scripture

Each state in the union prepares a guidebook on its points of interest and makes it available to tourists. Intelligent travelers study those guidebooks to learn more about the countryside through which they will be journeying. The Bible is such a guidebook that can make us more intelligent travelers through life. David H. C. Read said that the Bible "keeps us in the territory where we can really hear God speak." It is informative, reliable, and, when properly used, keeps us on the path that leads to our desired destination.

IV. You Find Your Way Through Confusing Times by Centering Everything in Jesus Christ

When the apostle talked about preaching the Word in and out of season, and about sound teaching based on this word, he was referring to the word of Jesus Christ, which is the gospel itself. If the good news of Jesus is the basis of everything we do and say, in the church and the world, then if ever we lose our way we shall not lose it for long. The idea is that we judge everything in relation to Christ and never judge Christ in relation to other things.

We are learning from some circles that it's a different world in which to be Christian. No one would contend that today is yesterday. Today's generation of believers faces a time marked by change and confusion. Old lessons from 2 Timothy are nonetheless helpful for this new day. Today's Christian can find the way through confusing times. (Mark E. Yurs)

PERSISTENCE PAYS OFF!

LUKE 18:1-8

Bellamy Partridge, in *Country Lawyer*, tells the story of a miraculous event that actually happened in a small town in upstate New York during the summer of 1885. It was a long, hot summer. Wells were drying up. Crops were wilting. But the new Presbyterian pastor in town had an idea: The townspeople ought to pray for rain.

He put out the word—not just in his church, but all over town. People went door to door—even to the saloons and pool halls—encouraging everyone to pause at a designated time and pray for rain. The response was overwhelming and unanimous—except for one cantankerous old farmer named Phineas Dodd.

The next day at noon, everything shut down for the prayer meeting. Then, they watched the sky. Clouds formed after an hour or so. A gusty wind arose after a couple of hours. Within four hours of the prayer meeting, the temperature dropped twenty degrees and the streets were drenched in water. Besides that, lightning struck the hay barn of Phineas Dodd, and it burned to the ground.

Phineas sued the Presbyterian church and its pastor, seeking $5,000 in damages for his barn. The trial lasted three days. Finally, the judge determined that the pastor and the townspeople had prayed only for rain and not lightning. The bolt that destroyed the barn was an act of God for which neither the pastor nor his congregation could be liable. The judged dismissed the suit but ordered Phineas Dodd to pay all court costs.

Jesus believed in the power of prayer. The text indicates that he believed also that people ought to persist in their prayers until they get an answer—even if they don't feel like it.

Recently, I heard a participant in an intercessory prayer ministry tell of a call she received on her church's prayer line. The caller was not even related to the church. She had experienced one loss after another: Her husband had left her for another woman. Her mother had died not long before. Her son had been arrested and was still in jail, charged with the possession and selling of drugs. She had been laid off from her job. She said, "I feel numb. I think I've even lost my faith in God. Frankly, I'm having trouble seeing any reason to go on living." In response, the prayer volunteer said: "Listen, don't give up. We'll hold on to you, and we'll hold on to your faith for you until you can take it back again. Until then, let our prayers and our faith carry you."

Sometimes, circumstances overwhelm us so much we think that we cannot possibly hold on. Sometimes, the darkness surrounding us becomes so thick we can't see the light at the end of the tunnel. The only thing that keeps us going is the faithfulness of those who refuse to give up, who are willing to pray—and to keep on praying—until the crisis passes.

Vince Lombardi once said, "Character is not made in a crisis. It's only displayed there." The character and strength of a Christian are literally made in times of prayer. That's when the genuineness of your faith and confidence in God are truly revealed—when, despite the apparent ineffectiveness of your prayers, you keep on praying anyhow. You keep on praying, until God answers! (Gary C. Redding)

OCTOBER 29, 1995

⤸

Twenty-first Sunday After Pentecost

Worship Theme: The Christian lives in anticipation of a positive future because of God's grace.

Readings: Joel 2:23-32; 2 Timothy 4:6-8, 16-18; Luke 18:9-14

Call to Worship (Psalm 65:1-2):
Praise is due to you,
  O God, in Zion;
and to you shall vows be performed,
  O you who answer prayer!
To you all flesh shall come.

Pastoral Prayer:
  Redeemer God, we pray this day for all who are lost, forlorn, and friendless. In a world that puts so much emphasis on love and intimacy, all around us are people starving for love, for friendship, for a caring word. Help us to be more loving. We pray for the sick and dying. In spite of medical advances, we cannot conquer death. Help those who face the end to have courage and hope in your eternal power. Be with the families and friends who grieve the loss of loved ones. And help those who seek answers to disease and illness to discover new avenues of healing and alleviating suffering.
  We pray this morning for missionary efforts around the world. May we all be drawn to a better understanding of the commitment we must have as disciples and churches to "go and make disciples of all nations." For we are committed first and foremost to our Lord Jesus Christ; help us to share his good news with all the world. And we offer these prayers in his name. Amen. (Steven R. Fleming)

SERMON BRIEFS

A NEW DAY COMING

JOEL 2:23-32

Joel means "Yahweh is God." It was a common name among the Hebrews. There are twelve persons in the Old Testament

351

named Joel in the history from Samuel to Nehemiah. We can only imagine how many others bore this name. We recognize this Joel readily. He was a prophet from the period in which the glory of Israel as a nation was fading. We remember him by the quote in Acts 2:16, explaining the experience of Pentecost.

Joel is not a long book. It is not complex. The first part, 1:1–2:27, is about present circumstances. The remainder is about the future.

The text we examine today spans the transition from the present to the future. Verses 23-27 concludes Joel's description of the present. Verse 28-32 are about the future. What is the image of the future that will overtake the people of God? What can it present to us today?

I. The Spirit Will Come to Everyone

There is such a hope expressed by Moses in Numbers 11:29. Moses assembled seventy elders. God placed his Spirit on them as well. While the Spirit was on them, these seventy prophesied. Their speaking for God ceased. Two were not present at the assembly, but they also began to prophesy. The people asked Moses to censure them. Moses replied that he wished that all of God's people were prophets and possessed the Spirit of God.

Joel believed God will fulfill this hope in his new world. All the people will possess the spirit of God and will be able to communicate the purposes of God.

II. There Will Be Signs of God's Coming Triumph

The coming of God will be noticed. For Joel, the signs are war and natural disasters. These signs are vivid; blood, death, fire, and smoke are signs of battle. The sun and moon will be dimmed. The day of the Lord is great and dreadful. Some describe a present disaster as a prelude to the end of the world. That is not Joel's intent. These signs are not here for dread and fear; they are given as signs of hope and change.

William Barclay, in a commentary on the temptation of Jesus, speaks of temptations as tests. The purpose is not to condemn but to provide conversion and strength. The followers of Christ are tested so their faith will be strong.

III. The Faithful in Jerusalem Will Be Delivered

The times of testing will pass. The future will be bright, not desolate. Behind each cloud is the ray of sun that brings hope and confidence.

A famous athlete was stricken with a disease that ended his career. When asked his feelings at having lost so much, he told of faith in the midst of tragedy. He said that his task was not to regret the past but to prepare for the future. Joel has a similar message. The future is coming, and with the new day comes God.

There are many difficulties in life. By God's Spirit we can see through the clouds to tomorrow's destiny. God's tomorrow is one in which we are delivered and brought to the fullness of God. Jesus said, "I came that they may have life, and have it abundantly" (John 10:10). Such is our hope; such is our faith; such is our assurance. (Harold C. Perdue)

A CHRISTIAN'S LIFE REVIEW

2 TIMOTHY 4:6-8, 16-18

Throughout most of 2 Timothy, the older apostle looks ahead to the future his younger colleague in ministry will face. He draws upon every resource he knows to feed that younger colleague with hope and courage. But now, near the end of his letter, Paul pauses and looks back upon his own life.

The older a person gets, the more prone that person is to conduct this sort of life review. It is part of the aging process. It is a way of coping with current limitations and of making sense out of one's existence.

Just as the author is helpful to every young Timothy looking out upon the future, so also he has wise counsel for every older saint who may be looking back. He provides a model for conducting a Christian life review.

I. The Christian Looks Back Without Regret

The lack of regret comes from attempts made, not successes won. It comes from faithfulness rather than achievement. The apostle clearly values what he puts under an athletic metaphor—fighting the good fight and finishing the race—but one senses that what he values most is that he has kept the faith. That transcends winning and losing and leads to a peaceful old age.

II. The Christian Looks Forward with Faith

Charles Spurgeon, writing on the fourth psalm in his *Treasury of David,* says, "It is not to be imagined that he who has helped us in six troubles will leave us in the seventh. God does nothing by halves, and he will never cease to help us until we cease to need. The manna will fall every morning until we cross the Jordan."

The apostle has the same faith. He sees through dying and death to glory, and has the hope that the crown of righteousness will be his. This is not the out-pouring of some sort of works righteousness, but the quiet trust of a confident soul who knows God is trustworthy. The future is certain because it is in the hands of the Lord.

III. The Christian Views All with Forgiveness

As the apostle looks back upon his life, he sees that he has been offended. But, in words close to those of the Lord from the cross, he says, "May it not be counted against them!" (v. 16). He forgives those who have wronged him.

Walter A. Maier said that Leonardo da Vinci initially had Judas resemble a personal enemy in his painting *The Last Supper.* Leonardo had to do Judas over again, though, when he found he could not paint the face of Jesus as long as he harbored hatred in his heart for his enemy.

A Christian should come to the end of his or her days with a heart full of forgiveness, not with a spirit that is a logjam of grudges. When we are clogged with complaints against others, the love of Christ cannot flow freely into us. The best way to empty the spirit of its grudges is to fill the heart with forgiveness.

When a seminarian was completing his intern year as a chaplain at a nursing home, the senior chaplain at that home, a retired pastor, gave him a book in which he had inscribed these words: "Blessed is the one who knows what to remember of the past, what to enjoy in the present, and what to hope for in the future." The apostle had that blessedness about him as he reviewed his life. May the Lord grant it to you as you review yours. (Mark E. Yurs)

THE STRANGE THINGS RELIGION WILL DO TO YOU

LUKE 18:9-14

In his book *The Hidden Value of a Man,* John Trent describes a period of time during his childhood:

> When my brothers and I were toddlers, my dad still lived at home—at least he slept there. He would work all day and then go out with his buddies at night. Sundays, however, were an exception. Back in the early fifties, many people in Phoenix took a stroll down Central Avenue after church on Sunday afternoons.
>
> All the nice shops were downtown at that time, and Central was the place to bump into all your friends and neighbors. Dad would be there, too, pushing us twins in the stroller and leading our older brother by the hand. We would all be dressed up in our cutest clothes, Dad in his best suit. For a couple of hours, we would stroll up and down old Central, Dad smiling, waving and greeting people.
>
> Why the Sunday devotion to the family? Frankly, it was good for business. As an insurance agent, Dad thought it would help him make contacts if people saw him as a devoted family man with cute little kids. The rest of the week, however, he didn't want any responsibility for us at all.
>
> My dad wanted two images, and he only kept the public one to enhance business. He thought that showing off . . . would bring him clients.

That's what the text is all about—keeping up appearances and pretending to be something you are not. Your children know when you're playing that game. Surely your wife knows. Don't you know that the Lord knows, too? Don't you ever wonder what he thinks about it—all the pretending, play-acting, and character?

Well, you don't have to wonder because Jesus told this story, and it dramatically reveals his attitude. Two men went to the Temple to pray. One was a Pharisee and the other a tax collector.

The Pharisee prayed about himself. He thanked God that the world was full of people whom he wasn't like, and he named

THE ABINGDON PREACHING ANNUAL 1995

some of them. He was thankful that he was better than extortioners, adulterers, the unjust, and even the tax collector.

The tax collector, on the other hand, was so deeply aware of his sinfulness that he wouldn't even lift his eyes toward heaven. And he prayed for mercy. He had absolutely no claim to worthiness. If God's mercy was not broad enough to include him, he was doomed!

Who are you most like? Most of us tend to identify with the humble man who confessed that he didn't deserve anything. However, there doesn't seem to be much in the story for us if we look at it from that perspective. I believe that more of us are like the Pharisee than the tax collector.

For instance, we often congratulate ourselves for the values we hold, the standards we cherish, the kind of life we live. We don't often engage in self-congratulation publicly. We are more apt to do so when we read the newspaper or watch television talk shows. That's when we're most likely to shake our heads in disgust and despair at perverted life-styles. That's when we're most apt to think that the world would be a lot better place if more people were like us.

Frankly, in lots of ways, we are better—more moral and civil— than lots of others. But God doesn't judge us against others. He never tells us to be at least as good as the next person or better than others. He demands that we become like him! Even if we use our best behavior as the measure, we all come in last when compared to God!

So let's stop pretending. More of us are in danger of the Pharisee's sins than those of the tax collector. Self-righteousness holds out precious little hope that we will ever experience the grace of God. For one thing, it's difficult to believe that we need his grace if we also believe that we're just naturally perfect, good, and upright people.

God heard the prayer of the tax collector and ignored the pretension of the Pharisee. In this story, Jesus reminds us that religion can do strange things to people. It can make you feel that you're perfectly all right, even when your sinful pride has completely shut you off from God. (Gary C. Redding)

NOVEMBER

❧

Replenishing the Well

Expecting Christ the King

The celebration of Christ the King occurs right after Pentecost and just before Advent. It is fitting that the church celebrates Christ as King immediately before Advent, in expectation of the King's entering into the world. This month's exercise is easy—we expect Christ the King in song.

Time: 30 minutes

Materials: A Bible and a hymnal.

Exercise:
Read Luke 23:38-43. Just as the secular preparation for Christmas begins, Christians are reminded that Christ the King was crowned during his crucifixion. The Child we await during Advent is heir to a crown of thorns. The King we follow leads us beyond Christmas to Good Friday and on to Easter.

For centuries, Christians have sung hymns to worship God. When we sing, several things happen at once—we confess our faith, pray, please God, and generally delight all the host of heaven.

In song today, expect an encounter with Christ the King. If you are timid about singing, you may want to find a place where no one can hear you. Open your hymnal and select four hymns that celebrate Christ the King. Before you begin singing, take a couple of minutes to imagine Christ the King standing in front of you. Now sing the hymns you selected to the Christ who stands before you. You may want to sing these hymns while on your knees, an appropriate posture to adopt in the presence of the King. Sing with all your heart, knowing that a chorus of angels joins you in praise. (Harriet Crosby)

NOVEMBER 5, 1995

✦

Twenty-second Sunday After Pentecost

Worship Theme: Divine grace changes our relationship with God and with others.

Readings: Habakkuk 1:1-4; 2:1-4; 2 Thessalonians 1:1-4, 11-12; Luke 19:1-10

Call to Worship (Psalm 119:137-138):

Leader: You are righteous, O LORD, and your judgments are right.

People: You have appointed your decrees in righteousness and in all faithfulness.

Pastoral Prayer:

Gracious God, in these quiet moments we gather our thoughts to give you thanksgiving and praise, as well as to intercede for others who are in need. We give you thanks, Lord, because we are richly blessed. There is the blessing of warm clothing on cool days, and the blessing of snug and dry homes. There is blessing in the technological achievements of our time: of miracle drugs and medical equipment; telephones and computers; manufacturing processes and the ability to create new things. All of these blessings, we know, come from you through the hands of individuals.

Yet, in spite of our great blessings, Lord, we know there are many who are not happy and many who suffer. We know there are those who lack the basics of life: warm clothing, adequate shelter, nutritious food, decent education. Our world is full of such people, and the thought often staggers our imagination and freezes us from action. Help us to be more compassionate and loving, willing to share of our possessions to help others less fortunate than ourselves. Help us to act with the love and charity of Christ, in whose name we pray. Amen. (Steven R. Fleming)

SERMON BRIEFS

A QUESTION AND ANSWER PERIOD

HABAKKUK 1:1-4; 2:1-4

In school, during the "question/answer period," we could ask the teacher any questions about the lessons. I needed that time, because I had a lot more questions than I had answers.

Habakkuk is a question/answer period with God. The situation was simple. The nation, Judah, was being faced with destruction by the Chaldeans, a very wicked people. Now Judah was bad, but not as bad as the Chaldeans. The people of Judah wanted to know what was going on. It was a question about the faithfulness of God. So Habakkuk raised his voice to God.

I. The Question: What Was God Doing?

"How long shall I cry for help, and you will not listen?" (1:1). Things were not going well for Judah. God's ways were ignored. The strong oppressed the weak, there was endless litigation, and destruction and violence ruled, justice did not. The wicked surrounded the righteous.

It was a vivid picture of what happens when God is ignored. What was God doing? Watching Judah reap what they had sown.

Today we have the same situation. Injustices that go unchallenged, wars that never end, corrupt governments, crime and violence in the streets, broken homes, hunger and poverty. What is going on? We are reaping what we have sown. We have not followed God seriously. Will we admit that? God has shown us a better way, but we have not followed.

A man had played fast and loose with his life. He had cheated on his wife and had lost his family. He had been unethical at work and was facing criminal charges. He had smoked three packs of cigarettes a day and now had serious lung cancer. "Why has God done this to me?" he cries. But the man did it to himself. How terrible the consequences of sin!

II. The Answer: God Will Act in Due Time

In spite of the terrible situation, Habakkuk expected God to answer. Like a watchman peering into the distance, Habakkuk looked expectantly for a word. And he got one! God told him to wait, but with hope. When the time was right, God would act. God had not forgotten them and would keep the vision of the kingdom alive. In the meantime, they were to live as God wanted; depend on God, be faithful (see 2:4).

We have that same word. We know that God has acted in Christ, and God's kingdom will never be defeated. God will do for us what we need. In the meantime, let us be faithful, living as God wants us to, depending on God for what we need.

A tamer of Bengal tigers would get into the cage with only a whip and chair to defend himself against them. One night during a performance, the lights went out! The tigers could see the tamer, but he could not see them. After thirty seconds, the lights came back on, and the tigers were exactly where they should have been. Asked later if he had been scared knowing the tigers could see him and not vice-versa, he said, "The tigers did not know I couldn't see them. So when the darkness came, I kept on cracking the whip and talking to them like I always do. They didn't know anything was wrong."

In a sense, that is the word from Habakkuk. In the midst of the darkness, keep on trusting and serving God as always. In due time, God will come and the darkness will be no more. (Hugh Litchfield)

A FORMULA FOR SUCCESS

2 THESSALONIANS 1:1-4, 11-12

The desire to be successful permeates our modern society. As members of the human race, we desire to be successful in all areas of our lives. We long to be successful at business, successful at parenting, successful at marriage, successful in friendship—the list goes on and on. As a Christian people, we also long to have success in our faith experience. We desire to have a deep and meaningful faith, one that changes our lives and influences the lives of those around us. It is equally important, however, that we possess a desire to see the church move forward with great success, measured not in terms of world standards, but rather in terms of Kingdom ministry.

Paul, Silas, and Timothy were three missionaries who first brought the gospel to Thessalonica. In this text, this trio is addressing the Church a second time offering thanksgiving and encouragement. In their words there is a formula for success to ensure the continued survival of the vibrant work.

In the mid 1800s, Basil Manly and John Broadus were two key players who helped to establish and strengthen theological education among Southern Baptists. Manly had been one of the founding faculty members of The Southern Baptist Theological Seminary. Through the turbulent days of the Civil War, and then through the pains of the Reconstruction era, Manly helped to keep the Seminary alive, only to become disheartened several years later. In 1871, he moved to Georgetown, Kentucky, to become the president of Georgetown College. He wrote to his good friend John Broadus at the Seminary about the struggles involved in keeping colleges alive with sound financial support. He wrote, "For a college to survive, its leaders must brag, beg, and grab."

Using those words of advice, coupled with the words of Paul, Silas, and Timothy, we see that a formula for success emerges for the local church. For a church to survive and have success, it must brag, beg, and grab.

I. The Church Must Have Members Who Will Brag

Like parents boasting over their children, Paul, Silas, and Timothy were boasting to other churches about the success in Thessalonica. The church, under the leadership of the Spirit of God, had accomplished much. As Paul outlines, their faith had grown, their mutual love for one another had increased, and their patient hope had allowed them to endure many trials. Paul's boasting was an encouraging word.

As children, we are taught that bragging is a fault. We learn from our earliest years that we are not to boast about who we are or what we possess. Instead we are taught to share and to be generous in our compliments of others. Yet if the church is to survive, there must be members within who can boast.

The boasting that is required, however, is never about self, but always about others. Every church family needs members who will boast about the accomplishments of others. Each church needs encouragers who will celebrate the good things that God is doing in the lives of other people. The ministry of encouragement is one of the most vital and needed ministries in the church today. No church will stand very long when there is an absence of encouragement.

II. The Church Must Have Leaders Who Will Beg

In the early church at Thessalonica, the founders did their begging in the form of a prayer. Paul states in verse 11, "We always pray for you." They petitioned God on behalf of the church family. The church of today must hear a similar call to prayer. There must be those within the walls who will truly become people of prayer, praying for the needs of others.

Recently, a missionary from Brazil spoke to a local congregation. He described many of the hardships of his work. There was a need for better health care, better sanitation, and better living conditions among the people with whom he worked. He described a number of areas that desperately needed careful attention. But when asked at the end of the presentation, "How can our church help you the most?" he replied, "Pray. Your prayers change lives, lift spirits, and open doors. There is no stronger tool anywhere." If the church is to survive, members must hear the call to pray without ceasing.

III. The Church Needs a Savior Who Grabs

Paul prayed that "the name of our Lord Jesus may be glorified in you, and you in him" (v. 12). To paraphrase: "May Jesus grab you, and you grab him!" It was Paul's fervent prayer that the members of the church would seek Jesus with all their hearts, with the wonderful assurance that as they did, they would discover his loving arms already extended in their direction. They were to be so closely aligned to Jesus that his glory would shine through them.

Our world needs embracing. The poor, the lonely, the grieving, the frightened, the sick, the disenfranchised—all need to feel the loving arms of the Savior. When his glory begins to shine through his people, their arms become his arms, grabbing those who need to be drawn into the fellowship of the church. The gospel must become flesh again, living and loving through the outstretched arms of the church. (Jon R. Roebuck)

A FACE IN THE CROWD

LUKE 19:1-10

Excitement mounted as John F. Kennedy made his way through the tightly assembled crowd. In those days before intense presidential Secret Service protection, he stopped on several occasions to touch and talk with individuals. A few days later, he was killed in Dallas.

Jesus must have caused the same high anticipation when he came to Jericho. The Bible makes it clear that Jesus walked among the people, touching and speaking with many of them. The great impact occurred as he stood under the sycamore tree and saw the small tax collector hiding in its branches, observing the procession down below. As Jesus called him out of the tree, the encounter was obviously life-changing for Zacchaeus.

I. A Man Seeking God

Zacchaeus had a God-shaped void in his life and had tried to fill it with many things. To become a tax collector for the Romans, he had given up his Jewish heritage, thus becoming an outcast. Even though he was rich, his riches did not satisfy his needs. He had been on the eternal search for meaning that all human beings take, and up to this point, none of the normal offerings from the culture—pleasure, position, wealth, prestige, or power—satisfied him.

The search for meaning—a search for God—had taken him from power and position of a Roman government to a sycamore tree in the streets of Jericho, where the Savior found him.

II. God Seeking Humans

The truth of the matter is that we do not find God. The Bible is not a picture of people searching for God. If you examine the

Bible with some sensitivity, you see in effect that God is seeking us. Since we were thrust out of the garden in the opening pages of Genesis, God has been coming to his people. He came to Abraham in the city of Ur; he came to Isaiah in the Temple; he came to Amos in the hills of Tekoa; he came to Hosea in the tragedy of his marital situation; and he has come to all of us in Jesus Christ. Jesus Christ is clearly God seeking man, for Jesus Christ was completely God and completely man simultaneously. God became human so he could communicate with humankind.

When Jesus was on the cross, he fiercely reached back into history and pulled all the sins that had ever been committed onto himself, and he reached forward into destiny and pulled in all the sins that ever would be committed. Then he spiritually took the hand of God, and he took the hand of humanity, and pulled God and humans together for the first time. Jesus Christ is God seeking humans.

III. People Seeking One Another

The symbol of the Christian faith has always been the cross, with its vertical beam pointing from God to humanity and its horizontal beam symbolizing person to person. Many people are certain they have their relationships correct with God. They have made their professions of faith and understand that Jesus is Savior. But faith is not complete until relationships are correct with other people. Zacchaeus quickly corrected his relationship with people: "Half of my possessions, Lord, I will give to the poor; and if I have defrauded anyone of anything, I will pay back four times as much" (v. 8). This was the immediate response on the part of Zacchaeus. When we have been found by God, we quickly move to make all relationships correct. (William L. Self)

NOVEMBER 12, 1995

～

Twenty-third Sunday After Pentecost

Worship Theme: The promise of God's presence and power is an encouragement to God's people.

Readings: Haggai 1:15*b*–2:9; 2 Thessalonians 2:1-5, 13-17; Luke 20:27-38

Call to Worship (Psalm 145:1-5, 17-21):

Leader: I will extol you, my God and King, and bless your name forever and ever.

People: Every day I will bless you, and praise your name forever and ever.

Leader: Great is the LORD, and greatly to be praised; his greatness is unsearchable.

People: One generation shall laud your works to another, and shall declare your mighty acts.

Leader: On the glorious splendor of your majesty, and on your wondrous works, I will meditate. . . .

People: The LORD is just in all his ways, and kind in all his doings.

Leader: The LORD is near to all who call on him, to all who call on him in truth.

People: He fulfills the desire of all who fear him; he also hears their cry, and saves them.

Leader: The LORD watches over all who love him, but all the wicked he will destroy.

All: My mouth will speak the praise of the LORD, and all flesh will bless his holy name forever and ever.

Pastoral Prayer:

We thank you, God, for the gift of life and the joy we find in living—its good times and bad, its sunny days and dark times. We each come today with our own load of uncertainty and confusion, sins and failures, worries and fears. We come to rest in your presence. Help us to relax and leave our heavy loads with you, because you are able to bear them. Help us to turn from anxiety to thanksgiving, from insecurity to confidence, from helplessness to strength, from despair to hope. Forgive us for our lack of faith. Let all our problems and doubts find their solution in the death of our Lord Jesus Christ on Calvary, in his resurrection from the grave, and in the eternal joy of life in his kingdom, which shall endure forever and ever. Amen. (Gary C. Redding)

SERMON BRIEFS

A SYMBOL FOR ENCOURAGEMENT

HAGGAI 1:15*b*–2:9

As you try to serve God, do you ever get discouraged, feel that nothing much good comes from all you do? Have you felt like quitting the work?

If so, you can understand the mood of the people during Haggai's time. They were back from the exile, trying to rebuild their lives—and the Temple! It wasn't going too well. The elders felt that no matter what they did, it would never match the splendor of the old Temple. They were discouraged.

Haggai spoke, calling them to get busy rebuilding the Temple because it would be a symbol of encouragement to them.

I. A Symbol of God's Presence (2:4)

Some had come to believe that God had abandoned them. Why worry about the Temple? God had deserted them! Not so, said Haggai. "I am with you, says the LORD of hosts" (v. 4). God had not deserted them. He was still involved in their lives. The Temple would stand as a symbol of God's presence among them. They were not forgotten.

Sometimes we wonder whether God knows what is going on in our lives. Does God know our pain, our frustration, our struggles? But when we go to worship, we get the answer: "I am with you." God comes to be with us. We are remembered. As we serve God, we are not alone.

A little girl was facing surgery. Her father asked, "Are you afraid?" She looked at him. "Will you be there with me?" "Yes, I will be there," he said. "Then," she said, "I am not afraid."

In life we ask, "God, will you be with us?" The Temple reminds us that God says yes!

II. A Symbol of God's Power (2:4-6)

Haggai called the people to take courage and get to work, because God was with them. "My spirit abides among you; do not fear" (v. 5). God's power would be with them, the power of the Spirit. If they depended on that power, nothing could stop them from doing the work.

God's power is with us. When we go to church, this is what we remember. To serve is not always easy; sometimes it is discouraging. But we don't do it alone. God's Spirit gives us the power. If we trust God, we will find power to live.

A boy was having trouble with a math problem. He threw up his hands and said, "I give up. I can't get it. I've tried everything. It's no use." His mother said, "There's one thing you haven't tried. You haven't asked me to help." We must never give up on anything until we ask God to help us.

III. A Symbol of God's Promise (2:6-9)

There will come a day, Haggai said, when God will shake the heavens and earth and sea and land. God will fill the house with splendor greater than before. And God will give them prosperity. In other words, God will bring in the Kingdom.

That means that every word and deed given for God's service will not be in vain. We serve a kingdom that will come. When it does, God will give us prosperity.

If you put one drop of blue dye in a glass of water, in a few seconds it disappears. But if you keep putting in the drops, eventually the water will be transformed into the color blue.

367

Sometimes, our efforts don't seem to change much, but if we keep at it, what we have done will one day transform the world.

Be encouraged! God's presence, power, and promises are ours. (Hugh Litchfield)

KEEPING YOUR GRIP

2 THESSALONIANS 2:1-5, 13-17

Grip strength can be a measure of overall fitness. How tightly a person can grip an object reveals much about upper body strength. At many sports testing facilities, a grip test is a key evaluating factor used to determine physical fitness.

A good grip is quite valuable. For the sportsman, a good grip is essential in holding a tennis racquet, a golf club, or a water skiing rope. Baseball players place a great deal of importance on how well a bat can be gripped. Parents, watching over their children, understand how necessary a good grip can be in ensuring the safety of a child crossing a street. Keeping your grip is important.

Paul, Silas, and Timothy were the founding missionaries for the first-century church at Thessalonica. Because they had played such a vital role in its birth and development, they continued to watch closely the factors at work in the life of the new church. Chapter 2 of 2 Thessalonians reveals a concern of these leaders for their Christian bothers and sisters in that congregation. It was their fervent hope, revealed in these verses, that these friends would keep a good grip on God's Word. How tightly they could hold to God's Word would be a true measure of their spiritual fitness.

In the challenge offered by the founding trio, there are three key instructions for gripping the Word of God.

I. Avoid Distractions (vv. 1-2)

Paul, Silas, and Timothy were addressing an apparent question or debate that had arisen in regard to the Second Coming of Christ. There was a sense of bewilderment among the members of the church. Many had received false reports and even inaccurate documents that stated that the Second Coming had already occurred. Such words and rumors were a great distraction, as well as being very upsetting, to the early church. Their practice of faith had become distracted to the point that much of their focus had been lost.

The challenge to the church is offered in verse 3, "Let no one deceive you in any way." In other words, "Do not be distracted." Paul had often taught these believers that certain events would occur first to point toward the Second Coming. Verse 5 is a not-so-gentle reminder: "Do you not remember that I told you these things when I was still with you?" Distractions can get in the way of Bible study and devotion.

Good, productive, and challenging Bible study must be done without distractions. The physical location is important; the time, place, and level of noise are important. The spiritual well-being is also vital; a sense of forgiveness, an open mind, a willing spirit are needed. All possible distractions must be avoided for good study to occur.

II. Get Serious (v. 15)

It is apparent that Paul, Silas, and Timothy had employed both a verbal and a written conveyance of Christ's teachings to the early church. The church at Thessalonica had received much of the oral tradition of the apostles as well as written documents. In a challenge to strengthen their grip on God's Word, Paul told them to "stand firm, hold fast to the traditions" (v. 15). Translation: Get serious with God's Word.

The Williams Translation states verse 15 this way, "Get a tight grip." The Cotton Patch version is even more direct, "Sink your teeth into the lessons taught you." The point is clear: One never drifts into discipleship, nor does one become a student of God's Word, without effort. Discipline is needed. Conscious effort is required. There is no "hit or miss" growth in God. Effective growth requires consistent discipline. Growth requires becoming serious about the decision to know God through the study of his Word.

III. Wait for the Blessing (vv. 16-17)

If your house in like ours, then the statement "Please wait for the blessing" is constantly repeated at mealtime. We are trying to teach our children the importance of saying a prayer of thanksgiving before eating. The idea is to teach a little patience before digging into the food.

That statement can be applied to the study of God's Word as well. Genesis 32:24ff. records the fascinating story of Jacob wrestling with an angel. As the night progressed the two engaged in a fierce battle. As the early light of dawn broke, the angel asked for freedom. Jacob replied, "I will not let you go unless you bless me" (Gen. 32:26). Sometimes, it is only as we wrestle patiently with God's Word that we receive the most blessing.

True Bible study is a very active process, and at times a very lengthy process. When the time is taken to study, to reflect, to ask questions, and to explore possibilities, then the true blessing of any Scripture begins to emerge. Paul, in 2 Timothy 3:16, states that "all Scripture is inspired by God and is useful for teaching, for reproof, for correction, and for training in righteousness." Sometimes it is only through the process of wrestling long enough with a passage that the biblical truth begins to emerge. We must learn to wait for the blessing.

A favorite and often-used expression issues a challenge to grip the Word of God. It states, "It is not so much the time that you spend in God's Word that is important, but rather the amount of time that God's Word spends in you!" Get a grip. Keep a grip. (Jon R. Roebuck)

WHEN BAD RELIGION HAPPENS TO GOOD PEOPLE
LUKE 20:27-38

Just as food spoils when stored improperly, so also does religion. This text gives the characteristics of religion gone sour.

The church has been plagued with unhealthy expressions of the Christian faith from David Koresh back to the Spanish Inquisition, and to Simon Magnus in the book of Acts.

There are several characteristics of religion gone sour.

I. More Judgment Than Forgiveness

Jesus made it very clear that our job is to forgive—not to judge. When we take the job of judging, we take God's place. "Vengeance is mine says the Lord."

Forgiveness is canceling the debt and taking the cost of repair on ourselves.

The world knows its need of forgiveness. We make the mistake of assuming it needs to be judged by us. People need to know that forgiveness is available. Forgiveness brings healing; judging brings wounding. Forgiveness takes courage; judgment is cowardly. Forgiveness brings restoration; judgment produces separation.

II. More Law Than Grace

The New Testament has a tension between law and grace. Paul preached grace, but Judaizers plagued him, trying to take new believers back into the law.

Our undue reliance upon rules and regulations, our need to legalize every portion of our religious life is a sign of immaturity.

Law is to the faith as bones are to the body. If you see the bones, the body is in trouble; it is unhealthy. But if you see the evidence of the bones, the body will be strong and the posture straight.

Grace can be trusted: " 'tis grace hath brought me safe thus far, and grace will lead me home."

III. More Pride Than Humility

Law and judgment produce pride. The essence of the gospel of Jesus is humility.

Humility is not weakness; it is teachableness. It is a word that pictures a horse ready to be used after the trainer has finished his or her work. The follower of Christ is ready to be used. She or he has been trained.

"Pride is moral insensitivity based on its own virtue and achievement. This is the foundation of all sin" (Augustine). Healthy religion will wash another's feet, go the second mile, sit at the foot of the table, and pray for the enemy. It does not push itself to the top or behave unseemly.

The Pharisees were clearly demonstrating that their religion had gone sour. They felt the need to trap Jesus in their spoiled theology.

There are two ways to look tall. You can cut everyone down, or you can stand up straight. Healthy religion stands straight; it does not need to destroy anyone else. (William L. Self)

NOVEMBER 19, 1995

❧

Twenty-fourth Sunday After Pentecost

Worship Theme: We anticipate a future of joy and peace because of God's promise.

Readings: Isaiah 65:17-25; 2 Thessalonians 3:6-13; Luke 21:5-19

Call to Worship (Isaiah 12:2-6):

Leader: Surely God is my salvation; I will trust, and will not be afraid,

People: for the LORD GOD is my strength and my might; he has become my salvation.

Leader: With joy you will draw water from the wells of salvation.

People: And you will say in that day: Give thanks to the LORD, call on his name;

Leader: make known his deeds among the nations;

People: proclaim that his name is exalted.

Leader: Sing praises to the LORD, for he has done gloriously; let this be known in all the earth.

All: Shout aloud and sing for joy, O royal Zion, for great in your midst is the Holy One of Israel.

Pastoral Prayer:

Father, you are worthy of praise. You have created us, and you have redeemed us for eternal life through Jesus. You continue to sustain us for confident living through your Holy Spirit. And yet, we confess, too often we keep from you the praise you deserve, especially when we excuse ourselves from worship for worldly reasons, give you the last fruits of our labor, accommodate false witnesses to your truth, and treat others without the esteem you have established for every person. Forgive us as we turn to you and ask, by the enabling of your Holy Spirit, to make our lives a perpetual psalm of praise to your glory through Jesus, in whose name we pray. Amen. (Robert R. Kopp)

SERMON BRIEFS

A NEW DAY COMING!
ISAIAH 65:17-25

"Will it ever end?" So asked the woman struggling with poverty, grief, suffering. She wondered whether the darkness would ever end.

So did the Hebrew people, undergoing the suffering and despair of their captivity. Would it ever end? Into their misery and despair, Isaiah spoke this exciting word: There's a new day coming! There will be a new heaven and a new earth. Isaiah told of a time when God will bring in a new day. It will get better! What will it be like?

I. A Day of Joy

Isaiah told of the day when the mourning that then filled the streets of Jerusalem would be replaced with rejoicing. No more the "sound of weeping" and the "cry of distress" (v. 19). Not only that, but people would live to a ripe old age. When God blesses them, they live long and will not "fall short" of a "hundred years." Life will be so good that they will not help rejoicing.

God promises us that one day there will be no more sorrow. God will wipe away the tears from our eyes (Rev. 21:4). Through Christ's resurrection, the day will come when the suffering and misery will be no more. A new day of rejoicing will come.

Clarence Darrow spoke at a black church in Chicago during the Depression. He said, "I don't understand it. You're poor, suffering, oppressed, but you still sing. What have you got to sing about?" Quick as a flash, a woman said, "We've got Jesus to sing about." Joy will come!

II. A Day of Reward

The new day will be a time when they will live in their houses, eat the fruit of their vineyards, enjoy the work of their hands. Their labor will not be in vain. Their service to God will be rewarded.

All that we do for God matters. Sometimes it doesn't seem so. When the new day comes, we will discover that all we have done for God has made a difference. We will reap the reward of the Kingdom for our faithful service.

A Sunday school teacher received a letter from a boy she taught thirty years earlier. He was thanking her for the difference she had made in his life. With joy she commented, "I guess what I did mattered." It always does!

III. A Day of Prayers Answered

Did God hear their prayers? "Before they call I will answer, / while they are yet speaking I will hear" (v. 24). God will hear and answer their prayers. God will do for them what they need.

Does God answer our prayers? In the new day coming, we will discover that God always has. In the new day, we will have everything we've ever needed. Our prayers are not wasted. God hears and answers.

IV. A Day of Peace

When the new day comes:

> The wolf and the lamb shall feed together,
>   the lion shall eat straw like the ox;
>   but the serpent—its food shall be dust!
> They shall not hurt or destroy
>   on all my holy mountain,
>   says the LORD. (v. 25)

No more war or fighting. Everyone will dwell together in peace.

Don't we long for that day? It's coming! One day, we "ain't going to study war no more." No more hate and violence. Peace will rule the day.

Will it ever get better? Yes, it will! God will bring in a new day. If we trust God, we will celebrate its coming. (Hugh Litchfield)

WHAT GOD SAYS ABOUT YOUR JOB

2 THESSALONIANS 3:6-13

We used to celebrate work. Now our society has begun to glorify pleasure. We have moved from a six-day work week to a five-day work week. Some businesses now have a four-day work week, and there is serious exploration of the idea of a three-day work week.

What, if anything, does God have to say about me and my job? How does work relate to my Christian faith?

I. There Is No Place for a Lazy Christian

Paul wrote to the Greek church at Thessalonica in strong words. Some of the Christians there had become lazy, in the name of Christianity. They loafed around, waiting for the return of Jesus Christ.

Yes, Jesus wants our worship and affection. Remember that incident at Bethany? Martha busied herself around the kitchen getting the meal. She became angry with Mary for her devotion to the Lord and her neglect of domestic responsibilities. Jesus chided Martha, encouraging her not to take her work too seriously, letting it get in the way of more important things.

Unfortunately, this can be mistaken for pious laziness. In no way does God want us to neglect our responsibility. The person who does not have an active job to do is one who is inclined to get involved in the affairs of others. What Jesus honored in Mary that day was her love, her adoration, her focus on human, relational values. He didn't refuse to eat the meal that Martha prepared. He was grateful for her hospitality. He wanted to infuse some joy into her work and to help her understand the spirit of sensitivity that Mary had toward other persons.

We are called to an energetic life of action and service.

II. We Are to Provide for Our Families

Verses 10-12 are tough words. Paul goes on to say that not only should we refrain from feeding persons who refuse to provide for themselves, but also we should stay away from them. Idleness and laziness are contagious diseases. They can destroy a family. They can eat like a cancer at the vitals of society.

This doesn't mean that we're not to provide welfare. The problem is that some people refuse to work. We should step in to help each other in need. God's Word speaks against indolence, not against poverty. Work is honorable. It is the calling of God.

III. Christians Should Produce Quality Workmanship

A Christian is called to quality performance. Our workmanship should be of the highest standards.

This doesn't mean that you and I are asked to do a better job than we are capable of doing. I can make myself inoperative, immobilized by self-doubt and self-questioning, when I compare what I can do to what others can do. God asks me to be only the best I can be. He doesn't ask me to compare myself to anyone else. He simply wants me to do the best job I am capable of doing. The same is true for you. He wants you to be the best that you can possibly be—no more, no less.

This perspective can change your whole approach to your work. Even a boring job can be transformed as you emphasize quality. Attitudes can be changed, even if the circumstances can't.

God has strategically placed you this week where no ordained clergy person could possibly go. You are God's representative. Your work is sacred. You are ordained to minister wherever you go. And you are called to bear witness by the way you work by God's love and grace in Jesus Christ. (John A. Huffman, Jr.)

A RIVER RUNS THROUGH IT

LUKE 21:5-19

No one argues that we live in a world that seems to be terribly impermanent. Most of us struggle to find a way to cope with this. Our frustration with this kind of world makes us vulnerable to the claims of many false messiahs who somehow give us an easy answer to a difficult situation. There has been no shortage of false messiahs, from the Reverend Moon to Jim Jones and his unfortunate followers in Guyana. When our world is coming apart at the seams, there are three ways we choose to live.

One is to be fearful. Those who are fearful seek every sign and listen to every false messiah. The clear message of Jesus is for us not to be led astray. When the time comes, it will be clear and obvious to all of us.

The second response is that we can adopt the "who cares" attitude. We can run to the world of hedonism. However, this does not protect us from the feelings of depression, discouragement, and loneliness. We do have a tendency to shrug our shoulders and sneak off into pleasure-seeking self-fulfillment. This is an easy, but dangerous, way to deal. The response Jesus recommends is to watch and pray. He asks us to be secure in our insecurities. We may be standing knee deep in thunder, broken dreams, and a broken heart, but he reminds us in verse 18 "not a hair of your head will perish."

In a world that is coming apart at the seams, the ways of coping generated by the nonbeliever give absolutely no security. Our security is in Christ and the power that rolled away the stone in front of the tomb. That is our only security.

In Robert Russell's *To Catch an Angel,* he tells of a blind man who lives alone on an island in the middle of a river. The blind man goes rowing on the river almost every day by a means of a fairly simple system. He attaches a bell with a timer to the end of the dock. The bell rings every thirty seconds. He can row up and down the river and every thirty seconds judge his distance by the sound of the bell. When he has had enough, he finds his way home by means of the bell. In the young man's words, "The river lies before me a constant invitation, a constant challenge, and my bell is the thread of sound along which I return to a quiet base."

The only way we can live in an impermanent world is to venture out where there is danger and excitement, but our security is in the living Word of Jesus himself. He is that living Word.

"Eventually, all things merge into one, and a river runs through it." (William L. Self)

NOVEMBER 26, 1995

✦

Christ the King

Worship Theme: Jesus Christ is a Savior who will meet all of life's needs.

Readings: Jeremiah 23:1-6; Colossians 1:11-20; Luke 23:33-43

Call to Worship (Luke 1:68-71, 76-79):

Leader: Blessed be the Lord God of Israel, for he has looked favorably on his people and redeemed them.

People: He has raised up a mighty savior for us in the house of his servant David,

Leader: as he spoke through the mouth of his holy prophets from of old,

People: that we would be saved from our enemies and from the hand of all who hate us. . . .

Leader: And you, child, will be called the prophet of the Most High; for you will go before the Lord to prepare his ways,

People: to give knowledge of salvation to his people by the forgiveness of their sins.

Leader: By the tender mercy of our God, the dawn from on high will break upon us,

All: to give light to those who sit in darkness and in the shadow of death, to guide our feet into the way of peace.

Pastoral Prayer:

Father, you have given us eternal life and abundant living through faith in Jesus. But while you never meant for us to keep Jesus only for ourselves, we confess the times we have not told family, friends, and neighbors about the love you have for them through Christ Jesus. Forgive us, O God, for keeping the gospel to ourselves when every person needs the wholeness, happiness, joy, and eternal security available through faith in Jesus. As led by your Holy Spirit, we recommit ourselves to the greatest mission of the church: introducing people to their Lord and Savior, Jesus Christ. Help us by creed and deed to point to Jesus as we pray in his great name. Amen. (Robert R. Kopp)

SERMON BRIEFS

THE WORTHY KING

JEREMIAH 23:1-6

Bad government! Bad leadership! The Jewish people faced that. As a result, they were going through bad times. Things weren't any better under the present king, Zedekiah. But Jeremiah spoke and gave them hope. God was going to send better leaders (or shepherds) who would help the people.

Then Jeremiah gave a messianic prophecy. A "righteous Branch" from the lineage of David would arise. He would be a worthy king to them. He would be called "the LORD is our righteousness" (v. 6) and would rule them in three ways.

I. Deal Wisely with Them

God would finish what was started, would do for the people what they needed. If they needed love, they would have it. If they needed forgiveness, it would come. If they needed power for living, they would discover it. God would provide for them what they needed.

II. Execute Justice and Righteousness

God would keep the promise of the covenant he made with them. God would right the wrong, defeat the power of evil, bring peace and joy and life to them all. It would be a kingdom where all would be equal and would treat each other with love and justice.

379

III. Provide Security for the People

God would save them. No longer would they have to fear other nations. God would keep them secure. No one or no nation could ever destroy them. The protection of God would never be defeated. They would be safe in God's arms.

They needed a king like that. Looking back, we feel such a worthy king has come. His name is Christ. In Christ, all the prophecies this "righteous Branch" would do can be seen. Christ dealt wisely with people. He came to meet our needs, to provide love and forgiveness and grace for our lives. Christ was and is sufficient for all our needs.

This Christ worked to execute justice and righteousness. He opposed injustice, mistreatment of others, sinful living. He called for them to love one another, meet the needs of the less fortunate, live as disciples of the Kingdom.

He provided salvation for all. If we put our lives in the hands of Christ, nothing can pry us loose from them. Christ will hold us tightly, keep us secure throughout eternity.

Today we are faced with a decision. Which king will we serve? There are plenty of earthly kings who promise much. Sometimes they carry names like materialism, pleasure, secular humanism, success, fame. They promise much, but when all is said and done, they will not deliver on their promises.

But Christ—here is a King who will! Christ promises love—and gives it. Christ promises forgiveness—and offers it. Christ promises life—and brings it abundantly and eternally. Christ promises salvation—and to all who believe, it will be given.

As we face this Advent season, we can celebrate the truth that the King of kings has come to offer himself to us. Will we follow that King?

A society in England studying comparative religions had an imprint on its note paper. Pictured are the founders of the great religions. Some are preaching, teaching, reading, meditating. Only one is suffering. Only one is hanging on the cross with hands outstretched. Only one cares enough to put his back under the burden of our sin and ignorance in order to free us from it. "I came that they may have life, and have it abundantly" (John 10:10).

Christ is the worthy King. He will rule us in the right way. Let us become part of his Kingdom! (Hugh Litchfield)

A SAVIOR'S RESUME

COLOSSIANS 1:11-20

In today's business world one of the most important documents used to aid in a person's upward mobility is a résumé. A
good, well-written résumé can open many doors for a person
hoping to be recognized by a potential employer. Much thought
and planning must be used in the preparation of a résumé to
accentuate the pluses of a person's career skills and accomplishments. It is critical to include items that compliment and never
those that detract.

In his letter to the Colossian church, Paul gives a wonderful
description of Jesus and his right to rule over the hearts and
minds of people. It is as though Paul offers a résumé, highlight-
ing the special qualities of Jesus that truly make him a Lord to be
worshiped. There are, of course, no negatives to avoid in such a
description, and the list of positive attributes is inexhaustible. Yet
in these words, Paul offers a brief description of four items
included on the Savior's résumé.

I. Jesus Is a Savior Who Rescues

Paul begins his list by describing the unique ability of Jesus to
rescue people from the darkness of their sinful state and bring
them into the Kingdom of light. The word *saved* is often used by
evangelical Christians to describe this rescuing ability of Jesus.
Because of his death on the cross on our behalf, Jesus is in the
position to save anyone from a life of disobedience and sin, which
will lead to ultimate and lasting death. He rescues his followers
from the domain of darkness and delivers them to the eternal
Kingdom of God.

After a five-day blizzard, a Red Cross rescue team was carried
by helicopter to a mountain cabin that was all but covered by
snow drifts. After knocking on the door, one rescuer stepped in
and said, "We're from the Red Cross." "Well," said the moun-
taineer, scratching his head, "it's been a tough winter, and I don't
see how we can give anything this year." It's hard to rescue some
people. Yet Jesus, as Savior, makes the offer to all.

II. Jesus Is a Savior Who Reveals

From the dawn of creation, humankind has longed to know what God is like. Many attempts have been made to describe God. Many have viewed God as a terrible agent of wrath who must constantly be appeased by ritualistic sacrifice. Others have seen God as a very nebulous being who is far away and removed from this world. Still others have described him in very anthropomorphic terms, such as "the big guy upstairs."

As Savior, Jesus came to give this world a glimpse of God. This is possible through the incarnation of God himself in the form of human flesh. Here Paul describes Jesus as "the image of the invisible God" (v. 15). God has been revealed to humankind through the heart and mind of Christ Jesus. Through his acts of compassion, his merciful forgiveness, his sufficient grace, and his sensibility to human need, Christ has revealed a very different portrait of God. Jesus describes God as a loving Father who cares for all of his children. Christ is a revealer of God to humans.

III. Jesus Is a Savior Who Rules

Paul is careful to remind the faithful at Colossae that Jesus is to have authority over both the church and each individual. His supremacy must be acknowledged in the church. It is not uncommon to hear of churches today going through stressful problems that lead to dissension and even division. Most church conflicts arise when certain people or groups of people begin to assert too much authority. Christ is to be the head of the church. The standard to raise above and beyond all else in defining the ministry of the church is never the opinion of the pastor or the dictates of a deacon board or the gossip that sometimes flows from the Sunday school class. The standard to raise is the mission of Christ. His Lordship over the church ought to be the determining factor for ministry.

Paul writes in the latter part of verse 18, "He is the beginning, the firstborn from the dead, so that he might come to have first place in everything." Surely this relates to individual conduct. It has never been the will of God for any human being to become his or her own authority. No person is the captain of his or her own soul. Human beings are called to live their lives under the control and authority of Christ Jesus. Christ is a ruling Savior.

IV. Jesus Is a Savior Who Reconciles

Paul writes in Ephesians 2:14, "For he [Jesus] is our peace; in his flesh he has made both groups into one and has broken down the dividing wall." Part of his reason for coming was to reunite God with humans. *Reconciliation* literally means "to bring together." As Savior, Jesus is involved in bringing sinful persons into a relationship with the Holy God. He becomes the device by which the two communicate and move into fellowship with each other.

By example, Jesus also calls his followers to be reconciled to each other. A preacher was trying to patch up a difference between two friends. "You must not develop hatred toward your neighbor," he said to the one who was complaining. "If your neighbor does you harm, you must forget it." "I do forget it, but I have such a bad memory that I keep forgetting that I forgot."

Jesus offers reconciliation. Centuries before his coming, Isaiah proclaimed him the "Wonderful Counselor, Mighty God, Everlasting Father, Prince of Peace" (Isa. 9:6). Jesus is a reconciler, a peace giver.

Such descriptive words should lead the faithful to rejoice as the hymn writer did: "Hallelujah, what a Savior!" (Jon R. Roebuck)

LESSONS FROM THE LEFT AND RIGHT SIDES OF THE CROSS
LUKE 23:33-43

A significant understanding of pain is given to us as we look at the three men on the cross. There are two ways of looking at pain. One is to see it without purpose, and the other is to see it with purpose. The way we react to pain is the way we look at life. Some would say, "Isn't it a pity roses have thorns?" while others would say, "Isn't it consoling that those thorns have roses?"

The lessons from the left side of the cross are clear. Pain in itself does not make us any better; it is apt to make us bitter. No one was ever better simply because she or he had an earache. Unspiritualized suffering does not improve us, it degenerates us. The thief at the left is no better because of his crucifixion. It sears him, burns him, and tarnishes his soul. He refuses to think of pain as being related to anything else. He thought only of himself and how to get off the cross. So it is with those who are faithless. There is no message of hope or proof of love here.

The thief on the right is the symbol of those for whom pain has meaning. The Savior's forgiveness opened his mind and heart in such a way that he understood the mercy of God. He understood that if pain had no reason, Jesus would not have embraced it. If the cross had no purpose, Jesus would not have climbed it. Surely, he who claimed to be God would never have taken that badge of shame unless it could have been transformed or transmuted to some holy purpose.

What does this means for us? Difficulty in itself is not unbearable. It is the failure to understand its meaning that is unbearable. Our dilemmas can be the death of our souls or they can bring us life. It all depends on whether we put our faith in him "who for the joy that was set before him endured the cross."

All the sickbeds in the world, therefore, are either on the left side of the cross or on the right. Their position is determined by whether, like the thief on the left, they ask to be taken down or, like the thief on the right, they ask to be taken up. It is all in the heart; it is all in the attitude within the heart.

The only way we can go through the difficulties of this life—the pain of living, disease, destruction, and despair in an empty and difficult world—is with the assurance that the Savior went there ahead of us and that he has made a way through it for us by the power of his resurrection. (William L. Self)

DECEMBER

❧

Replenishing the Well

Expect Healing

At the beginning of the Christian calendar, Advent sets the tone for the entire liturgical year: Expect encounters with the Lord of all life every day, in all seasons. The Gospels record that healing was one sign of the presence of the Lord. Not only did people receive healing, but even death itself was finally healed of the power to sting when the Lord of life came into the world.

Christians expect the Lord to be at work in our lives, and so we look for healing in ourselves and in others. This month's exercise will help you to focus on the healing aspect of your ministry.

Time: 30 minutes now, and 30 minutes on the last day of Advent.

Materials: A Bible, oil in a small glass container, your journal, a pen or pencil.

Exercise:
Read Matthew 11:2-11. Focus on verses 2-6. During Advent we ask with John the Baptist, "Are you the one who is to come, or are we to [expect] another?" The answer we get is that the presence of the Christ is heralded by healing. Not only is physical healing a sign of the Messiah, but the healing power of the gospel is preached to the poor, and even death itself is at last healed of its power to harm.

Take the small glass container you have filled with oil and place it before you on your desk. Anointing people with oil as an invocation of the healing power of God has been for centuries a part of Judeo-Christian practice. Place your hand above the oil and say the following prayer:

O Lord, giver of health and salvation,
Send your Holy Spirit to sanctify this oil
that those who receive this holy unction
be made whole.
In Jesus' name. Amen.

The oil before you will be a symbol throughout Advent of all the healing aspects of your ministry, including hospital and home visitation, counseling, and preaching. You may, of course, use this oil to anoint those seeking wholeness. But for our purposes this month, the oil serves as a constant reminder of how your ministry is one of healing.

Open your journal. For the next twenty minutes, write about how you experience your ministry as one of healing. For example, "I find that preaching helps my congregation through very difficult times in their lives. And preparing sermons sometimes heals me when I'm feeling wounded or exhausted."

As you minister throughout Advent, expect the healing power of God to be an integral part of your ministry.

The Last Day of Advent:

Read again Matthew 11:2-6. Open your journal. Across the top of the page, write: "Go tell John what you hear and see." Spend the next twenty-five minutes writing about any kind of healing you saw and heard in your ministry these past four weeks. For example, "I saw three new members join the church after years of absence from worship. I heard Mrs. Miller thank me for my prayers—she says my prayers help her through the grieving process." (Harriet Crosby)

DECEMBER 3, 1995

❧

First Sunday of Advent

Worship Theme: Advent is a time of personal and spiritual preparation to respond to God's gift of a Savior.

Readings: Isaiah 2:1-5; Romans 13:11-14; Matthew 24:36-44

Call to Worship (Psalm 122:1):
I was glad when they said to me,
  "Let us go to the house of the LORD!"

Pastoral Prayer:
O Lord, our Sovereign and Redeemer, as we enter this blessed season of Advent we rejoice at your grace and love, which provided for us a Savior. What the prophets could only dream of has become reality, and we are privileged to be able to know the Savior as a real and living presence in our own lives. And yet, Father, there are so many times when we take for granted this remarkable gift, when we go on with our daily thoughts and actions as if nothing had taken place in Bethlehem or at Calvary so many centuries ago. Sometimes it as if those events were so much ancient history, with no relevance to our own lives as we approach the end of the twentieth century.

Forgive us, Lord, for our shortsightedness, that sees so clearly the trivial events of our own days and overlooks the pivotal event of all history, which is ultimately far more important to our lives than anything else that will ever occur. And remind us, Lord, that Advent is not simply a time to recall past events but to prepare for that great and glorious event yet to come, when the Suffering Servant returns, this time as Lord of lords and King of kings. May these be days of preparation in our own hearts and lives, by the help of your Holy Spirit, that we might live in eager anticipation of the day when every knee will bow and every tongue confess that Jesus Christ is Lord. We ask it in his powerful name. Amen. (Michael Duduit)

SERMON BRIEFS

GETTING READY

ISAIAH 2:1-5

"Are you ready yet?" My parents said those words to me practically every Sunday morning. They had to ask me that question because I was always the last one to be dressed and ready to go to church. Now my wife and I ask the same question of our boys. Even as a child I knew that there is more to getting ready for church than putting on one's "Sunday best." We must also be spiritually prepared.

We should get ready for Christmas, too. Most people are already preparing for Christmas by hauling decorations down from the attic or up from the basement. The industrious among us have even purchased or made some of their gifts. But preparing for Christmas is also a spiritual matter. Since *advent* refers to the coming of Christ, and the season of advent is when we celebrate that coming, we must get ready to receive him.

The prophet Isaiah was getting ready for the coming of the Messiah eight hundred years before Christ's arrival. In the book that bears his name, Isaiah has provided help for us to get ready for the advent.

I. We Get Ready for Christmas by Believing God's Promises

In some ways, Isaiah's prophecies were fulfilled in the first advent of the Messiah. On the other hand, the complete fulfillment of God's promises concerning the last days will not come to pass until the second advent of Jesus. We live between the "already" and the "not yet." Nevertheless, we can be assured that God *will* keep all of his promises. The coming of the Messiah on that first Christmas night was in fulfillment of God's promises, and that event is our surety that the last days will occur according to his Word.

II. We Get Ready for Christmas by Sharing God's Priorities

During the lifetime of Isaiah, the worship of Jehovah and the teaching of his Word were confined to the Jewish people. However, God made it clear through the prophet that God's plan for the future included all the nations. His gospel is universal. When Jesus was born, an angel announced to shepherds outside Bethlehem, "I am bringing you good news of great joy for *all* the people" (Luke 2:10, emphasis added).

God's priority is to love every human being to himself. Is that your priority? Are you satisfied that the good news is confined to you and yours? Are you so caught up in the trappings of the season that God's missionary purpose is no longer a priority for you? If so, then you are not ready for Christmas.

III. We Get Ready for Christmas by Personifying God's Peace

Both Isaiah (2:4) and Micah (4:3) prophesied of a time when the nations would reshape their implements of war into implements of peace. This prophetic statement is prominently displayed in front of the United Nations building, but the preceding verses are omitted. The word of the prophets is that the nations will be at peace with one another when they are at peace with God.

The peace of which the prophets wrote began to be realized when Jesus was born. On the night he was born the angelic host announced, "Glory to God in the highest heaven, and on earth peace among those whom he favors" (Luke 2:14). The whole world is not yet at peace. In fact, the Messiah himself promised that until the end there would be "wars and rumors of wars" (Matt. 24:6). However, those who know him know his peace.

There's nothing like a deadline to motivate us to get ready. Our deadline is December 25. Will we be ready? (N. Allen Moseley)

GOD'S WAKE-UP CALL

ROMANS 13:11-14

Everyone who has done much traveling knows what a wake-up call is. You spend the night in a hotel but need to be up at a certain hour. You call the switchboard and ask for the operator to call you the next morning at your needed hour. With those instructions given, you can relax and enjoy a good night's rest.

The beginning of Advent is God's wake-up call to us. Notice how Paul puts it in verse 11: "It is now the moment for you to wake from sleep." What an unusual call this seems. But consider some of the implications of this mandate.

I. Wake Up to Theological Responsibilities

Faith is always lived in crisis times. That was true in Paul's day and in ours as well. The book of Romans addresses a church in theological conflict with its world. The Christ followers could not and did not fit into the theological molds of the first century. They were willing to give their lives if necessary to stand apart from their society.

Many people have observed that Christians today seem to stand for little that is different from society. If we profess to be Christian, that profession may mean little because we are often just like everyone else. We may attend church regularly and even tithe our income. But if the change is not on the inside, then the Advent/Christmas gospel means little.

Wake up because salvation is nearer now than when we first believed. That is a theological responsibility because it touches our need for vigilance.

II. Wake Up to Moral Responsibilities

Advent can be a crisis, so this is a good time to stake down the meaning of the season. You already know that it is not about packages and trees and wonderful food. It is not even about family and home. Advent is the time of paying attention to our moral responsibilities. As Paul put it, "Let us then lay aside the works of darkness" (v. 12). We need not spend much time imagining lurid tales of violence. Those are in today's headlines. Instead, let us remember that Christ comes as light in the darkness. As vermin scatter at the coming of the light, so do moral failures.

Keep a spiritual vigilance during this season. Also remember your moral responsibilities. What we do matters to God and to others.

III. Wake Up to Relational Responsibilities

The first half of verse 13 seems to describe some office Christmas parties: "Let us live honorably as in the day, not in reveling and drunkenness, not in debauchery and licentiousness." The second half seems to describe some church business meetings: "Not in quarreling and jealousy."

These are relational matters. The coming of Christ affects how we treat each other. We relate as whole persons to whole persons, not as objects to objects.

God is giving the world a wake-up call. His Son is coming. The light is dawning. Let us make no room for evil. (Don M. Aycock)

PREPARING FOR HIS COMING

MATTHEW 24:36-44

Don't you love a mystery? I grew up on "Perry Mason," watching that masterful legal strategist explore the various alternatives, then unmask the true villain (usually on the witness stand) in the final five minutes. Some people prefer an Agatha Christie mystery, or perhaps another writer. There is something in many of us that enjoys trying to put together the pieces of the puzzle; in such a story, we're just as delighted when we are completely surprised with the outcome. (Although we'll quickly begin to review the earlier clues and see how we could have easily come to the same conclusion earlier in the story!)

One of the great mysteries of the New Testament surrounds the return of Christ. We are told that there is a day coming when Christ will again enter our midst, this time to inaugurate his reign in human history. Countless writers and preachers have tried to identify the time when this second advent will take place; a couple of years ago, hundreds of thousands of copies of a book were distributed, purporting to identify the exact day when Christ would return. Of course, when that didn't happen, a sequel was soon available demonstrating conclusively that it was actually going to be a *different* day after all!

In these verses, Jesus emphasizes to his disciples that no one can know the time of this remarkable future event. Indeed, it will take humanity by surprise, much as the great flood came as an utter and total shock to a population that had made such fun of Noah and his boatworks.

In the face of such a mystery, Jesus nevertheless counseled his followers to take some practical steps in anticipation of his return. Not only are these good actions in anticipation of the second advent, but they are also actions that will contribute to victorious Christian lives in the here and now.

I. Watch for His Return (v. 42)

Have you ever watched and waited for a loved one you have not seen for a long time? Perhaps your spouse has been on a trip for several days; you have missed this special person in your life, and you've anxiously awaited the time of return. Now the expected time is fast approaching, and you keep looking at the clock; you keep going to the window to see if the car is entering the driveway.

That is the idea here. Jesus says, "Watch!" Live in expectancy of that great day. Live in a sense of anticipation that the One who loves you most, the One who gave his life for you, is about to return.

When we live in expectancy, we have a vivid sense of God's presence and direction in our lives. We are alert to his leading, alive to the Spirit's moving within us.

When we keep watch, it will lead to the second thing Jesus encourages us to do.

II. Prepare for His Return (v. 43)

This brief parable is not difficult to relate to our own time. We are growing more security conscious by the day. We carry poison sprays to fend off would-be attackers; we put alarms (or at least stickers threatening alarms) in our car windows; we install elaborate and expensive security systems in our homes, all because we fear those who would violate us or our belongings.

Imagine a person who receives a call one night that "A thief is on his way to your house, and is going to break in and steal your property." Can you imagine that same homeowner grunting at the phone, rolling over, and going back to sleep? I don't think so! I think the recipient of that warning would call the police, make sure the doors and windows were secured, and prepare for the potential thief.

In the same way we might prepare for such a negative event, Jesus says we ought to prepare for the positive event of his return.

How do we prepare? For a moment, imagine what specific steps you might take if you had concrete proof that Jesus was coming back twenty-four hours from now. You'd certainly try to set your own spiritual house in order; you'd probably have a sense of urgency about sharing your faith with some special friends and relatives; you'd be alert to be sure your thoughts and actions were positive and God-honoring. Sounds like we already know *how* to prepare; we just have to begin!

When we watch and prepare for his coming, we will inevitably follow the third action to which Jesus calls us.

III. Be Ready for His Return (v. 44)

A spirit of expectancy and a life-style of preparation will inevitably result in an attitude of readiness. We do not know when Christ's second advent may be, whether a day or a year or a century from now. We do know, however, that he challenges us to be ready for that day in every area of our lives.

In the earlier verses of this passage, Jesus talked about people in Noah's day, who were doing good things—the typical, every-day activities of life—but who had allowed those secondary activities to redirect their thoughts and priorities away from the most important thing: faithfulness and obedience to God. Jesus calls us to use the reality of his return as a constant reminder that we must be ready for his return, for when we live in readiness, then we are best prepared to serve faithfully and effectively in the days until he returns. (Michael Duduit)

DECEMBER 10, 1995

❧

Second Sunday of Advent

Worship Theme: Advent is a time to praise God for the hope we have in Christ.

Readings: Isaiah 11:1-10; Romans 15:4-13; Matthew 3:1-12

Call to Worship (Psalm 72:18-19):

Leader: Blessed be the LORD, the God of Israel, who alone does wondrous things.

People: Blessed be his glorious name forever; may his glory fill the whole earth. Amen and Amen.

Pastoral Prayer:

Father, your love for us in Jesus is the reason for this season. Your love for us in Jesus inspires us to praise you through all of the seasons of our lives. Because of Jesus, O Lord, every season and circumstance, good or bad or in between, can be filled with wonder, love, and praise. But sometimes, we confess, we act as if we don't know why he came or why we're here or where we're going through faith in him. Sometimes we let the little things of life get us down, aggravating and alienating us from each other and even from you. Forgive, O God, our sins. And as we move closer to Christmas day, help us by your Holy Spirit so that the little things of life don't distract us from the immeasurable joy of faith in Jesus. We pray this for your glory through Jesus, in whose name we pray. Amen. (Robert R. Kopp)

SERMON BRIEFS

CHRISTMAS GREATNESS

ISAIAH 11:1-10

Sometimes big things come in small packages. One man said that he had learned after years of marriage that when his wife says that she just wants something small for Christmas, it means that she wants jewelry. Some days seem small, but can later prove to be big. The day I met my future wife did not seem all that significant, but I did not know then that one day I would marry her; it proved to be a big day.

Christmas greatness is that way. It begins with what seems to be mundane and ends up being the most important thing in the world. It sneaks up on us. We don't realize how big it is until it's almost too late.

I. The Origin of Christmas Greatness Is Humble

During the lifetime of Isaiah, Judah was only a stump in comparison with the mighty forest of Assyria. Yet, in God's timing, by God's power, that stump became great. It started with just a twig—a shoot of new growth. No one would have voted for this unimpressive stump as "Most Likely to Succeed." But this small shoot changed the course of history, altered the nature of our world, and transformed millions of lives.

Isaiah used a fitting analogy for the birth of Jesus. The supernatural came in the form of the simple on the night that he was born. What appeared to be mundane was really miraculous. He was just a baby, but he was God in human form. Mary was just a plain Palestinian girl, but she was having a baby as a virgin. They were just ordinary shepherds, but an angelic host split the night sky to announce to them the birth of the Savior of humankind.

II. The Embodiment of Christmas Greatness Is Jesus

His greatness was not that of a celebrity, but of a servant. He went to the common people, not to the rich and royal. He touched the marginalized to manifest his power—a boy with fishes and loaves, a bleeding woman, a diminutive tax collector. He said, "Blessed are the meek," not "Blessed are the mighty." His followers were ordinary people, yet they changed the world. After all, he taught that his Kingdom would begin as a tiny mustard seed and would become a great tree. His death was the most ignominious possible, but through it he accomplished the redemption of the human race. Virtually everything Jesus ever did came in a small package, but it was really great. It started with an ordinary-looking infant—just a shoot from the stem of Jesse. But every Christian church, hospital, benevolence organization, and countless great things have come out of that small package.

III. The Nature of Christmas Greatness Is Determined by God

What made Jesus great? It was his character, and Isaiah gives us a glimpse of it. Jesus was great because the Spirit of the Lord was upon him (see Luke 4:18). According to Isaiah, this gave him wisdom and understanding, counsel and strength, and knowledge and the fear of the Lord. His delight was not in pleasing people, but in pleasing God. His character was marked with righteousness, compassion, fairness, truth, and faithfulness (vv. 3-5). The result of his life will be cosmic peace. Ultimately, through him God will restore the world to its intended order and beauty (vv. 6-9).

God wants to create this Christmas kind of greatness in us (Matt. 20:25-28). This is a typical-looking worship service. But it would be just like God to touch someone in this small service in a way that would make a great difference. (N. Allen Moseley)

AT CHRISTMAS TIME, DON'T MISS CHRISTMAS!

ROMANS 15:4-13

A man who lives in Hollywood says this to friends who come to visit: "When you are in Hollywood, don't miss Hollywood." He reminds his guests that his town is much more than a movie set. They won't see stars giving autographs or movie crews with cameras whirring. In a similar way the Scriptures seem to say to us, "At Christmas, don't miss Christmas." We can get so busy that the season passes over us like a plane at night, heard but not really seen.

I. Know the Hope That Comes with God

Christmas is a season of hope, and Advent is a message of the church, Santa Claus notwithstanding. The merchants have practically stolen this season by their message of "Buy, bye, bye!" Even so, this season is about God, who sent his Son into this world so that the world through him might be saved. Another word for this reality is *hope*.

We naturally think of this as a season of receiving, so think of what you can receive from God. One of his gifts is salvation from your sins. Another is a sense of belonging and purpose in life. A third gift is work to do in his Kingdom. All of this is part of the hope that is ours from our relationship with Christ.

II. Accept the People Who Come from God

"Welcome one another," said Paul. But this is more than just "buddy-buddy" feelings. Paul added the specification, "just as Christ has welcomed you" (v. 7).

Many people this time of year are already tired, broke, preoccupied, and cranky. Contrast this with the fact that Jesus came as the Prince of Peace. Why not accept some of his peace in your life during this season?

III. Give the Praise That Is Due to God

We also think of this season as a time of giving. What can you give this year that will express your faith and obedience? What about giving your life to Christ? We can also give gifts to the church to be used to spread the message about Christ and his love.

Perhaps the finest thing to give is praise to God. Paul breaks out into song in verses 9-13. Isn't that really the mood of Advent?

At Christmas, don't miss Christmas. There is meaning behind the madness. (Don M. Aycock)

A CALL TO NEW LIFE

MATTHEW 3:1-12

What a unique character John the Baptist must have been! The first prophet in Israel in four hundred years, he burst on the scene with a bizarre appearance and a powerful message: God is about to do a new thing among us, and you must prepare by coming to God in repentance.

What new thing does God want to do in your life? Have you experienced the things that John told the people they must do in order to prepare for God's presence?

I. Preparation for Christ Requires Confession (v. 6)

Have you ever known someone who had a lingering illness but who refused to seek a doctor's attention? You have to recognize that there's a problem before you will seek assistance from outside yourself.

Confession of sin is an acknowledgment that you have fallen short of God's perfect will for your life, that there is a spiritual sickness within you that requires the help of a Master Healer. Only in confession can we find authentic forgiveness.

II. Preparation for Christ Requires Obedience (v. 8)

John challenged the religious leadership to demonstrate their faith through specific, concrete acts of service. Just as a good tree produces fruit, so also a faithful life will produce actions of obedience and service for Christ.

Did you hear about the little boy who was acting up at the dinner table? He stood up in his chair, and despite his mother's demands, he continued to stand in the chair. Finally, she came around behind his chair and forced him to sit. After squirming for a time, he finally sat still, but he said defiantly, "I may be sitting on the outside, but I'm standing on the inside!" How like that child so many of us are—defiantly insisting on our own way, when all the time God wants to give us so much more if we will only trust and obey him.

III. Preparation for Christ Requires Dependence (v. 9)

It's little wonder that the religious establishment opposed John's work, for he was doing something unprecedented. Baptism was not new in Judaism; it was used as a step in the process of converting persons to the faith. But John wasn't simply baptizing converts; he was baptizing Jews! And he reminded his pious opponents that they couldn't rely on their religious heritage for salvation; repentance and faith involve recognition of their own inadequacy and a complete dependence on God.

For some people, the most difficult part of coming to Christ is acknowledging that they need help from beyond themselves, that they are not sufficient in and of themselves. That truth is at the heart of the gospel; it is only as we place ourselves in Christ's hands, relying on his love and grace as the only source of salvation, that we can find authentic peace.

John was preparing the way for Christ by preparing the hearts and lives of the people. Are you prepared for Christ to come into your life today? (Michael Duduit)

DECEMBER 17, 1995

Third Sunday of Advent

Worship Theme: Advent is a time to submit ourselves to Jesus Christ as Lord and Savior.

Readings: Isaiah 35:1-10; James 5:7-10; Matthew 11:2-11

Call to Worship (Luke 1:47-50):

Leader: My soul magnifies the Lord, and my spirit rejoices in God my Savior,

People: for he has looked with favor on the lowliness of his servant.

Leader: Surely, from now on all generations will call me blessed; for the Mighty One has done great things for me, and holy is his name.

All: His mercy is for those who fear him from generation to generation.

Pastoral Prayer:

O Lord, as we approach the wonderful day on which we celebrate the birth of our Lord and Savior, we come before you in wonder and praise. We do not understand such love, that would reach out to us while we were still filled with sin and rebellion, and pay such an awesome price for our deliverance. Even as we think of the miraculous star that shone over Bethlehem, our minds race forward to the darkness that enveloped Calvary, and we realize that Christmas has no meaning without Easter; the gift that began in a manger was completed on a cross. Thank you, Father, for such incredible love. As Christmas fast approaches, may these days be times of new and fresh surrender of our lives to the Savior who gave himself for us. Further, may they be days of witness to others of the love that has claimed and transformed our lives. Use us, O Lord, to spread your good news to others who have not yet experienced your love and grace in their own lives. We ask it in the name of the One who came to live among us, and even now intercedes for us in the heavenly courts. Amen. (Michael Duduit)

SERMON BRIEFS

CHRISTMAS AND HOPE

ISAIAH 35:1-10

A little girl in our city lived in a government housing project. She watched the drug deals and gang violence from her second-story window. A church started an outreach ministry in her complex, and after she became acquainted with one of the workers, the girl confided to her how she felt. "Mrs. Jones, when I see everything that goes on around here, sometimes I just don't want to live anymore." She was ten years old when she said that, and already she was feeling hopelessness.

She is not the only one. Successful business people sitting in mahogany-paneled offices are hoping that there is something more to life than what they feel inside day after day. People who feel themselves trapped in dead-end marriages are hoping that perhaps tomorrow their spouse will be willing to make the changes that will make life bearable again. Such stories could be multiplied endlessly.

Isaiah prophesied during a time when Judah's future looked bleak. Yet, the first word in the Hebrew text of chapter 35 is "rejoice." We too live in a world that seems to be growing darker all the time, but because of what God accomplished at Christmas we can have hope.

I. Christmas Gives Hope Because the Glory of God is Revealed.

With picturesque and vivid imagery, Isaiah wrote of a time in the future when the glory of God would be revealed. When the angels proclaimed the birth of Jesus, they said, "Glory to God in the highest" (Luke 2:14). John wrote of Jesus, "We have seen his glory, the glory as of a father's only son" (John 1:14; see 2:11).

401

The glory of God is the manifestation of his character, and Jesus manifested what God is like. At Christmas, when we reflect on the character of God as revealed in Jesus, we are given hope. As Corrie ten Boom once said, "When we look at the world we are distressed, when we look in ourselves we are depressed, but when we look at God we are at rest."

II. Christmas Gives Hope Because the Compassion of God Is Expressed

Isaiah prophesied that in the last days miracles would be performed. How do we know that God cares for our infirmities? We need only look at the ministry of compassion in the life of Jesus. Our greatest infirmity is sin, and he came as the Savior to die for our sin. Since he cares for us so, we should cast all our anxiety on him (1 Pet. 5:7; Heb. 4:15-16).

III. Christmas Gives Hope Because the Purpose of God Is Made Possible

Isaiah wrote of salvation (v. 4), holiness (v. 8), and the redeemed (v. 9). Since the Garden of Eden, God's purpose has been to reconcile persons to himself, and each of these words describes aspects of that reconciliation process. The purpose of God, which Isaiah expressed, was made possible through Jesus (John 3:16). Isaiah wrote of a highway in the wilderness—"the Holy Way" (v. 8). Jesus said that he is the Way (John 14:6).

When we go God's way, we have hope for reconciliation with God and eternity in heaven. As Good-will said to Christian in *Pilgrim's Progress,* "Look before thee; dost thou see this narrow way? That is the way thou must go: it was cast up by the Patriarchs, Prophets, Christ, and his Apostles; and it is as straight as a rule can make it: This is the way thou must go." (N. Allen Moseley)

WAITING FOR THE SON TO SHINE

JAMES 5:7-10

Waiting. We hate it! We don't want to wait in long lines for goods or services. Sometimes we even act like we should dictate

God's schedule. So today's Scripture arrests our attention with its first words: "Be patient."

The patience called for here is more than just killing time. It is the waiting of one in the dark awaiting daylight. We might say that this is a season of our waiting for the "son" to shine. How do we wait?

I. Anticipate His Coming

What if someone gave you a magnificent gift but you did not bother to open it? Jesus could very well be given the title, for many people, "The Unopened Gift." Christ's coming again is a natural result of his coming long ago as an infant in Bethlehem. Today we celebrate the first coming and anticipate his Second Coming.

We can help someone else to know who he is and what he offers. You could invite friends and family to church with you and let them hear about the word of grace. That is active waiting.

II. Work in the Meantime

Christianity is not a rocking-chair religion. While we are waiting we do not waste our time by doing nothing. Instead, as James says, we are farmers planting seeds in hope of a harvest. This is work. God expects us to be busy planting for him.

Many people wonder, "Does anyone really care about me? Does it matter whether I live or die?" The answer, according to Advent, is a resounding "Yes, it matters!" God's Son came to give life and meaning and hope to all who trust in him. What a joy to be about the work of telling people the reason for this season.

III. Give Others a Break

A five-year-old girl was trying to say the Lord's Prayer. When she got to the part about trespasses, she said, "And forgive us our Christmases as we forgive those who Christmas against us." We understand that sentiment! This time of year can be hectic. It can be a crisis that displays itself with frayed nerves and short tempers.

"Don't grumble against each other," say the Scriptures. Give other people a break. Our waiting is active and includes working for others and bearing with others. (Don M. Aycock)

THE SOURCE OF GREATNESS

MATTHEW 11:2-11

One of the most powerful characters in all of Scripture is John the Baptist. He steps onto the scene as a bold prophet, condemning the sin and corruption of the nation and calling Israel to repentance in preparation for the coming of Messiah. The crowds came to hear him, and many responded. When Jesus came to John at the Jordan, the prophet recognized that this was the "anointed one," the one God had sent to save the people.

Now John is in prison; the historian Josephus tells us that he was held at Machaerus, a hot desert fortress east of the Dead Sea. It must have been a difficult time for John, the hours of isolation must have caused doubts to creep into his thoughts. Was Jesus, in fact, the Messiah John was expecting? If so, why was John sitting in prison while his opponents lived in comfort?

Jesus reassures John and his followers by pointing to the deeds that surrounded the inauguration of this new age (v. 5). Then Jesus uses a tribute to John to explain the importance of this new Kingdom that was being ushered in, and to demonstrate that true greatness comes through following Christ.

I. People Judge Greatness Based on Achievement

Can you list some truly "great" people? If we think historically, we will tend to think of political or military leaders who accomplished significant things—perhaps Napoleon Bonaparte, George Washington, or Abraham Lincoln. We might think of people who did great things in science and technology—Madame Curie, Jonas Salk, George Washington Carver.

Could John the Baptist, locked up in a miserable dungeon, have been doing the same thing, wondering about Jesus' identity based on his lack of political or military initiatives? If Jesus was really the Messiah, would John still be locked up?

Obviously, we admire those who have achieved much; they serve as excellent models, and we respect the dedication and skill they have exhibited. But Jesus is making it clear that, in the light of eternity, human accomplishments are not the source of true greatness. If not, where is greatness to be found?

II. God Judges Greatness Based on Discipleship

Humanity judges greatness according to one standard, but God has an entirely different standard, a different measuring rod by which to judge greatness.

Notice how Jesus answers John's question about Jesus' identity (v. 5). Everything Jesus points to involves serving the poor and dispossessed, those who suffer from disease or physical handicaps. While John's contemporaries were awaiting a Messiah at the head of an army, Jesus is saying that God's new Kingdom doesn't work that way; it is a kingdom of love and compassion, of faithfulness and service.

Something new has come, and it supersedes every kingdom and rule before it. John stands at the pinnacle of the line of prophets; indeed, Jesus says that "there has not risen anyone greater than John the Baptist" (v. 11). But with the coming of Jesus and the inauguration of God's Kingdom in human history, everything has changed; now "he who is least in the kingdom of heaven is greater than" John.

Few minds in human history have been greater than that of Aristotle, but now the average high school student has knowledge far beyond that of Aristotle. How can that be? Because we live in a different era with a far greater body of knowledge—thanks in part to thinkers like Aristotle. We stand on the shoulders of giants, and thus can we see farther.

John the Baptist helped prepare the way for the coming of the Kingdom, although he would not live to see the remarkable events surrounding Jesus' death and resurrection. We are privileged to be able to look back and see, from a different vantage point, all that God has done to demonstrate his love for us. It is not enough simply to see, however; the key question is this: How will we respond to God's call? (Michael Duduit)

DECEMBER 24, 1995

❧

Fourth Sunday of Advent

Worship Theme: Christmas is a celebration of God's gift of salvation through Jesus.

Readings: Isaiah 7:10-16; Romans 1:1-7; Matthew 1:18-25

Call to Worship (Psalm 80:3, 19):

Leader: Restore us, O God; let your face shine, that we may be saved. . . .

People: Restore us, O LORD God of hosts; let your face shine, that we may be saved.

Pastoral Prayer:

O Lord, we gather today to celebrate the birth of a Savior, whose name is Jesus. In the midst of this season that has been so full of activities and distractions, so consumed with parties, shopping, and the other trappings of the holiday, we thank you that nothing can ultimately obscure the profound truth that in Jesus, you came to be a part of us in order to free us from our own sin and self-destruction, to restore us to the fellowship with you for which we were first created. Thank you for the love that overlooked our rebellious attitudes and for the forgiveness that is greater than our sin.

And now, Lord, the day for which we have been preparing is finally at hand. Be with those for whom this holiday is a difficult time, who are dealing with illness or family crisis or painful memories. Reach out to them with your comforting presence, and help us to be instruments of your peace in their lives as well. And use us, Lord, as translators of your good news; help us to speak your truth to those who know only tinsel and trees, but who have not yet experienced your transforming grace. Help us to celebrate the season by sharing your love with others, even as you shared your love with us through Jesus, in whose name we pray. Amen. (Michael Duduit)

SERMON BRIEFS

CHRISTMAS IS . . .

ISAIAH 7:10-16

During a past Christmas season a five-year-old boy was playing with our son and stayed at our house for lunch. As I served their meal I noticed our visitor's good manners, and I complimented him on them. His response was classic: "I'm being polite so that I can get what I want for Christmas." At least he was honest.

If we were as honest as my son's young friend, some of us would have to say, "For me, Christmas is getting what I want." Surely in our better moments Christmas means much more to us than that.

I. Christmas Is a Sign

God's sign to King Ahaz was the birth of a child. The birth of Jesus is also a sign to us. It signifies God's love, mercy, power, and grace. Sometimes it takes a sign to convince us of these realities, just as it did for Ahaz. For the main character in the movie *It's a Wonderful Life*, it took an angel to convince him of his worth. For Dickens's Scrooge it took a vivid nightmare. For the characters on the "Peanuts" Christmas special, it took Linus's recitation of the story of Jesus' birth.

When our oldest son was about four, we went through a stage of stretching out our arms as far as we could and saying, "I love you this much!" Once when we were in the car, our son made that gesture and said those words—first to my wife and then to me. My wife responded by doing the same thing. Then my son expected me to do it also. I explained to him that I was driving and that it would not be safe. "And besides," I added, "I could never stretch out my arms far enough to show you how much I love you." I was sure that would satisfy him, but in a few minutes he said, "Daddy, when we get out of the car, you can stretch your arms out to show me how much you love me." Sometimes we feel the need for a sign.

II. Christmas Is Grace

Ahaz had not been listening to God or to his prophet. He had not been a righteous king. This king was too busy with affairs of state to pay attention to spiritual things. He thought that problems such as the threat of invasion should be taken care of by practical means. To merely trust God, as Isaiah suggested, would be naive. It is proof of the grace of God that he continued to try to communicate with this errant king.

We, too, have gone astray (Isa. 53:6). We have disobeyed and rebelled. It is evidence of the grace of God that he would continue to seek us by sending his Son.

III. Christmas Is a Miracle

Jesus was born by impossible means—by a woman who was still a virgin. It was a miracle. In fact, Christmas is packed full of miracles—the angelic host, the guiding star, the escape from Herod, and more.

Perhaps the greatest miracle was that the little infant was God making himself known. During World War II a little boy kept a picture of his soldier father on his desk at school. The father had been at war for a long time. The boy's teacher asked him what he wanted for Christmas. He said that for Christmas he wanted his father to walk out of that picture. On the night Jesus was born, God walked out of eternity and into time; he has manifested himself through this sign-child.

(N. Allen Moseley)

LIKE FATHER, LIKE SON

ROMANS 1:1-7

Many people have been told they look just like their father. Family characteristics run deep. This is true of Christ, too. When it comes to his relation to God, we might quote the old proverb "Like Father like Son." On this Christmas Eve, let us hear the Word of God from Romans 1 and learn about God by getting to know his son.

I. The Promise

The gospel was promised long before it was delivered. The prophets were "seers" who knew something was coming long before it arrived. By the time Jesus was born, though, interest in the promised Messiah seemed low.

"Due to the lack of interest, Christmas has been canceled!" That statement was seen on a bumper sticker. We laugh at such a thought. Christmas may be many things, but a season of little interest it is not. Some companies spend eleven months gearing up for the one-month sale at Christmas time. Many other businesses make at least half of their profits from Christmas sales. They are very interested in this season!

Take stock of your own attitude. How are you feeling right now? Exhilarated? Bored? Excited? Depressed? Angry? Joyous? What is Christmas supposed to be? It was a promised event then and a promised blessing now.

II. The Fulfillment

What do you associate with Christmas? Gifts? Family and friends getting together? What about the special foods, like roast turkey and eggnog? In the flurry of activity around the holidays, we should keep this one fact in mind: Jesus did not come into the world to give us a Christmas holiday. He did not enter human history to give us a cause for celebration. So why did he come?

Verse 4 gives us the answer. It speaks of Christ's resurrection from the dead. The promised Savior came, was crucified, and was raised from the grave. That affects our destiny. The Gospels tell us that Mary bore a son and that she gave him the name Jesus "for it is he who will save his people from their sins."

III. The Blessing

"Mary Had a Little Lamb" is the title of a nursery song many of us sang as children. It is also a biblical reality. Mary's son Jesus grew up to be what God had intended him to be—the Savior of the world. John the Baptist said of him, "Behold, the Lamb of God who takes away the sin of the world!"

That gives us a tremendous blessing, one that is sketched in

verse 7. We receive grace and peace from God. That is what we see when we look into the life of Jesus. He is the giver of blessings. Like Father, like Son.
(Don M. Aycock)

THE MAN AT THE MANGER

MATTHEW 1:18-25

In the many elements that compose the Christmas story, the one we are most likely to overlook is Joseph. Certainly Mary and her special child are at the center of the story, and we love to recall the shepherds in the fields and the wise men bearing gifts. Look at the average nativity scene; Joseph is that guy standing in the back of the scene, looking on while everyone else gathers around the manger.

Yet Matthew reminds us here that Joseph was a central and essential character in the Christmas drama. The depth of character shown by Joseph serves as a model for each one of us during this time of celebration.

I. Joseph Was Righteous Before God

Matthew tells us that Joseph was a "righteous man" (v. 19), but I can't help thinking that was an understatement. God selected a special man to serve as the human father and model for Jesus, a man who would demonstrate integrity, honor, and virtue as the boy Jesus grew into a man.

The events described in this text offer one bit of evidence of the kind of man Joseph was. What a bitter blow it must have been to discover that young Mary, who was promised to him in marriage, was bearing a child. Can you imagine the thoughts and suspicions that would have gone through your mind in his situation? How would you have responded, especially in that culture, when you could certainly have exacted a dramatic measure of punishment for what you thought was a betrayal?

Yet Joseph's concern was for protecting Mary from public ridicule and punishment. Even at a moment in his life when he must have felt deeply hurt, he was anxious to protect the one he thought had hurt him. That is a depth of character not often found in his or any other day.

God could use Joseph because he had a compassionate heart and was a man of honor. Do we seek to demonstrate the kind of character in our lives that will enable God to more effectively use us?

II. Joseph Was Responsive to God

Imagine having the kind of dream Joseph had that night, and learning that the basis for his predicament was actually the work of God, and that the child your future wife is bearing is the Messiah, the "anointed one" of God. Yet Joseph's response was a simple one: "When Joseph woke up, he did what the angel of the Lord commanded him" (v. 24).

God isn't looking for the best and the brightest, the most handsome or beautiful, the most polished or popular. God is looking for men and women who will be responsive to his will; people who are willing to hear and obey. Look at the stories of those men and women who were used by God—people like Abraham and David and others like them; their common characteristic is a responsiveness to God. They were willing to do what God told them to do.

Are you responsive to God in your life? Do you spend time with the Lord in prayer and in the Word, seeking to recognize and follow God's will?

III. Joseph Was Responsible Before God

We don't learn much more here about Joseph than his personal discipline toward Mary until Jesus' birth (v. 25), and his obedience in giving the baby the name Jesus, as the angel had directed. The rest of Scripture doesn't tell us much, either; in fact, after Jesus' twelfth birthday, we never hear another word about Joseph. By the time of Jesus' public ministry at age thirty, his human father is apparently dead, for there's no mention of him as there is of other family members.

But you can learn about Joseph as you examine the life of Jesus. Could it be that Jesus learned to appreciate and honor the role of women by seeing how Joseph treated his mother, Mary?

411

Could it be that Jesus memorized so much of the Old Testament and was able to quote it as needed because he grew up in a home where his father honored and taught the Scripture to his family? Could it be that young Jesus learned the importance of honesty and hard work as he worked alongside Joseph in the carpenter's shop? Clearly, Joseph was a man who accepted the responsibility God had placed upon him, and gave himself to the task with commitment and faithfulness.

Perhaps today God is calling you to an important work, an important place of service. During this Christmas season, what better time to respond to God's call? (Michael Duduit)

DECEMBER 31, 1995

❧

First Sunday After Christmas

Worship Theme: This is a day of gratitude for the blessings of the past year and rededication to the service of Christ in the new year.

Readings: Isaiah 63:7-9; Hebrews 2:10-18; Matthew 2:13-23

Call to Worship (Psalm 148:1-4, 13):

Leader: Praise the LORD! Praise the LORD from the heavens; praise him in the heights!

People: Praise him, all his angels; praise him, all his host!

Leader: Praise him, sun and moon; praise him, all you shining stars!

People: Praise him, you highest heavens, and you waters above the heavens! . . .

Leader: Let them praise the name of the LORD, for his name alone is exalted;

All: his glory is above earth and heaven.

Pastoral Prayer:
   O God our Father, be with us throughout this coming year to bless us. As we pass from a season of celebration to begin a new year, make this time of worship something more than a worthy habit faithfully observed. May the piercing truth of your Word, sharper than any two-edged sword, stab us wide awake. Deliver us from weariness of mind and heaviness of heart, and into our bodies bring new life and joy in living. May this house of prayer shine today with your glory, O Lord, and speak to us new truths out of the old, old story. Above all, lead each one of us to where we may see you face to face and know your will for our lives. And thus seeing and knowing, help us to yield ourselves with joy to

your service, for the sake of Jesus Christ our Lord. Amen.
(John Bishop)

SERMON BRIEFS

THANKSGIVING DAY

ISAIAH 63:7-9

In this country, the last Thursday in November is celebrated as Thanksgiving Day. However, I would suggest that we also unofficially make the last day of the year a day of thanksgiving. On December 31, we spend a lot of time looking forward to the new year, and we should do that. Nevertheless, we should also look back to thank God for all he has done for us during the year. We said thank you to those who gave us Christmas gifts, but we should also thank God for what he has given us all year.

Remember is an important word in the Bible. Before the Hebrews crossed the Jordan into the Promised Land, Moses urged them to remember who was giving them the land. Before Christ died on the cross, he gave his disciples a symbol of his sacrifice and said, "This do in remembrance of me."

Maybe you have had a bad year. Yet there is always something for which we may be thankful. A boy in elementary school arrived late to school and was reprimanded for it. Later, he discovered that he had forgotten his homework, and he was scolded again. Then he began to feel sick, and ran in from the playground to go home. As he ran, he tripped and fell, breaking his arm. While he was on the ground, though, he found a quarter. While going home from the doctor's he told his parents, "This is the best day of my life! I have never found a quarter before!" We need to cultivate the spirit of that child so that we may remember the good things and be thankful, even when much has gone wrong. What may we remember and be grateful for on this thanksgiving day?

I. The Goodness of God

Isaiah mentioned God's "great goodness," which God expresses according to his compassion and lovingkindness (v. 7). The hymn writer said, "Count your blessings, name them one by one. Count your blessings, see what God has done." God has done and still does so much for us.

II. The Grace of God

Isaiah also referred to the fact that God had adopted Israel as his people and had become their Savior (v. 8). He did not do that because the Hebrews were the biggest and the best, but because of his grace. When was the last time you spent time thanking God for his salvation? It is all because of his grace. Think of where you would be, and what you would be, without him, and thank him for the difference he has made.

III. The Guidance of God

Isaiah painted a beautiful word portrait of the empathetic love of God. He hurts when we hurt, he sends his angel to help us, and he even picks us up and carries us (v. 9). Only God knows how many times we have been in danger, and he has protected us. Some of us are alive to face 1996 only because God has guided us out of some trouble. Certainly all of us can see the providential hand of God at work in our lives in some way.

Many times my wife and I have told our sons to say thank you when someone gives them a gift. God has given us many gifts this past year. Say, "Thank you, God." (N. Allen Moseley)

WHAT TO DO WHEN YOU'RE LOW AND BLUE

HEBREWS 2:10-18

Today is called "Low Sunday" in many churches. It is the Sunday following Christmas. The cantata has been presented, the finely prepared sermons delivered, the gifts exchanged, and the manger and bathrobes from the children's play put away. All the excitement of Christmas is gone already. People are traveling, and the attendance at church may be low.

But it is low in another sense as well. The sense of celebration and joy may be gone now. After all the hype around Christmas, what are we supposed to feel or to do? According to Hebrews 2, after the party comes the cleanup.

The Sunday after Christmas is a good time to learn to get on with life. Things are back to "normal," whatever that might be. We learn to participate in God's purposes for his people. Those purposes extend through periods of special events like Christmas and also the day-by-day existence of living, like today. After the party, here's what to do.

I. Consult the Author

Jesus is the "author" of salvation. He wrote the book on salvation! Jesus came as "God with us." This is the central conviction of the gospel message. In Jesus, God came to live among humankind. He lived with us and became vulnerable to our hurts and problems, and he died out of love for us.

During this season of the year Jesus can be Immanuel for you—God with you. Many people find this season to be a lonely time. But if God is with you, you will not find the loneliness so unbearable.

II. Lean on the Brother

Jesus is also called our brother. He was not a stronger brother of mythical proportions who could never be hurt. He was a man among men, and he accepted humanity's limitations.

Most of us enjoy old Christmas movies and have seen *Miracle on 34th Street* and *It's a Wonderful Life* several times. Many people have an image of Christmas that is straight out of Hollywood. The only problem is that the Hollywood version is all sweetness and spice, whereas the real events surrounding the birth of Jesus included murder and political intrigue.

When you are low you can lean on this brother who accepted humanity in full and who loves us still. Despite the tragic events in Christ's own life, he brings a word of love as an older brother. We can lean on him.

416

III. Trust the Victor

Jesus is a victor who made atonement for our sins. He is the Christ. Our word *Christ* is from the Greek word *Christos*, which is the same as the Hebrew word *Mashiach*. They both mean "Messiah." The Messiah was the "one who is anointed." Over long centuries of defeat and humiliation, the Jews began to look for one particular Messiah who would lead their nation out of tragedy and pain. The Jews could not agree who this Messiah would be, however. When Jesus came, some people thought he was the Messiah, while most did not.

The important thing for us to realize is that Christ came to save us from our most pressing problem—our sin. One person put it this way, "Man's greatest need is not for a new political or economic order. His primary problem is his sin. He is alienated from God, bearing the burden of this guilt and loneliness, facing a frightening future. He needs to be liberated from the tyranny of his sins, reconciled to God, and given a hope that transcends the circumstances of this life." This, in a nutshell, is what the gospel message is all about.

We can consult the Author of life. We can lean on our elder brother. And we can trust the Victor over tragedy and death. (Don M. Aycock)

WHEN DANGER THREATENS

MATTHEW 2:13-23

Sometimes celebration is quickly transformed into tragedy. During the long holiday celebration commemorating Christ's birth and the birth of a new year, how many lives will be lost, how many bodies maimed in accidents? How quickly joy can dissolve into sorrow!

Thus it is for us as we move from the story of the nativity to the terrible account of Herod's murder of Bethlehem's infant sons, often referred to as the "slaughter of the innocents." Twenty or thirty children were probably killed that day, but even one was too many. And all because King Herod was obsessed with eliminating any real or potential pretenders to his throne; he had sev-

417

eral members of his own family, including his three sons, murdered for the same reason.

Matthew wants us to understand that despite Herod's evil intentions, God is able to overcome the best efforts of those who would do us harm. God is able to protect his people.

Yet it was important that Joseph respond to God's direction. Three characteristics of authentic faith are demonstrated here that allowed Joseph to lead his family to safety with God's help. As we seek God's guidance and protection in our own lives, we need to understand these necessary actions.

I. Faith Acts Promptly

When Joseph was warned by the angel to seek safety in Egypt, he didn't decide to "sleep on it" or consult the experts or otherwise delay. Matthew tells us he gathered the family "during the night" and set out for the safety of Egypt (v. 14).

Faith doesn't delay unnecessarily. Once we understand what God would have us do, we need to act on it.

Immediately after the costly battle at Gettysburg, Lee's Confederate forces were in terrible shape and in full retreat. Crossing the Potomac to return to Virginia, the Southern army was split into two parts and vulnerable to an attack by Meade's Union army, which was superior in number thanks to prompt reinforcements. Yet Meade could not put his forces into action; he delayed, studied the situation, delayed some more, until finally he was ready to move his army into action. Unfortunately, by the time Meade was ready and the Union artillery began its attack, Lee's army had completed its river crossing and was safely back in Virginia. The result of Meade's delay may well have been to add considerable time to that already bloody war.

We must be ready to respond promptly to God's direction.

II. Faith Acts Obediently

In reponse to God's command, delivered through the angelic messenger, Joseph obeyed the directions precisely. It would have been tempting to choose another, more convenient location—perhaps somewhere Joseph or Mary had family, certainly not in an entirely different country with its own language and customs.

But there is no record of Joseph's raising the first objection; if God told him to go to Egypt, that's where he went.

How often we may be missing God's best for us by trying to second-guess his will and purpose for our lives. Faithful obedience to God allows him to work effectively in our lives, protecting us from dangers of which we may be unaware, and leading us into new and exciting opportunities we've never dreamed of.

III. Faith Acts with Trust

If it took faith to gather his family and escape into Egypt, I suspect it took even more faith to return to the land that held such danger. When the angel sounded an "all clear" and instructed Joseph to return to Israel, there must have been some real questions about the wisdom of such an action. But without hesitation, Joseph trusted God to protect them and provide for them, and the family set out to return to their homeland.

Have you ever sensed God's leadership into a particular course of action, but you just can't see how it will work? Does it seem too outlandish, too dangerous, too much of a risk? Some of the most exciting things that will ever happen in your life may be the result of God's asking you to walk where you can't yet see—but he can.

When we set out in faith—faith characterized by promptness, obedience, and trust—there are no limits to what God can do in and through us. As we begin a new year, with new opportunities and new challenges before us, that's an important truth for us to understand. (Michael Duduit)

BENEDICTIONS

❧

Advent and Christmas

We journey toward Bethlehem, O God, where you will reveal the glory of heaven and the hope of earth. May the light of your glory brighten our path to the future, and may the brilliance of your hope beckon us to new beginnings. **Amen.** [Year B]

The day is at hand; the savior draws near! Let us watch, and let our eyes be clear, lest the star appear and not be followed, lest the child be born and not be found. **Amen.** [Year C]

May the roots of your faith be deep during heavy winds, and may the fruits of your faith be plentiful during the harvest. May you prepare the way for the One who will come, being filled with all joy and peace. **Amen.** [Year A]

Somewhere in the night of our lives, a baby cries, and that cry is our hope. The grace of God has appeared for the salvation of our world. Glory to God in the highest and on earth, peace! **Amen.** [Year C]

Eternal God, as you gave yourself in Jesus to redeem us from all selfishness, give yourself through us for the redemption of others; and send us forth into the world, as you brought Jesus into the world, to fashion for yourself a people jealous of their love for you and zealous in their service to neighbor. **Amen.** [Year A]

New Year's Eve Day

O God of new beginnings, make us a people of new beginnings. Let the works of our hands reflect the works of your hand. Let us mirror the light that illumined the deep and brightened a cold, dark stable. **Amen.** [Year A]

O God of beginnings, encourage our hearts as we greet this new hour, this new day, this new year! Knit us gently together in love, so that when we go apart in body, we shall be one in spirit. **Amen.** [Year B]

Do not scan the clouds for a vision of the new heaven or search the skies for a glimpse of the new earth. Do not look up but look around, for the kingdom of God is in your midst. **Amen.** [Year A]

Lent and Easter

Look to God and be radiant; let your faces shine. For you who were lost have been brought home; go forth into the world. You who were dead have been raised; give life into the world. Go with God, and find! God with God, and live! **Amen.** [Year C]

We scanned the heavens, O God, in search of your likeness, but we did not find it there. We found it on earth in Jesus Christ, not as the result of our search for you, but as the result of your search for us. O Face whose light illumines our lives, let our lives illumine the world. **Amen.** [Year A]

May your hearts be strong, knowing that God hears your faintest prayer and will answer with an unexpected work in an unexpected place. Nothing can remove you from the love of God; the Lord will summon life from every darkened tomb. **Amen.** [Year A]

As the Lord sent Jesus into the world to manifest the grace of God, the Lord sends us into the world to manifest the love of Christ. Go now in the assurance that, as the Lord stood with Jesus in the hour of his trial, the Lord shall stand with us in the hour of our trial. As the Lord went with him, the Lord shall go with us. **Amen.** [Year B]

Receive now the blessed promise of Easter: Every night shall be broken by dawn, and every tear shall spring from joy; every step shall become a dance, and every word shall carry a song. This promise is yours to share. Carry it to those still standing on Golgotha; take it to those still trapped on Good Friday. Let your souls erupt in praise—let them not be silent! **Amen.** [Year C]

These benedictions have been selected from the three-volume work *Litanies and Other Prayers for the Revised Common Lectionary* (*Years A, B, and C*) by Phyllis Cole and Everett Tilson.

TEXT GUIDE

THE REVISED COMMON LECTIONARY (1995), CYCLE C

Sunday	First Lesson	Second Lesson	Gospel Lesson	Psalm
1/1/95	Eccles. 3:1-13	Rev. 21:1-6a	Matt. 25:31-46	Ps. 8
1/8/95	Isa. 43:1-7	Acts 8:14-17	Luke 3:15-17, 21-22	Ps. 29:10-11
1/15/95	Isa. 62:1-5	1 Cor. 12:1-11	John 2:1-11	Ps. 36:7-9
1/22/95	Neh. 8:1-3, 5-6, 8-10	1 Cor. 12:12-31a	Luke 4:14-21	Ps. 19:7-9
1/29/95	Jer. 1:4-10	1 Cor. 13:1-13	Luke 4:21-30	Ps. 71:15-16
2/5/95	Isa. 6:1-8, (9-13)	1 Cor. 15:1-11	Luke 5:1-11	Ps. 138:7-8
2/12/95	Jer. 17:5-10	1 Cor. 15:12-20	Luke 6:17-26	Ps. 1:1-2
2/19/95	Gen. 45:3-11, 15	1 Cor. 15:35-38, 42-50	Luke 6:27-38	Ps. 37:3-5
2/26/95	Isa. 55:10-13	1 Cor. 15:51-58	Luke 6:39-49	Ps. 92:1-2, 4
3/5/95	Deut. 26:1-11	Rom. 10:8b-13	Luke 4:1-13	Ps. 91:14-16
3/12/95	Gen. 15:1-12, 17-18	Phil. 3:17–4:1	Luke 13:31-35	Ps. 27:1-4, 13-14
3/19/95	Isa. 55:1-9	1 Cor. 10:1-13	Luke 13:1-9	Ps. 63:1-4
3/26/95	Josh. 5:9-12	2 Cor. 5:16-21	Luke 15:1-3, 11b-32	Ps. 32:11
4/2/95	Isa. 43:16-21	Phil. 3:4b-14	John 12:1-8	Ps. 126:3, 5-6
4/9/95	Isa. 50:4-9a	Phil. 2:5-11	Luke 19:28-40; 22:14–23:56	Ps. 118:1-2, 19-24
4/14/95	Isa. 52:13–53:12	Heb. 10:16-25	John 18:1–19:42	Ps. 22:26-31
4/16/95	Isa. 65:17-25	1 Cor. 15:19-26	John 20:1-18	Ps. 118:14-15, 19-24
4/23/95	Acts 5:27-32	Rev. 1:4-8	John 20:19-31	Ps. 118:14, 29
4/30/95	Acts 9:1-6, (7-20)	Rev. 5:11-14	John 21:1-19	Ps. 30:4-5
5/7/95	Acts 9:36-43	Rev. 7:9-17	John 10:22-30	Ps. 23
5/14/95	Acts 11:1-18	Rev. 21:1-6	John 13:31-35	Ps. 148:1-5a
5/21/95	Acts 16:9-15	Rev. 21:10, 22–22:5	John 14:23-29	Ps. 67:1-5
5/28/95	Acts 1:1-11	Eph. 1:15-23	Luke 24:44-53	Ps. 47:1-2, 6

12/10/95	Isa. 11:1-10	Rom. 15:4-13	Matt. 3:1-12	Ps. 72:18-19
12/17/95	Isa. 35:1-10	James 5:7-10	Matt. 11:2-11	Luke 1:47-50
12/24/95	Isa. 7:10-16	Rom. 1:1-7	Matt. 1:18-25	Ps. 80:3, 19
12/31/95	Isa. 63:7-9	Heb. 2:10-18	Matt. 2:13-23	Ps. 148:1-4, 13

CONTRIBUTORS

Don M. Aycock, Pastor, First Baptist Church of Gillis, Lake Charles, LA

Raymond Bailey, Professor of Christian Preaching, The Southern Baptist Theological Seminary, Louisville, KY

Greg Barr, Doctoral Candidate in Preaching, The Southern Baptist Theological Seminary, Louisville, KY

Barry J. Beames, Pastor, First Baptist Church, Jefferson, TX

John Bishop, Retired Methodist Pastor and Lecturer, Philadelphia, PA

Rick Brand, Pastor, First Presbyterian Church, Henderson, NC

Joseph Byrd, Pastor, Stewart Road Church of God, Monroe, MI

Gary L. Carver, Pastor, First Baptist Church, Chattanooga, TN

Harriet Crosby, Freelance Writer, San Francisco, CA

Earl C. Davis, Pastor, First Baptist Church, Memphis, TN

Michael Duduit, Editor, *Preaching* Magazine; Executive Director, American Academy of Ministry; and Adjunct Professor of Christian Preaching, The Southern Baptist Theological Seminary, Louisville, KY

Heather Murray Elkins, Assistant Professor of Worship & Liturgical Studies, The Divinity School, Drew University, Madison, NJ

Paul R. Escamilla, Pastor, First United Methodist Church, Heath, TX

Steven R. Fleming, Pastor, First United Presbyterian Church, Westminster, MD

Travis Franklin, Pastor, First United Methodist Church, Winters, TX

Mike Graves, Assistant Professor of Preaching, Midwestern Baptist Seminary, Kansas City, MO

E. Langston Haygood, Pastor, First Presbyterian Church, Gadsden, AL

Blake Harwell, Pastor, Mt. Herman Baptist Church, Bedford, KY

C. Thomas Hilton, Interim Minister, First Presbyterian Church, Wayne, PA

John A. Huffman, Jr., Pastor, St. Andrews Presbyterian Church, Newport Beach, CA

Mark A. Johnson, Pastor, First Baptist Church, Dillsboro, IN

Derl G. Keefer, Pastor, Three Rivers Church of the Nazarene, Three Rivers, MI

Eric Killinger, Presbyterian Minister, Birmingham, AL

John Killinger, Distinguished Professor of Religion & Culture, Samford University, Birmingham, AL

Gary G. Kindley, Pastor, St. Johns United Methodist Church, Georgetown, TX

Robert R. Kopp, Pastor, Logans Ferry Presbyterian Church, New Kensington, PA

Hugh Litchfield, Professor of Homiletics, North American Baptist Seminary, Sioux Falls, SD

Craig A. Loscalzo, Lester Professor of Christian Preaching, The Southern Baptist Theological Seminary, Louisville, KY

James Earl Massey, Dean, School of Theology, Anderson University, Anderson, IN

J. Lawrence McCleskey, Pastor, Myers Park United Methodist Church, Charlotte, NC

Rick McDaniel, Pastor, Abundant Life Christian Community, Durham, NC

Calvin Miller, Professor of Communication Studies and Writer-in-Residence, Southwestern Baptist Seminary, Fort Worth, TX

N. Allen Moseley, Pastor, First Baptist Church, Durham, NC

David N. Mosser, Pastor, First United Methodist Church, Georgetown, TX

Carol M. Norén, Associate Professor of Preaching, North Park Theological Seminary, Chicago, IL

Jerry E. Oswalt, Academic Vice President, Florida Baptist Theological College, Graceville, FL

Harold C. Perdue, Development Officer, Texas Methodist Foundation, Round Rock, TX

Gary C. Redding, Pastor, First Baptist Church, North Augusta, SC

John R. Roebuck, Pastor, South Avondale Baptist Church, Birmingham, AL

William L. Self, Pastor, Johns Creek Baptist Church, Atlanta, GA

Thomas R. Steagald, Pastor, Highlands United Methodist Church, Highlands, NC

Billy D. Strayhorn, Pastor, First United Methodist Church, Groesbeck, TX

Craig M. Watts, Pastor, First Christian Church, Louisville, KY

Mark E. Yurs, Pastor, Salem United Church of Christ, Verona, WI

INDEX